SPECIAL TOPICS ART 448 + 548
MADE IN U.S.A.
9¾ in. x 7½ in.

THE UNTHINKABLE MIND

WHAT IT IS

"MAKING COMICS"

"WRITE WHAT YOU SEE"

SYLLABUS

CLASS PROGRAM

NAME DRAWN & QUARTERLY

SCHOOL CLASS LYNDA BARRY

TIME FROM TO...

MONDAY
SUBJECT
ROOM
INSTRUCTOR

TUES
SUBJECT
ROOM
INSTRUCTOR

PERIOD 1 PERIOD 2 PERIOD 3 PERIOD 4 PERIOD 5 PERIOD 6 PERIOD 7 PERIOD 8

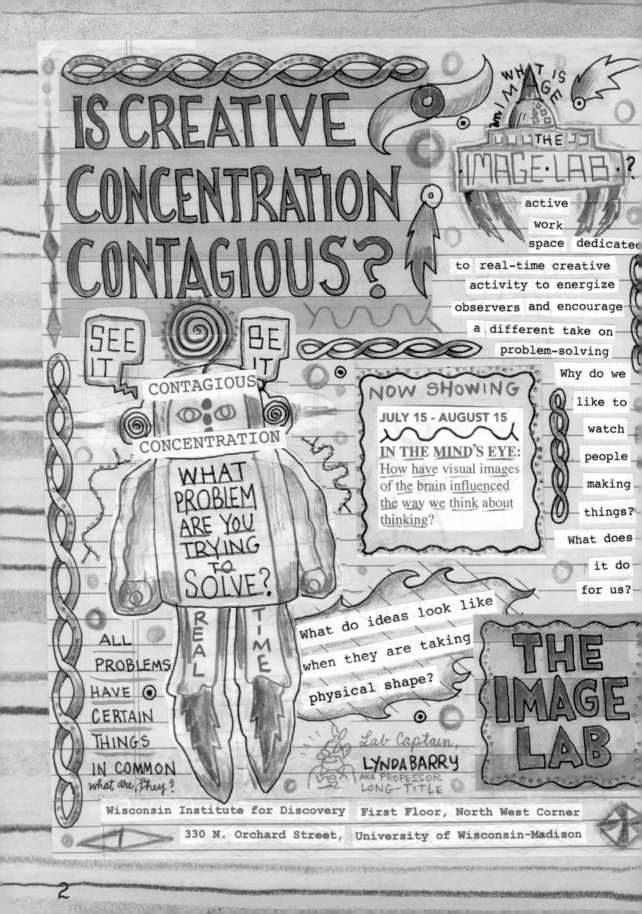

IS CREATIVE CONCENTRATION CONTAGIOUS?

WHAT IS THE IMAGE·LAB?

active work space dedicated to real-time creative activity to energize observers and encourage a different take on problem-solving

SEE IT · BE IT

CONTAGIOUS

CONCENTRATION

WHAT PROBLEM ARE YOU TRYING TO SOLVE?

REAL TIME

Why do we like to watch people making things? What does it do for us?

NOW SHOWING

JULY 15 - AUGUST 15

IN THE MIND'S EYE: How have visual images of the brain influenced the way we think about thinking?

What do ideas look like when they are taking physical shape?

ALL PROBLEMS HAVE CERTAIN THINGS IN COMMON what are they?

Lab Captain, LYNDA BARRY AKA PROFESSOR LONG-TITLE

THE IMAGE LAB

Wisconsin Institute for Discovery   First Floor, North West Corner
330 N. Orchard Street,   University of Wisconsin-Madison

2

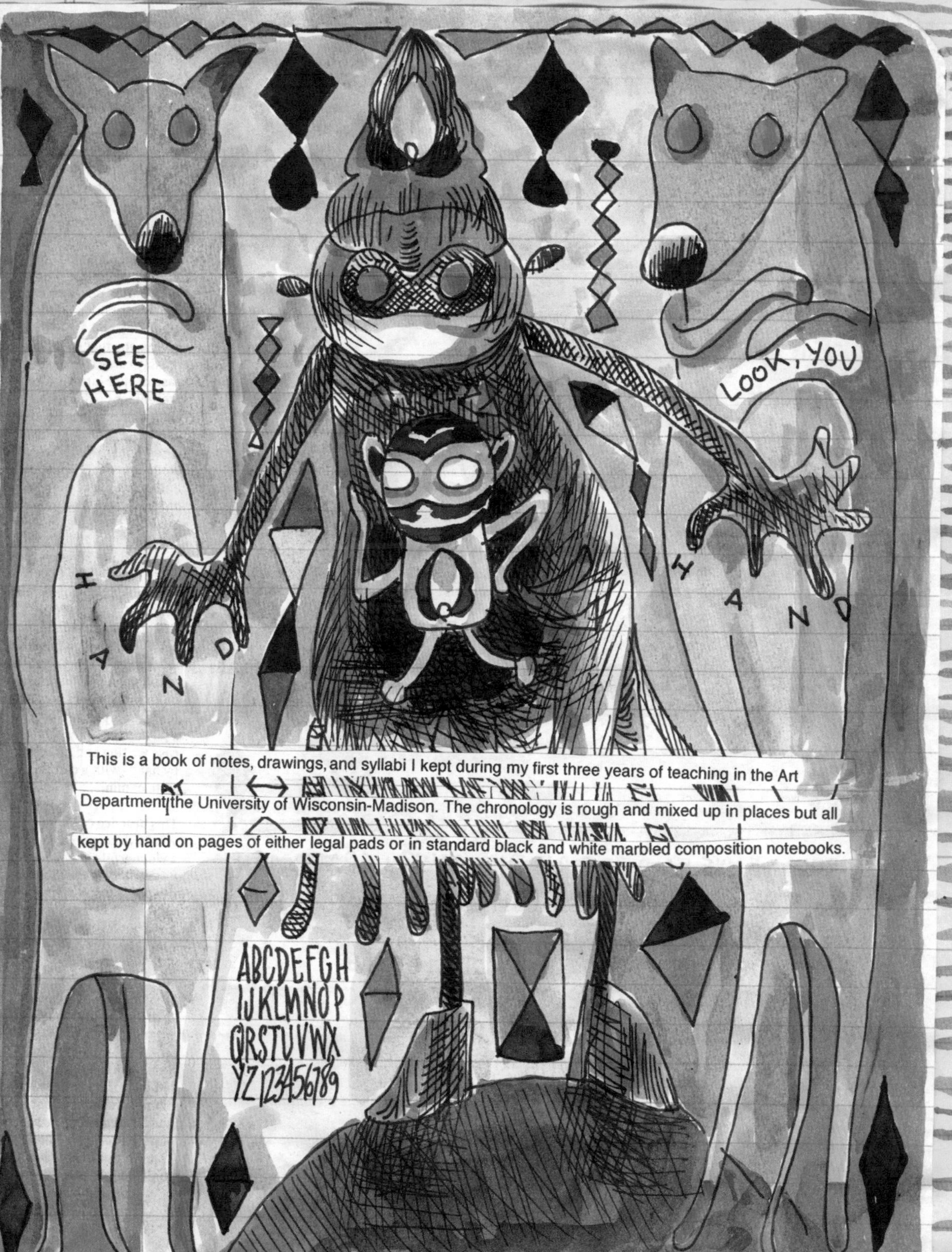
SEE HERE
LOOK, YOU
HAND
HAND
ABCDEFGH IJKLMNOP QRSTUVWX YZ123456789
COLORING THINGS IN BY HAND AS STUDY AID

This is a book of notes, drawings, and syllabi I kept during my first three years of teaching in the Art Department at the University of Wisconsin-Madison. The chronology is rough and mixed up in places but all kept by hand on pages of either legal pads or in standard black and white marbled composition notebooks.

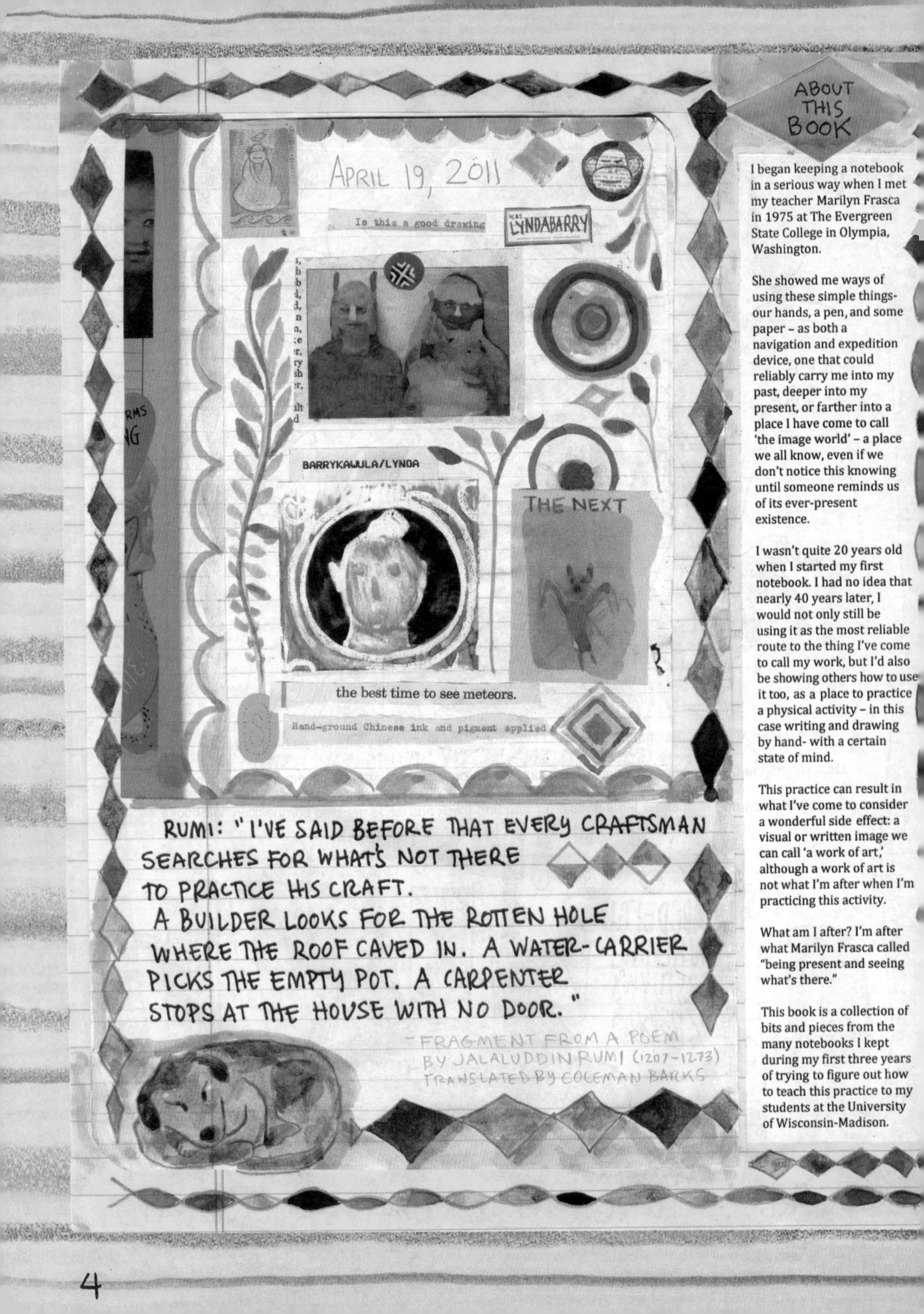
APRIL 19, 2011
Is this a good drawing
LYNDABARRY
BARRYKAWULA/LYNDA
THE NEXT
the best time to see meteors.
Hand-ground Chinese ink and pigment applied
RUMI: "I'VE SAID BEFORE THAT EVERY CRAFTSMAN SEARCHES FOR WHAT'S NOT THERE TO PRACTICE HIS CRAFT.
A BUILDER LOOKS FOR THE ROTTEN HOLE WHERE THE ROOF CAVED IN. A WATER-CARRIER PICKS THE EMPTY POT. A CARPENTER STOPS AT THE HOUSE WITH NO DOOR."
-FRAGMENT FROM A POEM BY JALALUDDIN RUMI (1207-1273) TRANSLATED BY COLEMAN BARKS

ABOUT THIS BOOK

I began keeping a notebook in a serious way when I met my teacher Marilyn Frasca in 1975 at The Evergreen State College in Olympia, Washington.

She showed me ways of using these simple things- our hands, a pen, and some paper – as both a navigation and expedition device, one that could reliably carry me into my past, deeper into my present, or farther into a place I have come to call 'the image world' – a place we all know, even if we don't notice this knowing until someone reminds us of its ever-present existence.

I wasn't quite 20 years old when I started my first notebook. I had no idea that nearly 40 years later, I would not only still be using it as the most reliable route to the thing I've come to call my work, but I'd also be showing others how to use it too, as a place to practice a physical activity – in this case writing and drawing by hand- with a certain state of mind.

This practice can result in what I've come to consider a wonderful side effect: a visual or written image we can call 'a work of art,' although a work of art is not what I'm after when I'm practicing this activity.

What am I after? I'm after what Marilyn Frasca called "being present and seeing what's there."

This book is a collection of bits and pieces from the many notebooks I kept during my first three years of trying to figure out how to teach this practice to my students at the University of Wisconsin-Madison.

April 25, 2011: A Monday. Trying to remember something someone said yesterday. Watched a Trilogy about an awful man going over his memories - He wasn't any more awful than I am, which is to say at times very awful. About to read another notebook of journal writing from the late 1970s - I'm not sure what it's doing beyond upsetting me but I want to read it - I want to have another look at that time...

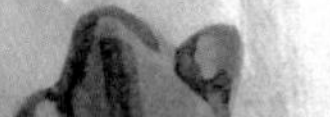

From my notes taken April 5, 1977

Marilyn:

How do you stop saying 'nothing happened.'

One way: pay attention, be quiet, and see what's there.

Not agree with, understand, like,

JUST SEE

24 hour period, moving back to see what was there.

The nature of this 24 hour period

Feeling/Tone

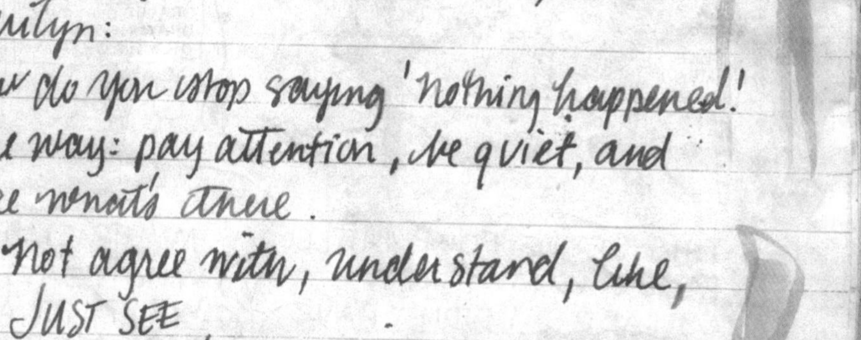

CRITICAL Friends AND

WHAT·IT·IS

manually shifting the image·

· ART/ENGLISH/THEATER and DRAMA 469
interdisciplinary studies in the arts

☘ INSTRUCTOR ❀
LYNDA BARRY
◇·····email lbarry@wisc.edu ·♥

STUDIO
OFFICE
HOURS!

WEDS 9:30-
RM
610!
NOON

our room 6101
TUES 4:30-7PM and THURS.
HUMANITIES Bld.

OFFICE
OFFICE
HOURS!
by
APPOINTMENT
ONLY

B150
LATHROP
WEDS
2PM-3:30

IC U2

·IF THE THING WE CALL 'THE ARTS'
·HAS A BIOLOGICAL FUNCTION,
·WHAT IS IT?

READY
or
NOT....

STARING
HERRING

✦EXPECTATIONS

PUNCTUALITY and
ATTENDANCE WILL
matter A LOT.

NO MATTER HOW
MUCH I DIG YOU OR
YOUR WORK, BEING
LATE OR
ABSENT
WILL
LOWER
YOUR
GRADE

FOR
REAL.

tick
tick
tick
tick

THERE ARE EXCEPTIONS
LIKE ? §§%, FOR

HIGH
FEVER
and

PROJECTILE

HORK

VOMITING D

BUT NOT FOR
☐ MOODY! ☐ HUNGOVER!
☐ IN LOVE! ☐ JUST 'CUZ!
☐ WHATEV! ☐ ALIENS!

WHAT IS WRONG

I WUV
YOU

WITH THIS PICTURE?

ANSWER: NOTHING
YOU WON'T BE
GRADED ON YOUR
DRAWING ABILITY
OR YOUR CHARM

YOU WILL BE SO
GRADED ON YOUR
EFFORT AND TIME
SPENT WITH PEN
OR PAINTBRUSH
ON EACH ASSIGNMENT

GO
DEEP!

THIS SET OF FOUR LITTLE
PAGES IS MY FIRST
SYLLABUS. I DIDN'T HAVE
MUCH OF AN IDEA ABOUT
WHAT TO INCLUDE. MY
TEACHER MARILYN FRASCA
GAVE ME A COPY OF A
SYLLABUS SHE USED FOR
ONE OF HER CLASSES AND
IT WAS JUST 2 SIDES OF
A SINGLE PAGE. ONE OF
THOSE SIDES WAS A LIST
OF ART MATERIALS NEEDED
FOR THE CLASS. THAT WAS IT.

MY FRIEND DAN CHAON,
WHO TEACHES CREATIVE
WRITING AT OBERLIN
COLLEGE, SENT ME HIS
SYLLABUS AND IT WAS
OVER 30 PAGES LONG.

ANOTHER FRIEND, THE
CARTOONIST AND TEACHER
IVAN BRUNETTI, HAD
PUBLISHED HIS SYLLABUS
IN THE FORM OF A LITTLE
BOOK: "CARTOONING:
PHILOSOPHY and PRACTICE"
(YALE UNIVERSITY PRESS: 2011)

SCHEDULE

Tuesdays and Thursdays
6101 HUMANITIES · 4:30-7:00 PM

Please come

BRING SOMEONE!

WEDNESDAY **SPECIAL EVENTS** WEDNESDAY
VISITING ARTISTS

IVAN BRUNETTI
FEBRUARY 15
4:30-5:45
L160 CHAZEN

RYAN KNIGHTON
FEBRUARY 22
4:30-5:45
L160 CHAZEN

also

PROFESSOR
LYNDA on MATT GROENING
MARCH 8, THURS.
7:00 PM MMOCA
LECTURE HALL
227 STATE

and

DAN CHAON
MAY 3, THURS
7:00 PM MMOCA
LECTURE HALL
227 STATE

our classroom is open to you as a work space except for the times listed below

MON + WEDS	TUES + THURS	I'LL BE in 6101 on WEDS 9:30-NOON FOR DROP-IN TIME
1:20-3:50	8:50-11:20 1:20-3:50	

CLASSROOM RULES

FOR OUR FIRST 8 CLASSES

TAKE NOTES HERE

YOUR CARD →

↖ DRAW THE SYMBOL HERE

ALL THREE OF THESE SYLLABI AND THE PEOPLE WHO CREATED THEM HAVE HAD A PROFOUND EFFECT ON MY WAY OF TEACHING AND MY VERY IDEA OF WHAT TEACHING IS. FROM THE MOST MUNDANE ASPECTS SUCH AS TAKING ATTENDANCE TO THE MORE SUBTLE CIRCUMSTANCE OF KNOWING WHEN TO STEP IN OR STAND BACK WHEN A STUDENT STRUGGLES WITH AN ASSIGNMENT, THESE THREE PROVIDED CRUCIAL GUIDANCE. THAT ALL THREE OF THEM ARE PRACTICING ARTISTS WITH DEEP CURIOSITY ABOUT IMAGES AND HOW THEY MOVE BETWEEN PEOPLE IS NO ACCIDENT. THEY WERE JUST THE TEACHERS I NEEDED.

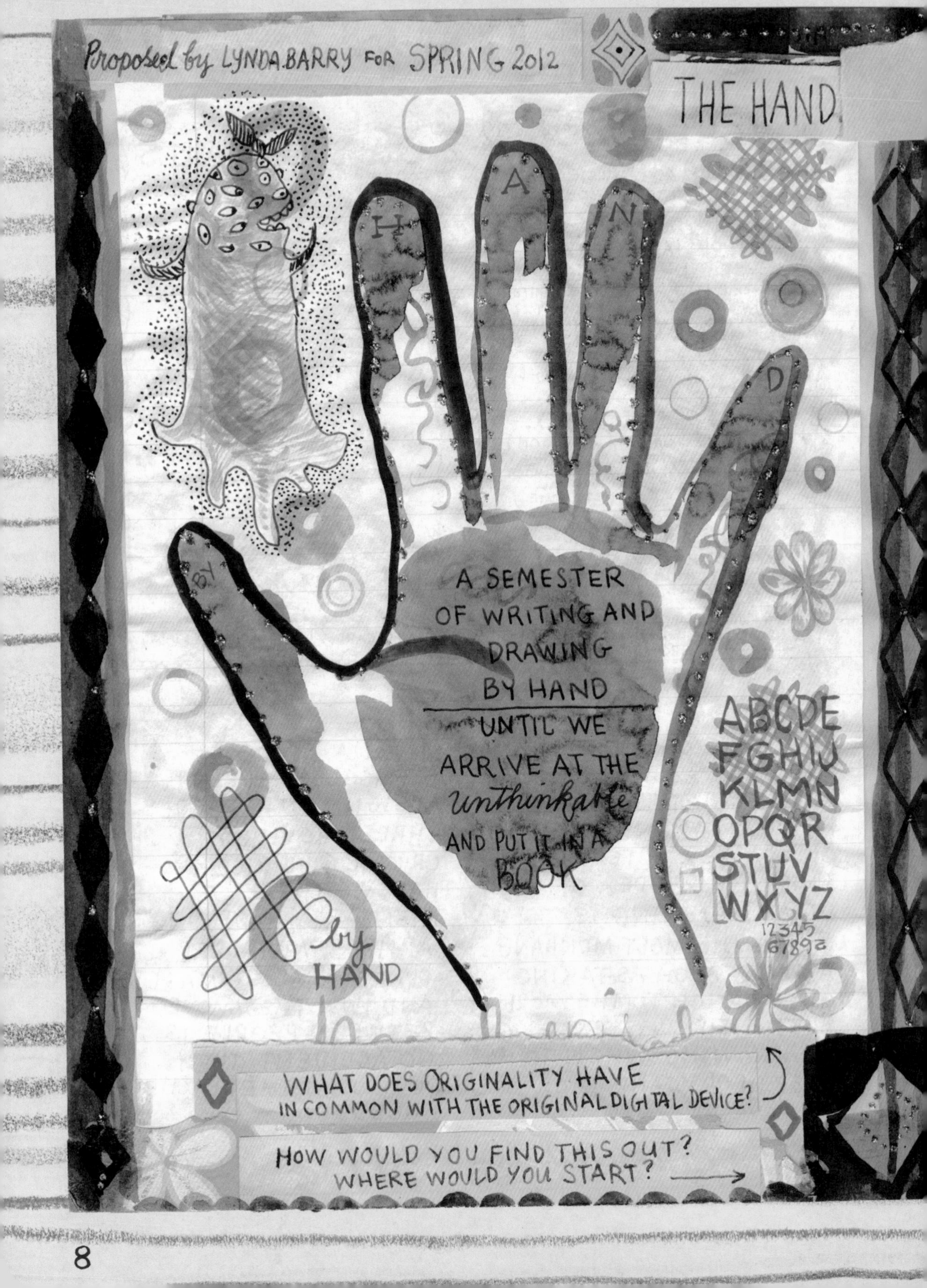
Proposed by LYNDA BARRY FOR SPRING 2012
THE HAND.
H A N D
BY
A SEMESTER OF WRITING AND DRAWING BY HAND
UNTIL WE ARRIVE AT THE unthinkable AND PUT IT IN A BOOK
ABCDE FGHIJ KLMN OPQR STUV WXYZ
12345 67890
by HAND
WHAT DOES ORIGINALITY HAVE IN COMMON WITH THE ORIGINAL DIGITAL DEVICE?
HOW WOULD YOU FIND THIS OUT? WHERE WOULD YOU START?

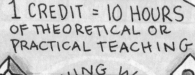

1 CREDIT = 10 HOURS OF THEORETICAL OR PRACTICAL TEACHING

DRAWING WORDS
SPEAKING PICTURES

"WHEN I START FEELING TOO CONCERNED THAT ALL THE WORDS I WRITE BE VERY SMART AND ABOUT SOMETHING WORTHWHILE, I FIND MY URGE TO WRITE REPLACED WITH AN URGE TO DRAW MONKEYS" FEB 10 '11 NOTEBOOK ENTRY

I need STUDENTS to HELP me FIGURE OUT how images MOVE

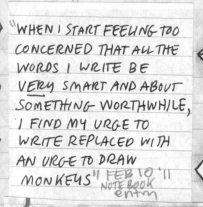

" I'm going to apply for the Artist-in-Residence position at the UW-Madison.

If I were going to get to seriously study something for a semester with a group of really smart students, what would it be?

The idea of the notebook being the core. Using comp books and handwriting and the natural human instinct for storytelling as a means of transferring something from one person to another. Transferring what?

Interested in handwriting, drawing, memorization of poetry, what's going on in the brain when we're in a certain image-making /mark-making frame of mind.

Need a room with tables for writing and drawing, tables we can move together so we can all be a group and move apart so we can do what Ira Progoff called "this solitary work we do together." Walls we can put things up on so we can stare at them.

Teaching this: To be able to accept what shows up. What do writing, drawing, dancing, music -- everything we call the arts—what do they have in common? Why do we group these things together? How do people who don't speak the same language communicate? How do we communicate with babies? When we translate something, what is being translated?

The ordinary is extraordinary. FEB 14 2011 NOTEBOOK ENTRY

HOW DO IMAGES MOVE AND TRANSFER?
SOMETHING INSIDE ONE PERSON TAKES EXTERNAL FORM – CONTAINED BY A POEM, STORY, PICTURE, MELODY, PLAY, ETC – AND THROUGH A CERTAIN KIND OF ENGAGEMENT, IS TRANSFERRED TO THE INSIDE OF SOMEONE ELSE. ART AS A TRANSIT SYSTEM FOR IMAGES

WHAT SORTS OF ACTIVITIES CAN DEMON- STRATE THIS?

HOW I GOT HOOKED

MY 'WHAT IT IS' CLASS

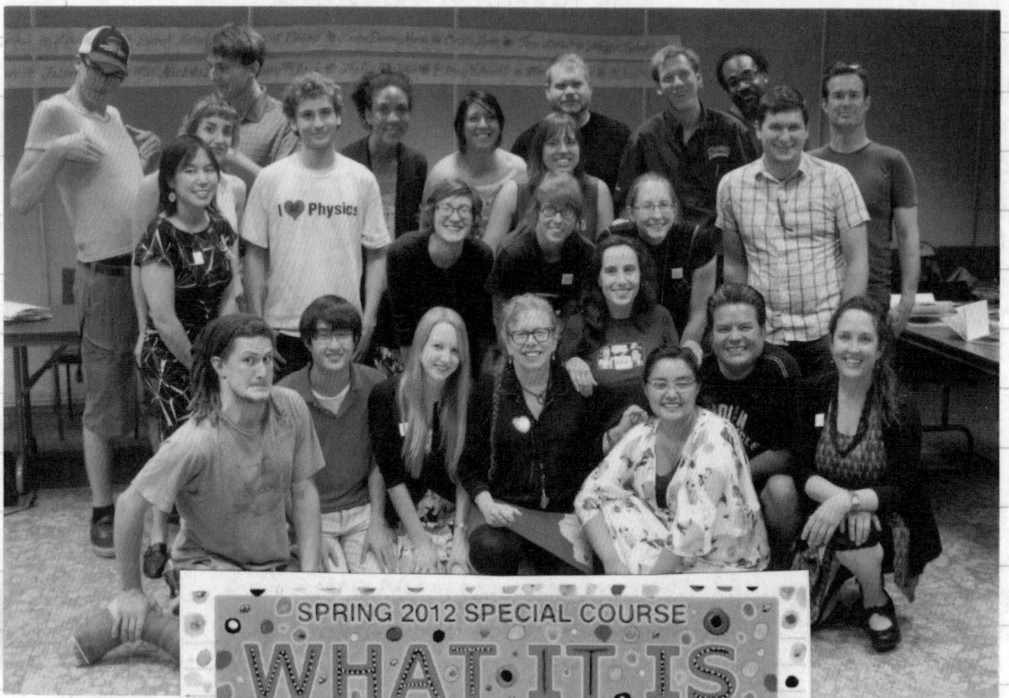

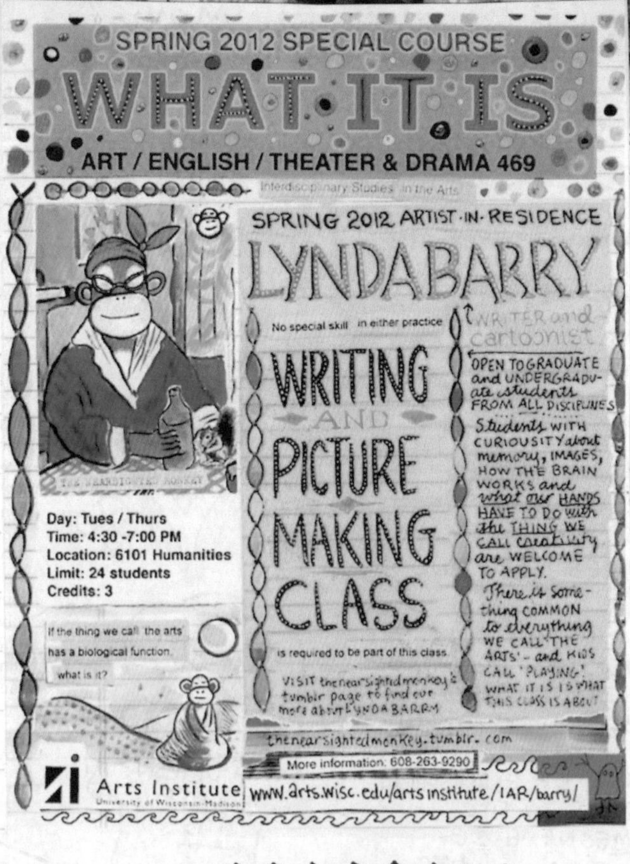
SPRING 2012 SPECIAL COURSE
WHAT IT IS
ART / ENGLISH / THEATER & DRAMA 469
Interdisciplinary Studies in the Arts
SPRING 2012 ARTIST-IN-RESIDENCE
LYNDA BARRY
WRITER and cartoonist
No special skill in either practice
WRITING AND PICTURE MAKING CLASS
is required to be part of this class.
OPEN TO GRADUATE and UNDERGRADUATE students FROM ALL DISCIPLINES
Students WITH CURIOUSITY about memory, IMAGES, HOW THE BRAIN WORKS and what our HANDS HAVE TO DO with the THING WE CALL creativity are WELCOME TO APPLY.
There is something COMMON to everything WE CALL 'THE ARTS' - and KIDS CALL 'PLAYING'. WHAT IT IS IS WHAT THIS CLASS IS ABOUT
Day: Tues / Thurs
Time: 4:30 -7:00 PM
Location: 6101 Humanities
Limit: 24 students
Credits: 3
If the thing we call the arts
has a biological function,
what is it?
VISIT thenearsightedmonkey's tumblr page to find out more about LYNDA BARRY
thenearsightedmonkey.tumblr.com
More information: 608-263-9290
Arts Institute
University of Wisconsin-Madison
www.arts.wisc.edu/arts institute/IAR/barry/

THESE ARE THE FIRST STUDENTS I WAS ABLE TO WORK WITH LONG ENOUGH TO GET AN IDEA OF HOW IMAGES MOVE BETWEEN PEOPLE AND PARTS OF OURSELVES - FROM THE BACK OF THE MIND ONTO THE PAGE: MADE VISIBLE

WHAT BEGAN AS A SEMESTER-LONG ARTS INSTITUTE RESIDENCY BECAME AN OBSESSION: WHAT HAPPENS WHEN STUDENTS FROM DIFFERENT DISCIPLINES GET TOGETHER TO WORK INTENSELY, USING BOTH DRAWING AND WRITING TO BRING ABOUT THE UNTHINKABLE?

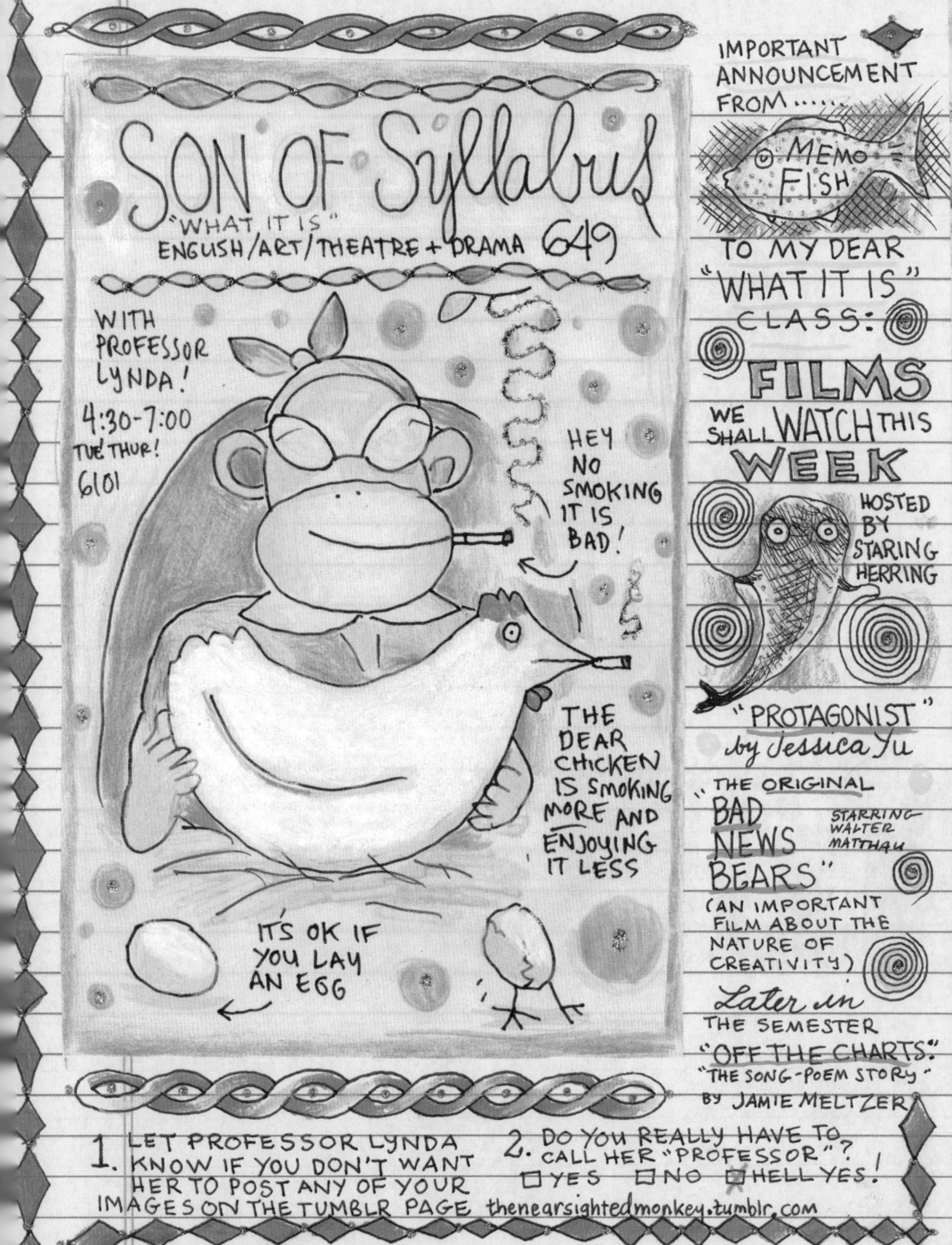
SON OF Syllabus
"WHAT IT IS"
ENGLISH/ART/THEATRE + DRAMA 649
WITH PROFESSOR LYNDA!
4:30-7:00
TUE THUR!
6101
HEY NO SMOKING IT IS BAD!
THE DEAR CHICKEN IS SMOKING MORE AND ENJOYING IT LESS
IT'S OK IF YOU LAY AN EGG
IMPORTANT ANNOUNCEMENT FROM......
MEMO FISH
TO MY DEAR "WHAT IT IS" CLASS:
FILMS WE SHALL WATCH THIS WEEK
HOSTED BY STARING HERRING
"PROTAGONIST" by Jessica Yu
"THE ORIGINAL BAD NEWS BEARS"
STARRING WALTER MATTHAU
(AN IMPORTANT FILM ABOUT THE NATURE OF CREATIVITY)
Later in THE SEMESTER "OFF THE CHARTS: "THE SONG-POEM STORY" BY JAMIE MELTZER
1. LET PROFESSOR LYNDA KNOW IF YOU DON'T WANT HER TO POST ANY OF YOUR IMAGES ON THE TUMBLR PAGE thenearsightedmonkey.tumblr.com
2. DO YOU REALLY HAVE TO CALL HER "PROFESSOR"?
☐ YES ☐ NO ☒ HELL YES!

THEORY

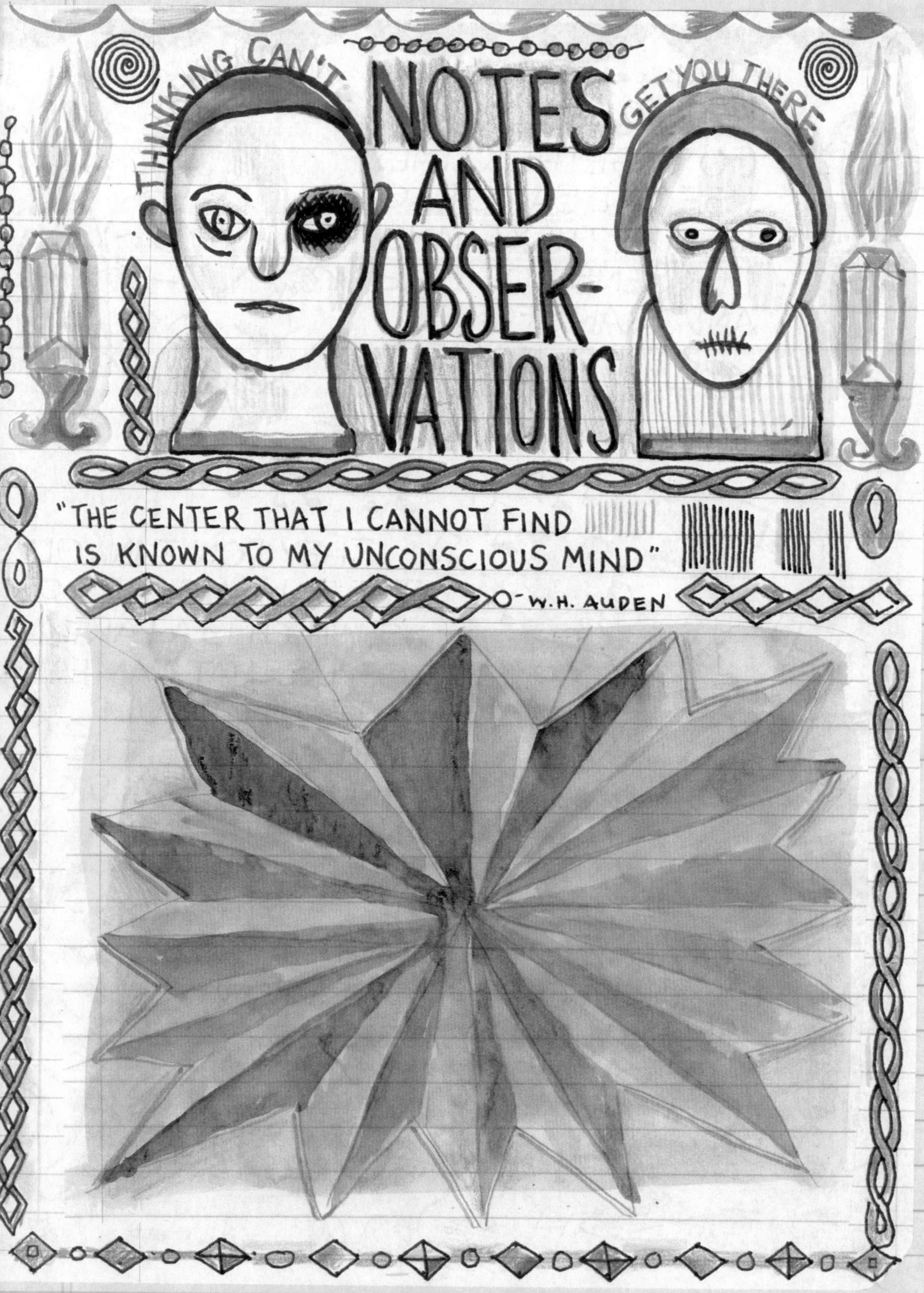
THINKING CAN'T
NOTES AND OBSERVATIONS
GET YOU THERE
"THE CENTER THAT I CANNOT FIND IS KNOWN TO MY UNCONSCIOUS MIND"
—W.H. AUDEN

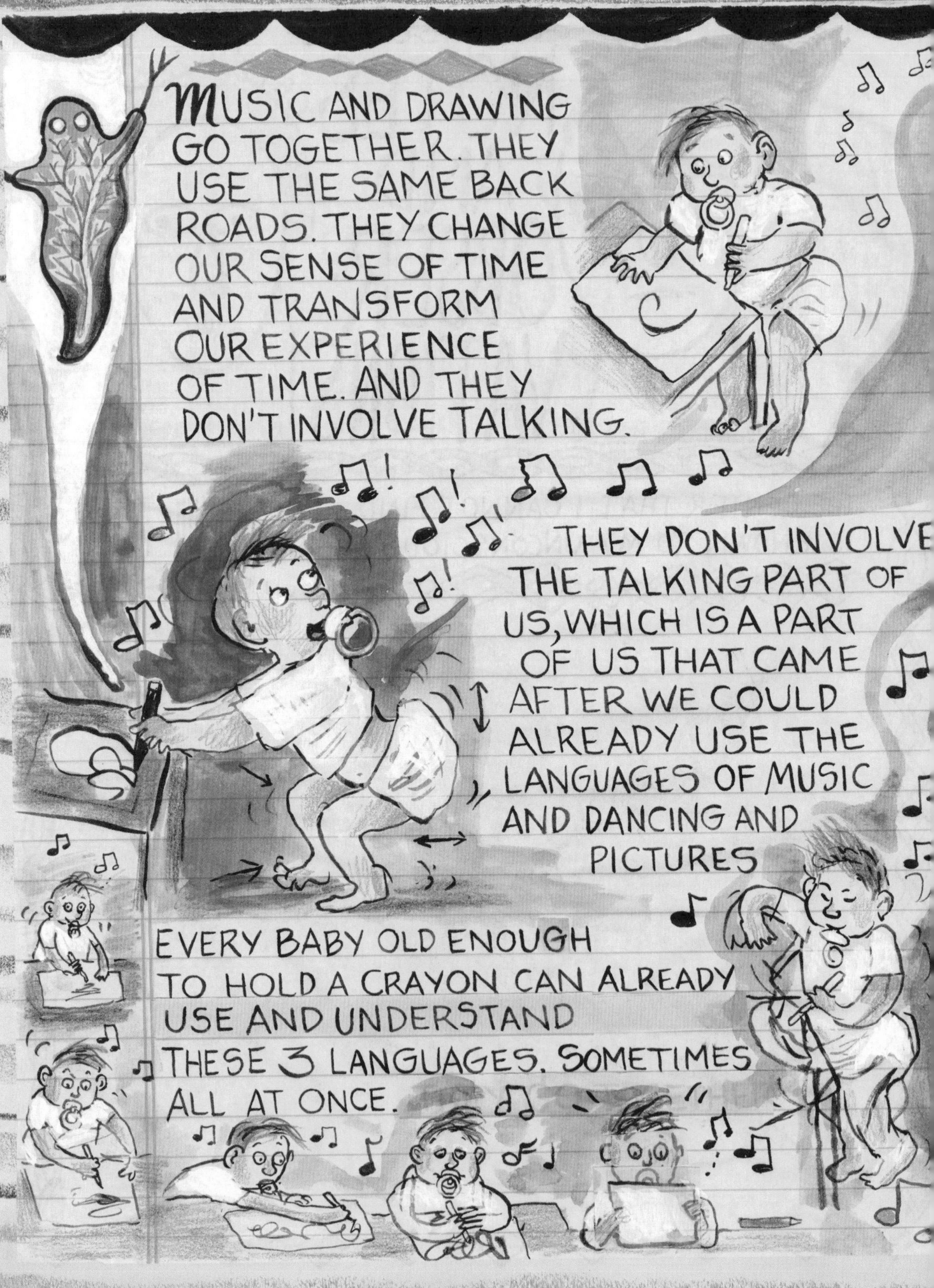
MUSIC AND DRAWING GO TOGETHER. THEY USE THE SAME BACK ROADS. THEY CHANGE OUR SENSE OF TIME AND TRANSFORM OUR EXPERIENCE OF TIME. AND THEY DON'T INVOLVE TALKING.
THEY DON'T INVOLVE THE TALKING PART OF US, WHICH IS A PART OF US THAT CAME AFTER WE COULD ALREADY USE THE LANGUAGES OF MUSIC AND DANCING AND PICTURES
EVERY BABY OLD ENOUGH TO HOLD A CRAYON CAN ALREADY USE AND UNDERSTAND THESE 3 LANGUAGES. SOMETIMES ALL AT ONCE.

How are our hands, images, and insight connected?

There is something common to everything we call the arts. What is it? It's not aesthetics. I've seen a squatting guy at a Minnesota 'Renaissance Faire' perform Romeo and Juliet using a cigarette butt and a bottle cap for the main characters, and I've seen Romeo and Juliet performed by Shakespearean actors in full period costume, and both times this 'it' I'm talking about was there. This ancient 'it' is something I call 'an image.'

By image I don't mean a visual representation, I mean something that is more like a ghost than a picture; something which feels somehow alive, has no fixed meaning and is contained and transported by something that is not alive- a book, a song, a painting— anything we call an 'art form.' Images are also contained by certain objects that young children become deeply attached to, like a certain blanket a certain child can't stand to be without. How is a piece of cloth transformed into something so directly tied to a child's sense of well-being that if it's missing, the child can't sleep? The blanket has come to contain something the child interacts with as if it were alive. How did this 'it' come to be located in the blanket? How was it put there?

Why do we have an innate ability to have a sustained and interactive relationship with an object/image well before we are able to speak? What kind of interaction is taking place?

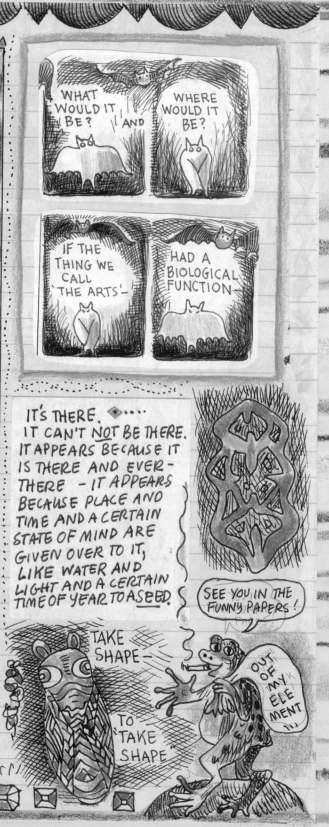

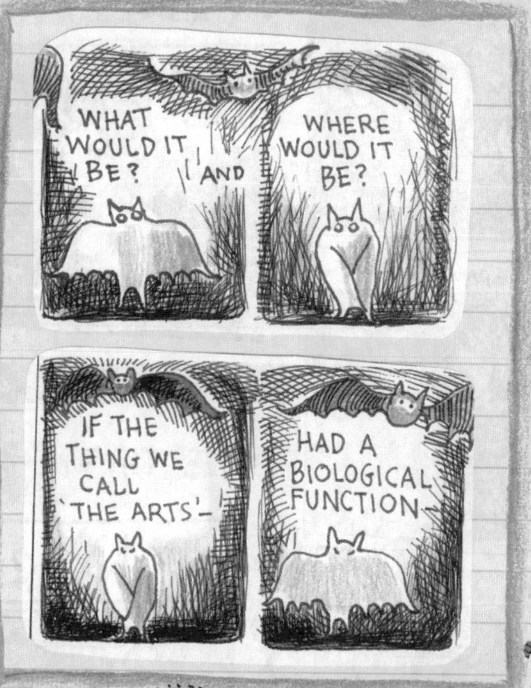
WHAT WOULD IT BE?
AND
WHERE WOULD IT BE?
IF THE THING WE CALL 'THE ARTS'—
HAD A BIOLOGICAL FUNCTION—

IT'S THERE....
IT CAN'T NOT BE THERE.
IT APPEARS BECAUSE IT IS THERE AND EVER-THERE - IT APPEARS BECAUSE PLACE AND TIME AND A CERTAIN STATE OF MIND ARE GIVEN OVER TO IT, LIKE WATER AND LIGHT AND A CERTAIN TIME OF YEAR TO A SEED.

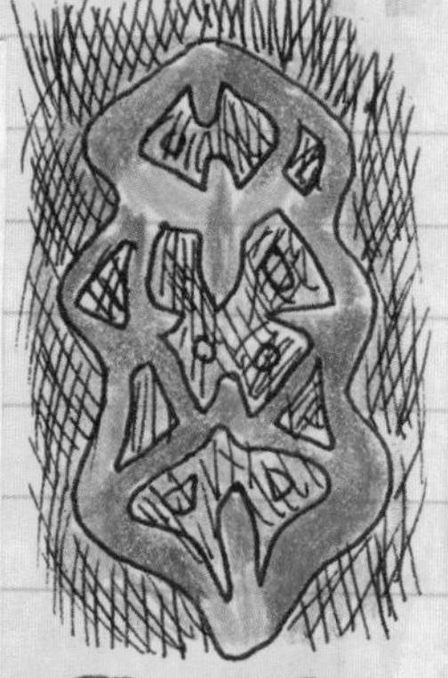

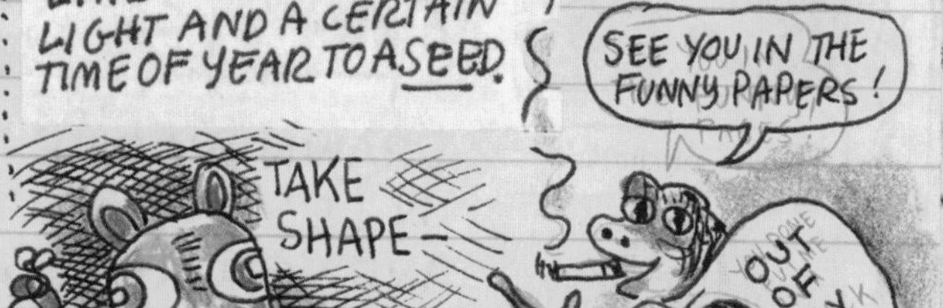
SEE YOU IN THE FUNNY PAPERS!
TAKE SHAPE—
TO 'TAKE SHAPE'
OUT OF MY ELEMENT

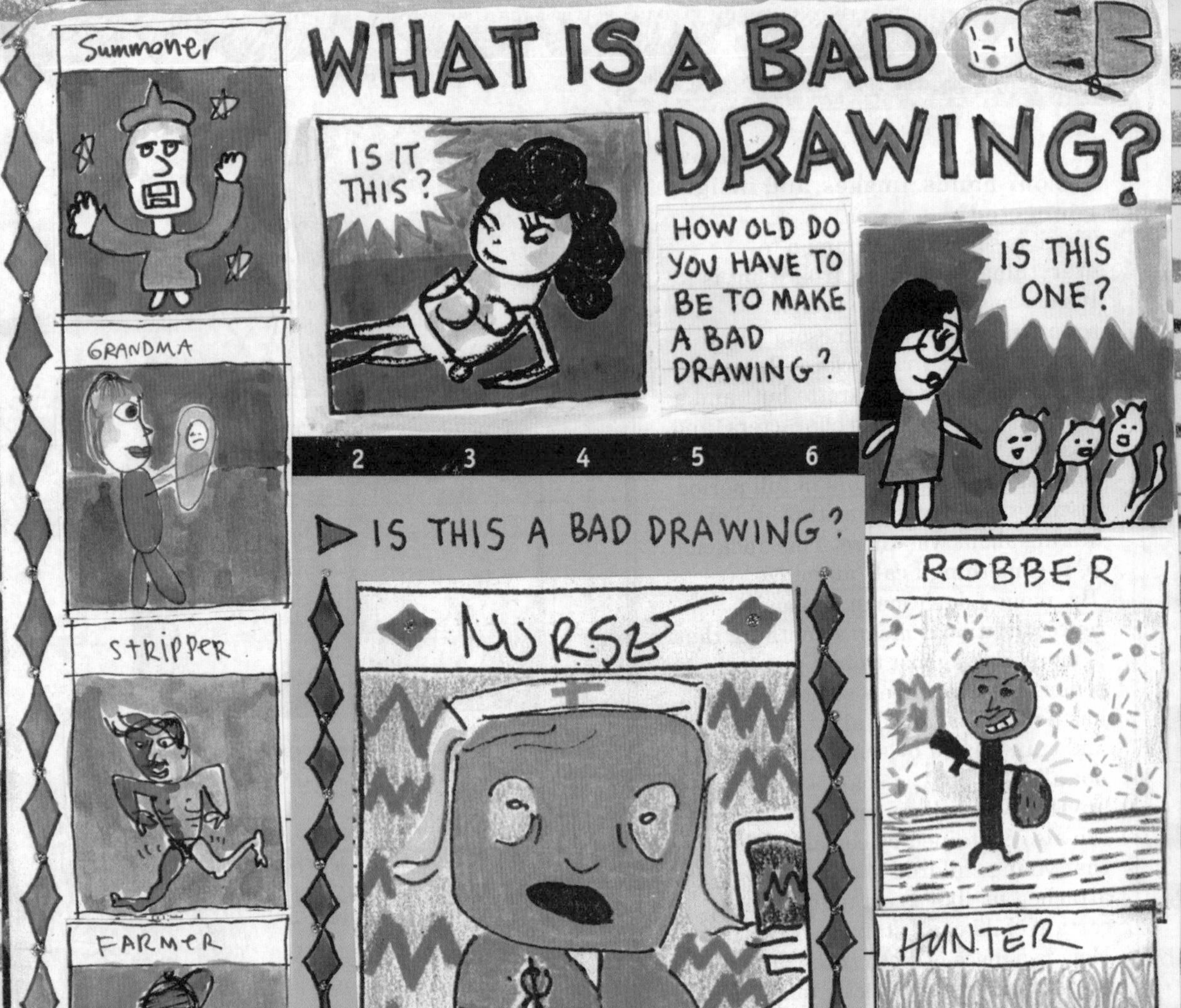

WHAT IS A BAD DRAWING?
Summoner
IS IT THIS?
HOW OLD DO YOU HAVE TO BE TO MAKE A BAD DRAWING?
IS THIS ONE?
GRANDMA
2 3 4 5 6
IS THIS A BAD DRAWING?
NURSE
ROBBER
stripper
FARMER
HUNTER
NEWS ANCHOR
DRAWN BY ONE STUDENT IN LESS THAN A MINUTE AND COLORED BY ANOTHER
– IS IT BAD???
DRUNK
THERE'S THE DRAWING YOU ARE TRYING TO MAKE AND THE DRAWING THAT IS ACTUALLY BEING MADE – AND YOU CAN'T SEE IT UNTIL YOU FORGET WHAT YOU WERE TRYING TO DO

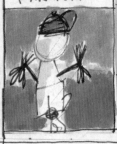

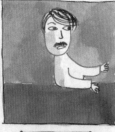

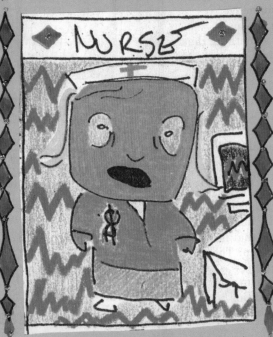

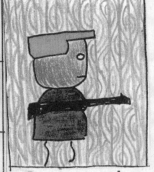

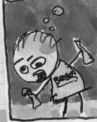

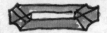

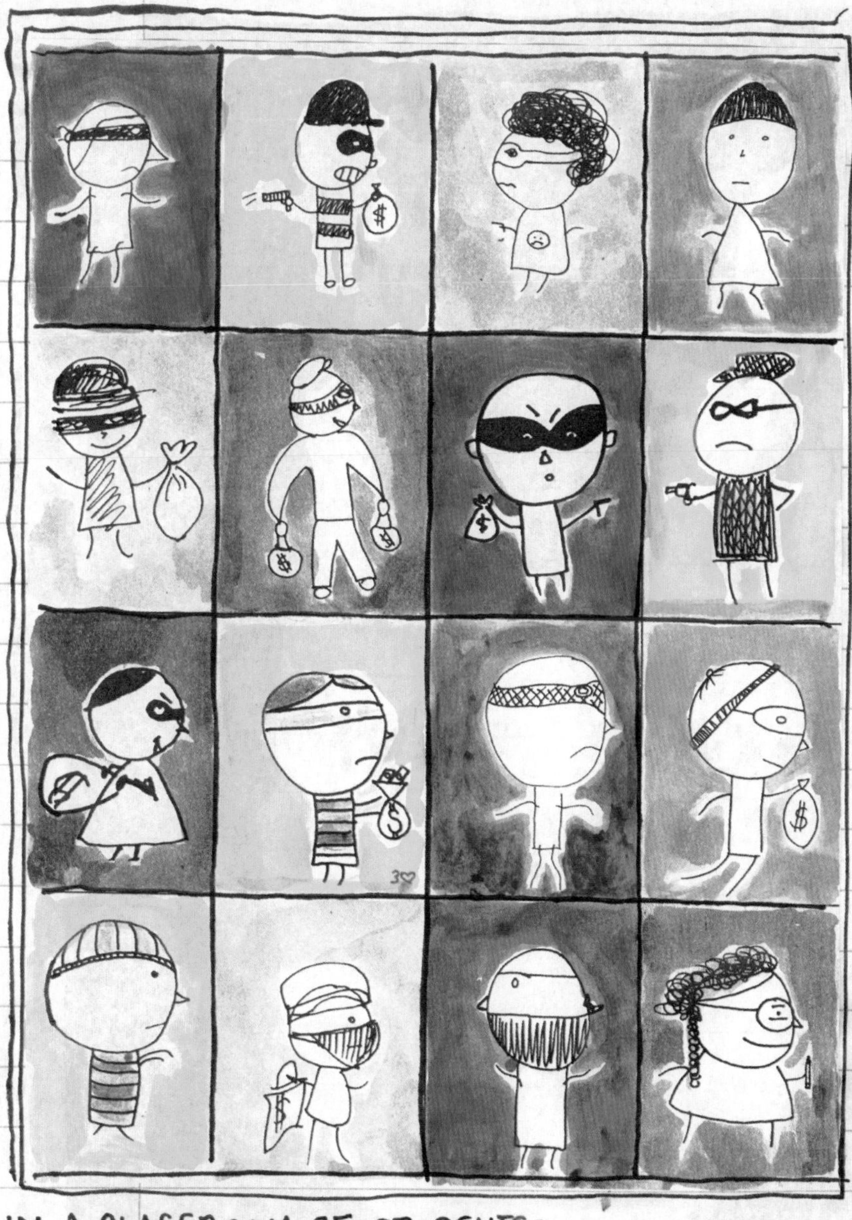

WHICH OF THESE IS A BAD DRAWING?

THEY WERE ALL DRAWN DURING THE SAME 60 SECONDS BY STUDENTS IN MY "WHAT IT IS" CLASS. I ASKED THEM TO DRAW A ROBBER IN THE STYLE OF IVAN BRUNETTI

his instructions:

"DRAW A CHARACTER BUILT OUT OF SIMPLE SHAPES: CIRCLES, TRIANGLES, RECTANGLES. MINIMAL FEATURES AND RUDIMENTARY LIMBS ARE OK, AS IS A BASIC PATTERN ON HIS OR HER CLOTHING."

IN A CLASSROOM OF STUDENTS WITH VARYING LEVELS OF DRAWING EXPERIENCE, THIS WAY OF DRAWING BRINGS US TO A COMMON STARTING PLACE THAT IS LIKE THE STARTING PLACE WE ALL SHARE: OUR FIRST DRAWINGS OF PEOPLE MADE WHEN WE WERE LITTLE

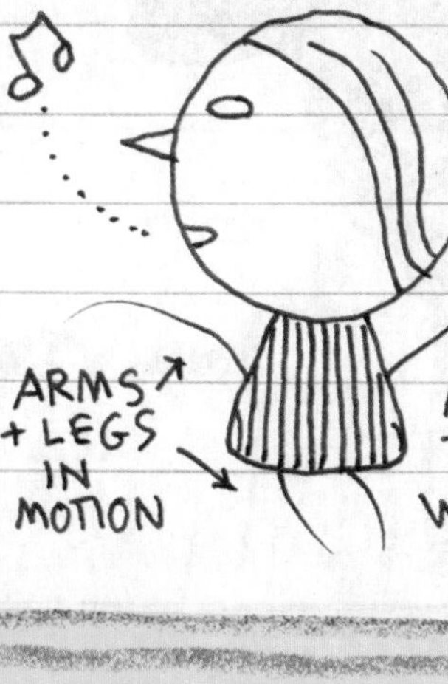
ARMS + LEGS IN MOTION

OVERSIZED HEAD, SIMPLE BODY AND FACIAL FEATURES. IT'S A QUICK AND WORKABLE ALTERNATIVE TO STICK FIGURES WITH A LOT MORE SOUL

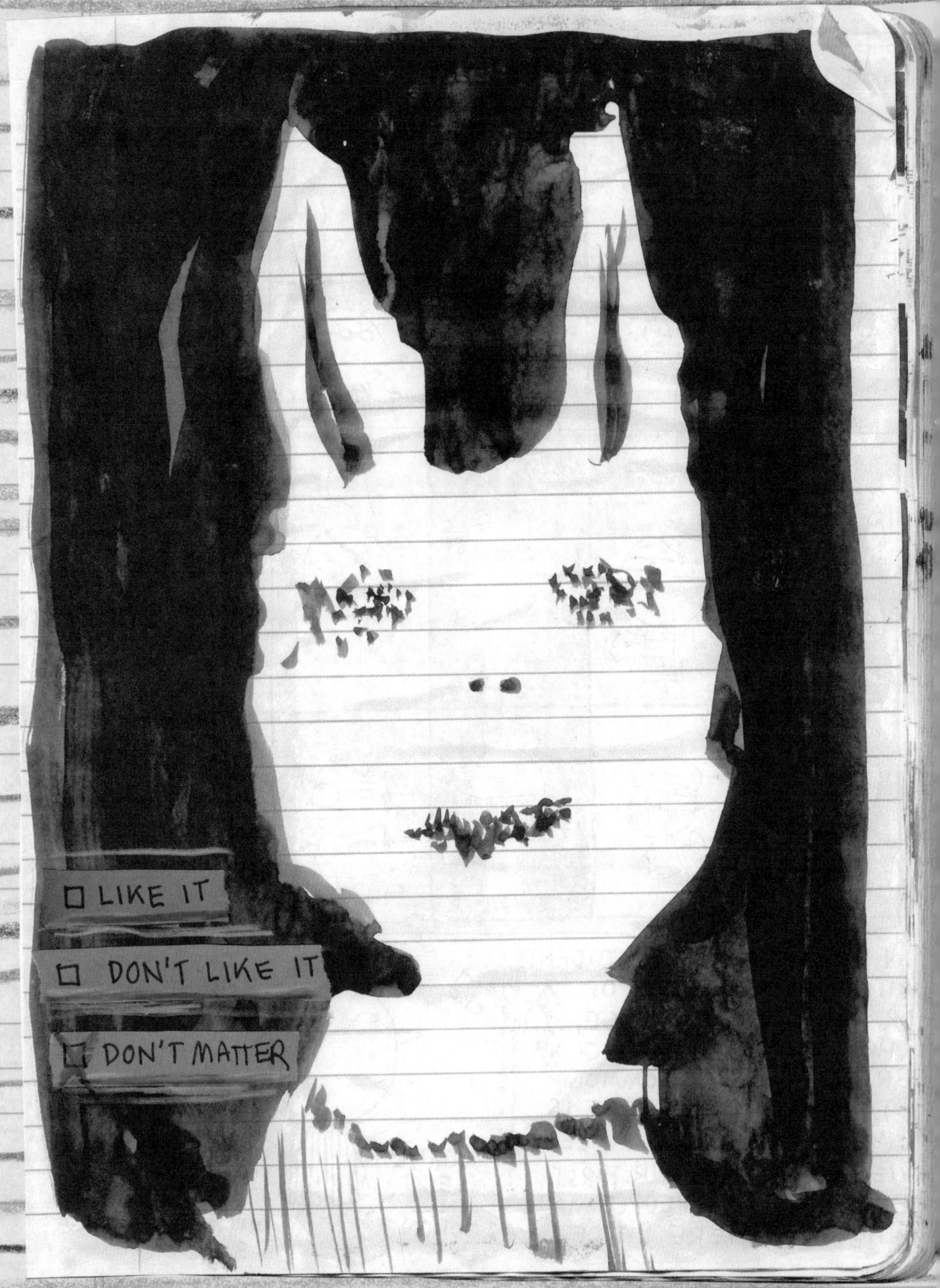
☐ LIKE IT
☐ DON'T LIKE IT
☐ DON'T MATTER

ON LIKING AND NOT LIKING

OUR DRAWINGS OUR DRAWINGS

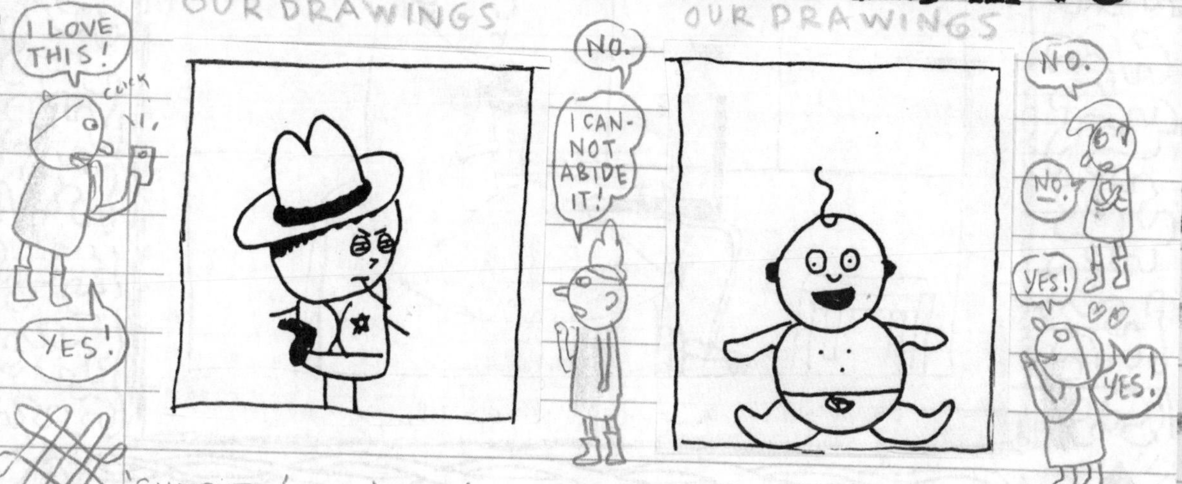

I LOVE THIS!
CLICK
YES!
NO.
I CANNOT ABIDE IT!
NO.
NO.
YES!
YES!

'SHERIFF' and 'BABY' – DRAWING JAM STUDENT DRAWINGS

OUR DRAWINGS

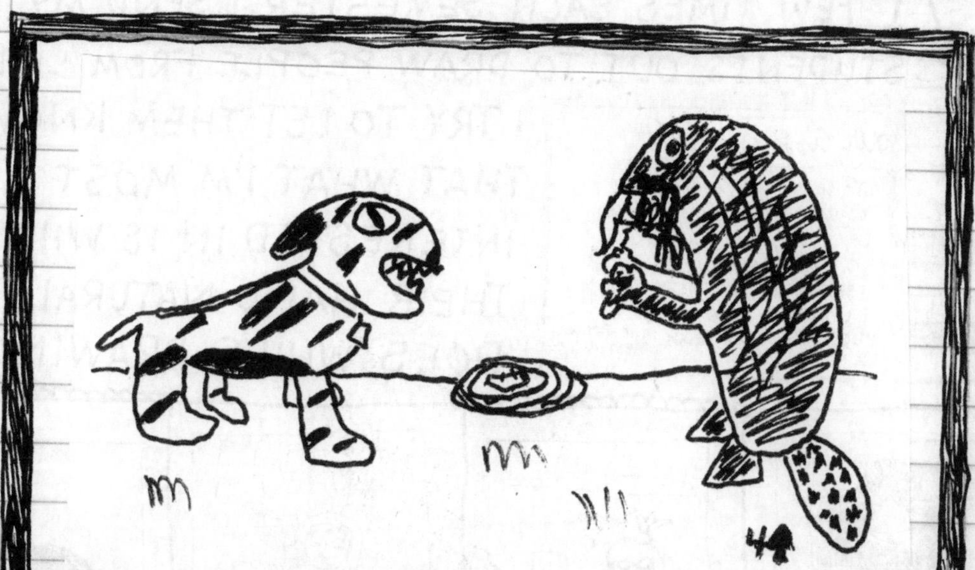

"DOG AND BEAVER" – INDEX CARD STUDENT DRAWING

WHAT HAPPENS TO A DRAWING WHEN WE DISLIKE IT?

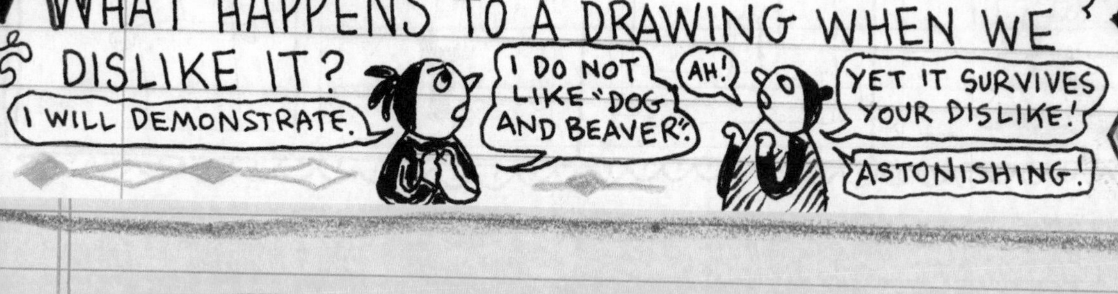

I WILL DEMONSTRATE.
I DO NOT LIKE "DOG AND BEAVER".
AH!
YET IT SURVIVES YOUR DISLIKE!
ASTONISHING!

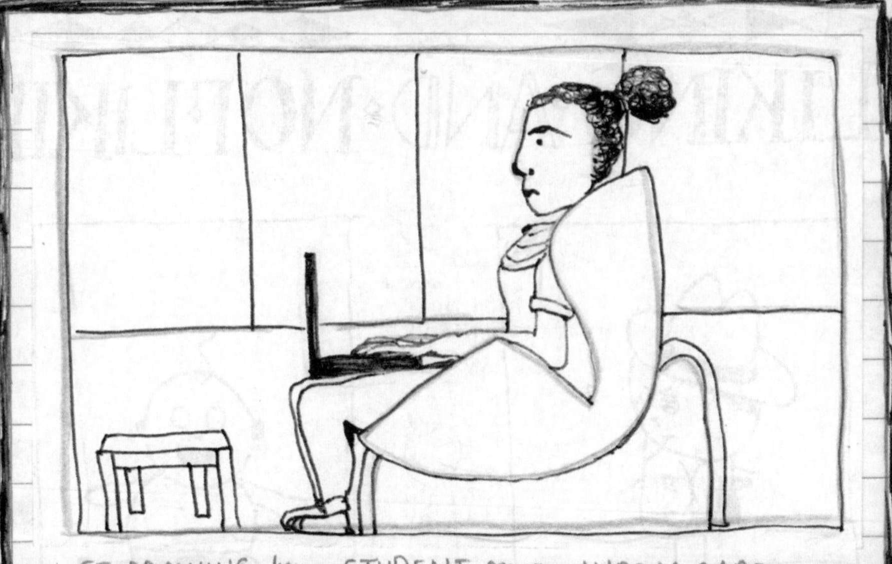

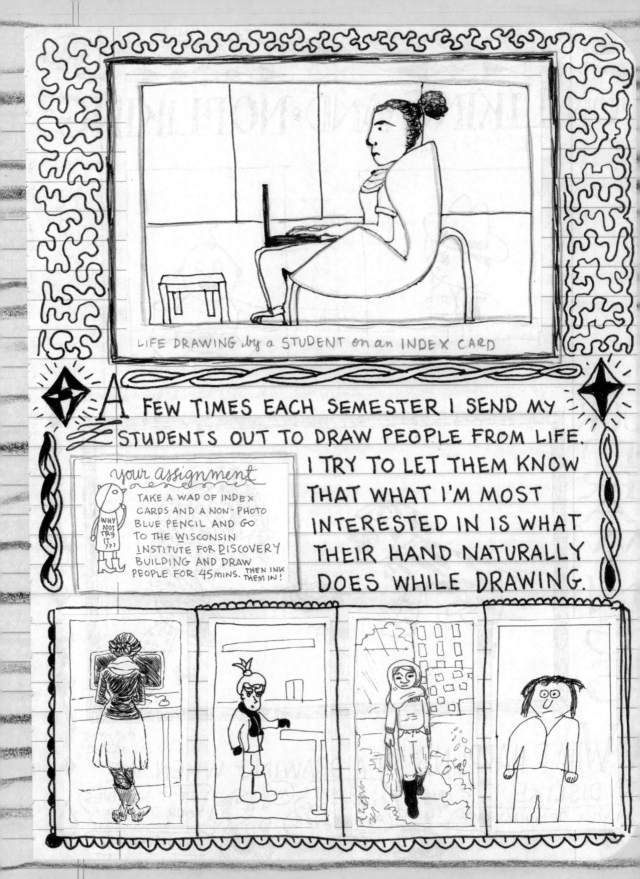

LIFE DRAWING by a STUDENT on an INDEX CARD

A FEW TIMES EACH SEMESTER I SEND MY STUDENTS OUT TO DRAW PEOPLE FROM LIFE.

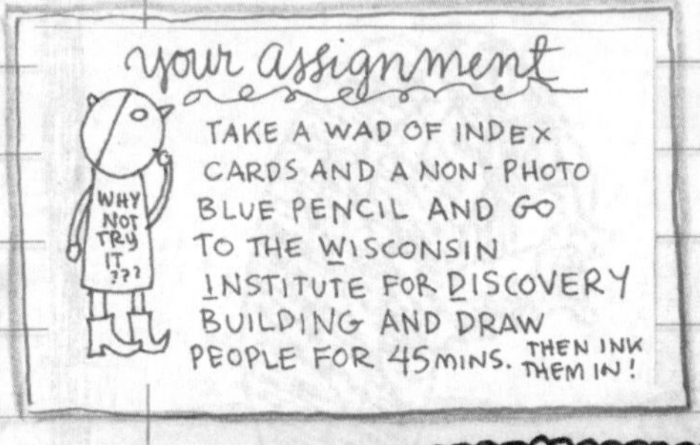
your assignment
WHY NOT TRY IT???
TAKE A WAD OF INDEX CARDS AND A NON-PHOTO BLUE PENCIL AND GO TO THE WISCONSIN INSTITUTE FOR DISCOVERY BUILDING AND DRAW PEOPLE FOR 45 MINS.
THEN INK THEM IN!

I TRY TO LET THEM KNOW THAT WHAT I'M MOST INTERESTED IN IS WHAT THEIR HAND NATURALLY DOES WHILE DRAWING.

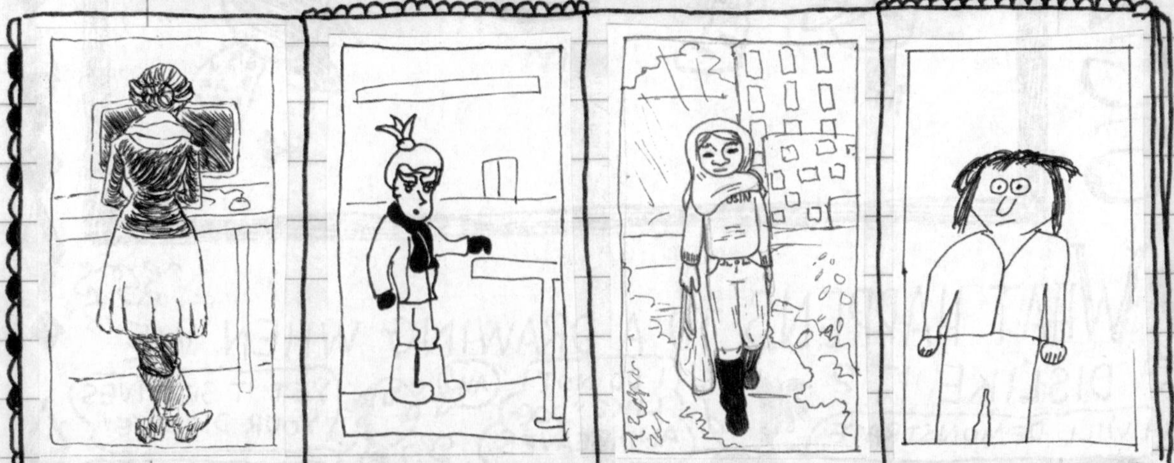

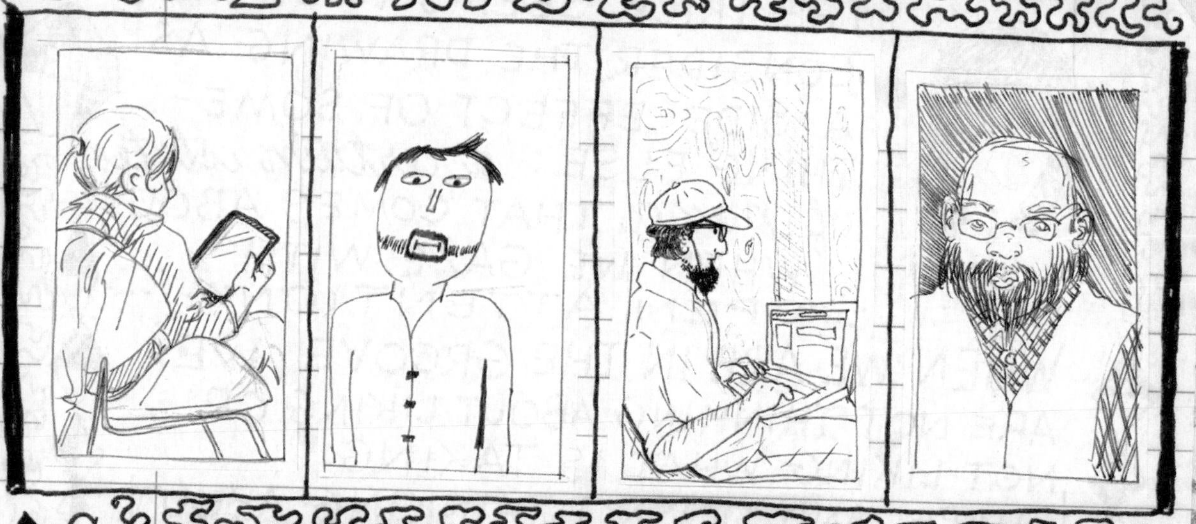

SOME HANDS HAVE BEEN AT IT FOR AWHILE BUT OTHERS ARE SO NEW TO THE GAME THAT NO PARTICULAR STYLE OF DRAWING HAS HAD A CHANCE TO TAKE ROOT

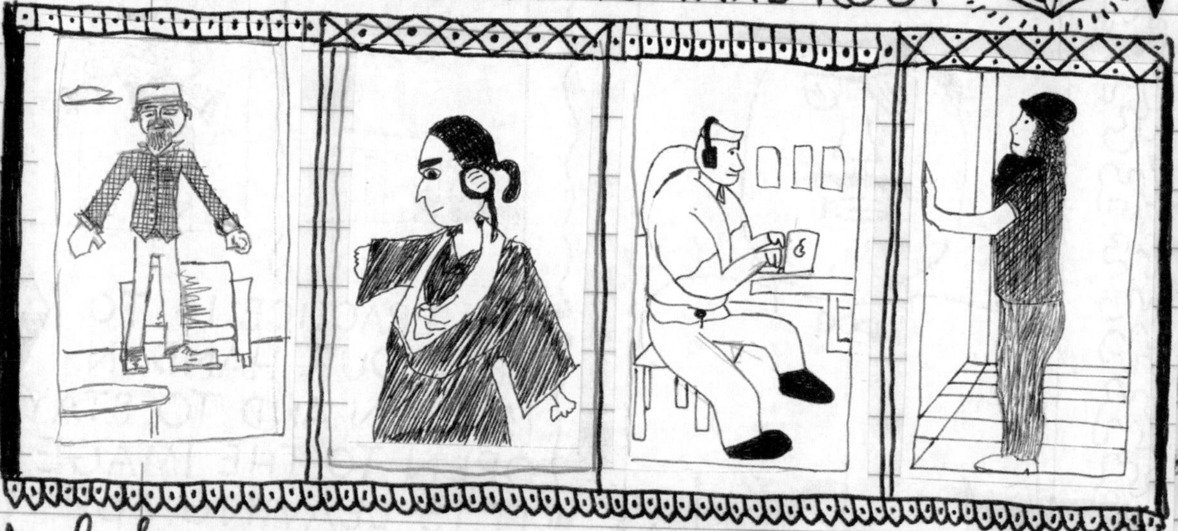

I know IF I CAN JUST KEEP THEM DRAWING WITHOUT THINKING ABOUT IT TOO MUCH, SOMETHING QUITE ORIGINAL WILL APPEAR... (ALMOST BY ITSELF)

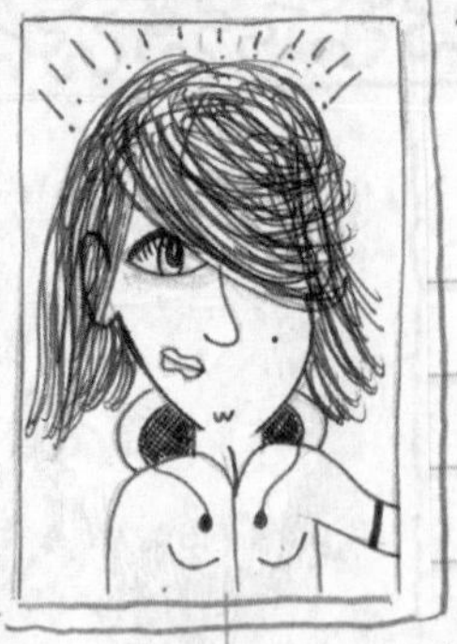

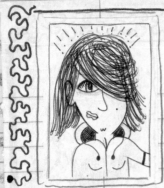

THE TRICK SEEMS TO BE THIS: CONSIDER THE DRAWING AS A SIDE EFFECT OF SOMETHING ELSE: *a certain state of mind* THAT COMES ABOUT WHEN WE GAZE WITH OPEN ATTENTION

WHEN WE ARE IN THE GROOVE, WE ARE NOT THINKING ABOUT LIKING OR NOT LIKING WHAT IS TAKING SHAPE, AND IT ISN'T THINKING ABOUT US EITHER. YET SOMETHING SHOWS UP---

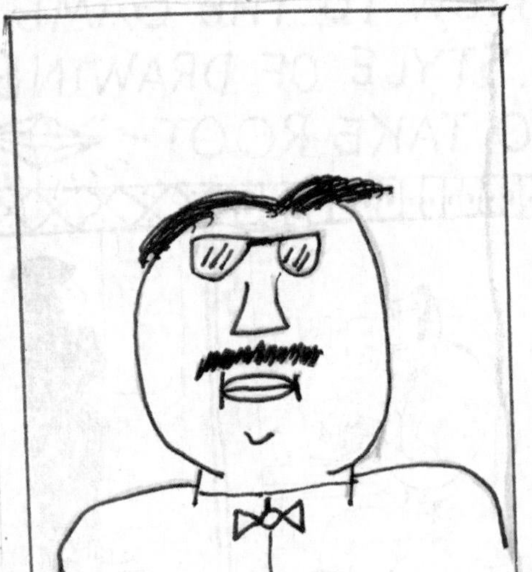

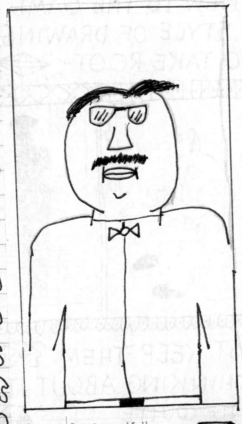

"LIFE DRAWING" – STUDENT IMAGE ON INDEX CARD

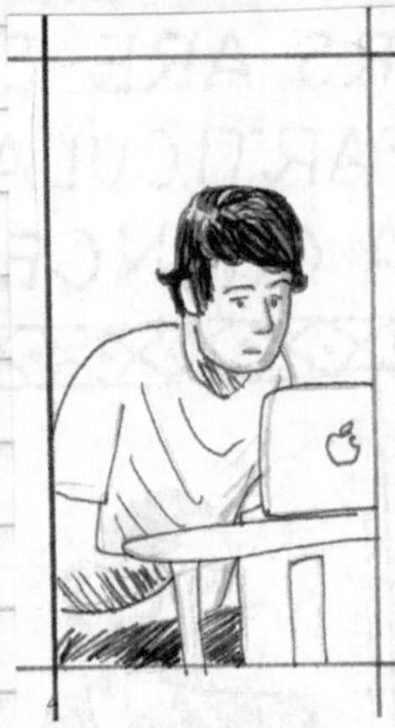

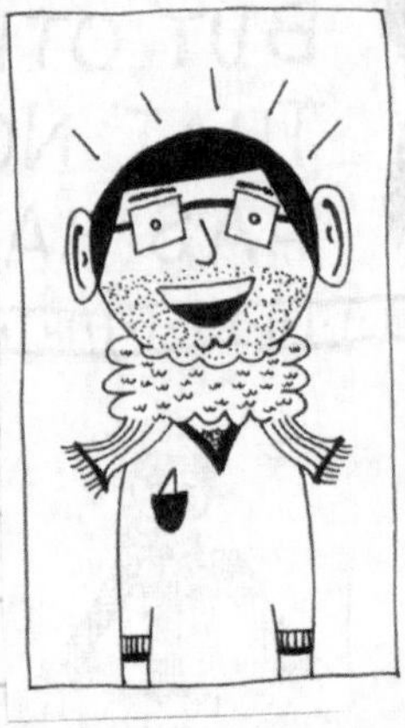

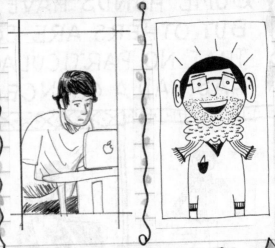

THE PRACTICE IS TO KEEP OUR HAND IN MOTION AND TO STAY OPEN TO THE IMAGE IT IS LEAVING FOR US: A MESSAGE-FRAGMENT WE MAY NOT RECOGNIZE UNTIL WE HAVE ENOUGH OF THEM TO UNDERSTAND.

LIKING AND NOT LIKING CAN MAKE US BLIND TO <u>WHAT'S</u> <u>THERE</u>. IN SPITE OF HOW WE FEEL ABOUT IT, IT IS MAKING ITS WAY FROM THE UNSEEN TO THE VISIBLE WORLD, ONE LINE AFTER THE NEXT, BRINGING WITH IT A KIND OF ALIVENESS I LIVE FOR: RIGHT HERE, RIGHT NOW. *All of these drawings* WERE MADE DURING THE SAME 45 MINUTES BY 14 OF MY STUDENTS ON A WINTER AFTERNOON IN 2014:

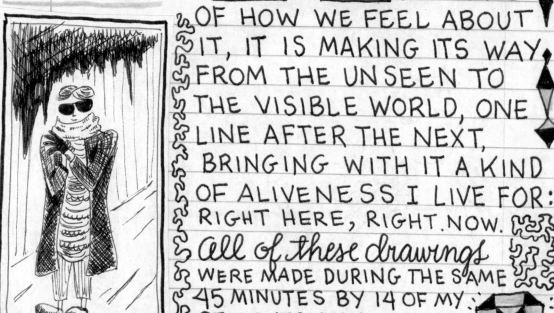

INDEX CARDS, NON-PHOTO BLUE PENCIL, UNIBALL PEN, HUMAN HAND, OPEN EYES, PHYSICAL MOTION.

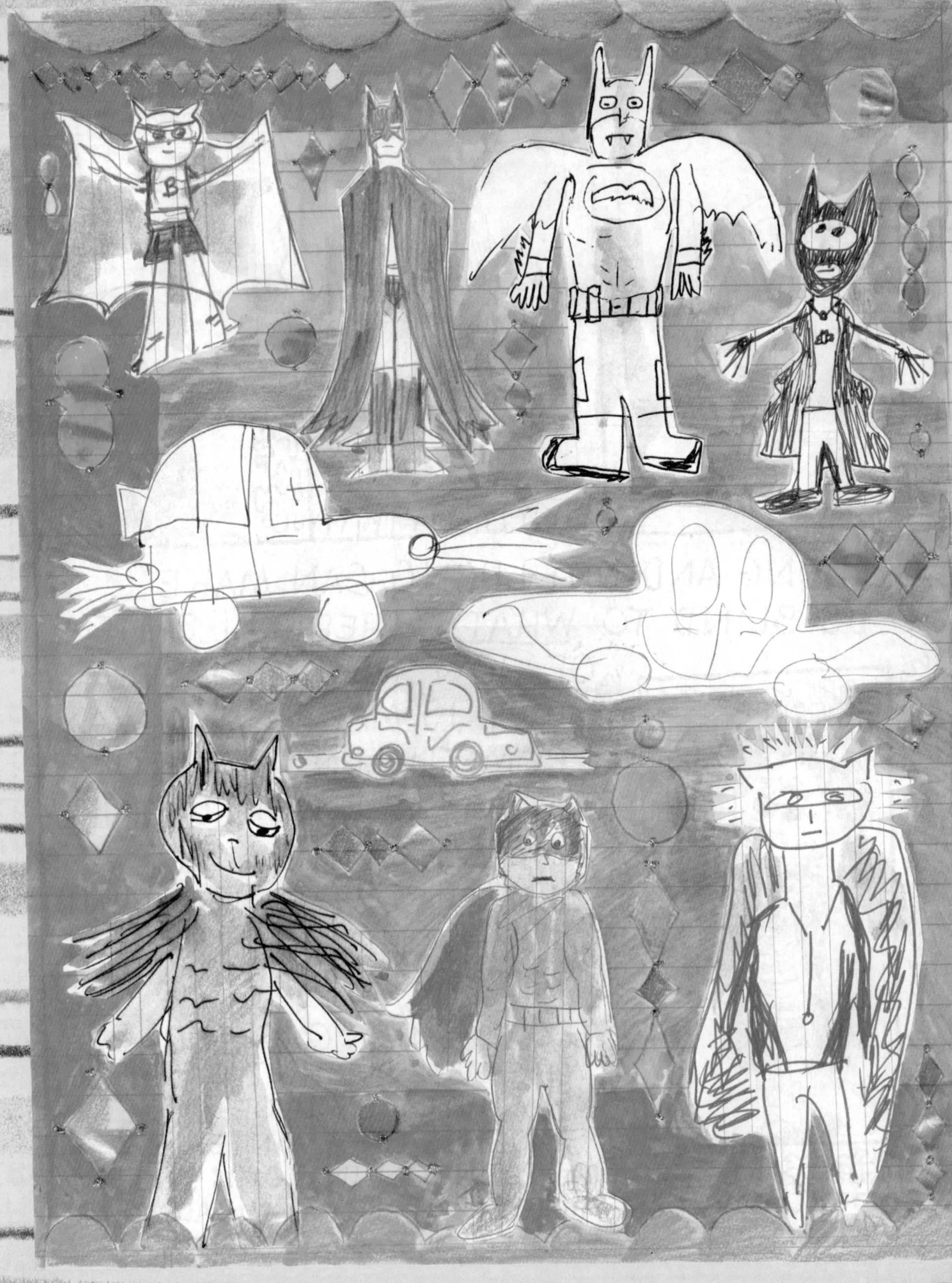

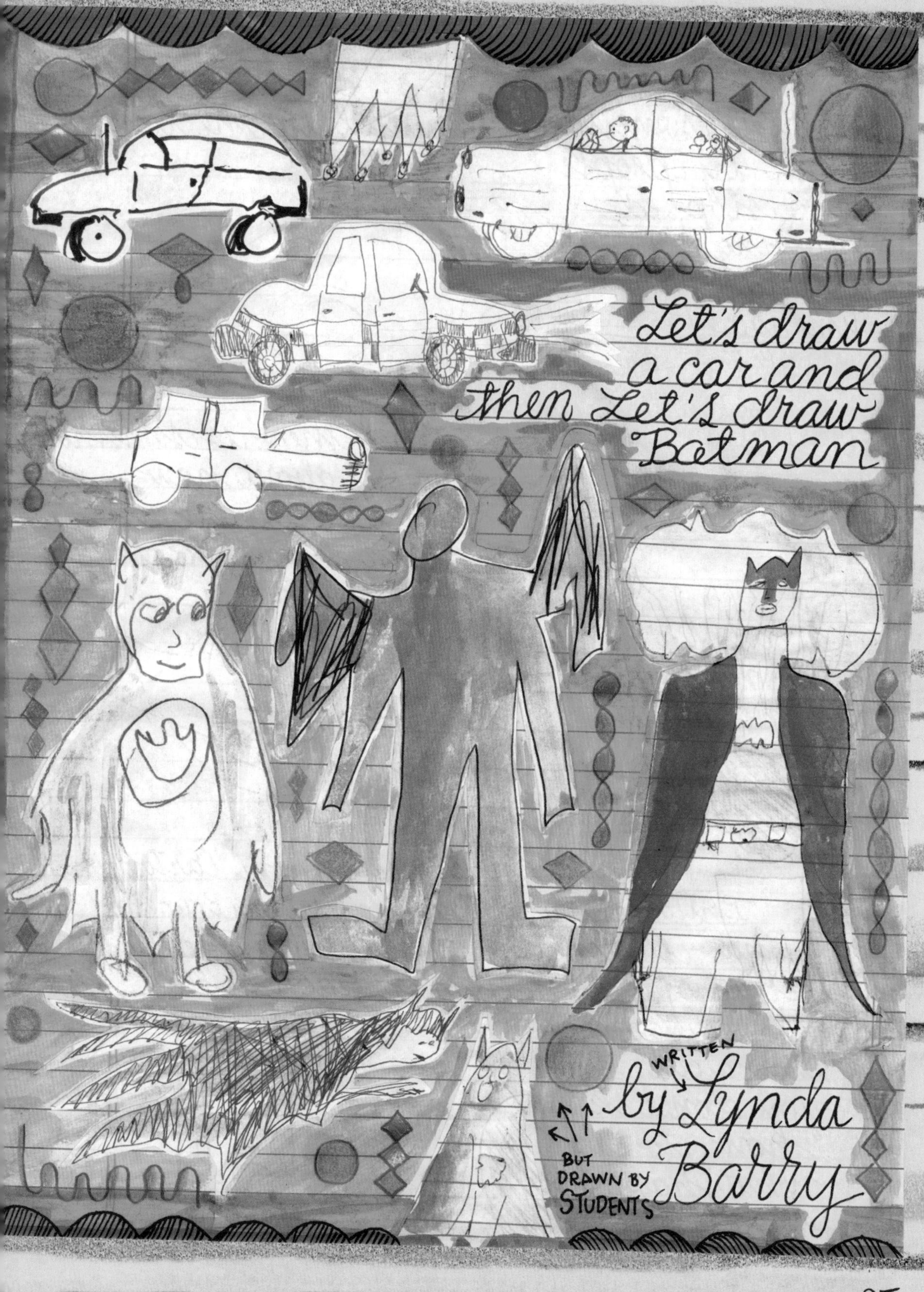
Let's draw a car and then Let's draw Batman
WRITTEN
by Lynda Barry
BUT DRAWN BY STUDENTS

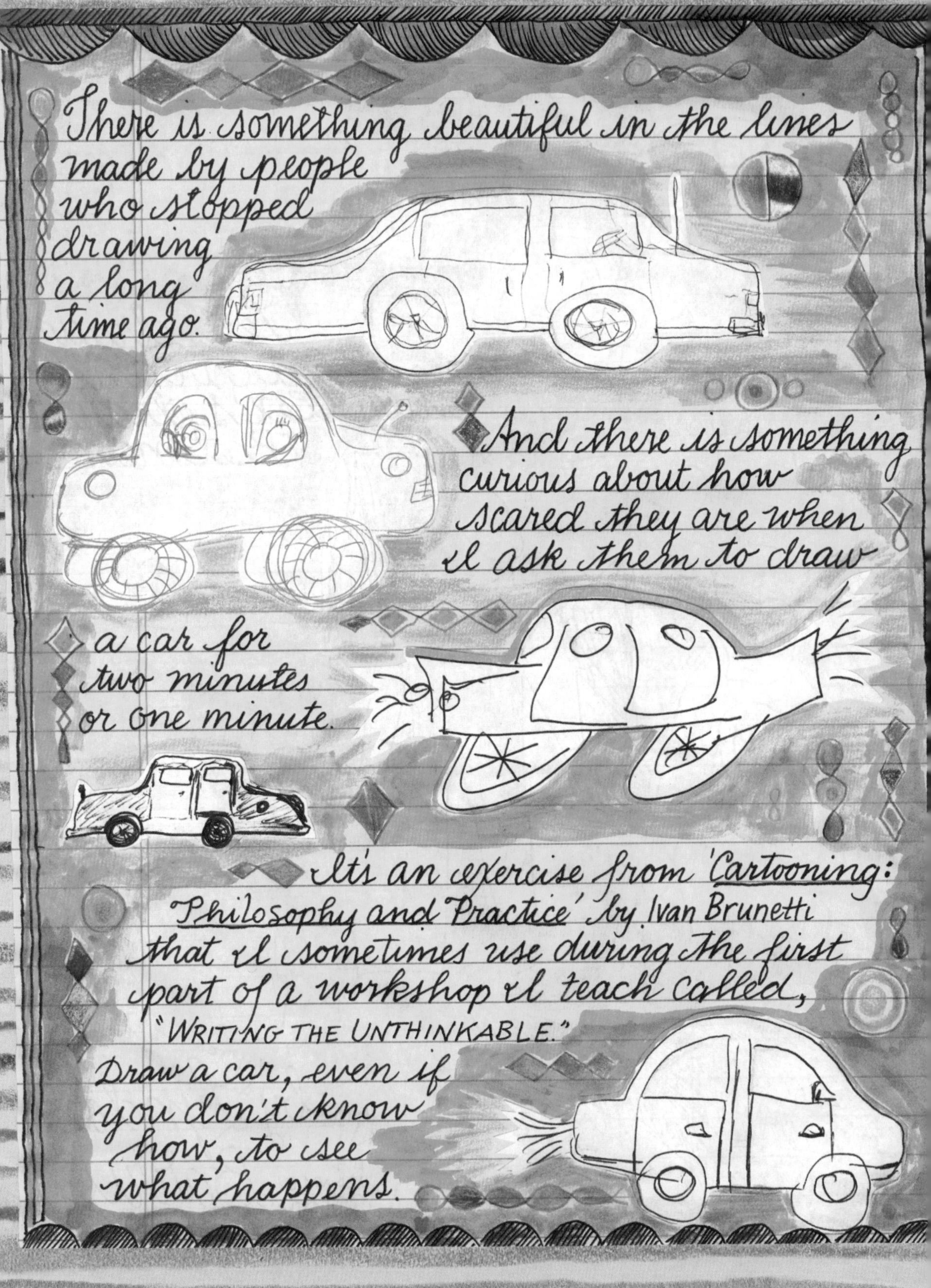
There is something beautiful in the lines made by people who stopped drawing a long time ago.
And there is something curious about how scared they are when I ask them to draw
a car for two minutes or one minute.
It's an exercise from 'Cartooning: Philosophy and Practice' by Ivan Brunetti that I sometimes use during the first part of a workshop I teach called, "WRITING THE UNTHINKABLE."
Draw a car, even if you don't know how, to see what happens.

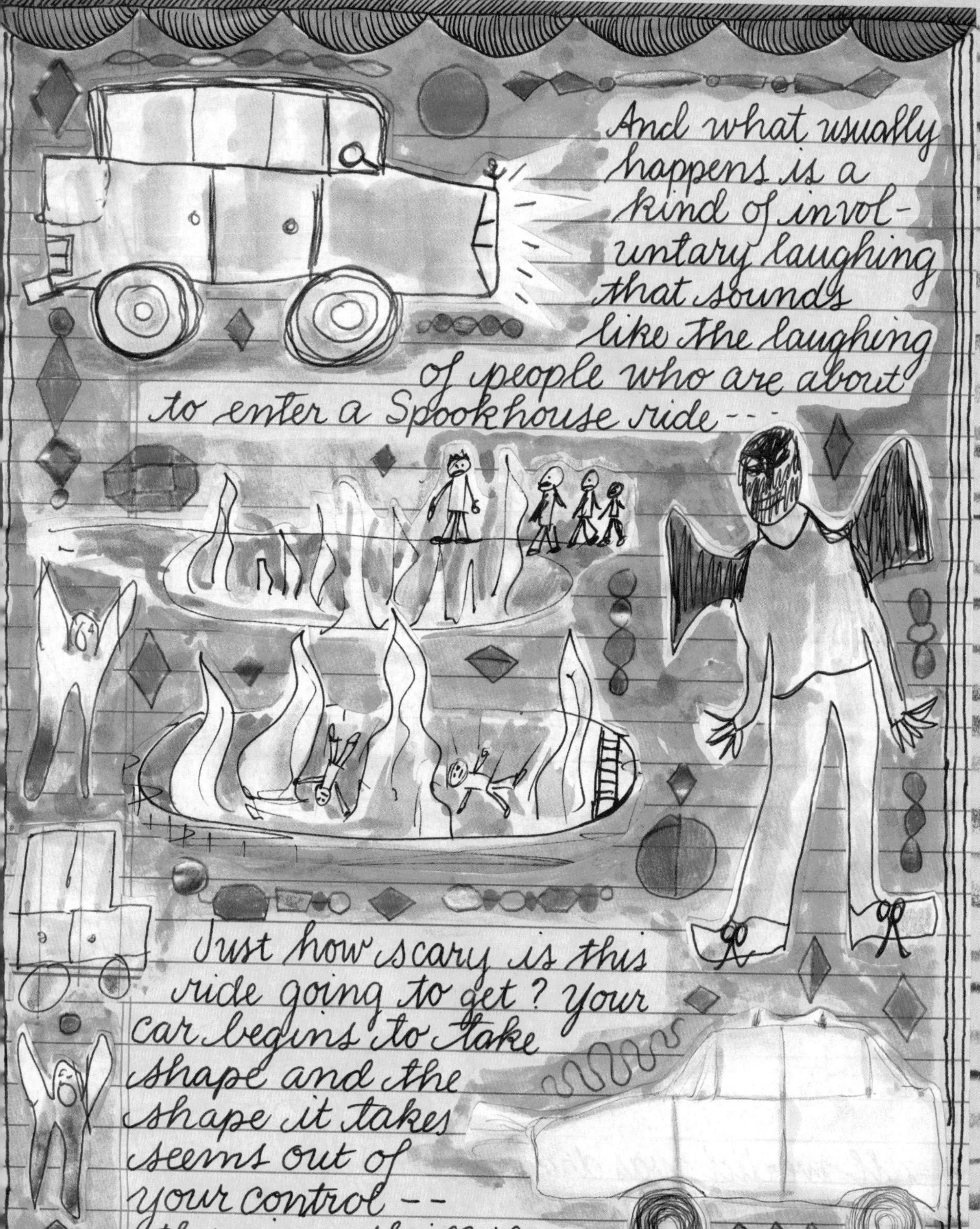
And what usually happens is a kind of invol- untary laughing that sounds like the laughing of people who are about to enter a Spookhouse ride---
Just how scary is this ride going to get? your car begins to take shape and the shape it takes seems out of your control -- there is a thrill there.

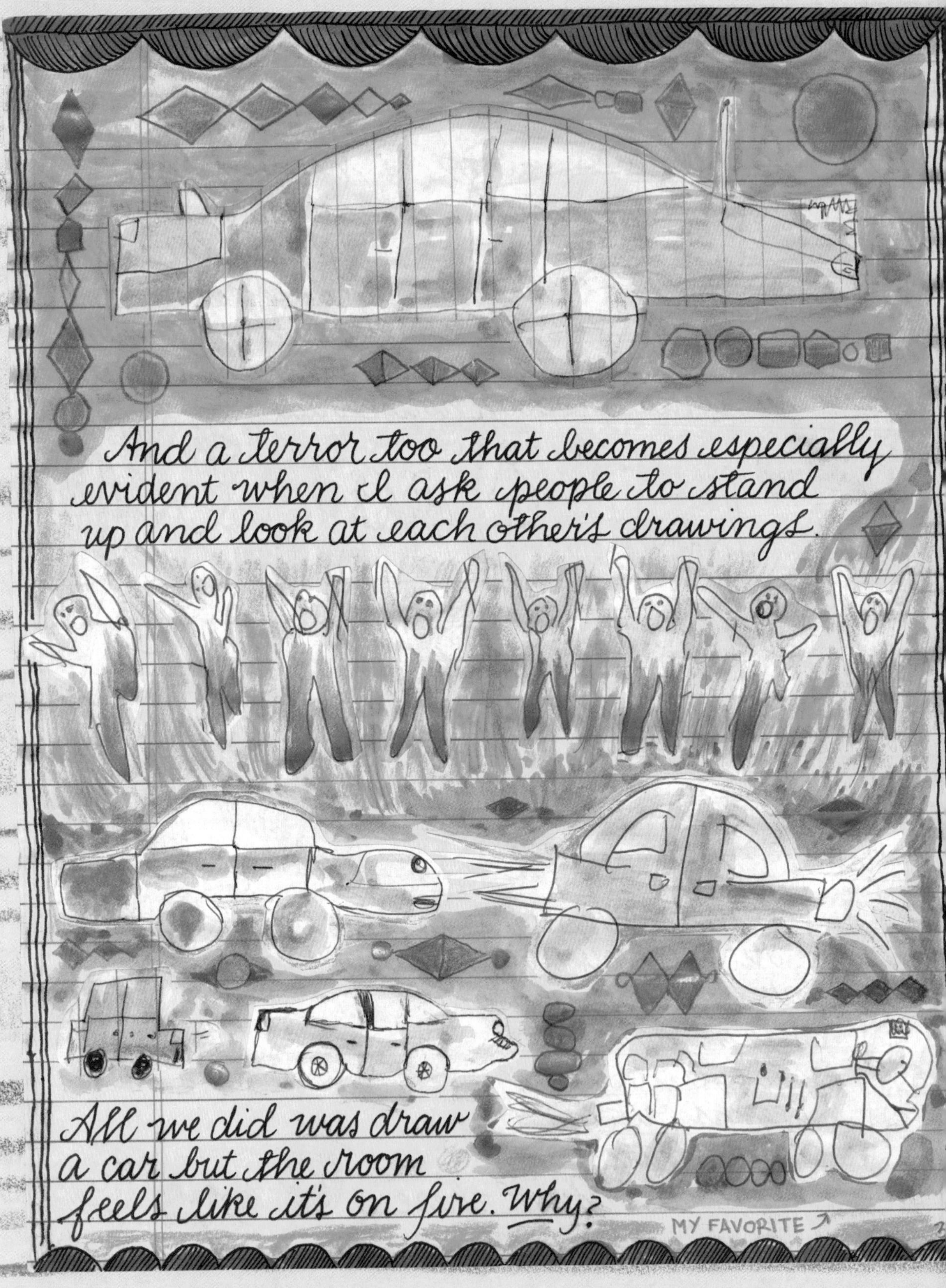
And a terror too that becomes especially evident when I ask people to stand up and look at each other's drawings.
All we did was draw a car but the room feels like it's on fire. Why?
MY FAVORITE

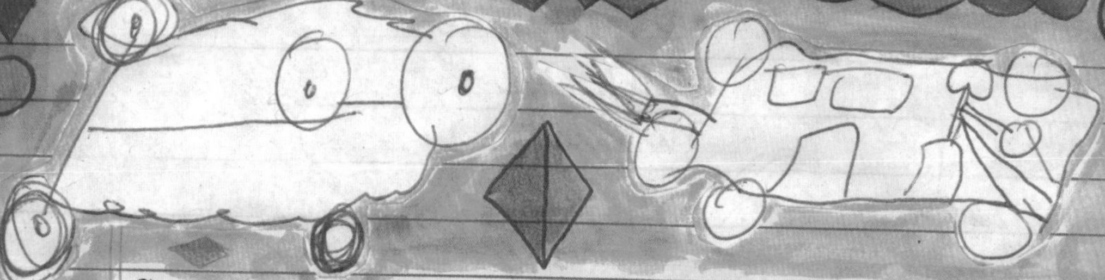

Some of the cars are quite far-out

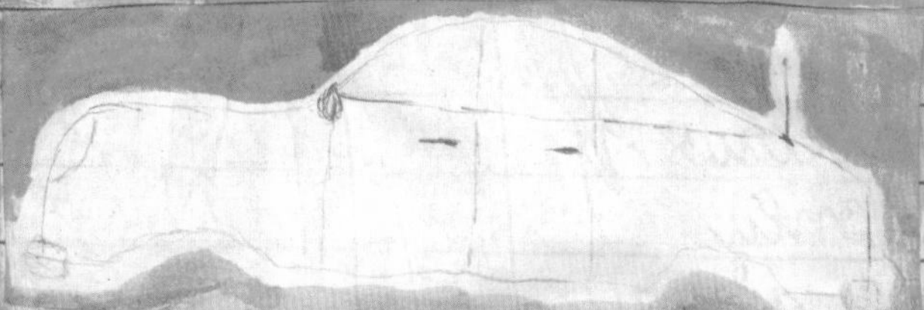

and some are barely there, like phantoms made of ghost lines.

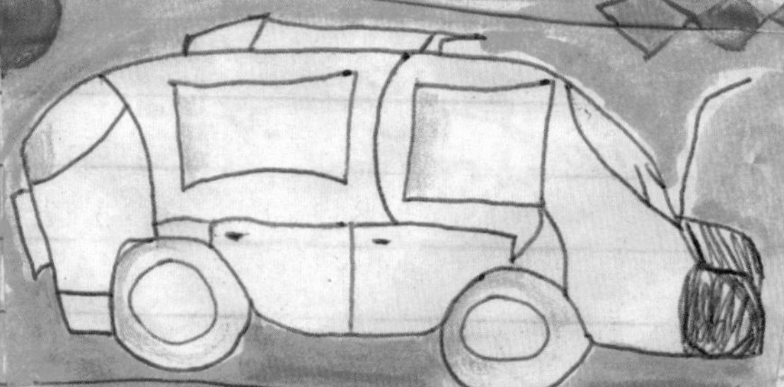

Others are more certain – and some seem to feel their way in.

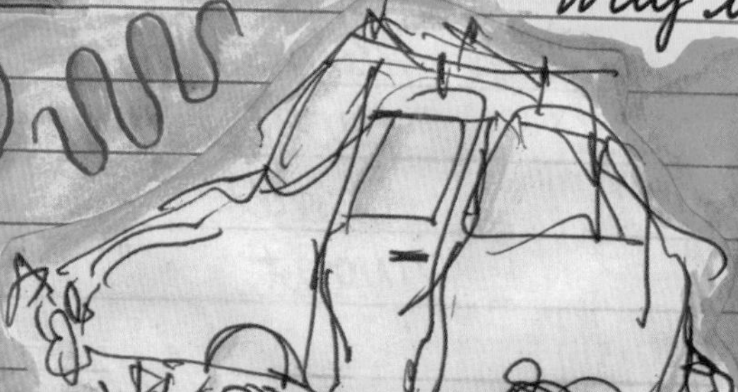

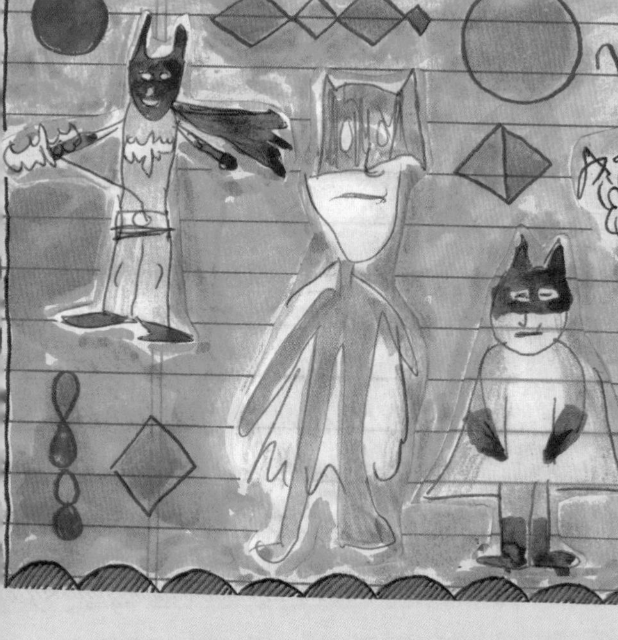

The same thing happens when I ask them to draw BATMAN

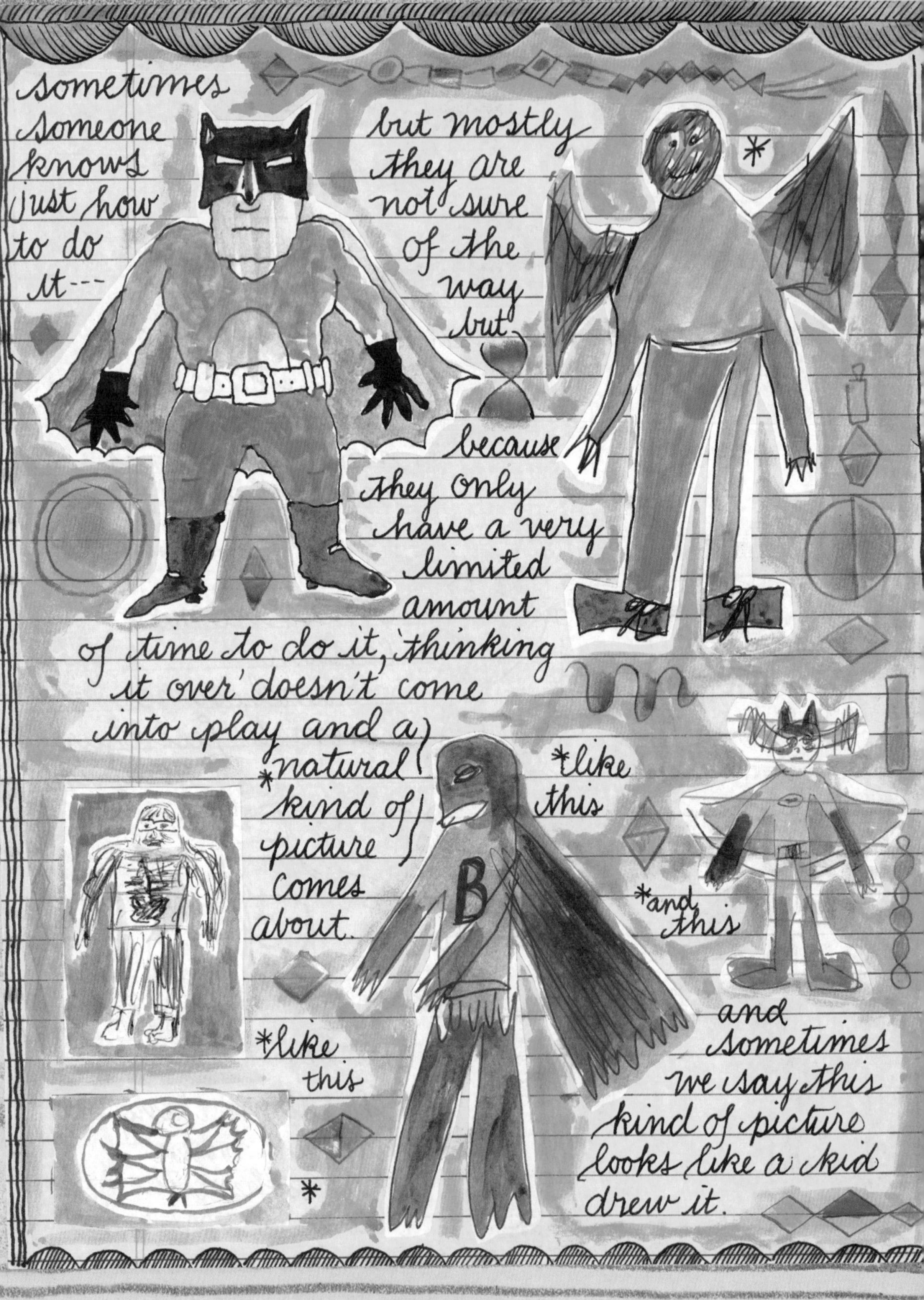
sometimes someone knows just how to do it---
but mostly they are not sure of the way but
because they only have a very limited amount of time to do it, thinking it over doesn't come into play and a *natural kind of picture comes about.
*like this
*like this
*and this
and sometimes we say this kind of picture looks like a kid drew it.

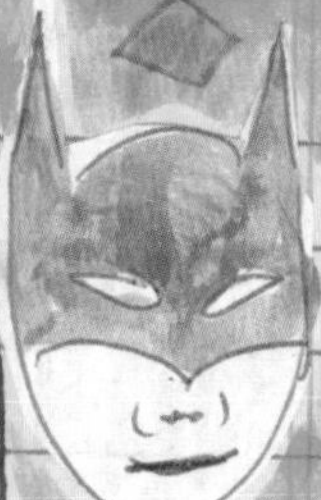

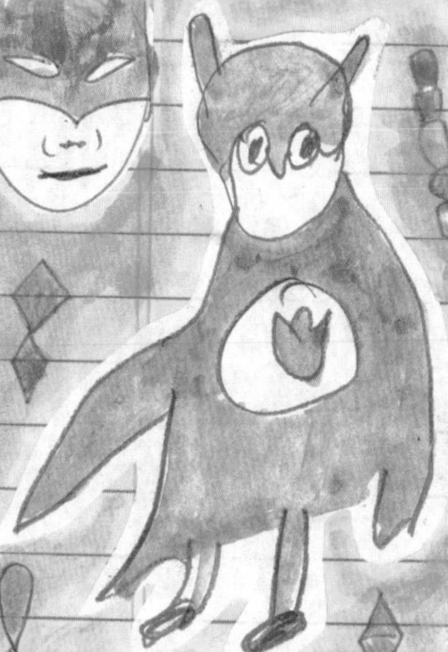

and people are dismayed by this and even ashamed enough to destroy the picture—get rid of it --- <u>immediately</u>

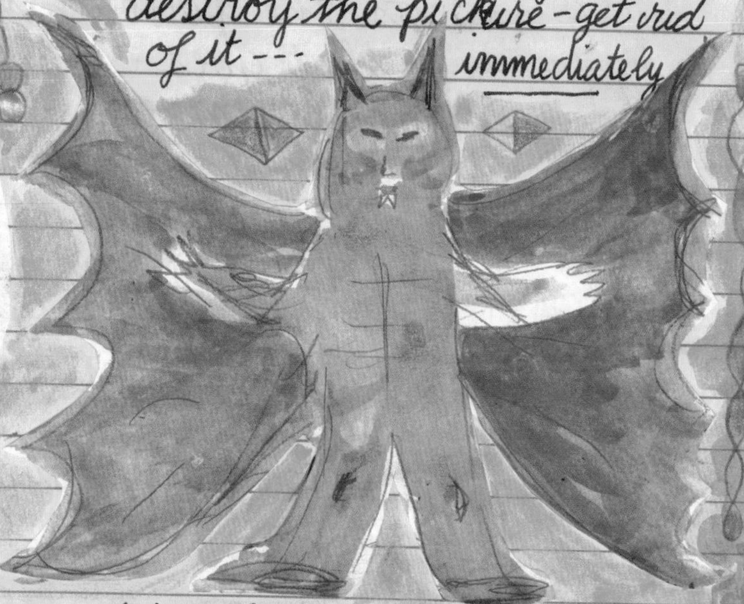

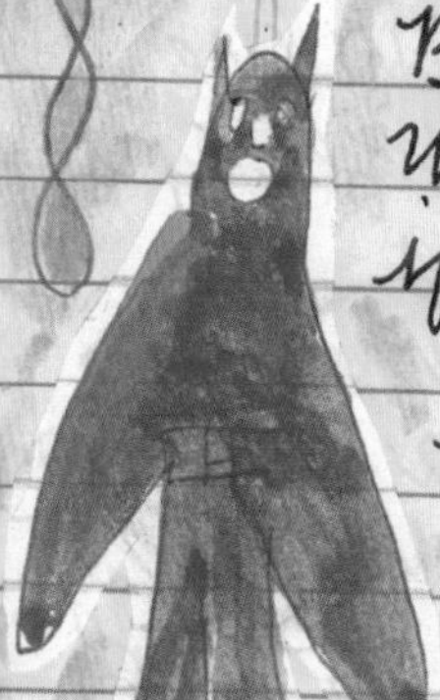

But what if the way kids draw -- that kind of line that we call 'childish' -- what if that is what a line looks like when someone is having an experience by hand? <u>A live wire</u>! There is an aliveness in these drawings that can't be faked, and when I look at them, that aliveness seems to come into me. I'm glad to see and feel them.

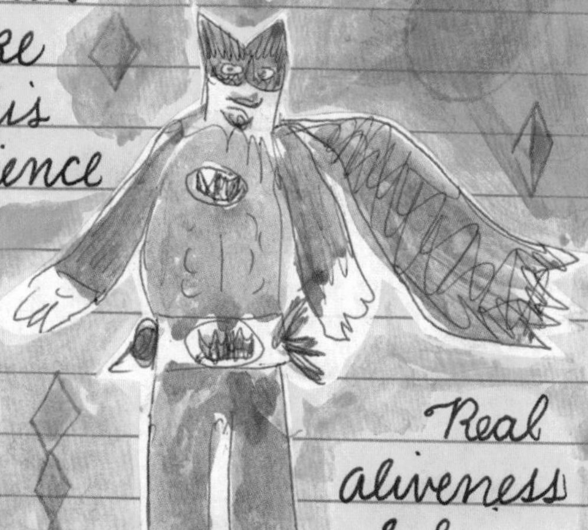

Real aliveness of line is hard to come by

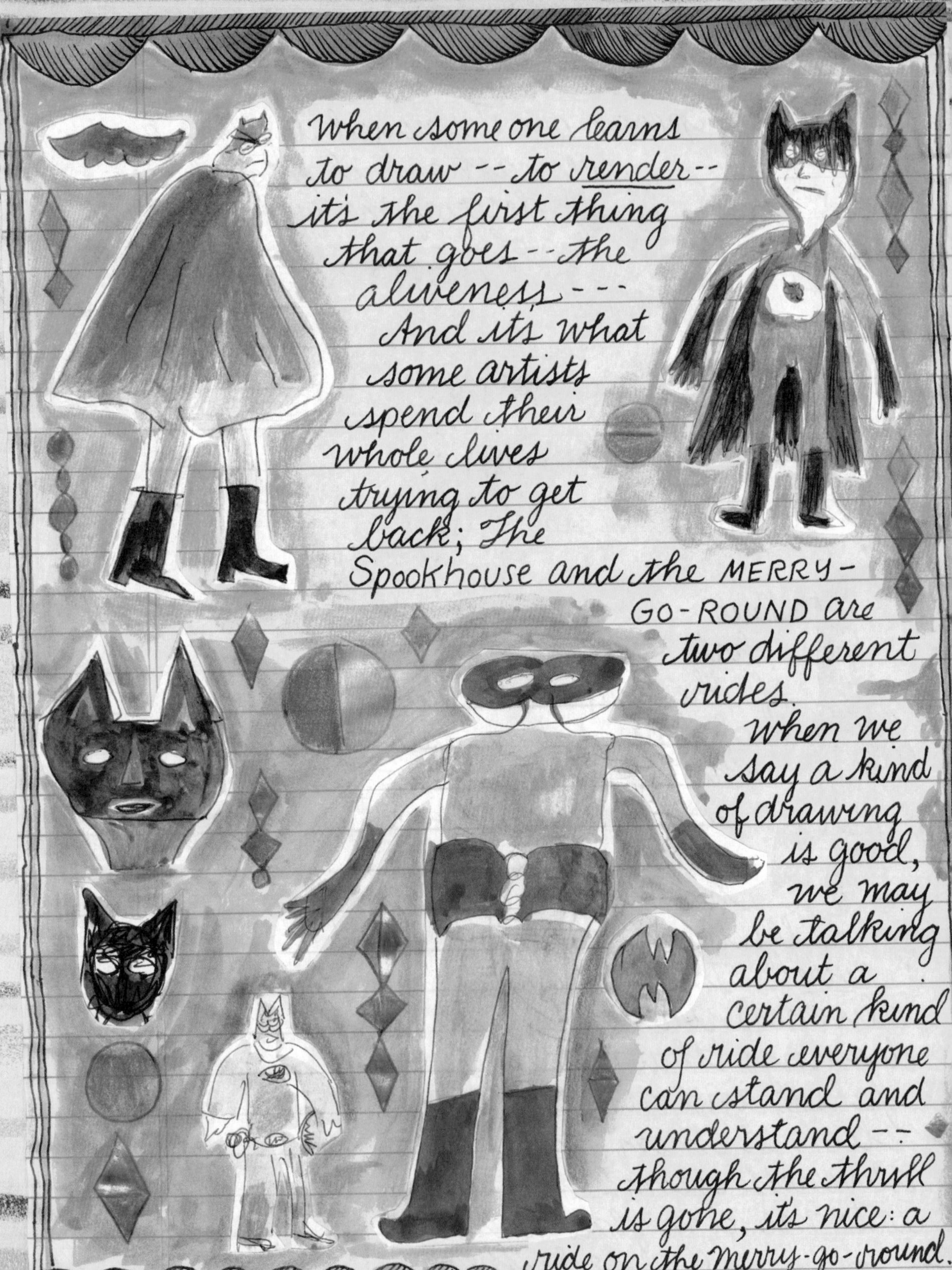
When some one learns to draw -- to render -- it's the first thing that goes -- the aliveness --- And it's what some artists spend their whole lives trying to get back; The Spookhouse and the MERRY-GO-ROUND are two different rides.
When we say a kind of drawing is good, we may be talking about a certain kind of ride everyone can stand and understand -- though the thrill is gone, it's nice: a ride on the merry-go-round.

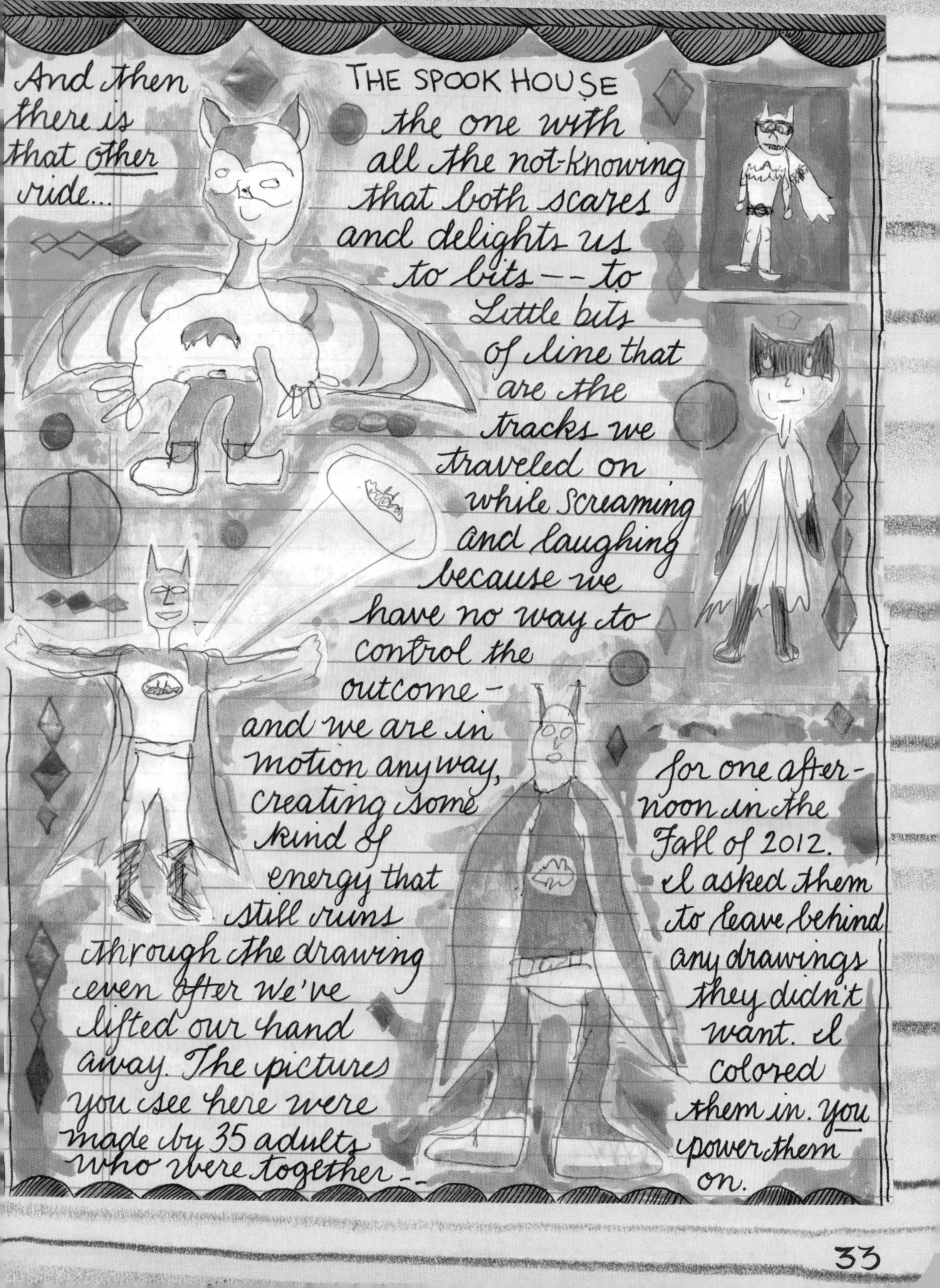
And then there is that other ride...
THE SPOOK HOUSE
the one with all the not-knowing that both scares and delights us to bits-- to Little bits of line that are the tracks we traveled on while Screaming and laughing because we have no way to control the outcome- and we are in motion anyway, creating some kind of energy that still runs through the drawing even after we've lifted our hand away. The pictures you see here were made by 35 adults who were together-- for one after-noon in the Fall of 2012. I asked them to leave behind any drawings they didn't want. I colored them in. You power them on.

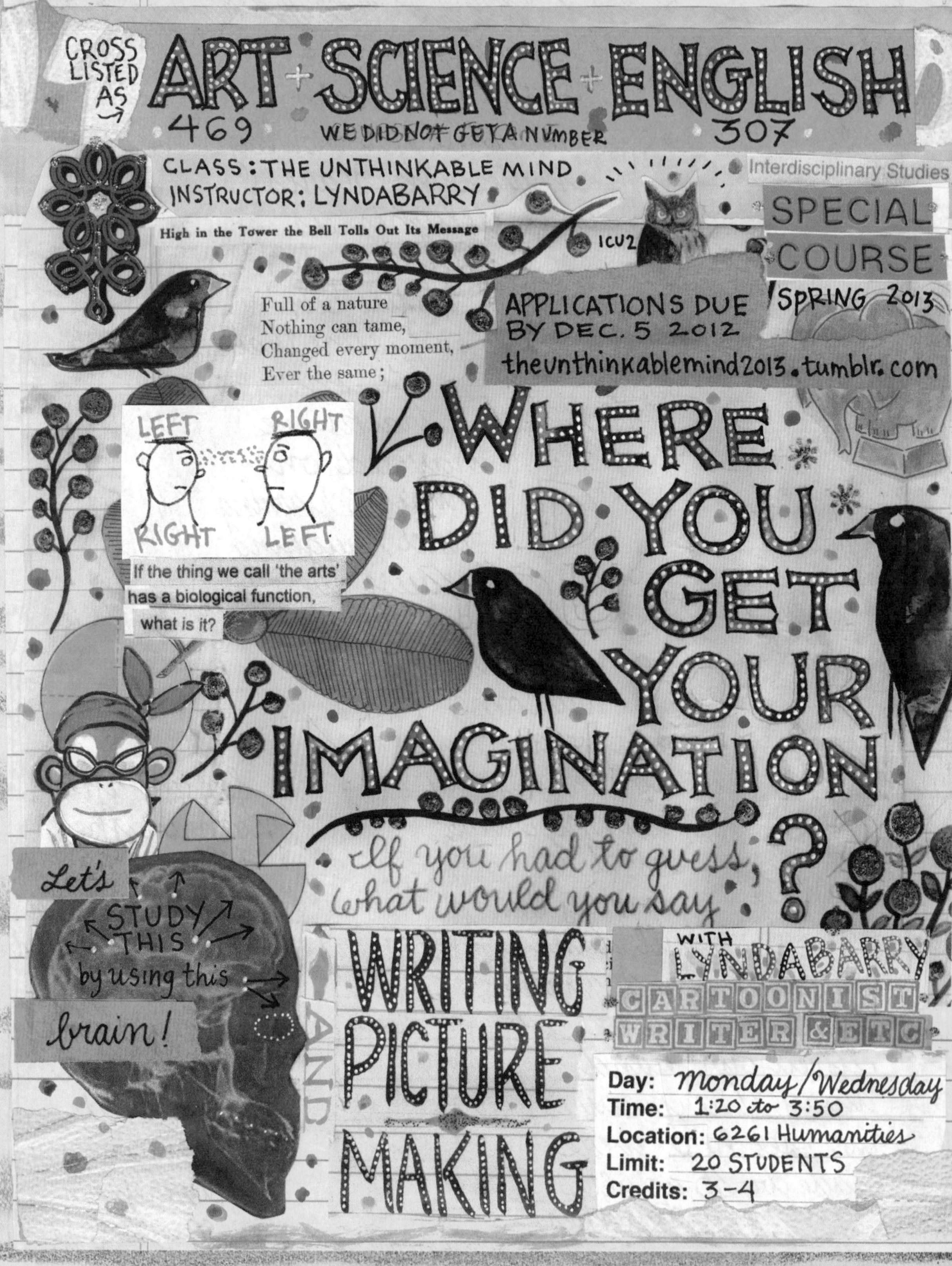
CROSS LISTED AS →
ART + SCIENCE + ENGLISH
469
WE DID NOT GET A NUMBER
307
CLASS: THE UNTHINKABLE MIND
INSTRUCTOR: LYNDABARRY
Interdisciplinary Studies
SPECIAL COURSE
SPRING 2013
High in the Tower the Bell Tolls Out Its Message
ICU2
Full of a nature
Nothing can tame,
Changed every moment,
Ever the same;
APPLICATIONS DUE BY DEC. 5 2012
theunthinkablemind2013.tumblr.com
LEFT
RIGHT
RIGHT
LEFT
If the thing we call 'the arts'
has a biological function,
what is it?
WHERE DID YOU GET YOUR IMAGINATION?
If you had to guess, what would you say
Let's STUDY THIS by using this brain!
WRITING AND PICTURE MAKING
WITH LYNDABARRY
CARTOONIST WRITER & ETC
Day: Monday/Wednesday
Time: 1:20 to 3:50
Location: 6261 Humanities
Limit: 20 STUDENTS
Credits: 3-4

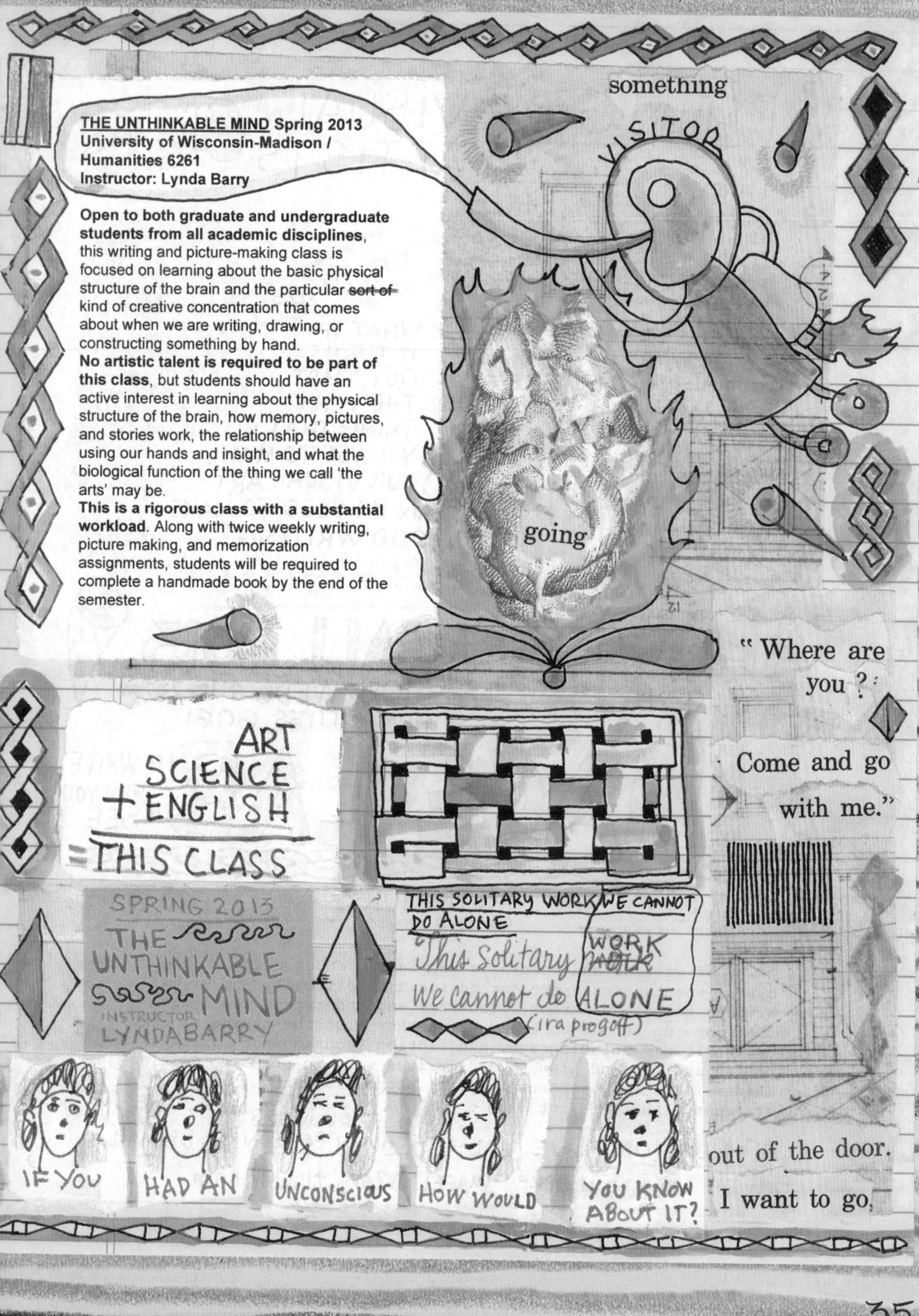
THE UNTHINKABLE MIND Spring 2013
University of Wisconsin-Madison /
Humanities 6261
Instructor: Lynda Barry
Open to both graduate and undergraduate students from all academic disciplines, this writing and picture-making class is focused on learning about the basic physical structure of the brain and the particular ~~sort of~~ kind of creative concentration that comes about when we are writing, drawing, or constructing something by hand.
No artistic talent is required to be part of this class, but students should have an active interest in learning about the physical structure of the brain, how memory, pictures, and stories work, the relationship between using our hands and insight, and what the biological function of the thing we call 'the arts' may be.
This is a rigorous class with a substantial workload. Along with twice weekly writing, picture making, and memorization assignments, students will be required to complete a handmade book by the end of the semester.
something
VISITOR
going
"Where are you ?
Come and go with me."
ART
SCIENCE
+ENGLISH
=THIS CLASS
SPRING 2013
THE UNTHINKABLE MIND
INSTRUCTOR LYNDA BARRY
THIS SOLITARY WORK WE CANNOT DO ALONE
This Solitary WORK
We cannot do ALONE
(ira progoff)
IF YOU
HAD AN
UNCONSCIOUS
HOW WOULD
YOU KNOW ABOUT IT?
out of the door.
I want to go,

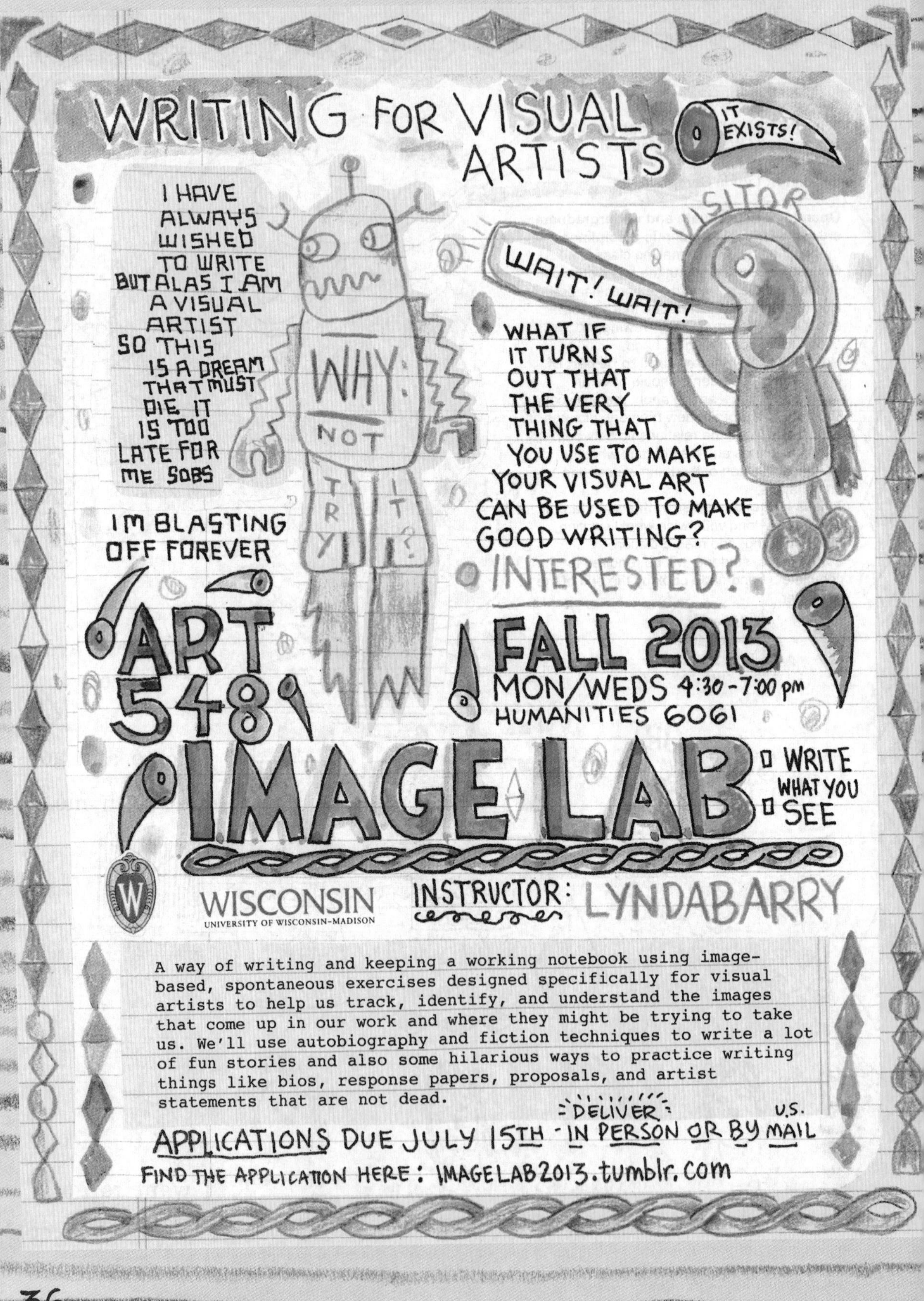
WRITING FOR VISUAL ARTISTS
IT EXISTS!
I HAVE ALWAYS WISHED TO WRITE BUT ALAS I AM A VISUAL ARTIST SO THIS IS A DREAM THAT MUST DIE IT IS TOO LATE FOR ME SOBS
WHY: NOT TRY IT?
I'M BLASTING OFF FOREVER
VISITOR
WAIT! WAIT!
WHAT IF IT TURNS OUT THAT THE VERY THING THAT YOU USE TO MAKE YOUR VISUAL ART CAN BE USED TO MAKE GOOD WRITING?
INTERESTED?
ART 548
FALL 2013
MON/WEDS 4:30-7:00 pm
HUMANITIES 6061
IMAGE LAB
WRITE WHAT YOU SEE
WISCONSIN
UNIVERSITY OF WISCONSIN-MADISON
INSTRUCTOR: LYNDA BARRY
A way of writing and keeping a working notebook using image-based, spontaneous exercises designed specifically for visual artists to help us track, identify, and understand the images that come up in our work and where they might be trying to take us. We'll use autobiography and fiction techniques to write a lot of fun stories and also some hilarious ways to practice writing things like bios, response papers, proposals, and artist statements that are not dead.
APPLICATIONS DUE JULY 15TH - DELIVER IN PERSON OR BY U.S. MAIL
FIND THE APPLICATION HERE: IMAGELAB2013.tumblr.com

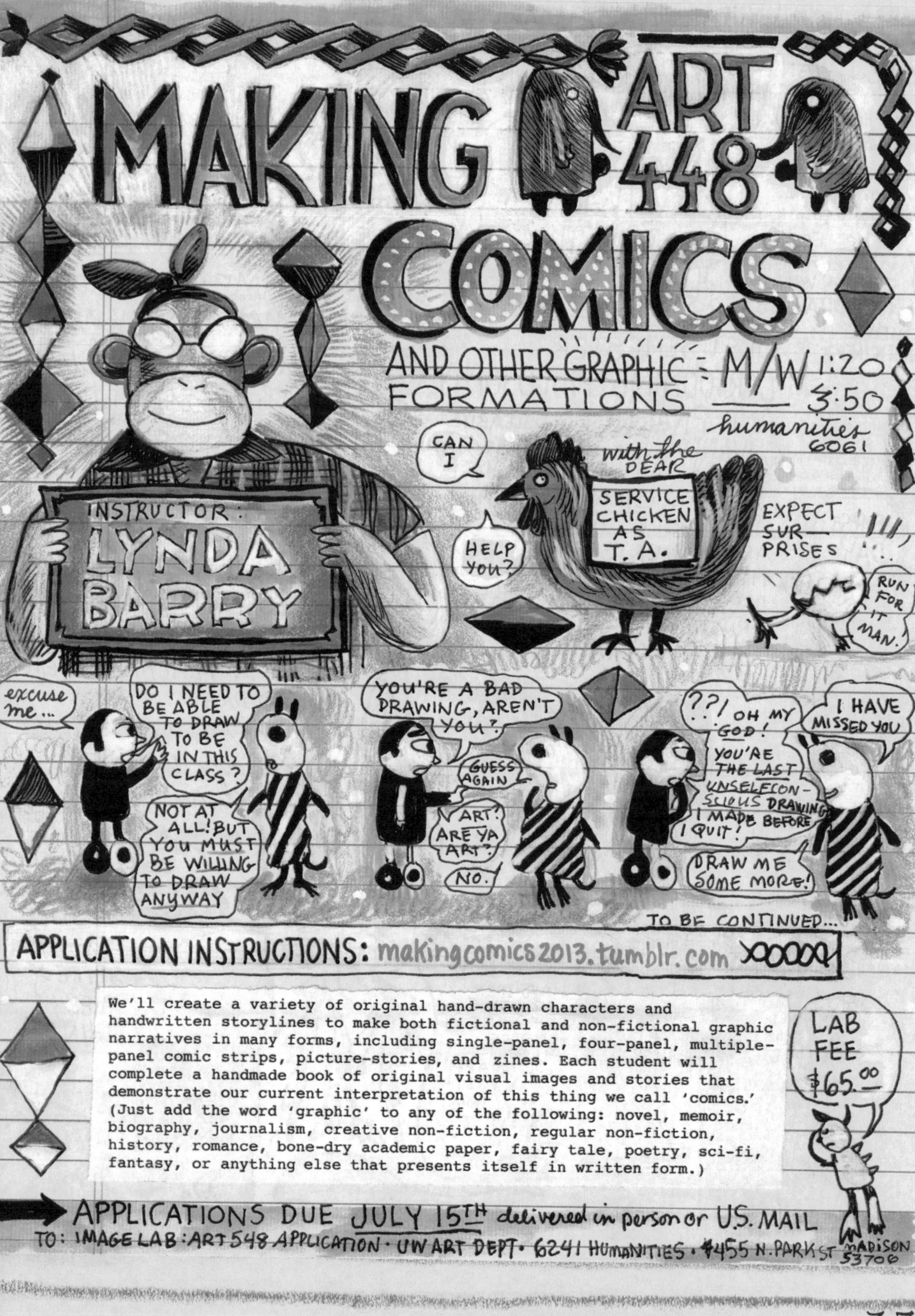
MAKING COMICS
ART 448
AND OTHER GRAPHIC FORMATIONS
M/W 1:20 — 3:50
humanities 6061
INSTRUCTOR: LYNDA BARRY
CAN I HELP YOU?
with the DEAR
SERVICE CHICKEN AS T.A.
EXPECT SUR-PRISES
RUN FOR IT MAN.
excuse me...
DO I NEED TO BE ABLE TO DRAW TO BE IN THIS CLASS?
NOT AT ALL! BUT YOU MUST BE WILLING TO DRAW ANYWAY
YOU'RE A BAD DRAWING, AREN'T YOU?
GUESS AGAIN
ART? ARE YA ART?
NO.
??! OH MY GOD! YOU'RE THE LAST UNSELFCONSCIOUS DRAWING I MADE BEFORE I QUIT!
I HAVE MISSED YOU
DRAW ME SOME MORE!
TO BE CONTINUED...
APPLICATION INSTRUCTIONS: makingcomics2013.tumblr.com
We'll create a variety of original hand-drawn characters and handwritten storylines to make both fictional and non-fictional graphic narratives in many forms, including single-panel, four-panel, multiple-panel comic strips, picture-stories, and zines. Each student will complete a handmade book of original visual images and stories that demonstrate our current interpretation of this thing we call 'comics.' (Just add the word 'graphic' to any of the following: novel, memoir, biography, journalism, creative non-fiction, regular non-fiction, history, romance, bone-dry academic paper, fairy tale, poetry, sci-fi, fantasy, or anything else that presents itself in written form.)
LAB FEE $65.00
APPLICATIONS DUE JULY 15TH delivered in person or U.S. MAIL
TO: IMAGE LAB: ART 548 APPLICATION · UW ART DEPT · 6241 HUMANITIES · 455 N. PARK ST MADISON 53706

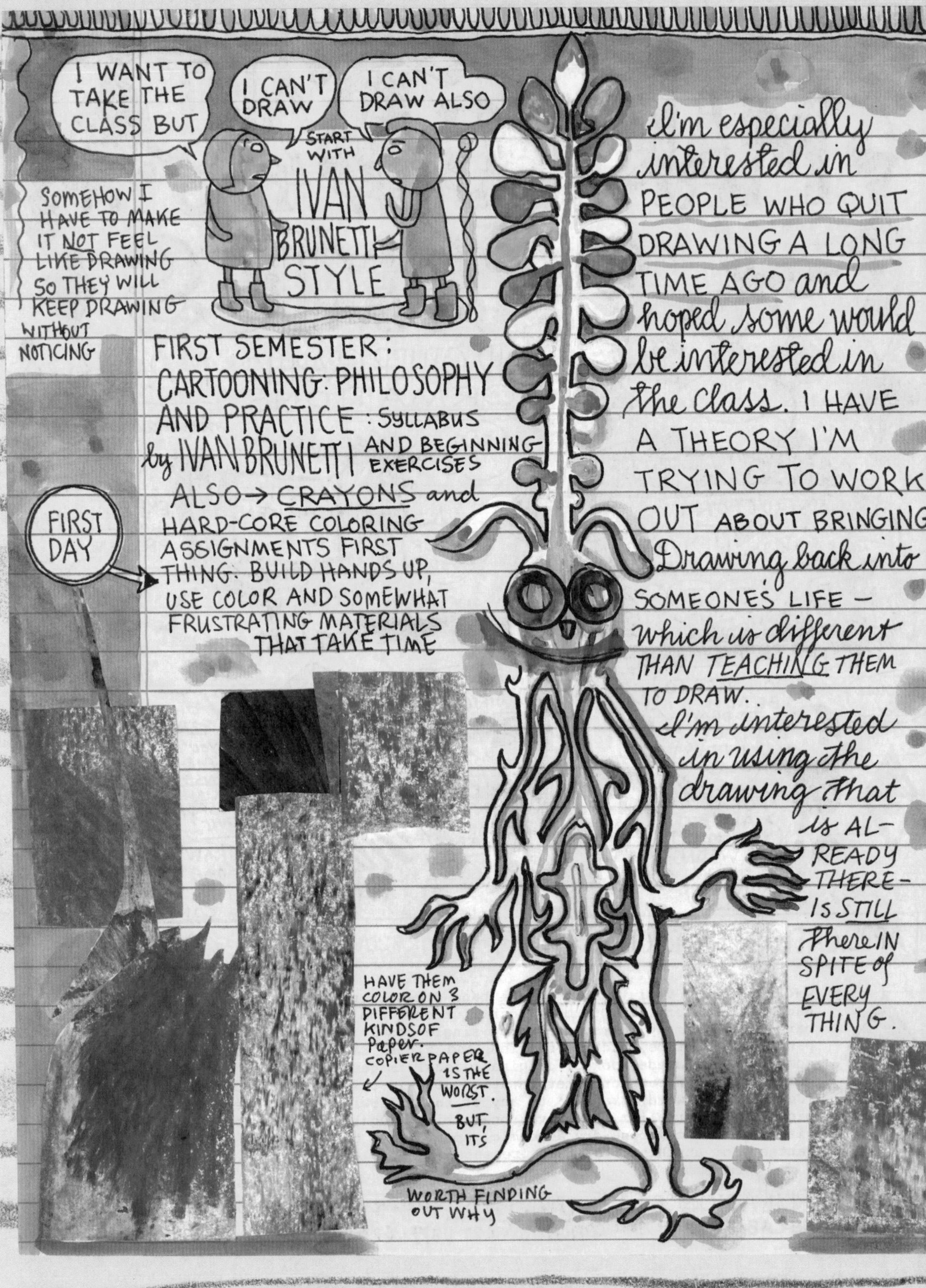
I WANT TO TAKE THE CLASS BUT
I CAN'T DRAW
I CAN'T DRAW ALSO
START WITH IVAN BRUNETTI STYLE
SOMEHOW I HAVE TO MAKE IT NOT FEEL LIKE DRAWING SO THEY WILL KEEP DRAWING WITHOUT NOTICING
FIRST SEMESTER: CARTOONING: PHILOSOPHY AND PRACTICE by IVAN BRUNETTI : SYLLABUS AND BEGINNING EXERCISES
ALSO → CRAYONS and HARD-CORE COLORING ASSIGNMENTS FIRST THING. BUILD HANDS UP, USE COLOR AND SOMEWHAT FRUSTRATING MATERIALS THAT TAKE TIME
FIRST DAY
I'm especially interested in PEOPLE WHO QUIT DRAWING A LONG TIME AGO and hoped some would be interested in the class. I HAVE A THEORY I'M TRYING TO WORK OUT ABOUT BRINGING Drawing back into SOMEONE'S LIFE — which is different THAN TEACHING THEM TO DRAW.
I'm interested in using the drawing that is ALREADY THERE — IS STILL there IN SPITE of EVERY THING.
HAVE THEM COLOR ON 3 DIFFERENT KINDS OF Paper. COPIER PAPER IS THE WORST. BUT, IT'S WORTH FINDING OUT WHY

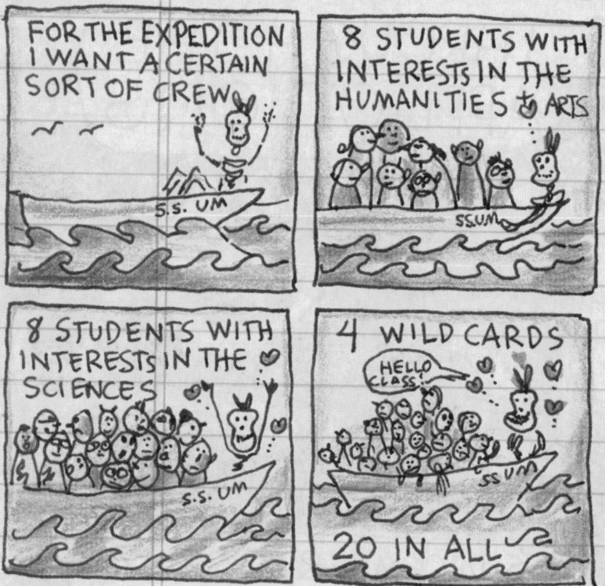

FOR THE EXPEDITION I WANT A CERTAIN SORT OF CREW
S.S. UM
8 STUDENTS WITH INTERESTS IN THE HUMANITIES & ARTS
SS.UM
8 STUDENTS WITH INTERESTS IN THE SCIENCES
S.S. UM
4 WILD CARDS
HELLO CLASS!
SS UM
20 IN ALL

Prospective students should answer each of the questions below without putting too much thought into it. The first answers that come to mind are the ones I'm most interested in.

Questions for Students Applying to "The Unthinkable Mind"

1. Full Name:
2. Student ID Number (10 digits, no dashes or spaces)
3. Email address: (please use your wisc.edu email address)
4. Degree program or area of study and year (eg BFA, Dance, Junior)
5. This course is offered through different departments. Select the department through which you would like to take the course.
6. Art 469 —-English/Creative writing 307 —— Science *(Course number to come)*
7. What classes did you take during Fall Semester of 2012? Why?
8. What classes will you be taking Spring Semester of 2013? Why?
9. What were some of the books you read as a kid?
10. What were some of the games you played?
11. What were some of your favorite fictional characters when you were growing up. (These can be any kind of fictional characters at all, from literary to cartoon to video game characters.)
12. Who was your favorite elementary school teacher? Why?
13. Who was your least favorite elementary school teacher? Why?
14. Was there an object or thing that disturbed you as a kid? Why?
15. Was there an object or thing that did the opposite for you? Why?
16. Was there something you made by hand as a kid that frustrated you?
17. Was there something you made by hand as a kid that made you happy?
19. What was your least favorite kind of fictional creature?
20. What would be your least favorite kind of fictional environment?
21. How do you feel about writing by hand?

THE PAST. THE SEEDLING PAST THAT KEEPS GROWING AND CHANGING. NOT FIXED AT ALL.

A PART OF OURSELVES WE HAVE NOT FORGOTTEN BUT HAVE FORGOTTEN HOW TO REMEMBER,

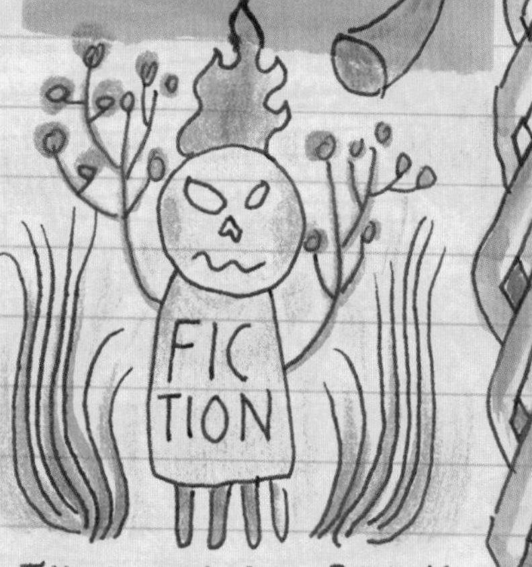

FIC TION

THIS HAS SOMETHING TO DO WITH FICTION —FICTION AS MEMORY WITHOUT REMEMBERING— experiences that don't have to pass through THINKING [redacted]

REFORMULATED by A series of images — written, drawn, sung, SCULPTED — ART FORMS — →FOR THE class TO START PRACTICING THIS right away. PUT images INTO BOTH PICTURE AND WORD — WOULD BE GOOD

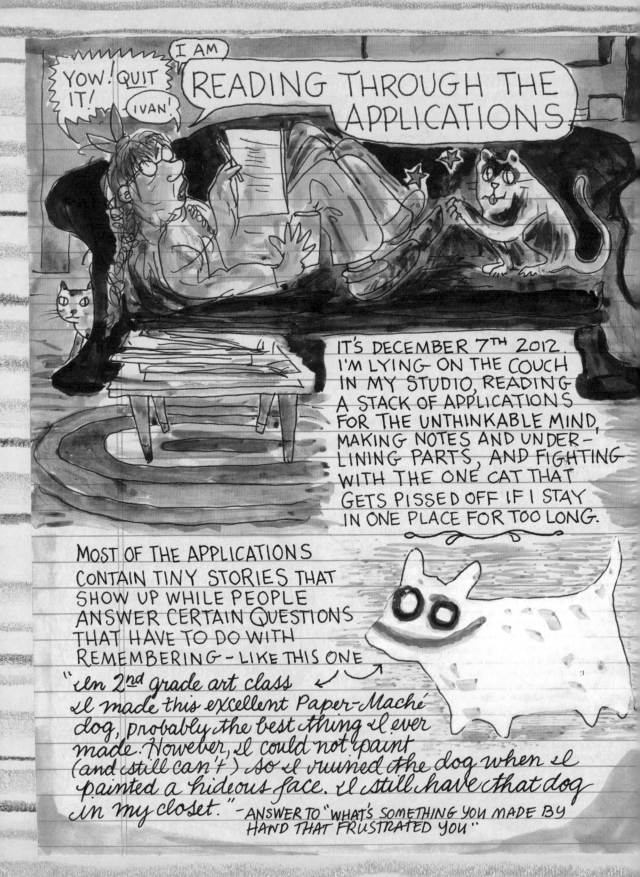

YOW! QUIT IT!

IVAN!

I AM READING THROUGH THE APPLICATIONS

IT'S DECEMBER 7TH 2012. I'M LYING ON THE COUCH IN MY STUDIO, READING A STACK OF APPLICATIONS FOR THE UNTHINKABLE MIND, MAKING NOTES AND UNDER-LINING PARTS, AND FIGHTING WITH THE ONE CAT THAT GETS PISSED OFF IF I STAY IN ONE PLACE FOR TOO LONG.

MOST OF THE APPLICATIONS CONTAIN TINY STORIES THAT SHOW UP WHILE PEOPLE ANSWER CERTAIN QUESTIONS THAT HAVE TO DO WITH REMEMBERING - LIKE THIS ONE

"In 2nd grade art class I made this excellent Paper-Maché dog, probably the best thing I ever made. However, I could not paint (and still can't) so I ruined the dog when I painted a hideous face. I still have that dog in my closet." - ANSWER TO "WHAT'S SOMETHING YOU MADE BY HAND THAT FRUSTRATED YOU"

RESPONSES TO APPLICATION QUESTIONS *illustrated with* UNRELATED STUDENT INDEX CARD DRAWINGS I HAPPEN TO DIG

Lincoln logs bothered me the way station wagons bothered me. Not sure why. Just rubbed me the wrong way.

I always hated those baby dolls that actually wet themselves. They unnerved me. They cried and some even threw up. Who wants a toy that throws up?

When I was six I was in a fight with a 12-year-old girl who kept pulling my hair.

I had a thing against consonants being together so all my evil characters had names like "Malzr" (the dark lord) and "Zlfodk" (his henchman)

My dad kept this object wrapped in packing tape in his freezer. It was about the size of a mummified gerbil. I only asked him about it once. He told me it was Charlie's balls. Those were his words. Charlie was our dog.

I used to make collages from old magazines and calendars. I had a Brett Farvre one, a Lord of the Rings one, a Destiny's Child one. They are the most beautiful things I've ever created and possibly will ever create.

I have a small, lumpy, stuffed clown-like doll that I won at the fair. His name is "Mr. Try It"

I cut the eyelashes off of several of my dolls.

41

When I was a kid I didn't know The Weekly World News was a fake thing. When I saw the devil's face photoshopped into smoke billowing out of a factory in Mexico, it burned into me.

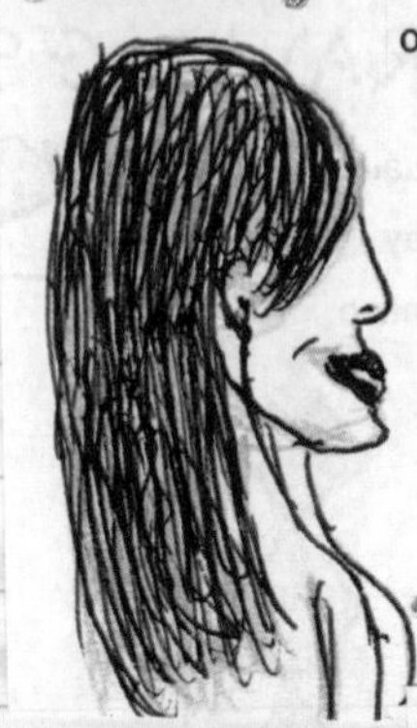

I never really wrestled with my sister all that much. We mostly screamed, bit each other's arms, and played mind games with each other.

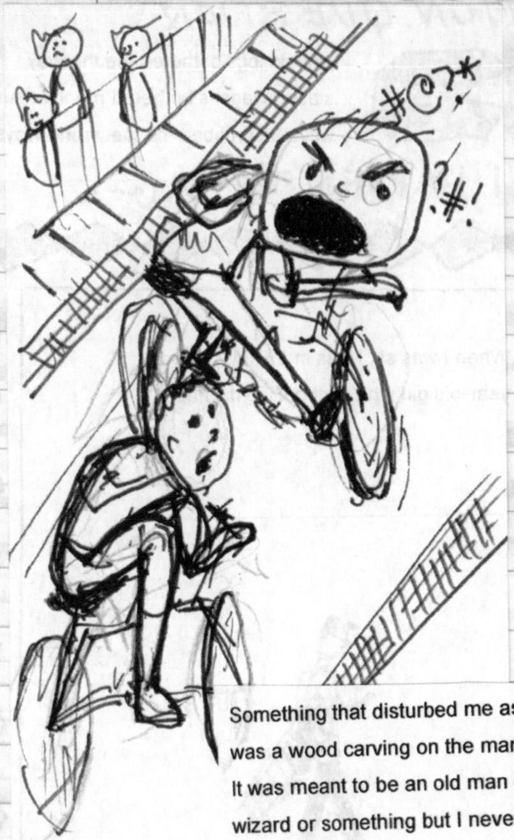

When I was about eight, my neighbor and I made a zine about life as cavemen and women. It had an ad in it for how to deal with unmanageable Paleolithic hair.

Something that disturbed me as a kid was a wood carving on the mantelpiece. It was meant to be an old man or a wizard or something but I never knew where it came from or what it was doing there.

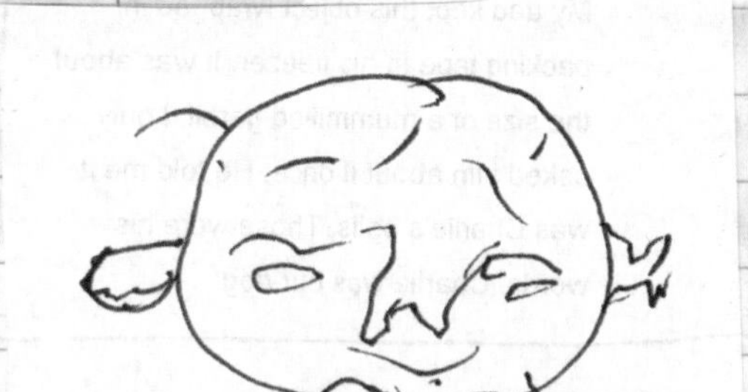

I just drew people with their arms behind their backs or with mittens and gloves to avoid drawing hands.

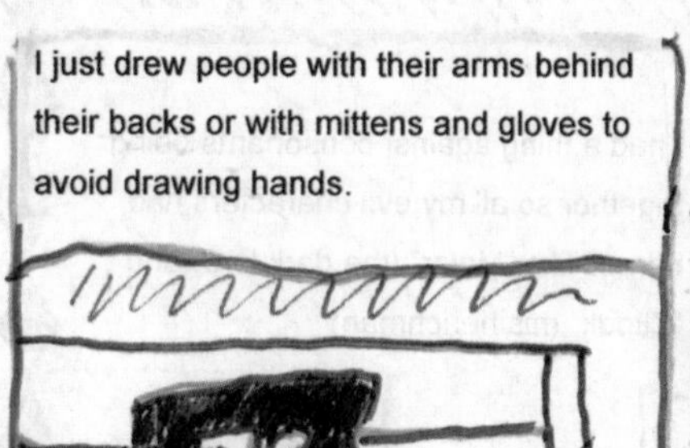
76

Sometimes I draw the faces of characters I want to write about before I've written about them. I also draw dream chairs of unimaginable comfort. These chairs and character faces look pretty similar.

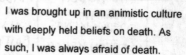

When I was six we moved to a new house and there was a bird skull in my bedroom. My mom told me to get rid of it. I threw it in the bushes in the front yard. Whenever I walked by I thought the bird skull was watching me, trying to figure out how to get back into my bedroom.

I was brought up in an animistic culture with deeply held beliefs on death. As such, I was always afraid of death.

I was scared of being home alone, the dark, grocery stores—especially ones with tall shelving populated by cans of which there wasn't more than a few feet between the top and the ceiling.

I was a die-hard Trekkie. I liked to quote lines of dialogue. I still do. My favorite line is from the series finale: "We are what we are and we do the best that we can." In college, when my girlfriend and I broke up, that line was the last thing I said to her. The last thing she said to me was "Steve, you're an asshole."

Every trip to grandma's meant a trip to see The Clown. She painted The Clown's emotions, The Clown's life, The Clown's soul. And, oh my god. The Clown was just despondent. The Clown's eyes made me just shiver.

As a child I read the entire series of <u>Goosebumps</u> books by R.L. Stine. My best friend in third grade, ███████, and I read them together and I would while away class-time drawing the <u>oozing Goosebumps logo</u> onto every piece of paper I saw. When we finished reading all the books we started to write our own. At one point we wanted to make a Goosebumps movie, which we decided would star Wesley Snipes.

BOOKS	OBJECTS	FICTIONAL CHARACTERS	TEACHERS
Goosebumps	GRANDMOTHER'S 'TOUCH' LAMP	RONIA THE ROBBER'S DAUGHTER	MR. LEBEDA
JUNIE B. JONES	GARBAGE PAIL KIDS TRADING CARDS	SATSUKI (FROM MY NEIGHBOR TOTORO)	Mrs. Irelyn Paras
HAMILTON'S MYTHOLOGY	SISTER'S CURLING IRON	ANY OF THE ORIGINAL POKEMON	MRS. JACKSON
HARRY POTTER SERIES	A SANTA CLAUS MADE FROM AN OLD MILK JUG	MICHELLE Pfeiffer's turn as CATWOMAN IN BATMAN RETURNS	mrs. COTTAM
THE HOBBIT	SHARKS		MRS. KEPROS
WHERE THE SIDEWALK ENDS	BOTTLE ROCKETS	DONATELLO FROM TEENAGE MUTANT NINJA TURTLES	MRS. SCHORAK
STEVEN KELLOGG PICTURE BOOKS	TINY GREY STEIFF RABBIT	HERMIONE GRANGER	MS. DAVIES
DR. SUESS	TORNADOES	SPONGEBOB SQUAREPANTS	Ms. Imhoff
SURVIVAL GUIDE FOR LGBT YOUTH	PAPER-MACHE DOG IN CLOSET	A GUY WHOSE MOTHER DIED WHEN HE WAS A CHILD AND HE PUT HER SKULL ON AS A HAT AND IT GOT STUCK THERE PERMANENTLY.	KIRBY BROWN
THE TROUBLE WITH TROLLS	STUFFED DOLPHIN		MRS. COLBURN
WHERE'S WALDO	ROBOT CLAW		MR. CAPOZI
A SERIES OF UNFORTUNATE EVENTS	LEGOS COWS		YUNG-RAE HWANG
	PURPLE PENS	ALPHONSE THE MYSTERIOUS TADPOLE	Ms. DE GUZMAN
BABY-SITTERS LITTLE SISTER	BIG STUFFED TIGER WITH NO NECK	SCOOBY DOO	MR. NIECHWANDER
CHOOSE YOUR OWN ADVENTURE	A WEREWOLF MASK THAT MY COUSINS SCARED ME WITH	SPOT THE DOG	MRS. PEACOCK
FOREVER		SONIC THE HEDGEHOG	MRS. SCHEDDAR
BETTY + VERONICA DIGESTS	NEEDLES	GHOST FROM GHOST WRITER	MRS. BROWN
CALVIN AND HOBBES COLLECTION	BUGS BUNNY'S FRESHLY PULLED CARROTS	THE WITCH FROM THE WIZ WHO GOT FLUSHED DOWN THE GIGANTIC TOILET AT THE END OF THE MOVIE	MRS. LUSSMYER
CAPTAIN UNDERPANTS	MY GROUND-FLOOR BEDROOM WINDOWS		MRS. NOONAN
THE VELVETEEN RABBIT	BIG BEAR	THE LITTLE MERMAID ARIEL	MRS. HURST
RUSSIAN FAIRY TALES		MACGYVER	MRS. SWIFT
ROALD DAHL'S BOOKS	MOUTHWASH	VIOLET BAUDELAIRE	MR. MUELLER
SHERLOCK HOLMES	GREY ELECTRICAL BOX W/ PICTURE OF GIANT ELECTRICITY MONSTER FIGURE WITH MEAN FACE ELECTROCUTING A PERSON	C.J. PARKER	MRS. SCHROEDEL
CHARLOTTE'S WEB		RASPUTIN THE BLOB	MS. HARRIS
THE BLACK CAULDRON		ROBIN HOOD	Ms. McKENNA
SMURF COMICS		SLEEPING BEAUTY	MRS. STANKEVICH
A POCKET FOR CORDUROY		GOBLINS	MR. SHONE
		LATKA AND SIMKA	MR. CHURCHILL
		ANIMORPHS	MRS. WILKE
		RUGRATS BABIES	MRS. HUGHES
			MR. PATNOE

GAMES	ACTIVITIES	STUDYING	OBSERVATIONS
MILDRED THE FLY, ABADU—A PIECE OF LINT	MY SISTER HAD A PET RAT. WE PLAYED 'MAILMAN' WITH HIM.	GENETICS	• TROLLS ARE AWESOME
TUMBANG PRESO: FILIPINO GAME THAT INVOLVES STRIKING DOWN TIN CAN WITH FLIP FLOPS.	I HAD THIS LITTLE FAMILY MADE OUT OF ERASER HEADS	• PSYCHOLOGY SOUTHEAST ASIAN LITERATURE IN TRANSLATION DANCE GRAPHIC DESIGN	• FLAUBERT'S MADAME BOVARY (WHICH I GOT FROM MY AUNT'S LIBRARY) MADE ME WANT TO BE EMMA BOVARY FOR ABOUT A YEAR.
SORRY! CLUE, CANDY LAND, MONOPOLY, MARIO PARTY GO FISH • D + D CLUE RISK	I WAS OBSESSED WITH THE CAST OF SAVED BY THE BELL AND WROTE THEM ALL LETTERS BUT MY PACKAGE GOT RETURNED BECAUSE I SENT THEM TO THEIR FICTIONAL HIGH-SCHOOL, 'BAYSIDE HIGH"	COMMUNICATION ARTS GLOBAL HEALTH POETRY • CHEMISTRY ENGLISH LITERATURE	• I WAS DISTURBED BY THE VACUUM WHEN I WAS A KID • TROLLS ARE PRETTY AWFUL
MONOPOLY, STAR WARS EDITION! DRAWING WARS GHOST IN THE GRAVEYARD UNO KICKBALL FREEZE TAG SPY GAMES	A DIARAMA MY AUNT HAD THE IDEA TO MAKE: A SHOE BOX AQUARIUM	• CREATIVE WRITING CURRICULUM AND IN-STRUCTION, CURRICULUM THEORY + RESEARCH PRINTMAKING ANTHROPOLOGY	• FOR SOME REASON I REALLY LIKED SEBASTIAN, THE CAT THAT TRIES TO EAT TWEETY BIRD
CHINESE GARTER: LEAP OR CARTWHEEL OVER MAKESHIFT ROPE MADE OF RUBBER BANDS STRUNG TOGETHER	COPS AND ROBBERS WAS ALWAYS FUN. WHEN I WAS THE ROBBER I WOULD HIDE IN THE SHED, OR MY NEIGHBORS' YARD.	ZOOLOGY ART REHABILITATION—PSYCHOLOGY NEUROBIOLOGY	BX PFEIFFER'S PERFORMANCE [AS CATWOMAN] MADE ME DREAM OF BEING ALL LEATHER-CLAD AND UNHINGED AND MALEVOLENT. (IT HASN'T HAPPENED YET) •
TWISTED METAL YS ON SEGA DRESS-UP TELEPHONE	I MADE STARS OUT OF POPSICLE STICKS I WROTE A STORY CALLED "THE SCARY	ECONOMICS • HISTORY PHILOSOPHY	I DID NOT LIKE WHEN LARGE INSECTS WERE IN STORIES
CARD GAME I MADE UP CALLED "JELLO" WHERE THE RULES CHANGED EVERY TIME	MUSKELLUNGE" I PLAYED WITH BEANIE BABIES. THEY GOT INTO ALL	• BOTANY WEB AND INTERACTIVE DESIGN • BUSINESS	TELETUBBIES ARE JUST COMPLETELY POINTLESS
ICE AND HAMMER WHO CAN FIND THE MOST DINOSAUR BONES	KINDS OF TROUBLE PLAYED LOTS OF SPORTS FORMED MUSICAL GROUPS AND I BELIEVE FOUGHT EACH OTHER ALL THE TIME	ORGANIC CHEMISTRY • ENGINEERING	I DIDN'T LIKE SEEING HAIR IN THE BATH-ROOM DRAIN

My favorite fictional characters growing up were Scorpion and Sub-Zero from Mortal Kombat, Sonic the Hedgehog, Megaman, Hercules, and Goku from Dragon Ball Z.

45

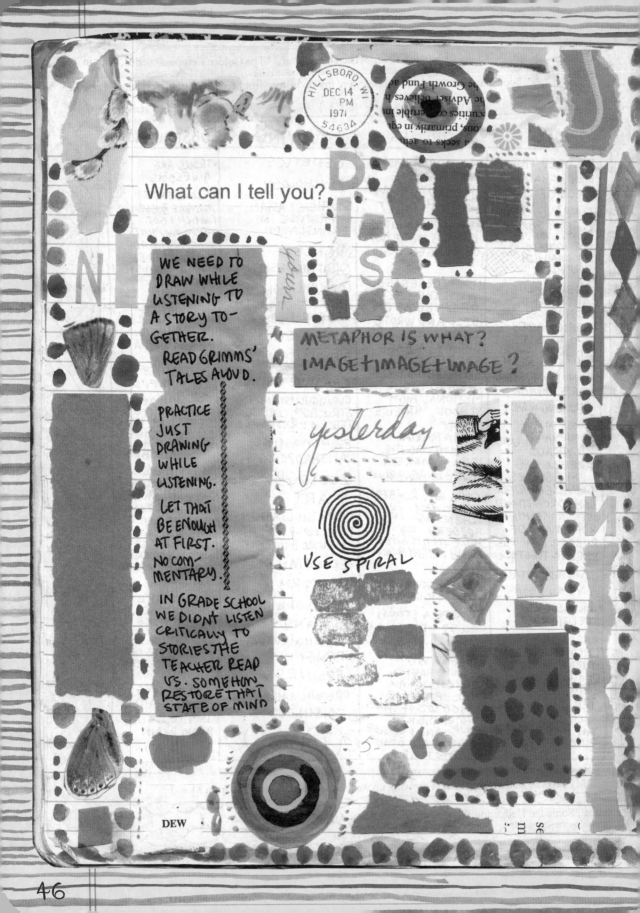

Postmark: HILLSBORO, WI / DEC 14 / PM / 1971 / 54634

What can I tell you?

WE NEED TO DRAW WHILE LISTENING TO A STORY TOGETHER. READ GRIMMS' TALES ALOUD.

PRACTICE JUST DRAWING WHILE LISTENING.

LET THAT BE ENOUGH AT FIRST. NO COMMENTARY.

IN GRADE SCHOOL WE DIDN'T LISTEN CRITICALLY TO STORIES THE TEACHER READ US. SOMEHOW RESTORE THAT STATE OF MIND

METAPHOR IS WHAT? IMAGE + IMAGE + IMAGE?

yesterday

USE SPIRAL

- 5 -

DEW

46

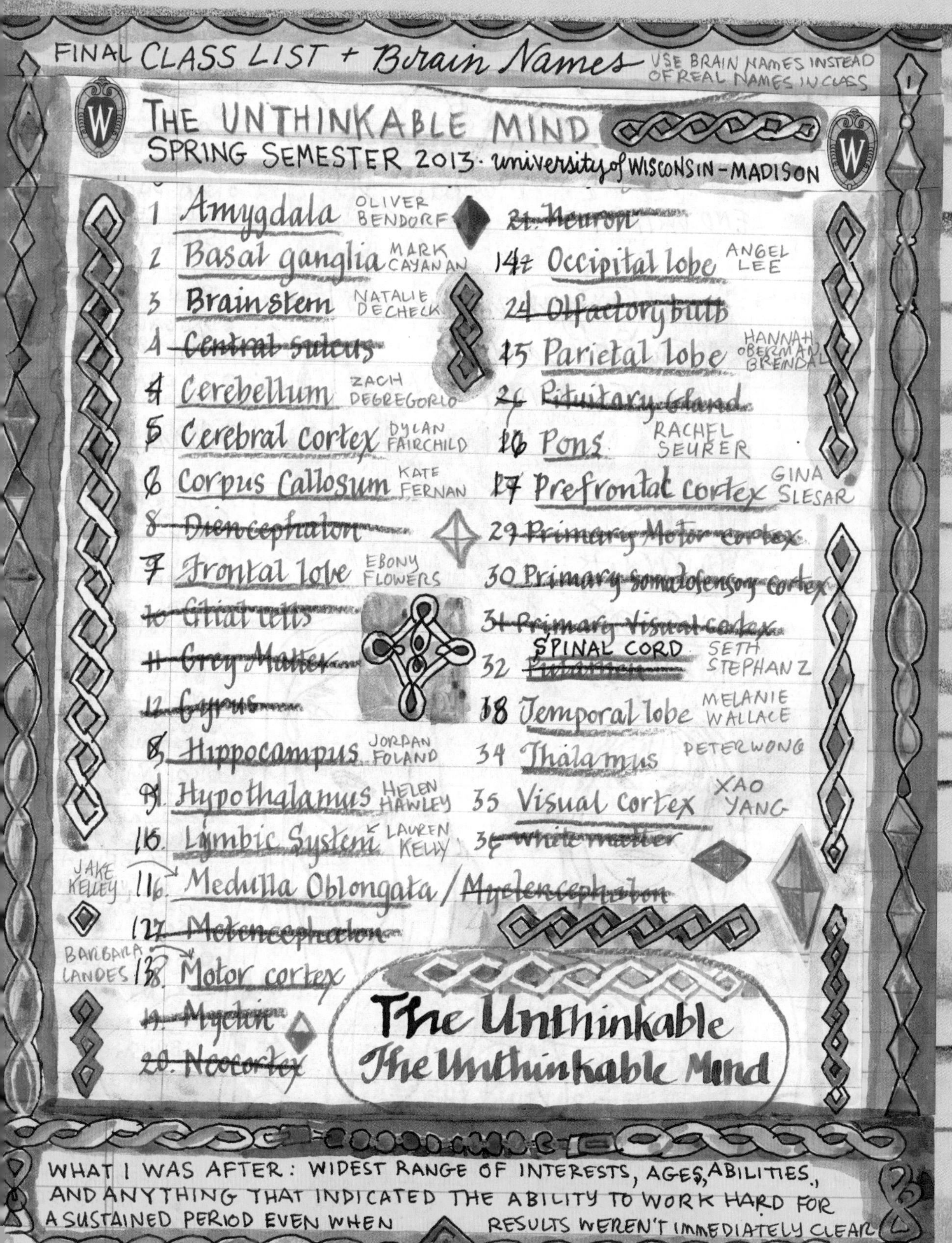
FINAL CLASS LIST + Brain Names
USE BRAIN NAMES INSTEAD OF REAL NAMES IN CLASS
THE UNTHINKABLE MIND
SPRING SEMESTER 2013 · university of WISCONSIN-MADISON
1 Amygdala OLIVER BENDORF
2 Basal ganglia MARK CAYANAN
3 Brainstem NATALIE DECHECK
4 Central Sulcus
4 Cerebellum ZACH DEGREGORIO
5 Cerebral cortex DYLAN FAIRCHILD
6 Corpus Callosum KATE FERNAN
8 Diencephalon
7 Frontal lobe EBONY FLOWERS
10 Glial cells
11 Grey Matter
12 Gyrus
8 Hippocampus JORDAN FOLAND
9 Hypothalamus HELEN HAWLEY
10 Limbic System LAUREN KELLY
JAKE KELLEY 11 Medulla Oblongata / Myelencephalon
12 Metencephalon
BARBARA LANDES 13 Motor cortex
19 Myelin
20 Neocortex
21 Neuron
14 Occipital lobe ANGEL LEE
24 Olfactory bulb
15 Parietal lobe HANNAH OBERMAN BREINDAL
26 Pituitary Gland
16 Pons RACHEL SEURER
17 Prefrontal cortex GINA SLESAR
29 Primary Motor cortex
30 Primary somatosensory cortex
31 Primary Visual cortex
32 SPINAL CORD Putamen SETH STEPHANZ
18 Temporal lobe MELANIE WALLACE
34 Thalamus PETER WONG
35 Visual cortex XAO YANG
36 White matter
The Unthinkable
The Unthinkable Mind
WHAT I WAS AFTER: WIDEST RANGE OF INTERESTS, AGES, ABILITIES, AND ANYTHING THAT INDICATED THE ABILITY TO WORK HARD FOR A SUSTAINED PERIOD EVEN WHEN RESULTS WEREN'T IMMEDIATELY CLEAR

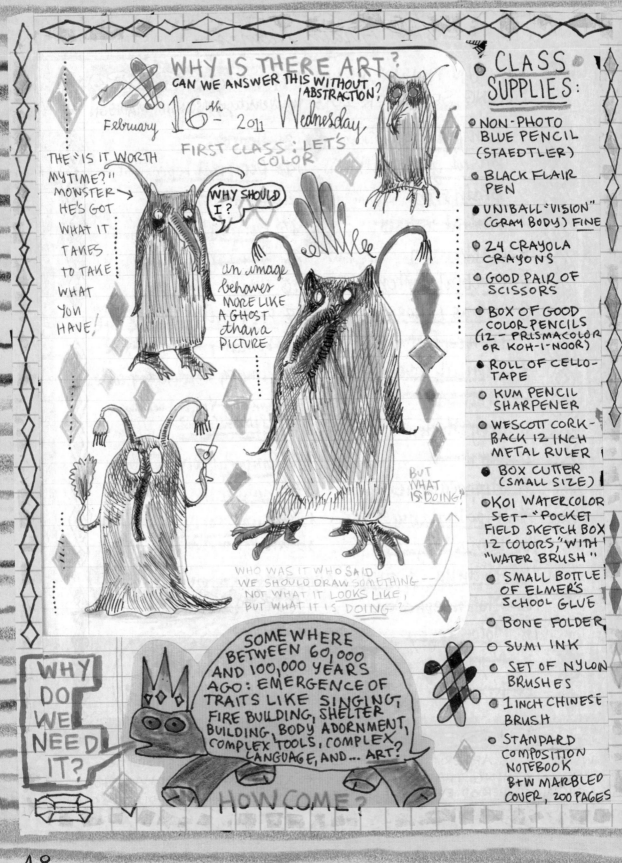

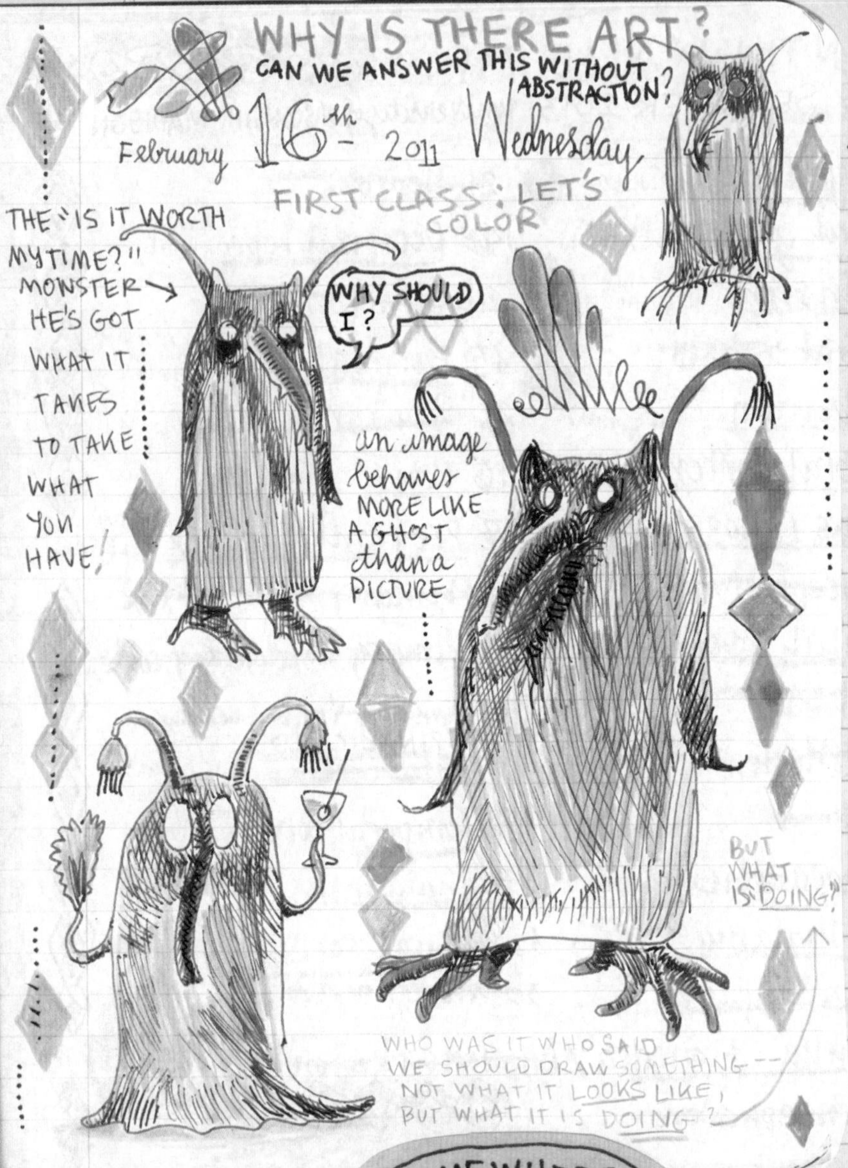
WHY IS THERE ART?
CAN WE ANSWER THIS WITHOUT ABSTRACTION?
February 16th - 2011 Wednesday
FIRST CLASS: LET'S COLOR
THE "IS IT WORTH MY TIME?" MONSTER
HE'S GOT WHAT IT TAKES TO TAKE WHAT YOU HAVE!
WHY SHOULD I?
an image behaves MORE LIKE A GHOST than a PICTURE
BUT WHAT IS DOING?
WHO WAS IT WHO SAID WE SHOULD DRAW SOMETHING -- NOT WHAT IT LOOKS LIKE, BUT WHAT IT IS DOING?

CLASS SUPPLIES:

- NON-PHOTO BLUE PENCIL (STAEDTLER)
- BLACK FLAIR PEN
- UNIBALL "VISION" (GRAY BODY) FINE
- 24 CRAYOLA CRAYONS
- GOOD PAIR OF SCISSORS
- BOX OF GOOD COLOR PENCILS (12 - PRISMACOLOR OR KOH-I-NOOR)
- ROLL OF CELLO-TAPE
- KUM PENCIL SHARPENER
- WESCOTT CORK-BACK 12 INCH METAL RULER
- BOX CUTTER (SMALL SIZE)
- KOI WATERCOLOR SET - "POCKET FIELD SKETCH BOX 12 COLORS," WITH "WATER BRUSH"
- SMALL BOTTLE OF ELMER'S SCHOOL GLUE
- BONE FOLDER
- SUMI INK
- SET OF NYLON BRUSHES
- 1 INCH CHINESE BRUSH
- STANDARD COMPOSITION NOTEBOOK B+W MARBLED COVER, 200 PAGES

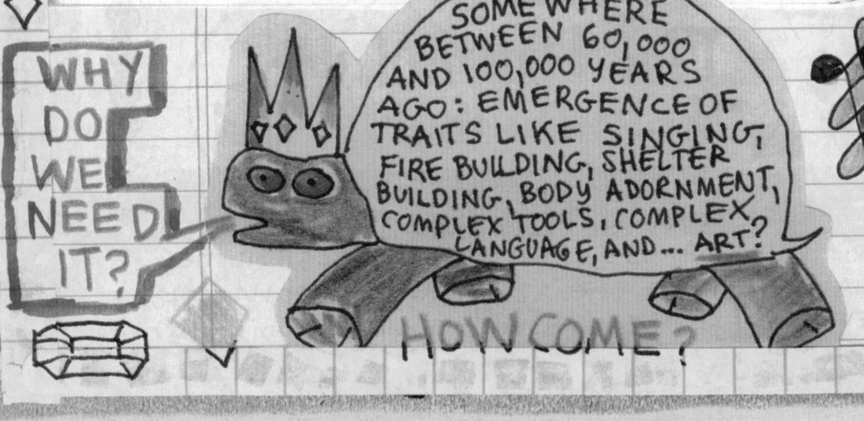
WHY DO WE NEED IT?
SOMEWHERE BETWEEN 60,000 AND 100,000 YEARS AGO: EMERGENCE OF TRAITS LIKE SINGING, FIRE BUILDING, SHELTER BUILDING, BODY ADORNMENT, COMPLEX TOOLS, COMPLEX LANGUAGE, AND... ART?
HOW COME?

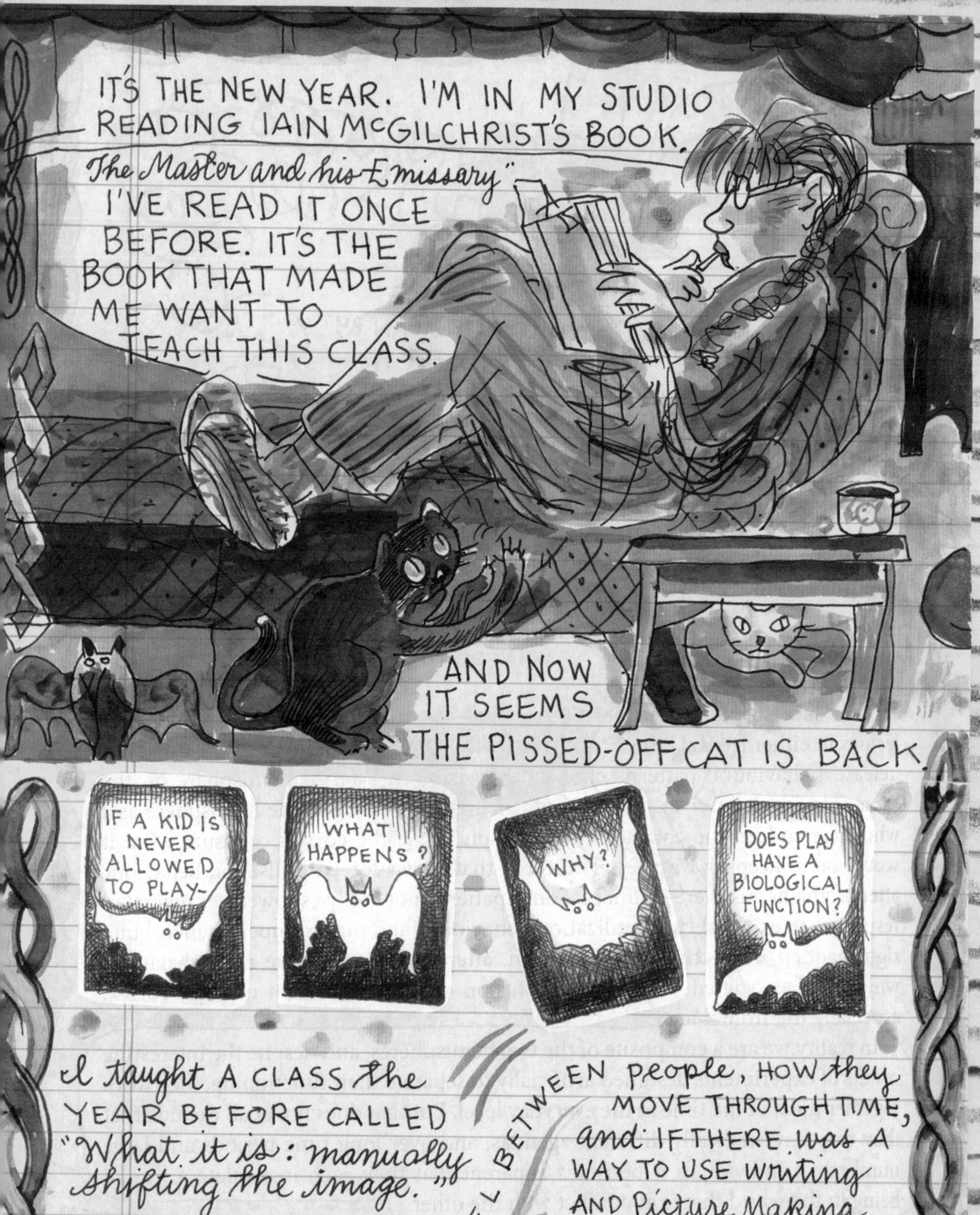
IT'S THE NEW YEAR. I'M IN MY STUDIO READING IAIN McGILCHRIST'S BOOK.
"The Master and his Emissary"
I'VE READ IT ONCE BEFORE. IT'S THE BOOK THAT MADE ME WANT TO TEACH THIS CLASS.
AND NOW IT SEEMS THE PISSED-OFF CAT IS BACK.
IF A KID IS NEVER ALLOWED TO PLAY-
WHAT HAPPENS?
WHY?
DOES PLAY HAVE A BIOLOGICAL FUNCTION?
I taught A CLASS the YEAR BEFORE CALLED "What it is: manually shifting the image." I WAS TRYING TO UNDERSTAND HOW IMAGES TRAVEL BETWEEN people, HOW they MOVE THROUGH TIME, and IF THERE was A WAY TO USE writing AND Picture Making TO FIGURE OUT MORE ABOUT how images WORK.

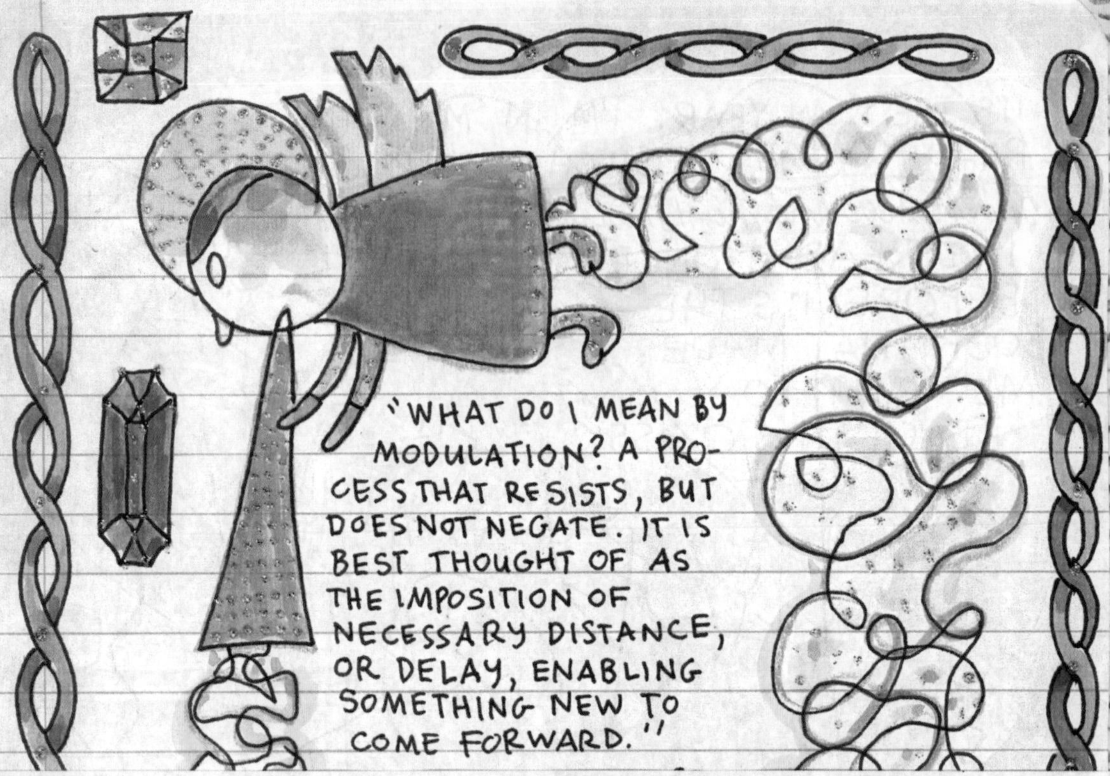
"WHAT DO I MEAN BY MODULATION? A PROCESS THAT RESISTS, BUT DOES NOT NEGATE. IT IS BEST THOUGHT OF AS THE IMPOSITION OF NECESSARY DISTANCE, OR DELAY, ENABLING SOMETHING NEW TO COME FORWARD."

THE MASTER AND HIS EMISSARY

IAIN MCGILCHRIST

END OF CHAPTER TWO

further data provided by Lhermitte is that the syndrome is as common after lesions in either frontal lobe;[529] and a lesion in either frontal lobe may, in any case, ‘release’ behavioural patterns characteristic of the posterior hemisphere on the same side (see below), as much as impair the functioning of the hemisphere as a whole (or indeed the contralateral hemisphere via the corpus callosum). But it would be in keeping with other research that shows forced utilisation behaviour after right-hemisphere damage: one patient not only showed exaggerated responses to external cues (utilization behaviour), and motor impersistence, but a right-handed instinctive grasp reaction, after an infarct in the right thalamus, which was associated with under-perfusion of the entire right cerebral cortex, especially the frontal area.[530]

In reality we are a composite of the two hemispheres, and despite the interesting results of experiments designed artificially to separate their functioning, they work together most of the time at the everyday level. But that does not at all exclude that they may have radically different agendas, and over long time periods and large numbers of individuals it becomes apparent that they each instantiate a way of being in the world that is at conflict with the other.

CODA: THE ‘FRONT-BACK’ PROBLEM

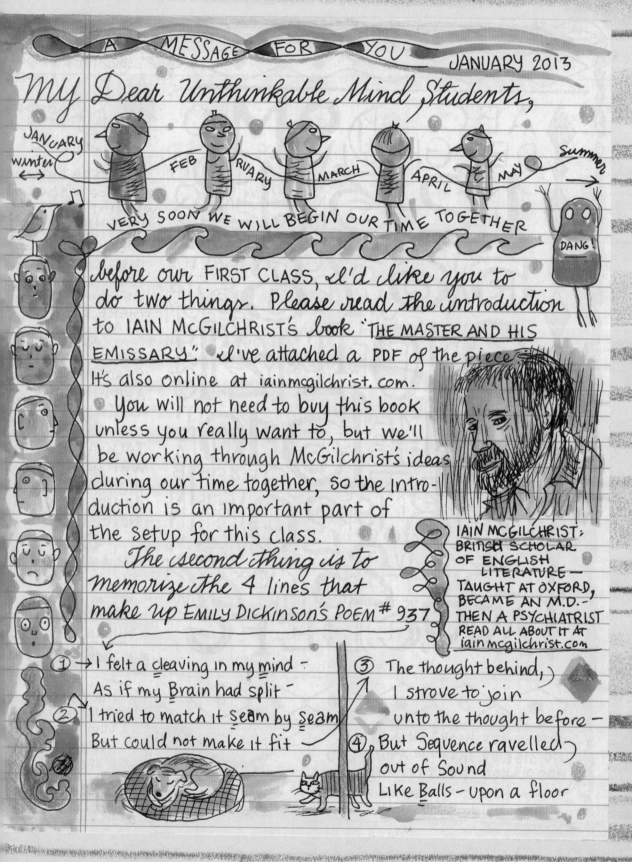

JANUARY 2013

MY Dear Unthinkable Mind Students,

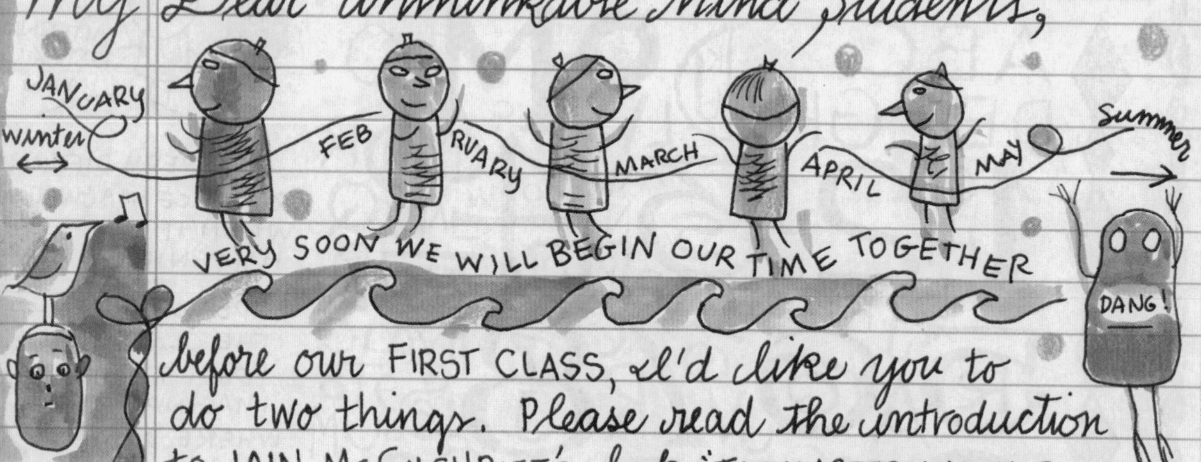
JANUARY
winter
FEB
RUARY
MARCH
APRIL
MAY
summer
VERY SOON WE WILL BEGIN OUR TIME TOGETHER
DANG!

before our FIRST CLASS, I'd like you to do two things. Please read the introduction to IAIN McGILCHRIST'S book "THE MASTER AND HIS EMISSARY." I've attached a PDF of the piece. It's also online at iainmcgilchrist.com.

You will not need to buy this book unless you really want to, but we'll be working through McGilchrist's ideas during our time together, so the introduction is an important part of the setup for this class.

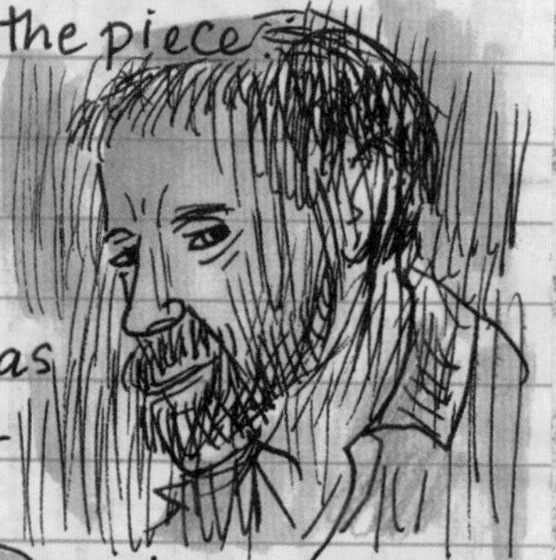

IAIN MCGILCHRIST: BRITISH SCHOLAR OF ENGLISH LITERATURE — TAUGHT AT OXFORD, BECAME AN M.D. - THEN A PSYCHIATRIST READ ALL ABOUT IT AT iainmcgilchrist.com

The second thing is to memorize the 4 lines that make up EMILY DICKINSON'S POEM # 937

① → I felt a cleaving in my mind -
As if my Brain had split -

② I tried to match it seam by seam
But could not make it fit

③ The thought behind,
I strove to join
unto the thought before -

④ But Sequence ravelled
out of Sound
Like Balls - upon a floor

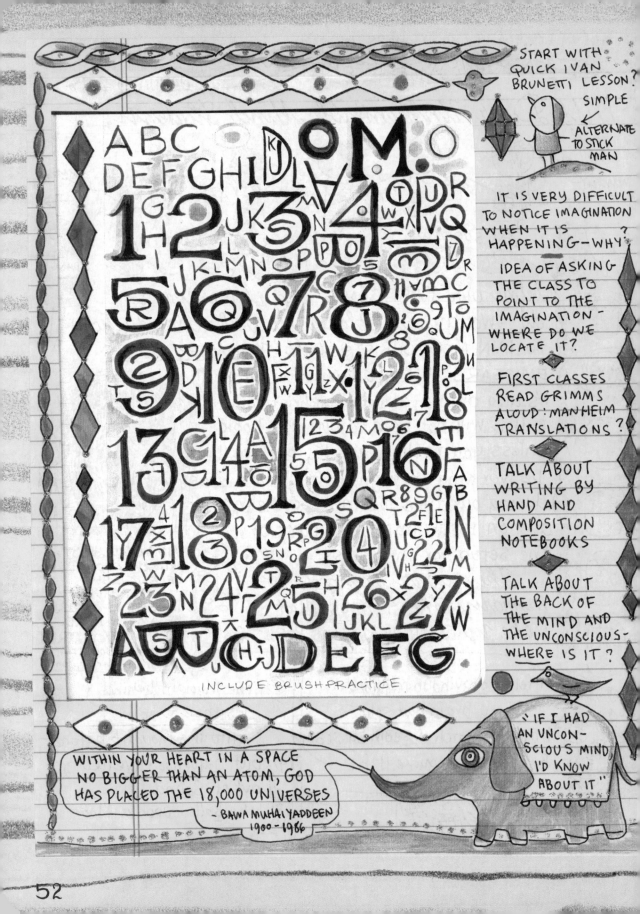

START WITH QUICK IVAN BRUNETTI LESSON?

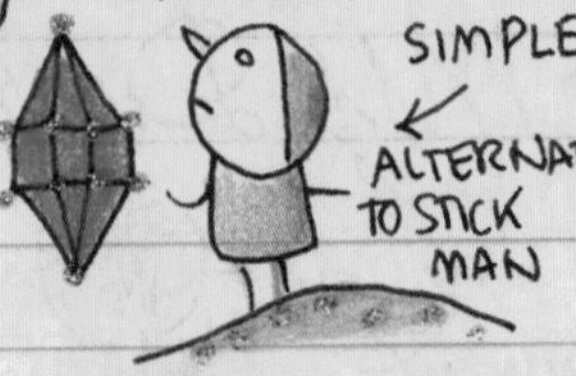
SIMPLE
ALTERNATE TO STICK MAN

IT IS VERY DIFFICULT TO NOTICE IMAGINATION WHEN IT IS HAPPENING—WHY?

IDEA OF ASKING THE CLASS TO POINT TO THE IMAGINATION—WHERE DO WE LOCATE IT?

FIRST CLASSES READ GRIMMS ALOUD: MANHEIM TRANSLATIONS?

TALK ABOUT WRITING BY HAND AND COMPOSITION NOTEBOOKS

TALK ABOUT THE BACK OF THE MIND AND THE UNCONSCIOUS—<u>WHERE</u> IS IT?

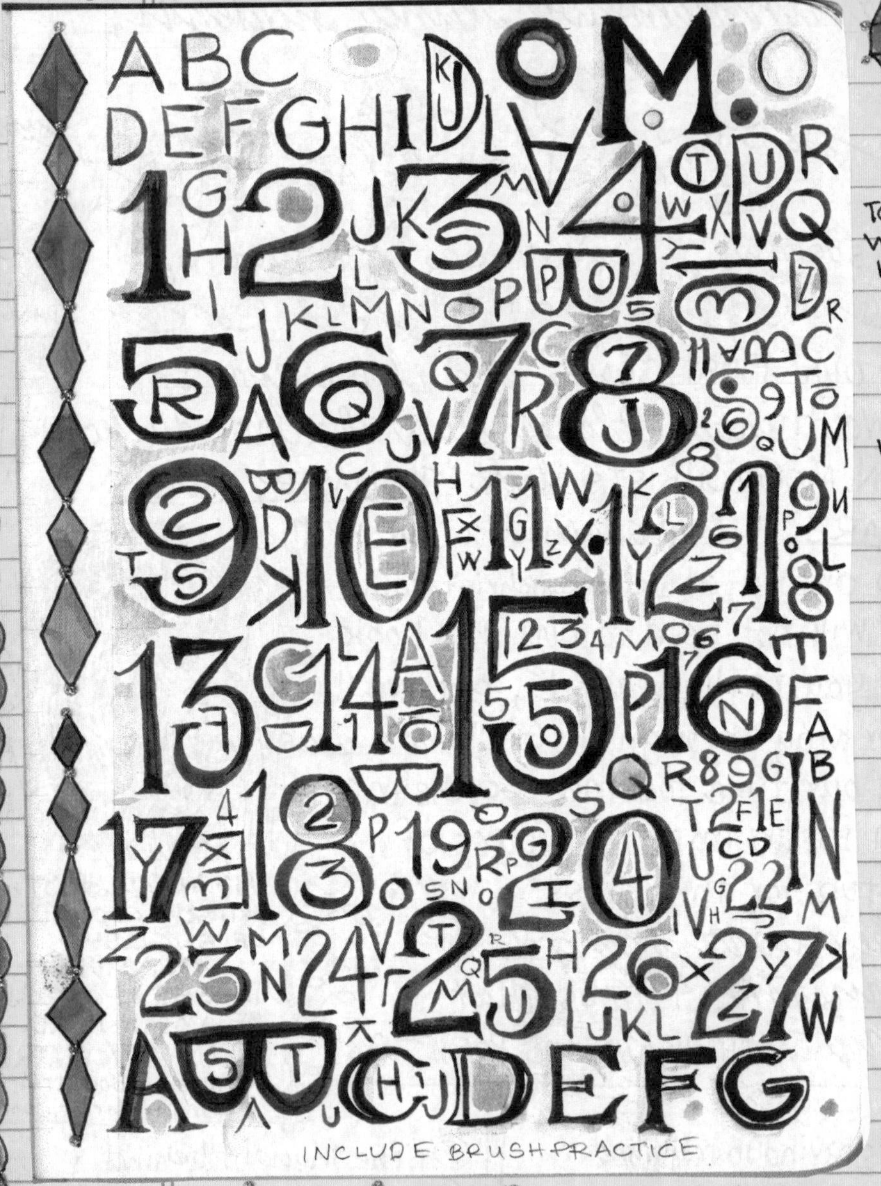

INCLUDE BRUSH PRACTICE

WITHIN YOUR HEART IN A SPACE NO BIGGER THAN AN ATOM, GOD HAS PLACED THE 18,000 UNIVERSES

– BAWA MUHAIYADDEEN 1900–1986

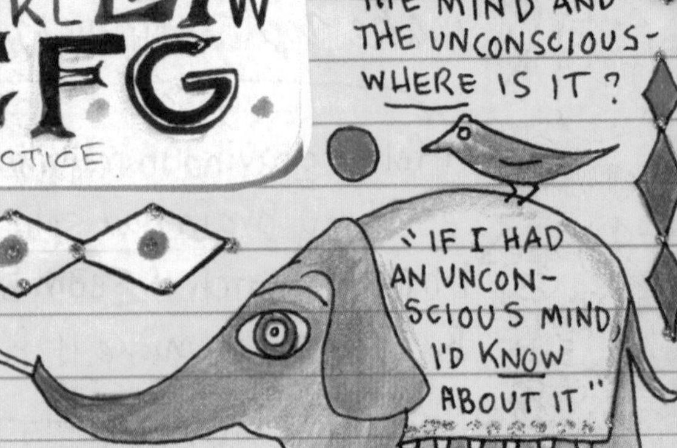
"IF I HAD AN UNCON-SCIOUS MIND, I'D KNOW ABOUT IT"

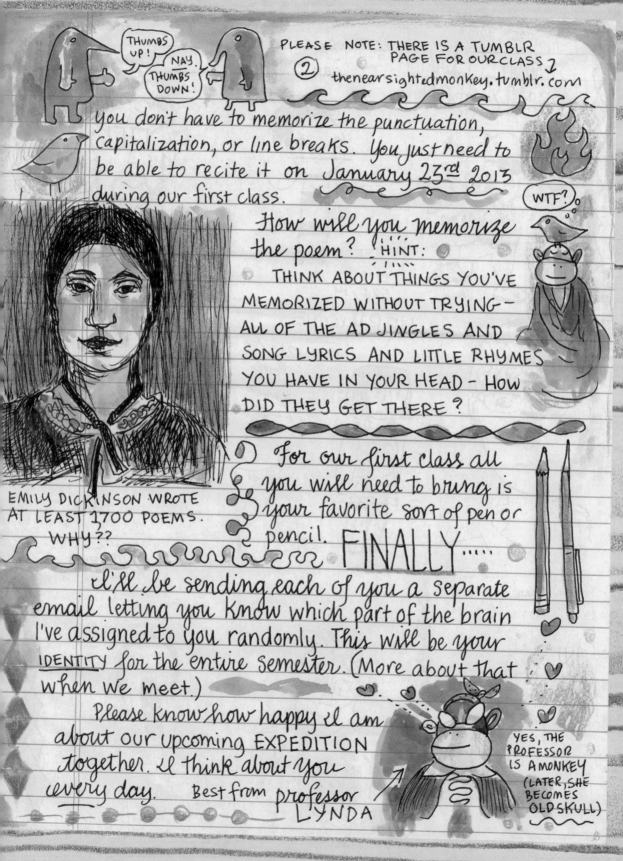

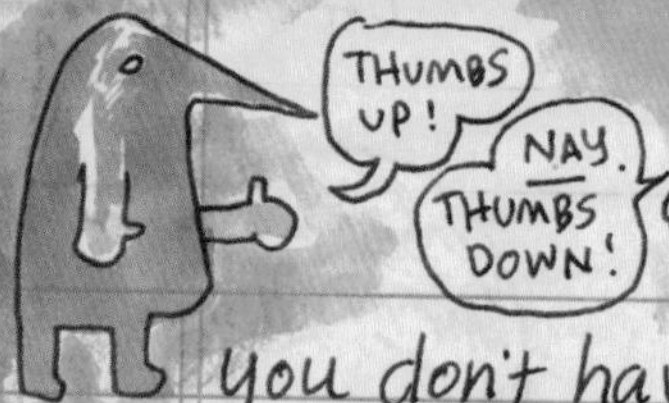
THUMBS UP!
NAY. THUMBS DOWN!

PLEASE NOTE: THERE IS A TUMBLR PAGE FOR OUR CLASS

② thenearsightedmonkey.tumblr.com

you don't have to memorize the punctuation, capitalization, or line breaks. You just need to be able to recite it on January 23rd 2013 during our first class.

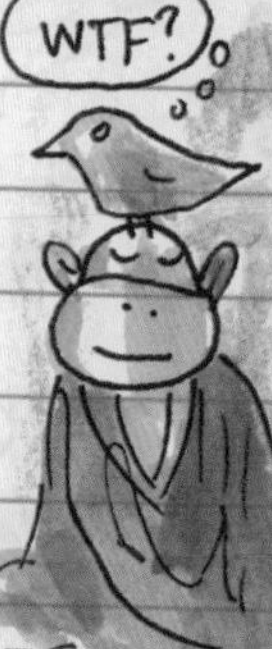
WTF?

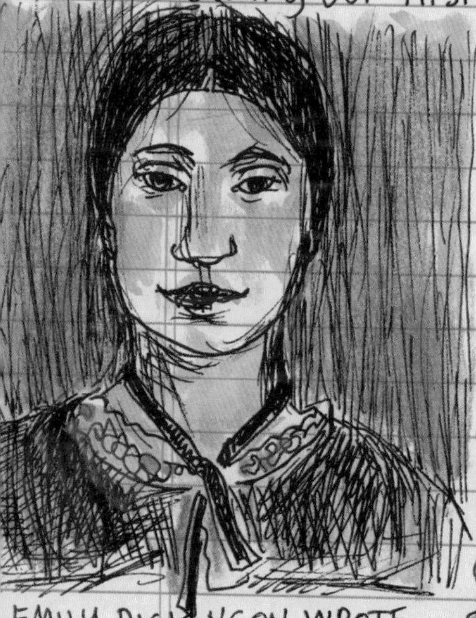

EMILY DICKINSON WROTE AT LEAST 1,700 POEMS. WHY??

How will you memorize the poem? HINT: THINK ABOUT THINGS YOU'VE MEMORIZED WITHOUT TRYING— ALL OF THE AD JINGLES AND SONG LYRICS AND LITTLE RHYMES YOU HAVE IN YOUR HEAD — HOW DID THEY GET THERE?

For our first class all you will need to bring is your favorite sort of pen or pencil. FINALLY.....

I'll be sending each of you a separate email letting you know which part of the brain I've assigned to you randomly. This will be your IDENTITY for the entire semester. (More about that when we meet.)

Please know how happy I am about our upcoming EXPEDITION together. I think about you every day. Best from professor LYNDA

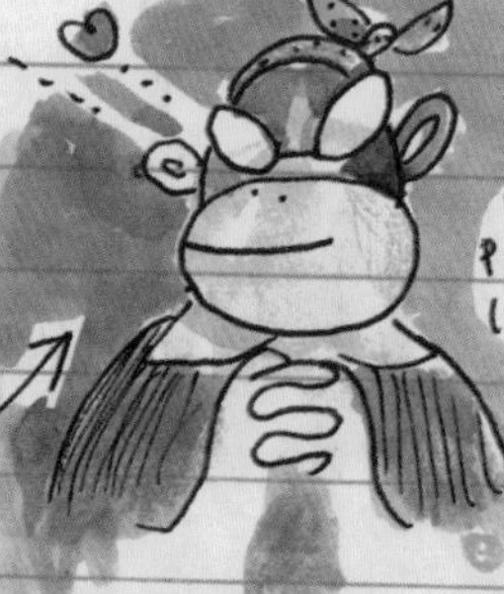

YES, THE PROFESSOR IS A MONKEY (LATER, SHE BECOMES OLD SKULL)

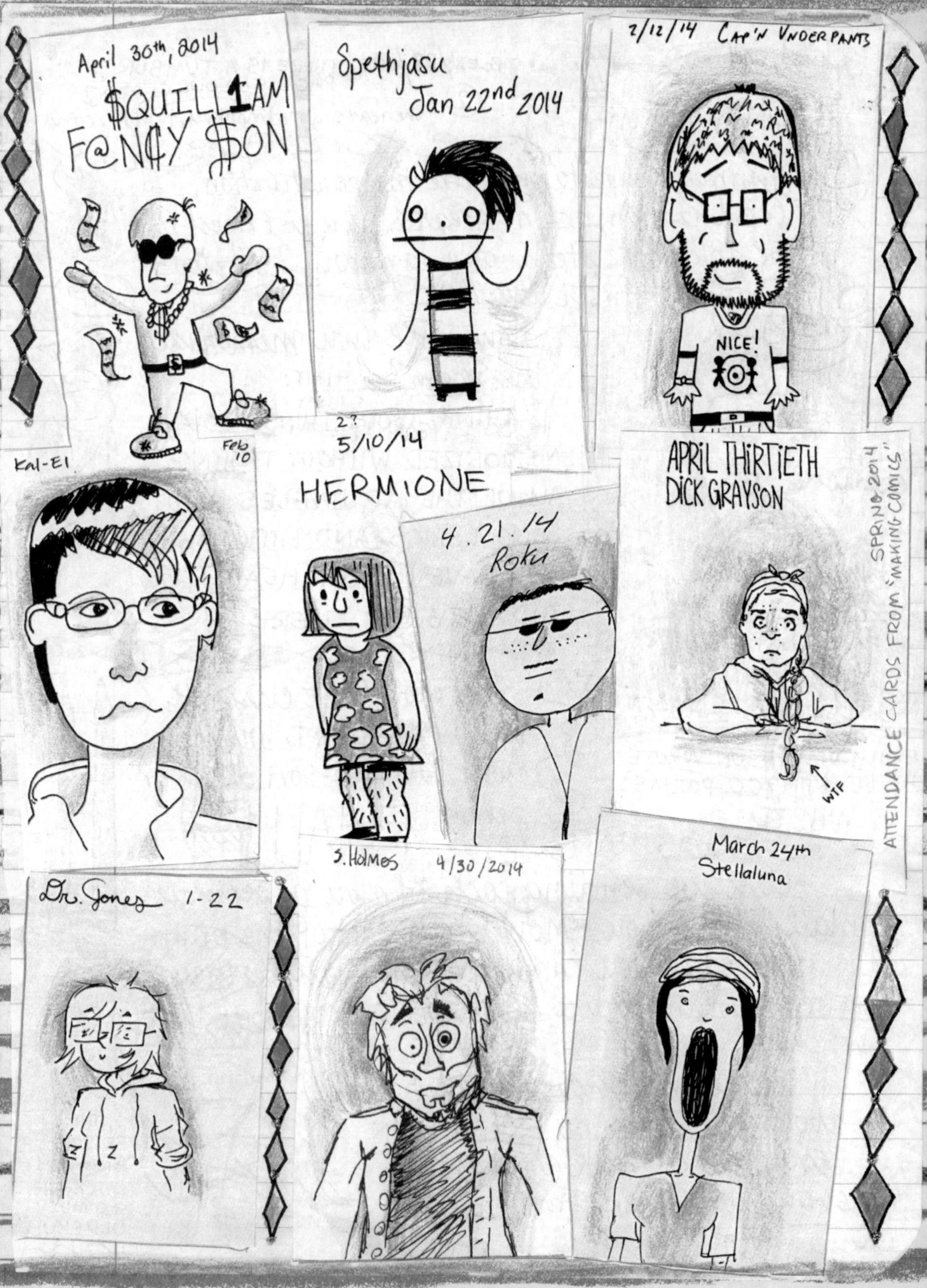
April 30th, 2014
$QUILL1AM F@N¢Y $ON
Feb 10
Spethjasu
Jan 22nd 2014
2/12/14 Cap'n Underpants
NICE!
Kal-El
2?
5/10/14
HERMIONE
4.21.14
Roku
APRIL THIRTIETH
DICK GRAYSON
SPRING 2014
ATTENDANCE CARDS FROM "MAKING COMICS"
WTF
S. Holmes 4/30/2014
Dr. Jones 1-22
z z
March 24th
Stellaluna

CLASSROOM RULES

WE DON'T USE OUR REAL NAMES IN CLASS. WE GO BY CHARACTER NAMES; EITHER ASSIGNED OR CHOSEN

WHEN CLASSMATES READ ALOUD, WE DO NOT LOOK AT THEM. INSTEAD, WE DRAW TIGHT SPIRALS SLOWLY.

WE NEVER TALK ABOUT THE WORK THAT IS READ ALOUD - EITHER IN OR OUT OF CLASS.

WE DO NOT PUT OUR NAMES ON THE FRONT SIDE OF OUR DRAWINGS OR STORIES.

WE DO NOT ASK WHO MADE WHICH PICTURE OR WROTE WHICH STORY.

WE DO NOT ACTIVATE ANY ELECTRONIC DEVICES IN CLASS OR USE THEM FOR OUR ASSIGNMENTS

WE BRING OUR COMPOSITION NOTEBOOKS AND ALL OUR ART SUPPLIES TO EVERY CLASS

WE DON'T OFTEN CHAT. INSTEAD, WE GET TO KNOW EACH OTHER THROUGH THE IMAGES IN OUR WORK.

WE SIT IN A DIFFERENT SEAT FOR EACH CLASS BESIDE DIFFERENT CLASSMATES

WE BEGIN EACH CLASS BY DRAWING A 2 MINUTE SELF-PORTRAIT ON AN INDEX CARD AND TURN IT IN, DATED.

WE DON'T GIVE ADVICE OR OPINIONS ON THE WORK OF OUR CLASSMATES

WE FILL OUR COMPOSITION NOTEBOOKS AND THEN START ANOTHER. AIM FOR 3 TO 4 DURING THE SEMESTER

ATTENDANCE CARDS FROM "WRITE WHAT YOU SEE" SPRING 2014

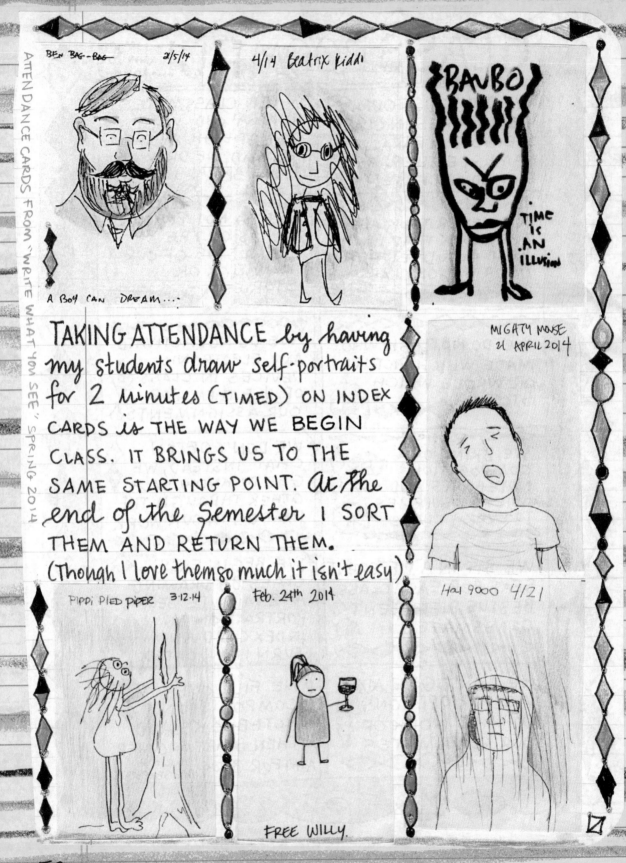

BEN BAG-BAG
2/5/14
A BOY CAN DREAM...

4/14 Beatrix Kiddo

BAUBO
TIME IS AN ILLUSION

TAKING ATTENDANCE by having my students draw self-portraits for 2 minutes (TIMED) ON INDEX CARDS is THE WAY WE BEGIN CLASS. IT BRINGS US TO THE SAME STARTING POINT. At the end of the Semester I SORT THEM AND RETURN THEM. (Though I love them so much it isn't easy)

MIGHTY MOUSE
21 APRIL 2014

PIPPI PIED PIPER 3.12.14

Feb. 24th 2014
FREE WILLY.

Hal 9000 4/21

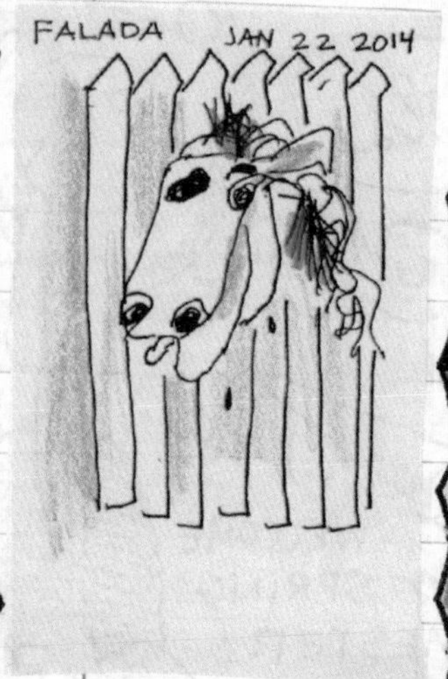
FALADA
JAN 22 2014

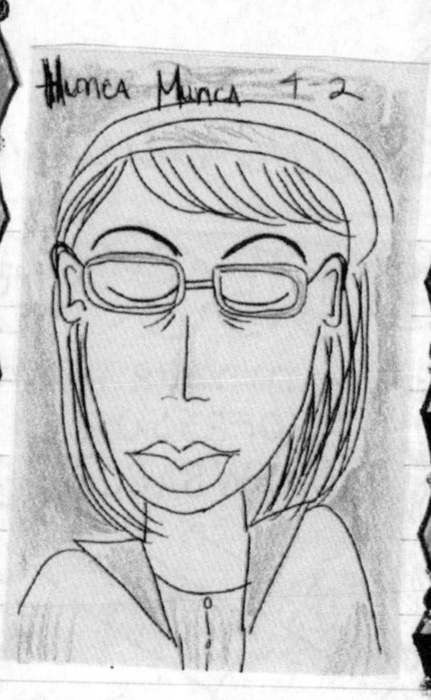
Hunca Munca 4-2

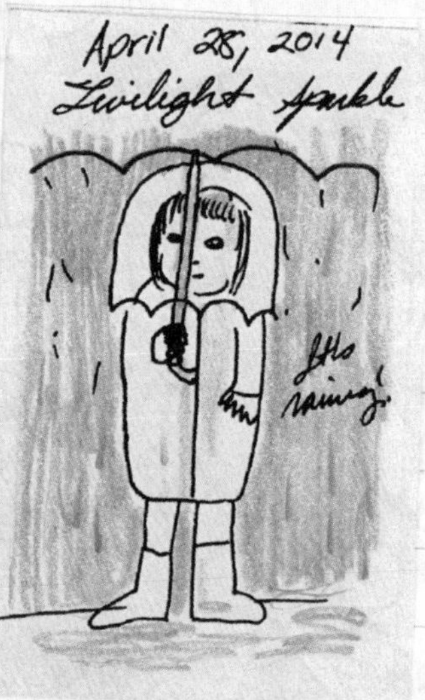
April 28, 2014
Twilight Sparkle
It's raining!

THERE ARE USUALLY ABOUT 30 DRAWINGS IN ALL, MOST OF THEM COMPLETELY FORGOTTEN UNTIL OUR LAST DAY OF CLASS. MY HOPE IS THAT THEY KEEP THEM. MY HOPE IS THAT THEY SEE THE EXTRAORDINARY RESULT OF DOING SOMETHING AS ORDINARY AS DRAWING A 2-MINUTE SELF-PORTRAIT ON AN INDEX CARD TWICE A WEEK.

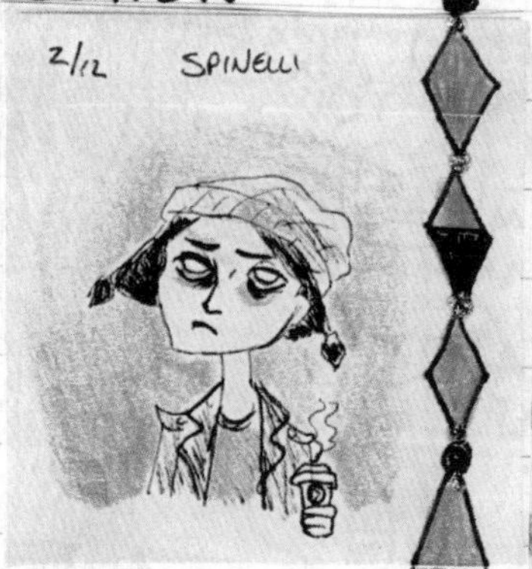
2/12
SPINELLI

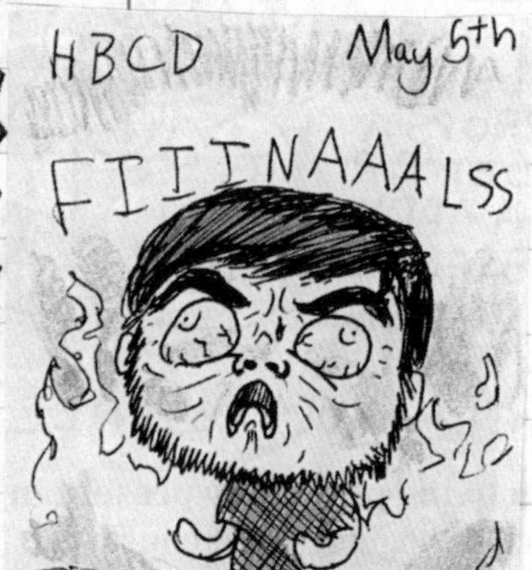
HBCD
May 5th
FIIINAAALSS
AAAAAAAAA

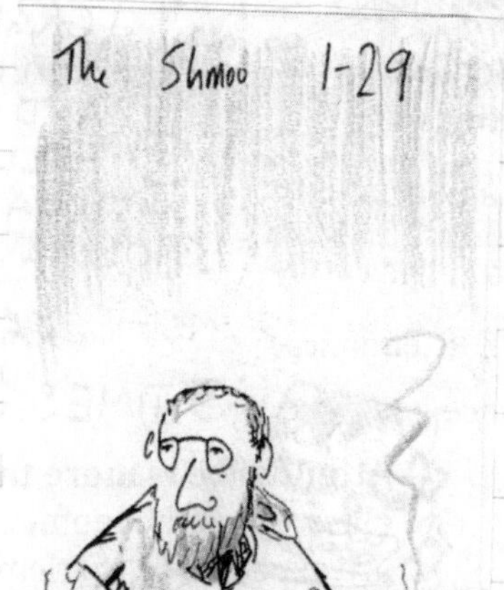
The Shmoo 1-29
BURKE WRESTLING

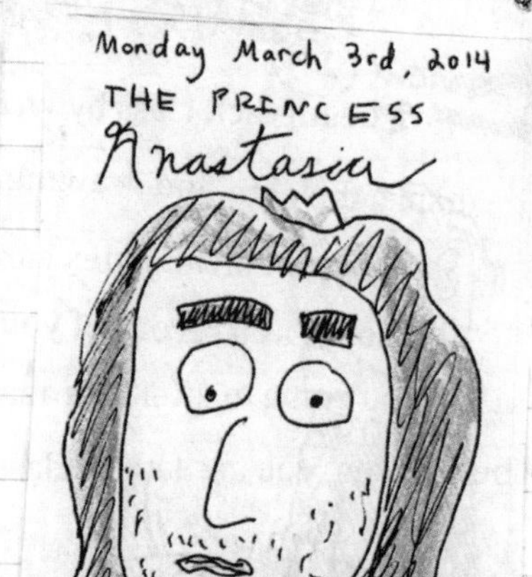
Monday March 3rd, 2014
THE PRINCESS
Anastasia

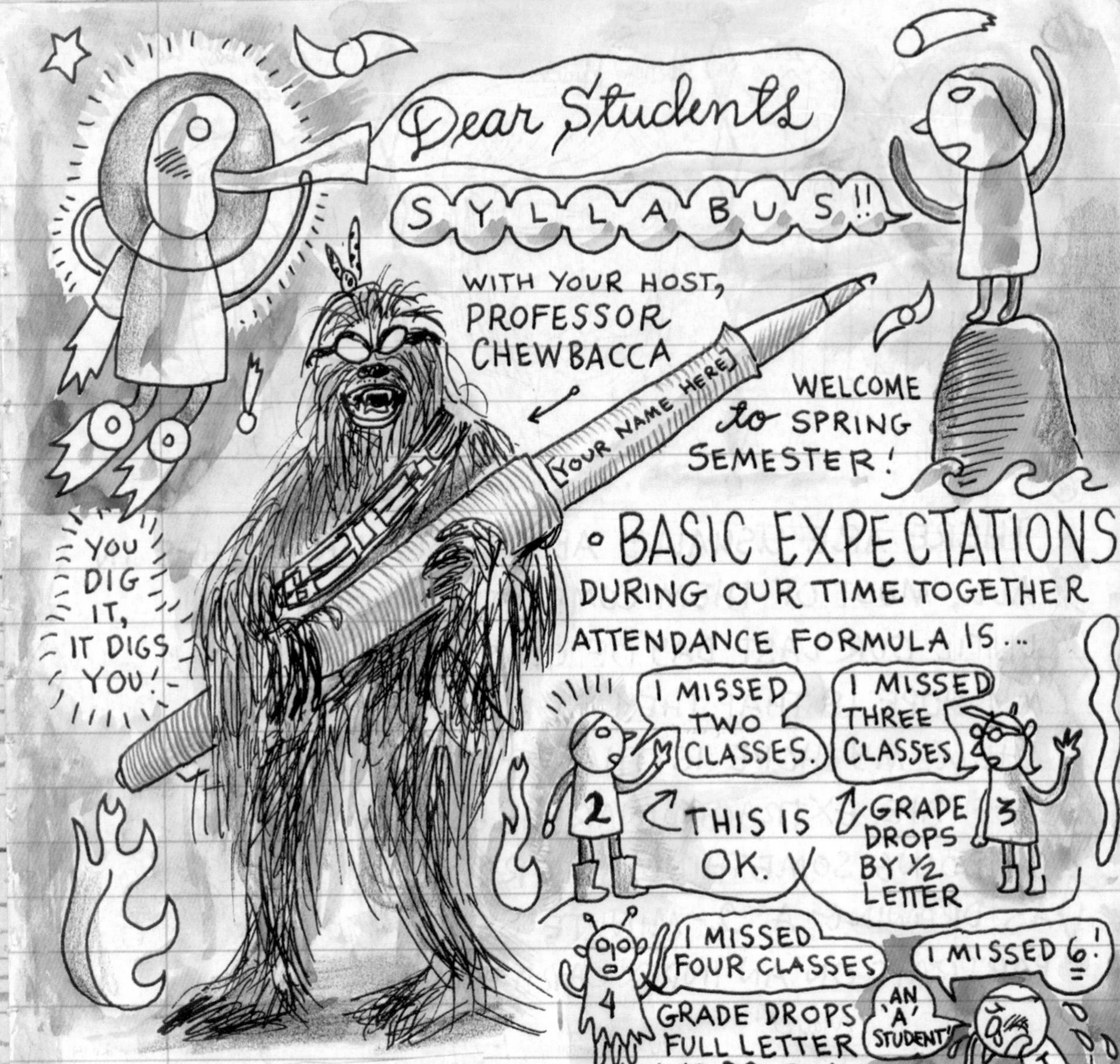
Dear Students
SYLLABUS!!
WITH YOUR HOST, PROFESSOR CHEWBACCA
[YOUR NAME HERE]
WELCOME to SPRING SEMESTER!
YOU DIG IT, IT DIGS YOU!
• BASIC EXPECTATIONS
DURING OUR TIME TOGETHER
ATTENDANCE FORMULA IS...
I MISSED TWO CLASSES.
I MISSED THREE CLASSES
THIS IS OK.
GRADE DROPS BY ½ LETTER
I MISSED FOUR CLASSES
I MISSED 6!

We begin each class by writing our name, the date, and drawing a two-minute self-portrait on an index card. The cards will serve as a record of your attendance. If you come in after attendance has been taken, you are late to class.

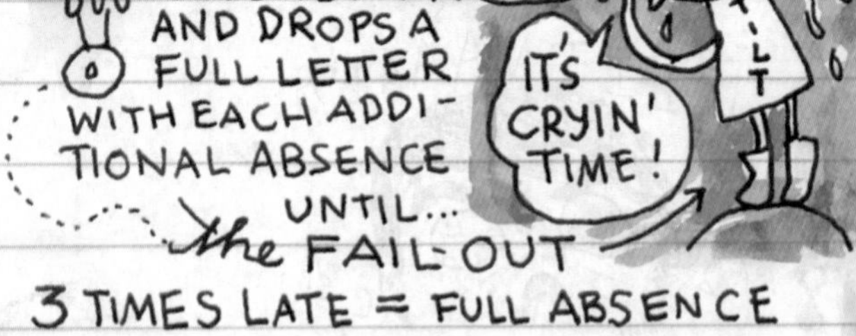
GRADE DROPS FULL LETTER AND DROPS A FULL LETTER WITH EACH ADDITIONAL ABSENCE UNTIL... the FAIL-OUT
AN 'A' STUDENT!
IT'S CRYIN' TIME!
TILT
3 TIMES LATE = FULL ABSENCE

Attendance is more than being physically present in class. From the moment class begins until it ends, you are expected to participate fully in class activities. During the entire 150 minutes of each class session I ask that you not check personal devices, use your computer, wear headphones, etc. This includes breaks and field trips.

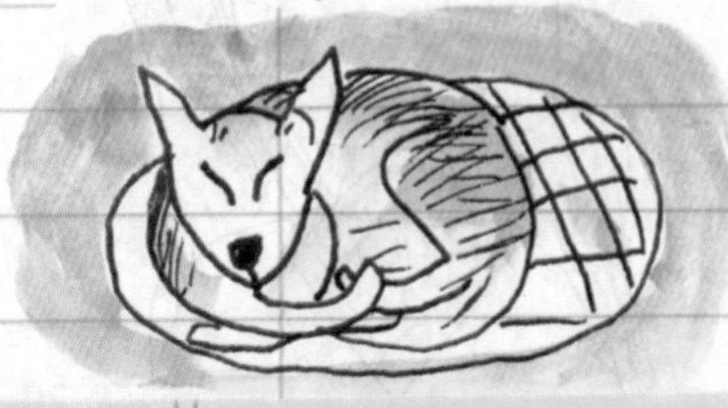

GRADES!

Your final grade will be based on

-Attendance and punctuality
-Class participation
-Content and use of composition notebooks
-Timely completion of weekly assignments
-Final Project

To get an **A**, you must not only spend more time on assignments and demonstrate active engagement with the work, you must also find something original during the course of the semester.

What I mean by 'finding something* original" may be hard to define on paper, but it's unmistakable when it starts to happen. The whole class feels it. A new way of seeing comes about, a new approach to problem-solving and working that extends beyond the limits of our class time into other aspects of daily life.

my experience has been that this *SOMETHING can be found by ANY STUDENT –regardless OF TECHNICAL ABILITY– who TAKES each assignment SERIOUSLY AND WORKS HARD.

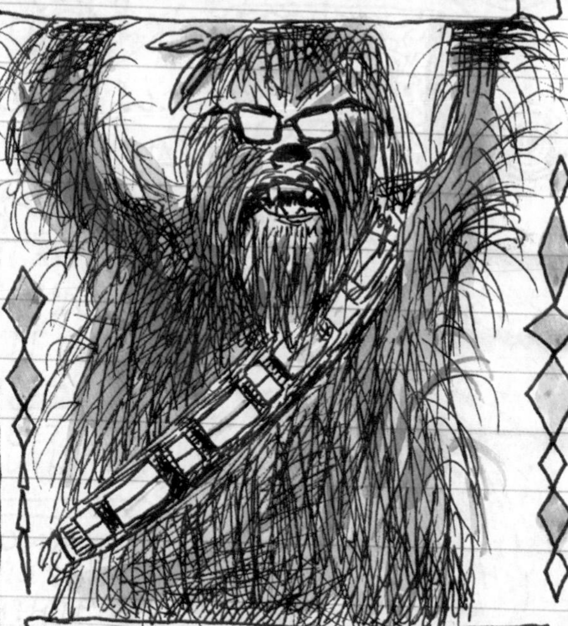

Those who do the minimum amount of required work will get a **C**.

Those who spend more time on assignments and demonstrate engagement with the work will get a **B**.

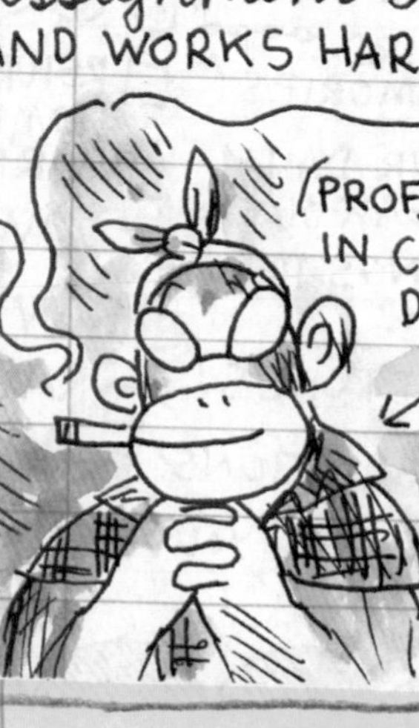

(PROF. CHEWBACCA IN CIVILIAN DRESS)

ON GRADING INDIVIDUAL ASSIGNMENTS

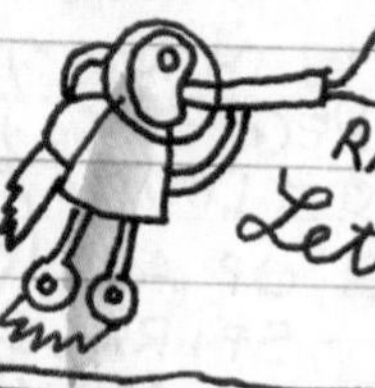

I USE √- √ and √+ ON ASSIGNMENTS RATHER THAN Letter grades

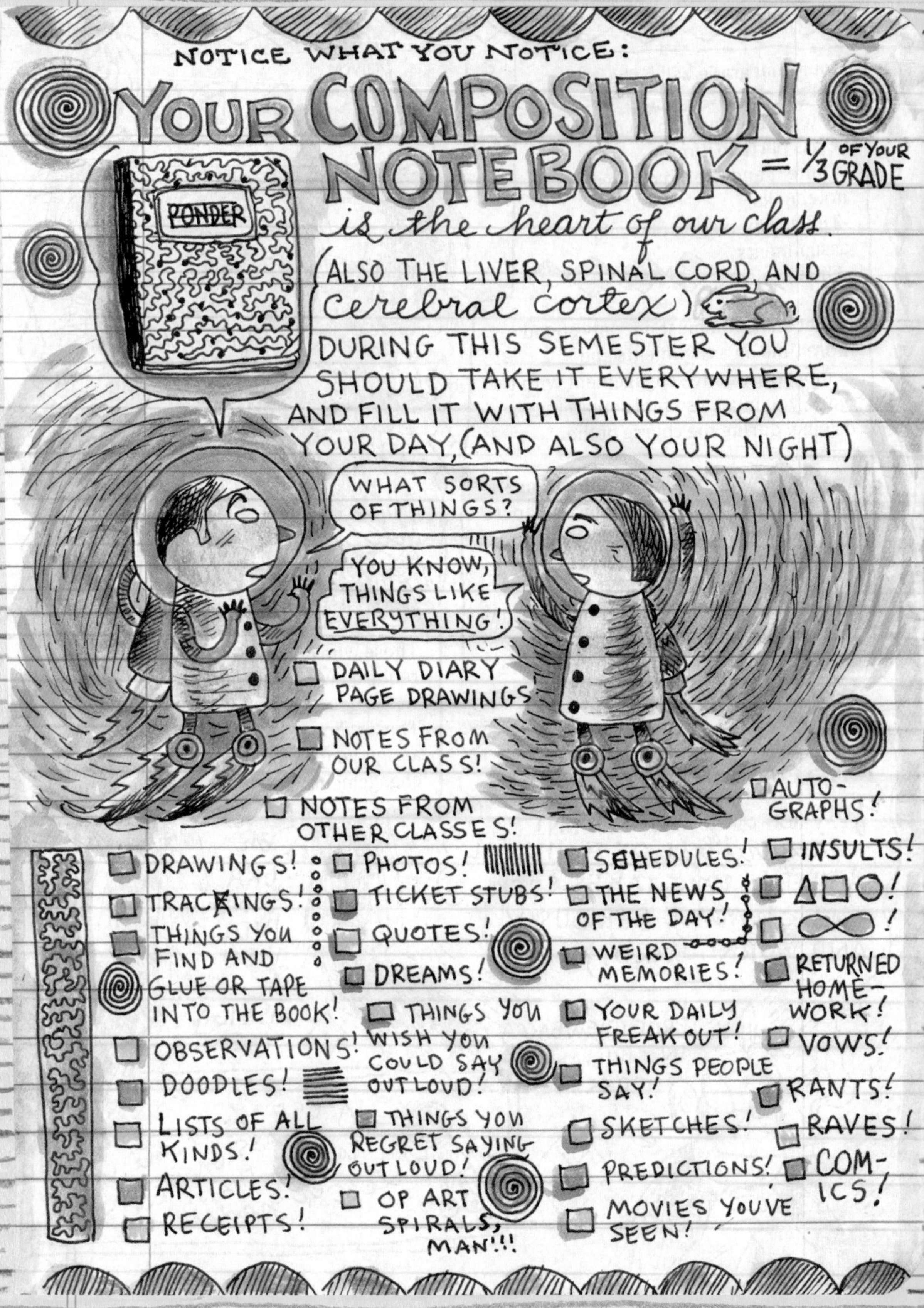
NOTICE WHAT YOU NOTICE:
YOUR COMPOSITION NOTEBOOK = 1/3 OF YOUR GRADE
PONDER
is the heart of our class.
(ALSO THE LIVER, SPINAL CORD, AND cerebral cortex)
DURING THIS SEMESTER YOU SHOULD TAKE IT EVERYWHERE, AND FILL IT WITH THINGS FROM YOUR DAY, (AND ALSO YOUR NIGHT)
WHAT SORTS OF THINGS?
YOU KNOW, THINGS LIKE EVERYTHING!
DAILY DIARY PAGE DRAWINGS
NOTES FROM OUR CLASS!
NOTES FROM OTHER CLASSES!
AUTO-GRAPHS!
DRAWINGS!
TRACKINGS!
THINGS YOU FIND AND GLUE OR TAPE INTO THE BOOK!
OBSERVATIONS!
DOODLES!
LISTS OF ALL KINDS!
ARTICLES!
RECEIPTS!
PHOTOS!
TICKET STUBS!
QUOTES!
DREAMS!
THINGS YOU WISH YOU COULD SAY OUT LOUD!
THINGS YOU REGRET SAYING OUT LOUD!
OP ART SPIRALS, MAN!!!
SCHEDULES!
THE NEWS OF THE DAY!
WEIRD MEMORIES!
YOUR DAILY FREAK OUT!
THINGS PEOPLE SAY!
SKETCHES!
PREDICTIONS!
MOVIES YOU'VE SEEN!
INSULTS!
△□○!
∞!
RETURNED HOME-WORK!
VOWS!
RANTS!
RAVES!
COM-ICS!

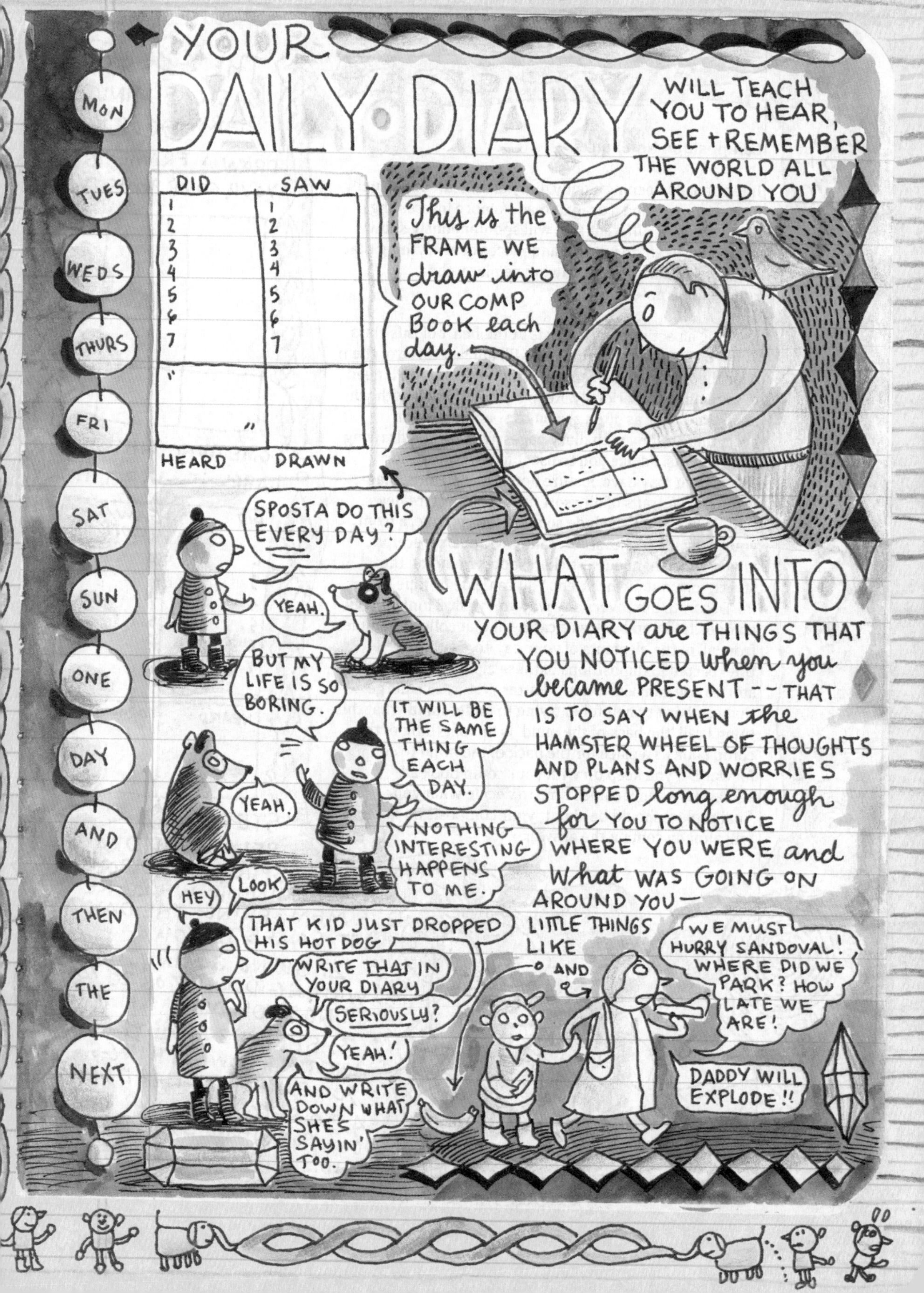

YOUR DAILY DIARY WILL TEACH YOU TO HEAR, SEE + REMEMBER THE WORLD ALL AROUND YOU
MON
TUES
WEDS
THURS
FRI
SAT
SUN
ONE
DAY
AND
THEN
THE
NEXT
DID
SAW
1 2 3 4 5 6 7
1 2 3 4 5 6 7
HEARD
DRAWN
This is the FRAME WE draw into OUR COMP Book each day.
SPOSTA DO THIS EVERY DAY?
YEAH.
BUT MY LIFE IS SO BORING.
IT WILL BE THE SAME THING EACH DAY.
YEAH.
NOTHING INTERESTING HAPPENS TO ME.
WHAT GOES INTO YOUR DIARY are THINGS THAT YOU NOTICED when you became PRESENT -- THAT IS TO SAY WHEN the HAMSTER WHEEL OF THOUGHTS AND PLANS AND WORRIES STOPPED long enough for YOU TO NOTICE WHERE YOU WERE and What WAS GOING ON AROUND YOU—
LITTLE THINGS LIKE
AND
HEY
LOOK
THAT KID JUST DROPPED HIS HOT DOG
WRITE THAT IN YOUR DIARY
SERIOUSLY?
YEAH!
AND WRITE DOWN WHAT SHES SAYIN' TOO.
WE MUST HURRY SANDOVAL! WHERE DID WE PARK? HOW LATE WE ARE!
DADDY WILL EXPLODE!!

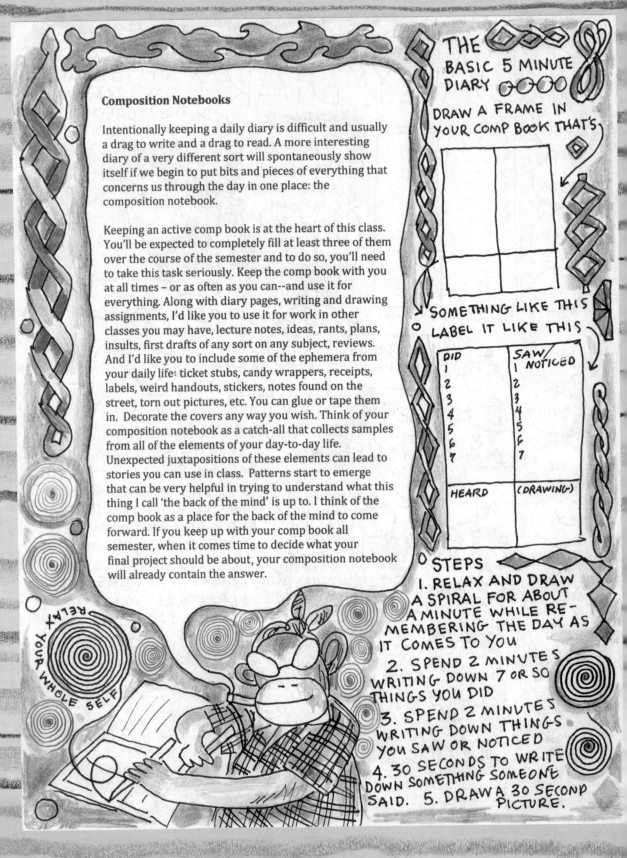

Composition Notebooks

Intentionally keeping a daily diary is difficult and usually a drag to write and a drag to read. A more interesting diary of a very different sort will spontaneously show itself if we begin to put bits and pieces of everything that concerns us through the day in one place: the composition notebook.

Keeping an active comp book is at the heart of this class. You'll be expected to completely fill at least three of them over the course of the semester and to do so, you'll need to take this task seriously. Keep the comp book with you at all times – or as often as you can--and use it for everything. Along with diary pages, writing and drawing assignments, I'd like you to use it for work in other classes you may have, lecture notes, ideas, rants, plans, insults, first drafts of any sort on any subject, reviews. And I'd like you to include some of the ephemera from your daily life: ticket stubs, candy wrappers, receipts, labels, weird handouts, stickers, notes found on the street, torn out pictures, etc. You can glue or tape them in. Decorate the covers any way you wish. Think of your composition notebook as a catch-all that collects samples from all of the elements of your day-to-day life. Unexpected juxtapositions of these elements can lead to stories you can use in class. Patterns start to emerge that can be very helpful in trying to understand what this thing I call 'the back of the mind' is up to. I think of the comp book as a place for the back of the mind to come forward. If you keep up with your comp book all semester, when it comes time to decide what your final project should be about, your composition notebook will already contain the answer.

THE BASIC 5 MINUTE DIARY

DRAW A FRAME IN YOUR COMP BOOK THAT'S

SOMETHING LIKE THIS

LABEL IT LIKE THIS

DID	SAW/ NOTICED
1	1
2	2
3	3
4	4
5	5
6	6
7	7
HEARD	(DRAWING)

STEPS

1. RELAX AND DRAW A SPIRAL FOR ABOUT A MINUTE WHILE RE-MEMBERING THE DAY AS IT COMES TO YOU

2. SPEND 2 MINUTES WRITING DOWN 7 OR SO THINGS YOU DID

3. SPEND 2 MINUTES WRITING DOWN THINGS YOU SAW OR NOTICED

4. 30 SECONDS TO WRITE DOWN SOMETHING SOMEONE SAID. 5. DRAW A 30 SECOND PICTURE.

RELAX YOUR WHOLE SELF

◆BASIC QUICK DIARY FORMAT◆

what you did	What you saw
1.	1.
2. SPEND	2. SPEND
3. 2½	3. 2½
4. MINUTES MAKING	4. MINUTES MAKING
5. THIS	5. THIS
LIST	LIST
6.	6.
7.	7.
Something you heard someone say	draw a picture OF SOMETHING you saw
30 SECONDS	30 SECONDS

START BY NOTICING WHAT YOU NOTICE AS YOU GO ABOUT YOUR DAY, YOU DO THINGS— SOMETIMES INTENTIONALLY AND OTHER TIMES BY ACCIDENT. BOTH SORTS OF EVENTS SHOULD BE WELCOME IN YOUR LIST OF THINGS YOU DID. INCLUDE 7 TO 10 THINGS EACH DAY.

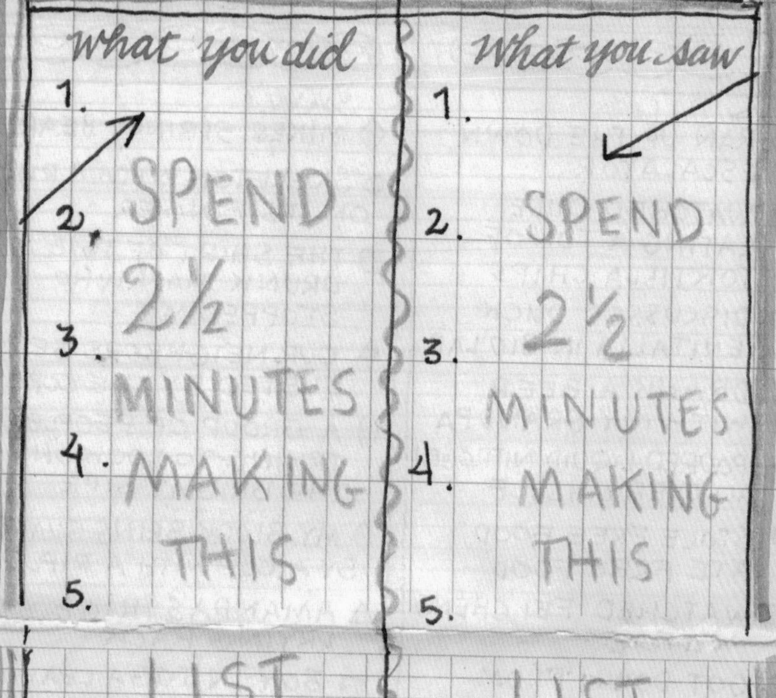

AND LISTEN TO WHAT PEOPLE ARE SAYING — OVERHEARD CONVERSATIONS ARE FULL OF GOOD LINES. PAY ATTENTION TO HOW PEOPLE REALLY SPEAK. WRITE DOWN WHAT THEY SAY.

YOU MAY FIND YOURSELF STARING AT SOMETHING FOR "NO REASON", A LABEL ON A BOTTLE OF JUICE, A PIGEON, A WISP OF HAIR ON THE NAPE OF SOMEONE'S NECK -- OR YOU MAY SEE SOMETHING SPECTACULAR: A FIGHT OR A FIRE OR AN ACCIDENT. ALL ARE WELCOME ON YOUR LIST OF THINGS YOU SAW. DRAW ONE OF THEM HERE. JUST A QUICK SKETCH. AVOID PICKING THE EASIEST THING TO DRAW- PICK SOMETHING THAT'S A CHALLENGE

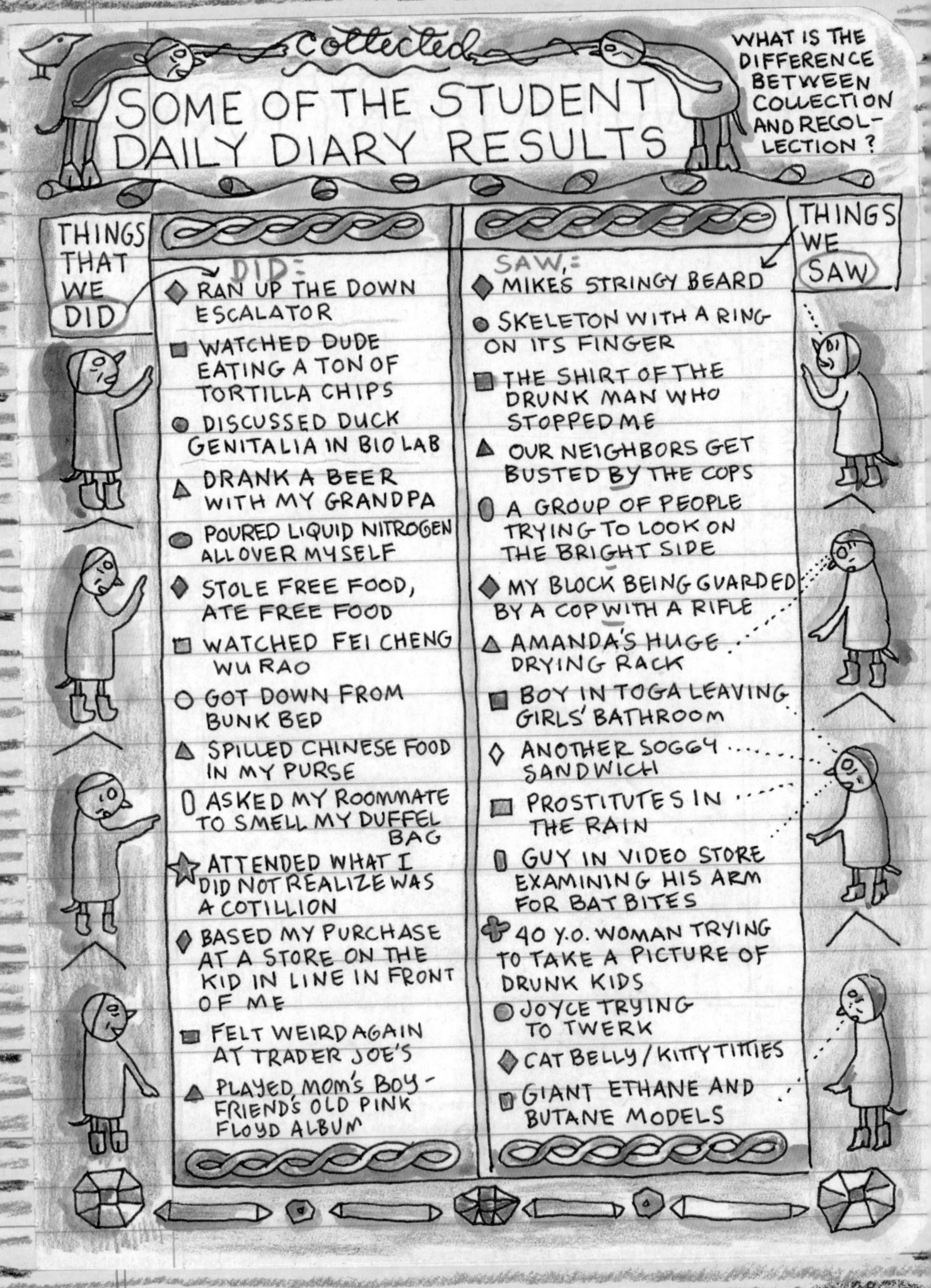

collected
SOME OF THE STUDENT DAILY DIARY RESULTS
WHAT IS THE DIFFERENCE BETWEEN COLLECTION AND RECOLLECTION ?
THINGS THAT WE DID
DID:
RAN UP THE DOWN ESCALATOR
WATCHED DUDE EATING A TON OF TORTILLA CHIPS
DISCUSSED DUCK GENITALIA IN BIO LAB
DRANK A BEER WITH MY GRANDPA
POURED LIQUID NITROGEN ALL OVER MYSELF
STOLE FREE FOOD, ATE FREE FOOD
WATCHED FEI CHENG WU RAO
GOT DOWN FROM BUNK BED
SPILLED CHINESE FOOD IN MY PURSE
ASKED MY ROOMMATE TO SMELL MY DUFFEL BAG
ATTENDED WHAT I DID NOT REALIZE WAS A COTILLION
BASED MY PURCHASE AT A STORE ON THE KID IN LINE IN FRONT OF ME
FELT WEIRD AGAIN AT TRADER JOE'S
PLAYED MOM'S BOY-FRIEND'S OLD PINK FLOYD ALBUM
THINGS WE SAW
SAW:
MIKE'S STRINGY BEARD
SKELETON WITH A RING ON ITS FINGER
THE SHIRT OF THE DRUNK MAN WHO STOPPED ME
OUR NEIGHBORS GET BUSTED BY THE COPS
A GROUP OF PEOPLE TRYING TO LOOK ON THE BRIGHT SIDE
MY BLOCK BEING GUARDED BY A COP WITH A RIFLE
AMANDA'S HUGE DRYING RACK
BOY IN TOGA LEAVING GIRLS' BATHROOM
ANOTHER SOGGY SANDWICH
PROSTITUTES IN THE RAIN
GUY IN VIDEO STORE EXAMINING HIS ARM FOR BAT BITES
40 Y.O. WOMAN TRYING TO TAKE A PICTURE OF DRUNK KIDS
JOYCE TRYING TO TWERK
CAT BELLY / KITTY TITTIES
GIANT ETHANE AND BUTANE MODELS

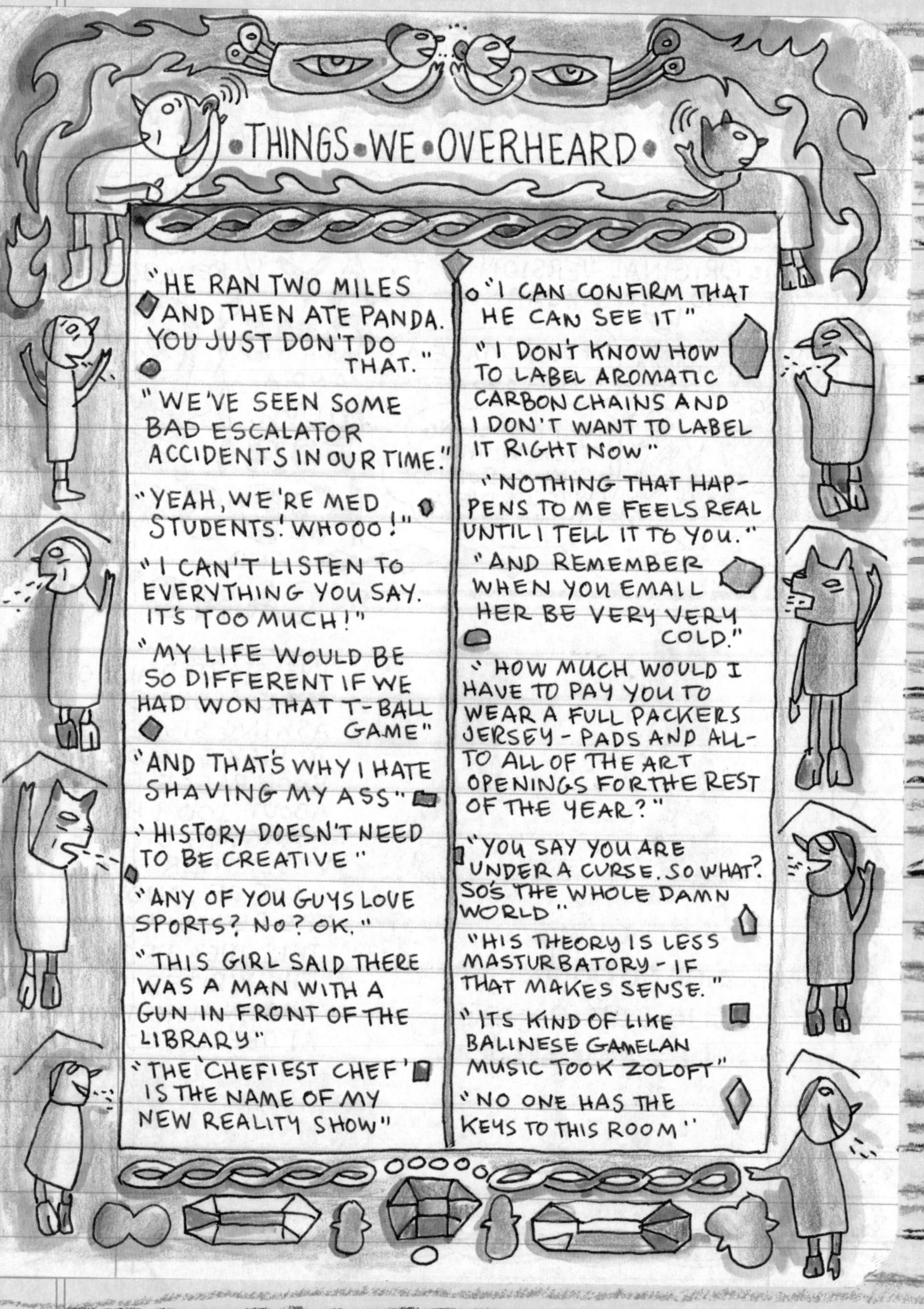
THINGS WE OVERHEARD
"HE RAN TWO MILES AND THEN ATE PANDA. YOU JUST DON'T DO THAT."
"WE'VE SEEN SOME BAD ESCALATOR ACCIDENTS IN OUR TIME."
"YEAH, WE'RE MED STUDENTS! WHOOO!"
"I CAN'T LISTEN TO EVERYTHING YOU SAY. IT'S TOO MUCH!"
"MY LIFE WOULD BE SO DIFFERENT IF WE HAD WON THAT T-BALL GAME"
"AND THAT'S WHY I HATE SHAVING MY ASS"
"HISTORY DOESN'T NEED TO BE CREATIVE"
"ANY OF YOU GUYS LOVE SPORTS? NO? OK."
"THIS GIRL SAID THERE WAS A MAN WITH A GUN IN FRONT OF THE LIBRARY"
"THE 'CHEFIEST CHEF' IS THE NAME OF MY NEW REALITY SHOW"
"I CAN CONFIRM THAT HE CAN SEE IT"
"I DON'T KNOW HOW TO LABEL AROMATIC CARBON CHAINS AND I DON'T WANT TO LABEL IT RIGHT NOW"
"NOTHING THAT HAPPENS TO ME FEELS REAL UNTIL I TELL IT TO YOU."
"AND REMEMBER WHEN YOU EMAIL HER BE VERY VERY COLD."
"HOW MUCH WOULD I HAVE TO PAY YOU TO WEAR A FULL PACKERS JERSEY - PADS AND ALL - TO ALL OF THE ART OPENINGS FOR THE REST OF THE YEAR?"
"YOU SAY YOU ARE UNDER A CURSE. SO WHAT? SO'S THE WHOLE DAMN WORLD"
"HIS THEORY IS LESS MASTURBATORY - IF THAT MAKES SENSE."
"ITS KIND OF LIKE BALINESE GAMELAN MUSIC TOOK ZOLOFT"
"NO ONE HAS THE KEYS TO THIS ROOM"

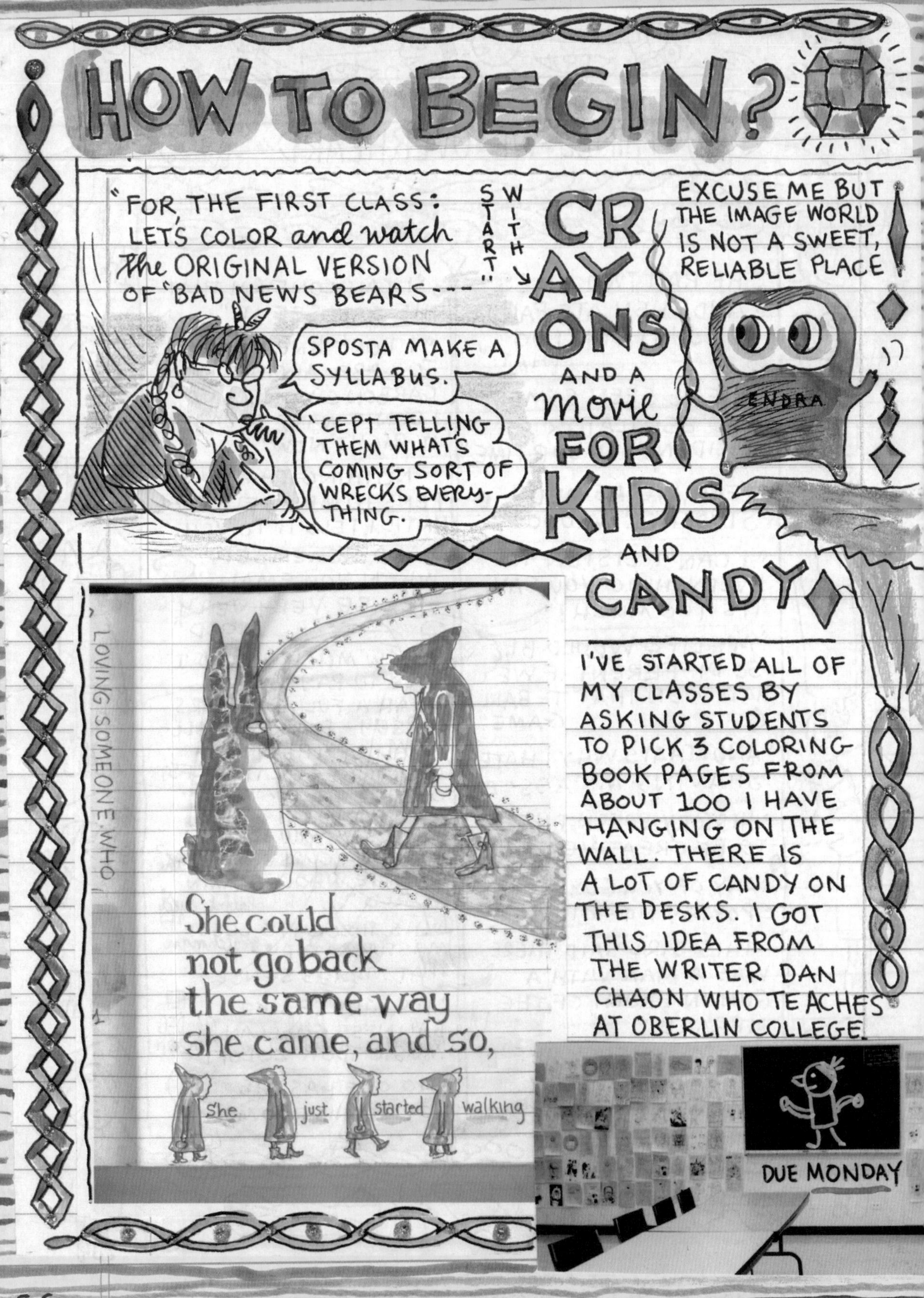
HOW TO BEGIN?
"FOR THE FIRST CLASS: LET'S COLOR and watch the ORIGINAL VERSION OF 'BAD NEWS BEARS---
SPOSTA MAKE A SYLLABUS.
'CEPT TELLING THEM WHAT'S COMING SORT OF WRECKS EVERYTHING.
START WITH"
CRAYONS AND A movie FOR KIDS AND CANDY
EXCUSE ME BUT THE IMAGE WORLD IS NOT A SWEET, RELIABLE PLACE
ENDRA
LOVING SOMEONE WHO
She could not go back the same way she came, and so,
She just started walking
I'VE STARTED ALL OF MY CLASSES BY ASKING STUDENTS TO PICK 3 COLORING BOOK PAGES FROM ABOUT 100 I HAVE HANGING ON THE WALL. THERE IS A LOT OF CANDY ON THE DESKS. I GOT THIS IDEA FROM THE WRITER DAN CHAON WHO TEACHES AT OBERLIN COLLEGE.
DUE MONDAY

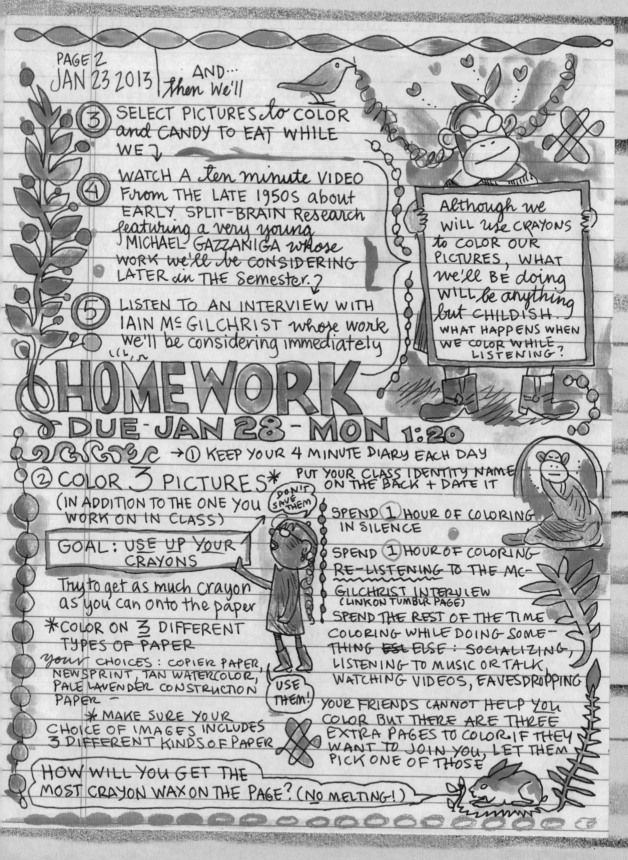

AND... then We'll

③ SELECT PICTURES to COLOR and CANDY TO EAT WHILE WE

④ WATCH A ten minute VIDEO From THE LATE 1950s about EARLY SPLIT-BRAIN Research featuring a very young MICHAEL GAZZANIGA whose WORK we'll be CONSIDERING LATER in THE Semester.

⑤ LISTEN TO AN INTERVIEW WITH IAIN MᶜGILCHRIST whose work we'll be considering immediately

Although we WILL use CRAYONS to COLOR OUR PICTURES, WHAT we'll BE doing WILL be anything but CHILDISH. WHAT HAPPENS WHEN WE COLOR WHILE LISTENING?

HOMEWORK
DUE · JAN 28 · MON 1:20

→① KEEP YOUR 4 MINUTE DIARY EACH DAY

② COLOR 3 PICTURES* PUT YOUR CLASS IDENTITY NAME ON THE BACK + DATE IT

(IN ADDITION TO THE ONE YOU WORK ON IN CLASS)

DON'T SAVE THEM

GOAL: USE UP YOUR CRAYONS

Try to get as much crayon as you can onto the paper

*COLOR ON 3 DIFFERENT TYPES OF PAPER

your CHOICES: COPIER PAPER, NEWSPRINT, TAN WATERCOLOR, PALE LAVENDER CONSTRUCTION PAPER —

USE THEM!

*MAKE SURE YOUR CHOICE OF IMAGES INCLUDES 3 DIFFERENT KINDS OF PAPER

SPEND ① HOUR OF COLORING IN SILENCE

SPEND ① HOUR OF COLORING RE-LISTENING TO THE MC-GILCHRIST INTERVIEW (LINK ON TUMBLR PAGE)

SPEND THE REST OF THE TIME COLORING WHILE DOING SOMETHING ~~ESL~~ ELSE: SOCIALIZING, LISTENING TO MUSIC OR TALK, WATCHING VIDEOS, EAVESDROPPING

YOUR FRIENDS CANNOT HELP YOU COLOR BUT THERE ARE THREE EXTRA PAGES TO COLOR. IF THEY WANT TO JOIN YOU, LET THEM PICK ONE OF THOSE

HOW WILL YOU GET THE MOST CRAYON WAX ON THE PAGE? (NO MELTING!)

STUDENTS ARE SURPRISED BY HOW LONG IT TAKES TO COLOR SOMETHING IN: CRAYONS ARE HARD TO WORK WITH.

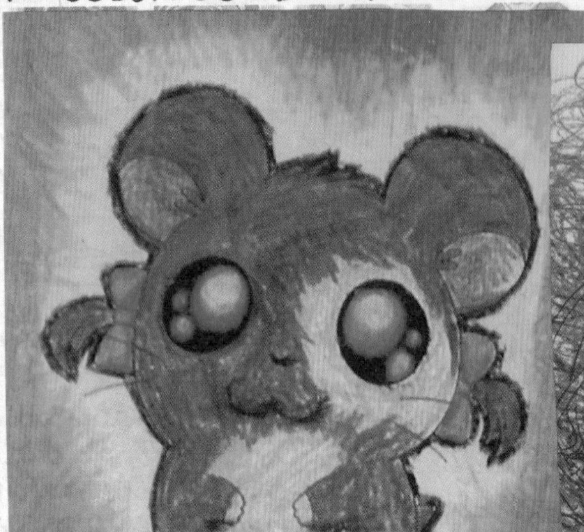

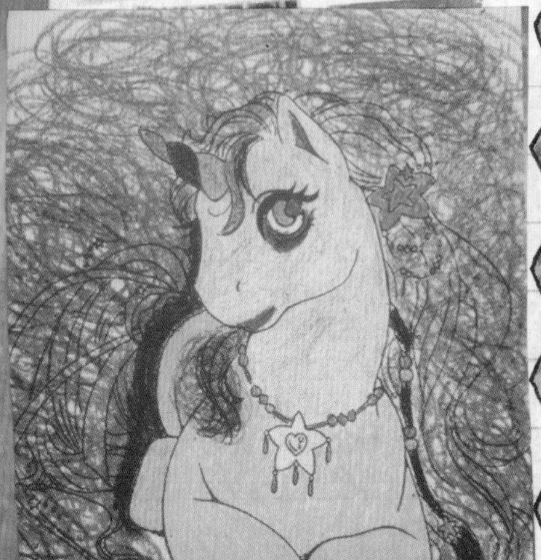

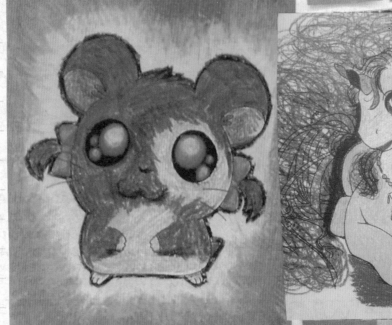

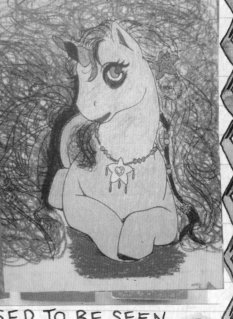

THEY ARE ALSO EMBARRASSED TO BE SEEN COLORING. *and this embarrassment* IS SOMETHING I WANT THEM TO WONDER ABOUT.

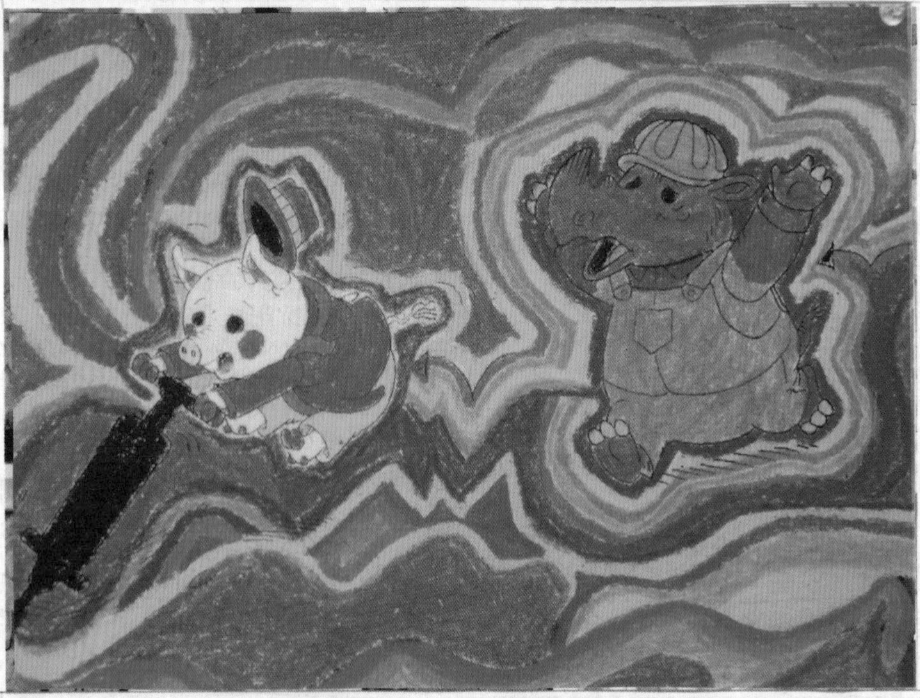

WHAT'S THE SOURCE OF IT? WHY IS IT THERE?

MON DAY

PROF. LYNDA'S Self-Portrait DRAWN IN THE STYLE OF IVAN BRUNETTI

UM...

Dear UM... STUDENTS

UM... UM... JANUARY 28 20 15

Class #2 OF THE UNTHINKABLE MIND

UM...

THIS DRAWING IS NOT in the STYLE OF IVAN BRUNETTI

AGENDA

HEY MAN DON'T PULL MY TAIL

WHAT'S THE DEAL WITH THIS PICTURE ANYWAY?

When you arrive, please pin your work up on the wall Place your 3 pictures away from each other

IVAN BRUNETTI cartoonist AUTHOR OF "CARTOONING: PHILOSOPHY AND PRACTICE"

IVAN BRUNETTI STYLE IN A NUTSHELL

MAKE SURE YOUR BRAIN IDENTITY IS ON THE BACK and it's dated then......

ALSO DRAWN IN MODIFIED IVAN BRUNETTI STYLE

UM UM UM

CIRCLE HEAD

RECTANGLE BODY

SIMPLE FEATURES

SIMPLE LIMBS

SPEND SOME TIME WORKING ON JUST LOOKING AT THE COLORING PAGES

then WE WILL PRACTICE 'INFORMATION RETRIEVAL' (AKA: A TEST) then ...... I COLLECT THEM

old skull		old skull neocortex		
WRITE YOUR CLASS IDENTITY ON BLANK SIDE OF INDEX CARD	FLIP IT OVER AND WRITE ONE THING YOU REMEMBER FROM THE MCGILCHRIST INTERVIEW	PASS CARD TO PERSON ON ® WRITE YOUR IDENTITY ON BACK	FLIP IT OVER WRITE ANOTHER THING FROM THE INTERVIEW - NO REPEATS	REPEAT PROCESS TWO MORE TIMES - THEN REVIEW

69

FEBRUARY 19 2012

ALTHOUGH WE ALL START OUT BY DRAWING IN THE SAME STYLE, SOMETHING STARTS TO SHOW UP PRETTY QUICK: OUR OWN STYLE. THERE IS A WAY OF MAKING LINES AND SHAPES THAT IS OURS ALONE, AND THE MORE WE DRAW, THE CLEARER IT BECOMES, NOT JUST TO OURSELVES BUT TO OTHERS: A STYLE UNIQUE AND RECOGNIZABLE.

SIMON SPARROW:
when I draw a person
I'm drawing the
mystery form of
that person

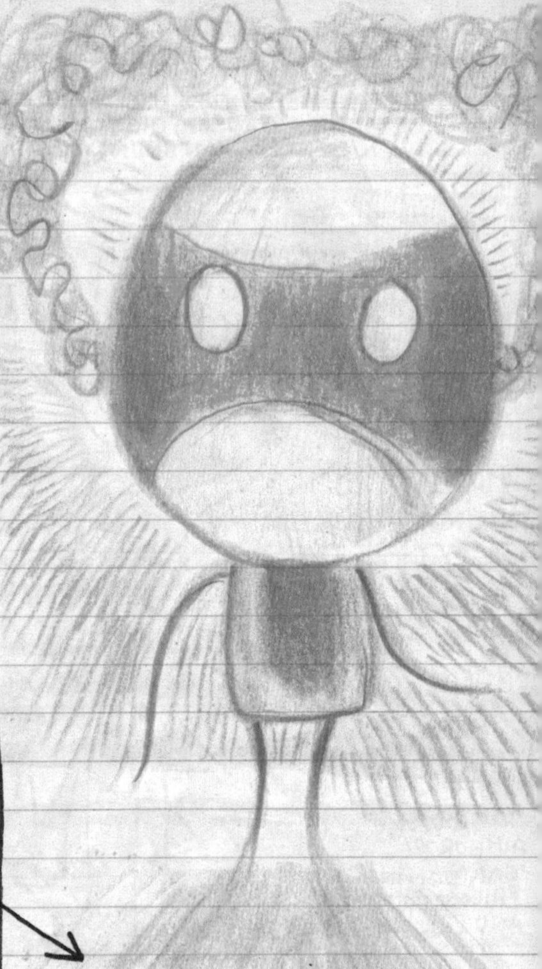

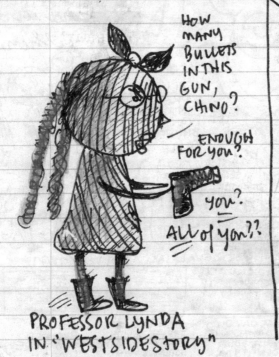

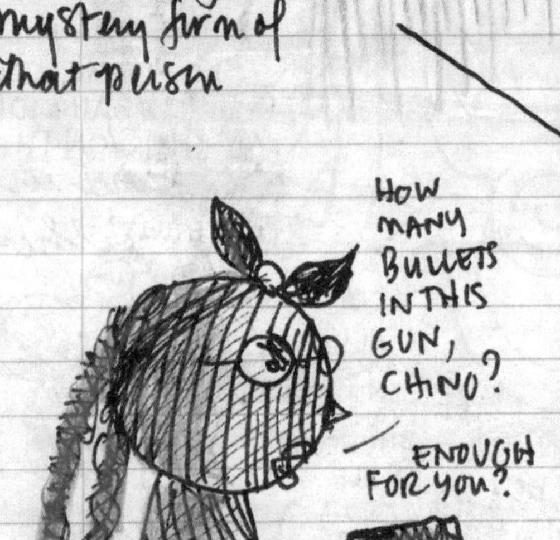
HOW MANY BULLETS IN THIS GUN, CHINO?
ENOUGH FOR YOU?
YOU?
ALL of you??

PROFESSOR LYNDA IN "WESTSIDESTORY"

WHEN WE DRAW A PERSON, ALONG WITH WHAT SIMON SPARROW CALLS 'THE MYSTERY FORM OF THAT PERSON,' WE ARE ALSO DRAWING THE MYSTERY FORM OF OUR LINE AND OUR URGE TOWARD COMPOSITION. THE TRICK IS TO FIND A WAY TO KEEP OURSELVES FROM REJECTING IT BEFORE IT CAN FULLY PRESENT ITSELF.

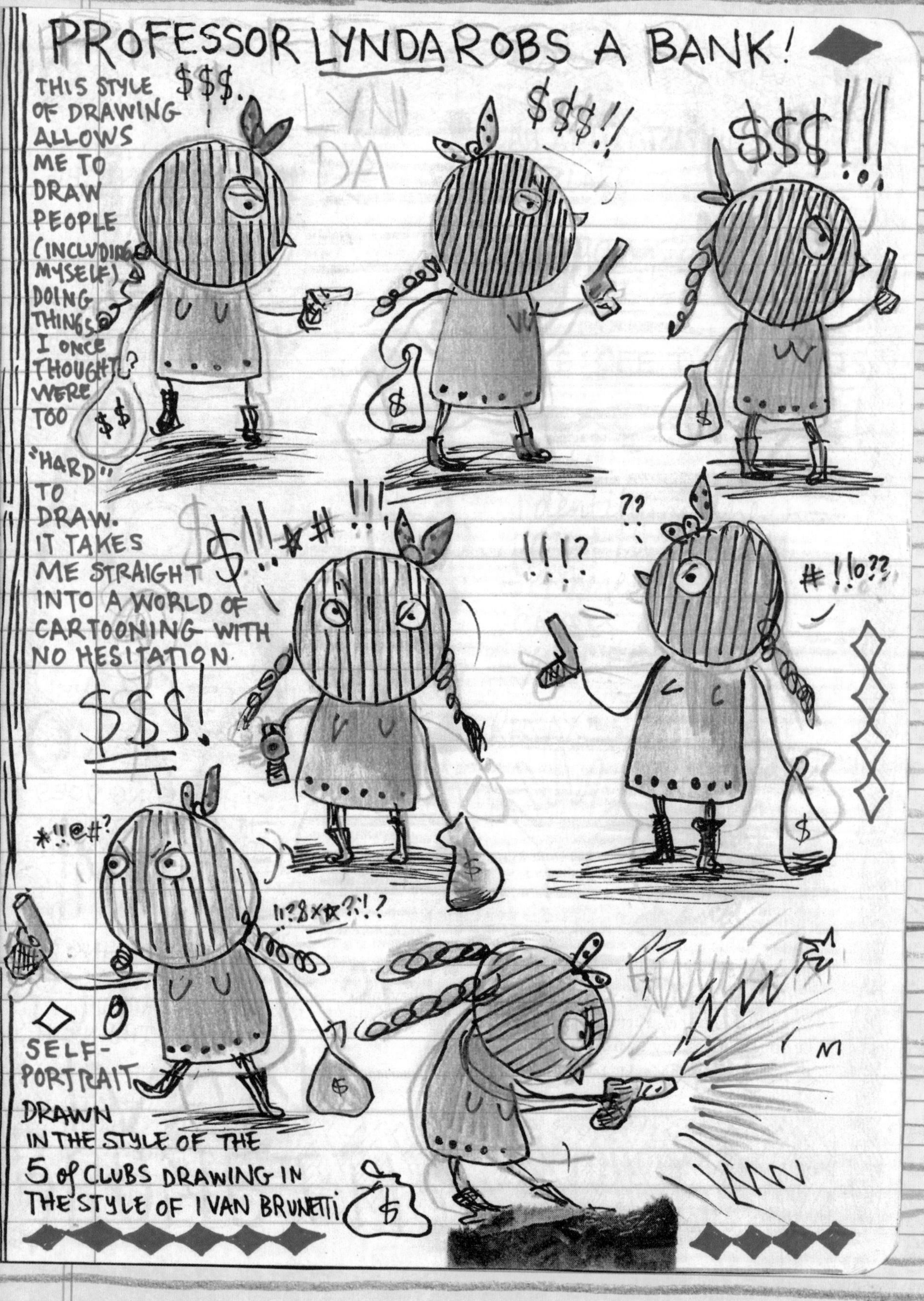
PROFESSOR LYNDA ROBS A BANK!
THIS STYLE OF DRAWING ALLOWS ME TO DRAW PEOPLE (INCLUDING MYSELF) DOING THINGS I ONCE THOUGHT WERE TOO "HARD" TO DRAW. IT TAKES ME STRAIGHT INTO A WORLD OF CARTOONING WITH NO HESITATION.
$$$.
$$$!!
$$$!!!
$$$!
???
!!!?
#!!@??
SELF-PORTRAIT DRAWN IN THE STYLE OF THE 5 of CLUBS DRAWING IN THE STYLE OF IVAN BRUNETTI

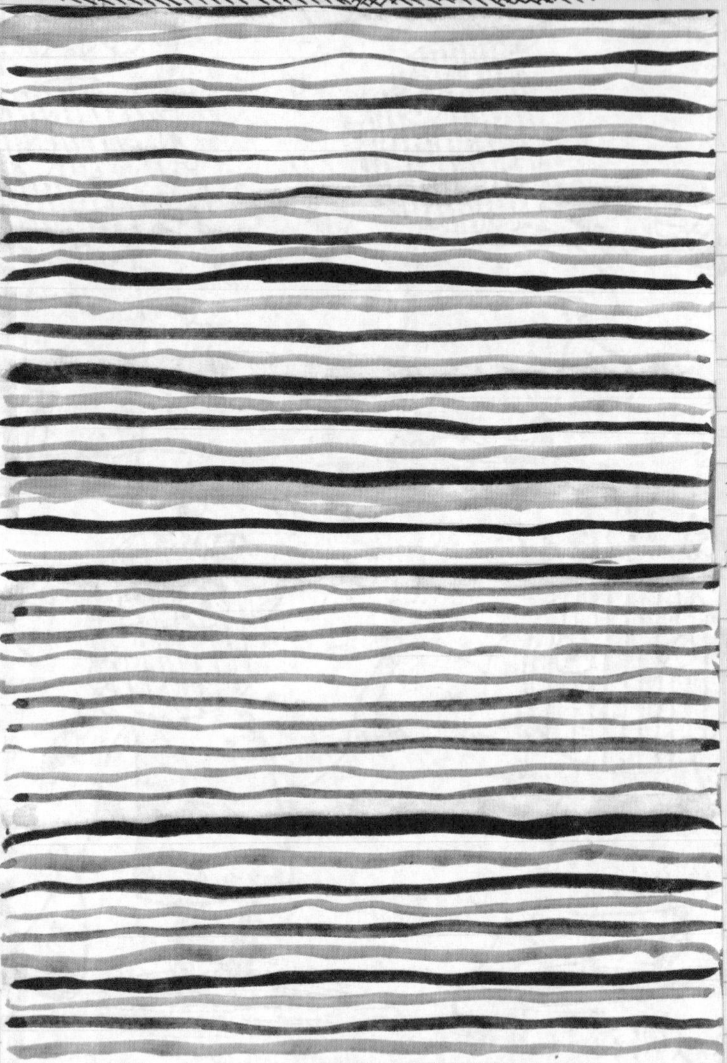

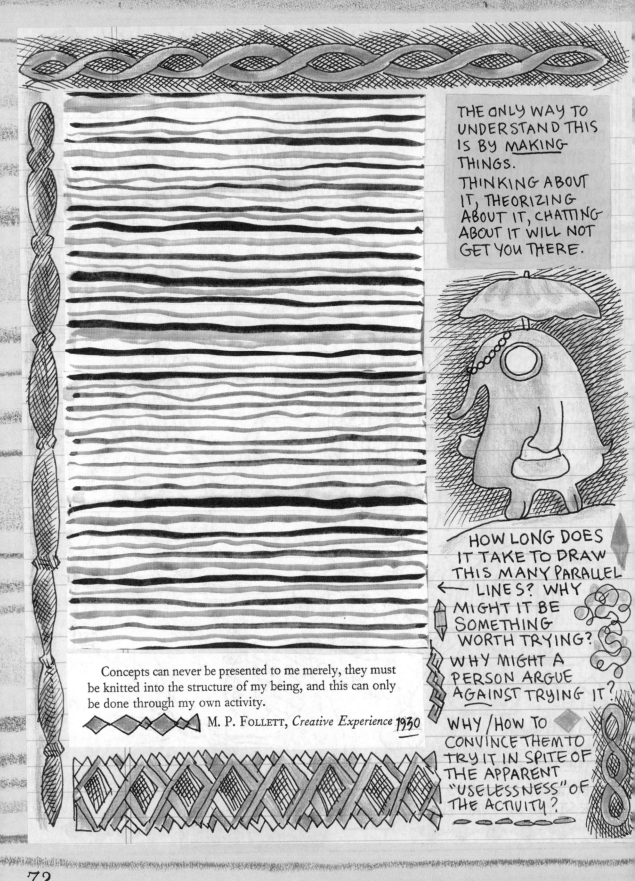

THE ONLY WAY TO UNDERSTAND THIS IS BY <u>MAKING</u> THINGS.
THINKING ABOUT IT, THEORIZING ABOUT IT, CHATTING ABOUT IT WILL NOT GET YOU THERE.

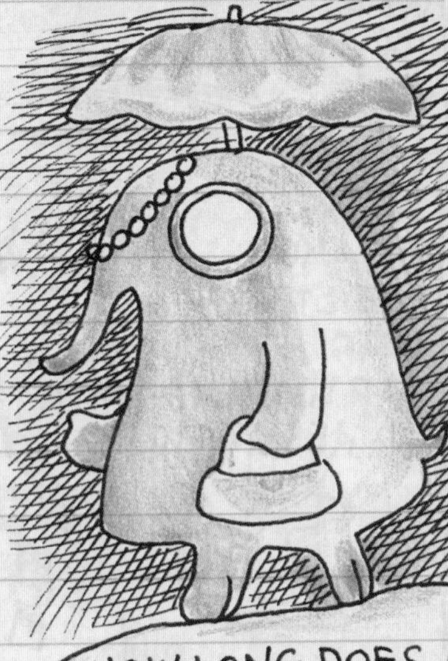

HOW LONG DOES IT TAKE TO DRAW THIS MANY PARALLEL ← LINES? WHY MIGHT IT BE SOMETHING WORTH TRYING?

WHY MIGHT A PERSON ARGUE <u>AGAINST</u> TRYING IT?

WHY/HOW TO CONVINCE THEM TO TRY IT IN SPITE OF THE APPARENT "USELESSNESS" OF THE ACTIVITY?

Concepts can never be presented to me merely, they must be knitted into the structure of my being, and this can only be done through my own activity.

M. P. FOLLETT, *Creative Experience* 1930

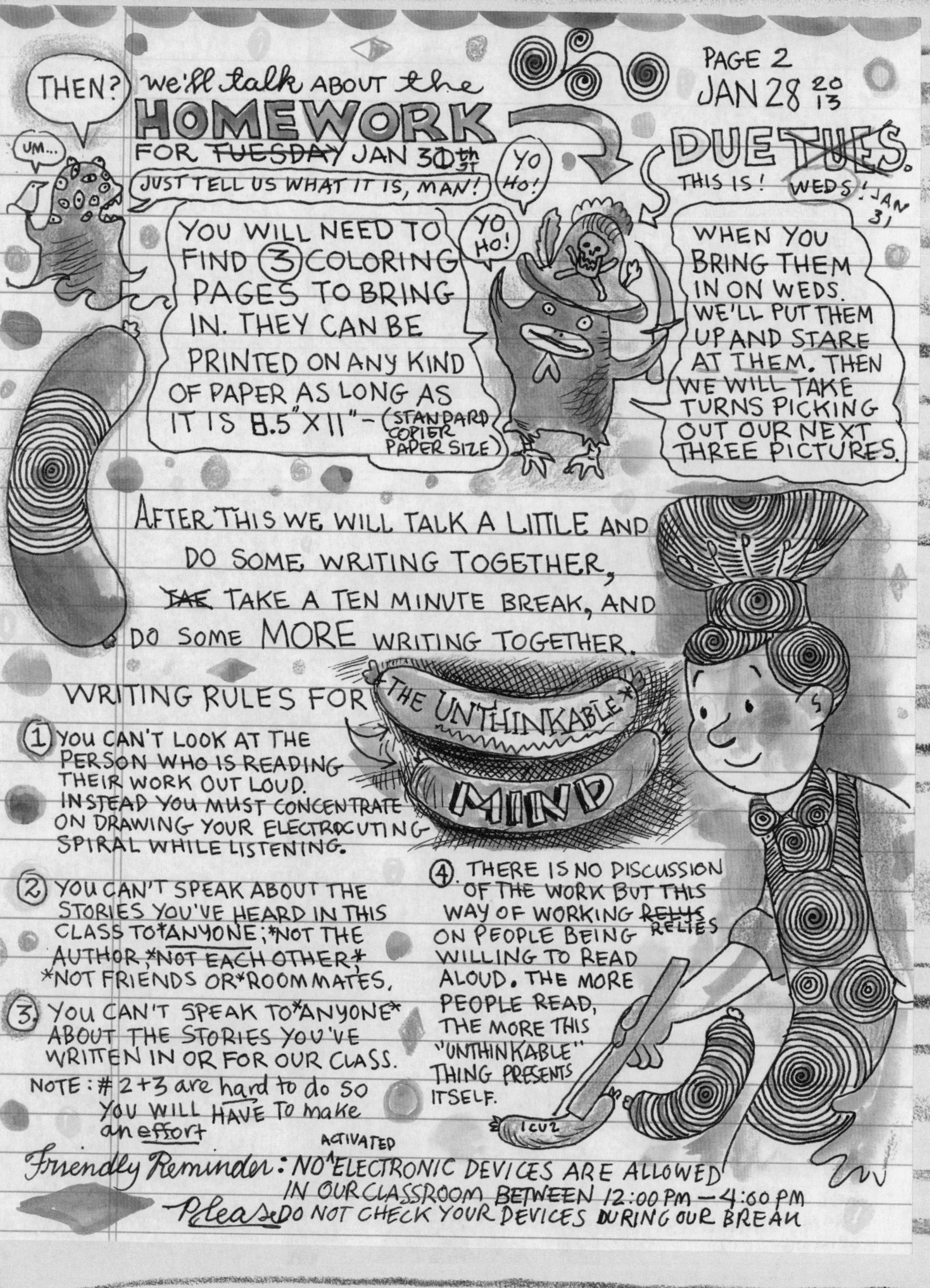

THEN?
UM...
we'll talk ABOUT the
HOMEWORK
FOR ~~TUESDAY~~ JAN 30th 31st
JUST TELL US WHAT IT IS, MAN!
YO HO!
PAGE 2
JAN 28 2013
DUE ~~TUES~~ WEDS! JAN 31
THIS IS!
YO HO!
YOU WILL NEED TO FIND ③ COLORING PAGES TO BRING IN. THEY CAN BE PRINTED ON ANY KIND OF PAPER AS LONG AS IT IS 8.5" X 11" - (STANDARD COPIER PAPER SIZE)
WHEN YOU BRING THEM IN ON WEDS. WE'LL PUT THEM UP AND STARE AT THEM. THEN WE WILL TAKE TURNS PICKING OUT OUR NEXT THREE PICTURES.
AFTER THIS WE WILL TALK A LITTLE AND DO SOME WRITING TOGETHER, ~~TAE~~ TAKE A TEN MINUTE BREAK, AND DO SOME MORE WRITING TOGETHER.
WRITING RULES FOR *THE UNTHINKABLE* MIND
① YOU CAN'T LOOK AT THE PERSON WHO IS READING THEIR WORK OUT LOUD. INSTEAD YOU MUST CONCENTRATE ON DRAWING YOUR ELECTROCUTING SPIRAL WHILE LISTENING.
② YOU CAN'T SPEAK ABOUT THE STORIES YOU'VE HEARD IN THIS CLASS TO *ANYONE; *NOT THE AUTHOR, *NOT EACH OTHER* *NOT FRIENDS OR *ROOMMATES.
③ YOU CAN'T SPEAK TO *ANYONE* ABOUT THE STORIES YOU'VE WRITTEN IN OR FOR OUR CLASS.
NOTE: # 2+3 are hard to do so you will have to make an effort
④ THERE IS NO DISCUSSION OF THE WORK BUT THIS WAY OF WORKING ~~RELYS~~ RELIES ON PEOPLE BEING WILLING TO READ ALOUD. THE MORE PEOPLE READ, THE MORE THIS "UNTHINKABLE" THING PRESENTS ITSELF.
ICU2
Friendly Reminder: NO ACTIVATED ELECTRONIC DEVICES ARE ALLOWED IN OUR CLASSROOM BETWEEN 12:00 PM — 4:00 PM
- Please DO NOT CHECK YOUR DEVICES DURING OUR BREAK

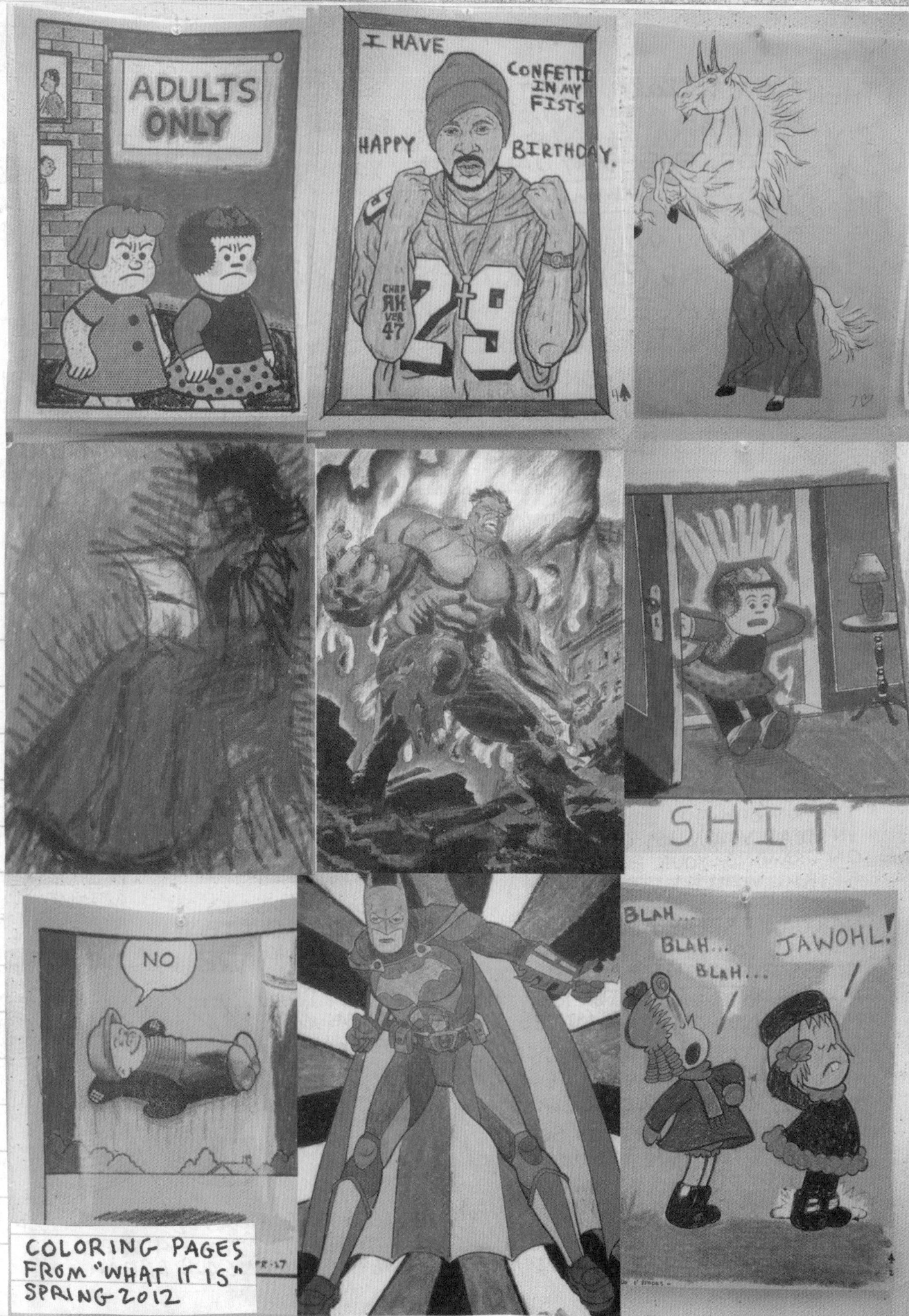
ADULTS ONLY
I HAVE
CONFETTI IN MY FISTS
HAPPY BIRTHDAY.
29
SHIT
NO
BLAH... BLAH... BLAH...
JAWOHL!

COLORING PAGES FROM "WHAT IT IS" SPRING 2012

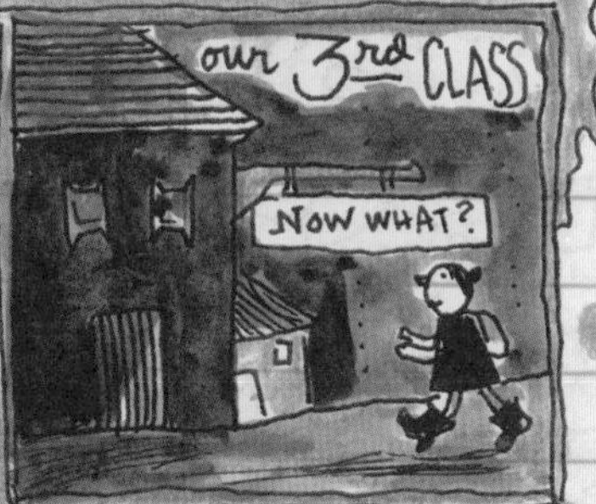

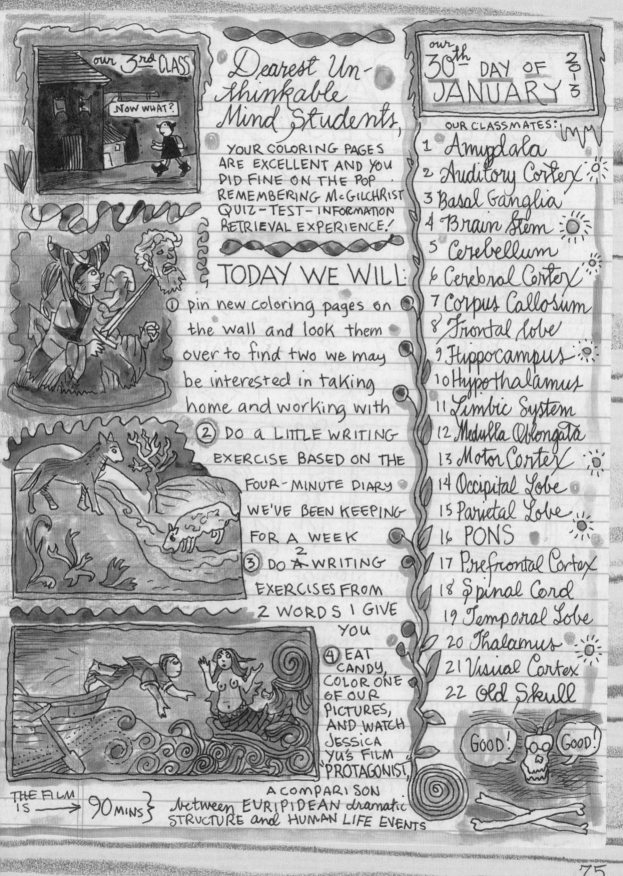

our 3rd CLASS
NOW WHAT?

Dearest Un-thinkable Mind Students,

YOUR COLORING PAGES ARE EXCELLENT AND YOU DID FINE ON THE POP REMEMBERING McGILCHRIST QUIZ-TEST-INFORMATION RETRIEVAL EXPERIENCE!

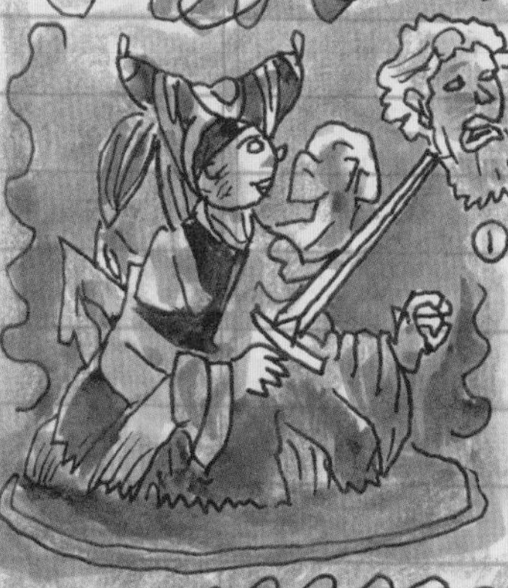

TODAY WE WILL:

1. pin new coloring pages on the wall and look them over to find two we may be interested in taking home and working with
2. DO A LITTLE WRITING EXERCISE BASED ON THE FOUR-MINUTE DIARY WE'VE BEEN KEEPING FOR A WEEK
3. DO ~~A~~ 2 WRITING EXERCISES FROM 2 WORDS I GIVE YOU
4. EAT CANDY, COLOR ONE OF OUR PICTURES, AND WATCH JESSICA YU'S FILM "PROTAGONIST," A COMPARISON between EURIPIDEAN dramatic STRUCTURE and HUMAN LIFE EVENTS

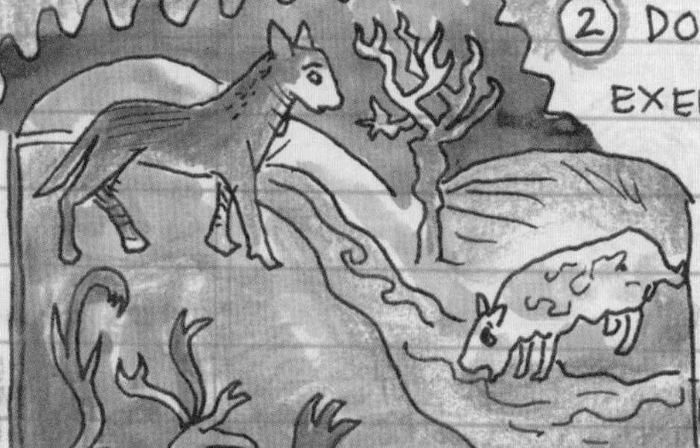

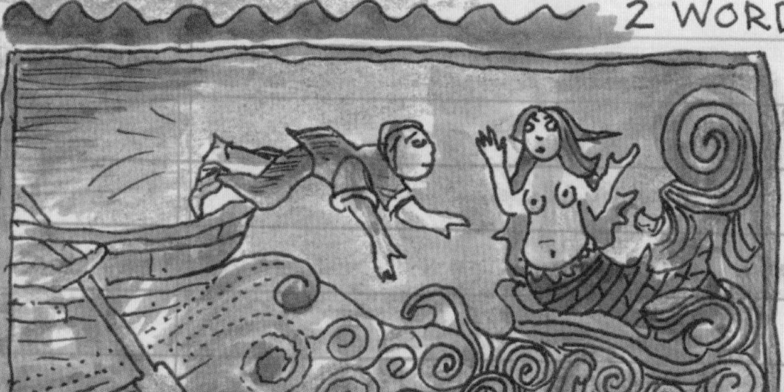

THE FILM IS ⟶ 90 MINS }

our 30th DAY OF JANUARY 2013

OUR CLASSMATES:

1 Amygdala
2 Auditory Cortex
3 Basal Ganglia
4 Brain Stem
5 Cerebellum
6 Cerebral Cortex
7 Corpus Callosum
8 Frontal Lobe
9 Hippocampus
10 Hypothalamus
11 Limbic System
12 Medulla Oblongata
13 Motor Cortex
14 Occipital Lobe
15 Parietal Lobe
16 PONS
17 Prefrontal Cortex
18 Spinal Cord
19 Temporal Lobe
20 Thalamus
21 Visual Cortex
22 Old Skull

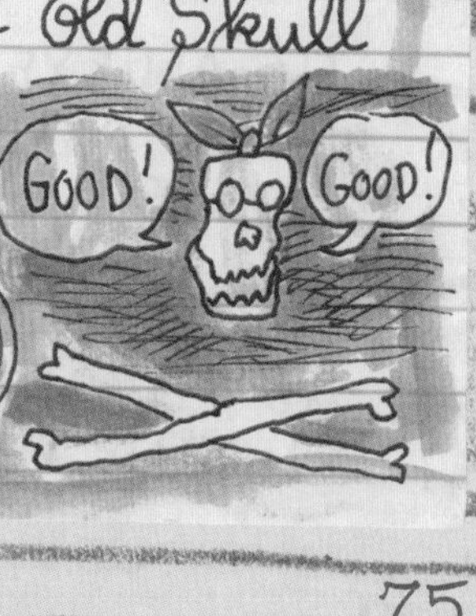

GOOD!
GOOD!

X-PAGE EXERCISES!!

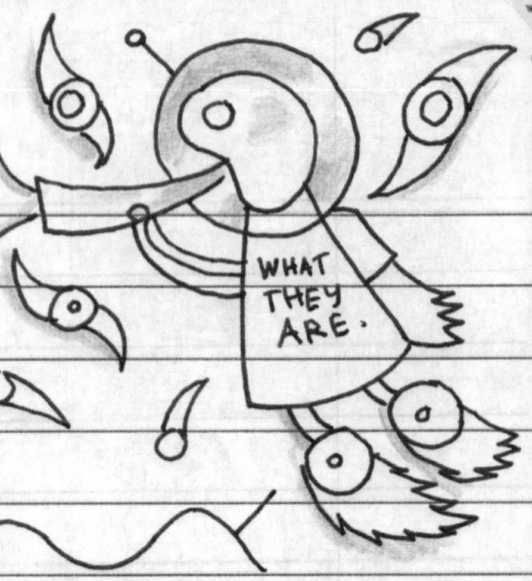
WHAT THEY ARE.

YOU WILL NEED

YOUR COMPBOOK

A PEN

AT LEAST 20 MINUTES OF UNINTERRUPTED TIME

WE BEGIN BY OPENING OUR COMPBOOKS TO A CLEAN TWO PAGE SPREAD

DATE THE PAGE

NUMBER THIS SIDE FROM ONE TO TEN

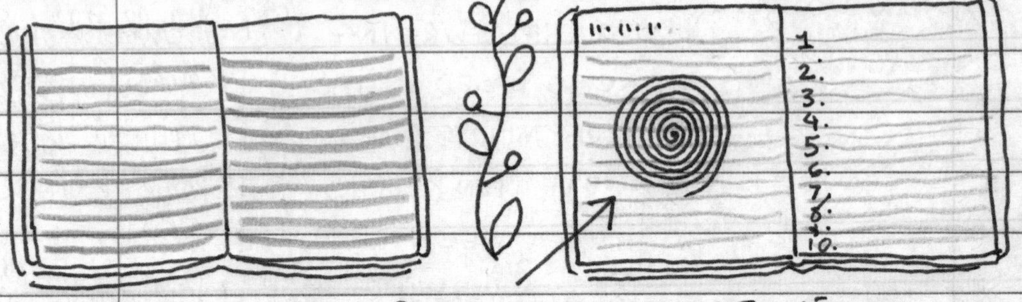
1.
2.
3.
4.
5.
6.
7.
8.
9.
10.

ON THIS SIDE OF THE PAGE WE BEGIN OUR SPIRAL

START WITH A DOT

SPIRAL A LINE AROUND IT

KEEP GOING

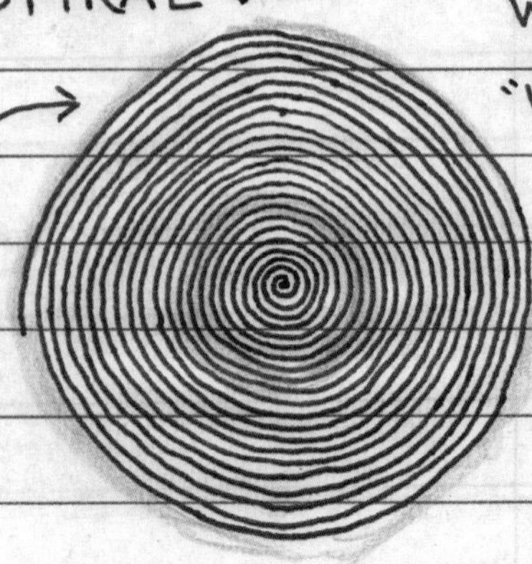

IT'S AN EXERCISE IN BOTH RELAXATION AND CONCENTRATION — YOUR TASK IS TO GET THE LINES AS CLOSE TOGETHER AS POSSIBLE WITHOUT LETTING THEM TOUCH. IF THEY TOUCH, YOU GET ELECTROCUTED.

DON'T WORRY ABOUT "WASTING" PAPER. OUR COMPBOOKS DON'T MIND BEING USED UP.

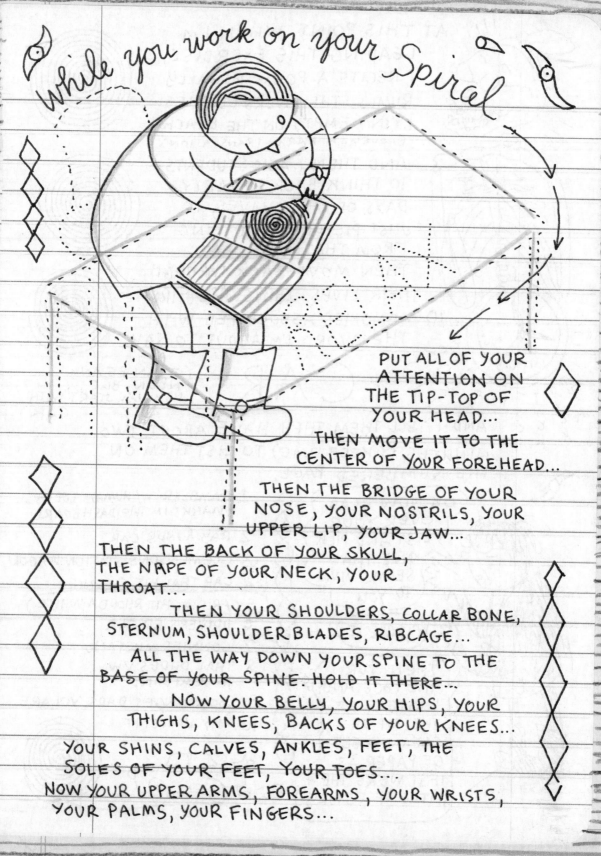

while you work on your Spiral

RELAX

PUT ALL OF YOUR
ATTENTION ON
THE TIP-TOP OF
YOUR HEAD...
THEN MOVE IT TO THE
CENTER OF YOUR FOREHEAD...
THEN THE BRIDGE OF YOUR
NOSE, YOUR NOSTRILS, YOUR
UPPER LIP, YOUR JAW...
THEN THE BACK OF YOUR SKULL,
THE NAPE OF YOUR NECK, YOUR
THROAT...
THEN YOUR SHOULDERS, COLLAR BONE,
STERNUM, SHOULDER BLADES, RIBCAGE...
ALL THE WAY DOWN YOUR SPINE TO THE
BASE OF YOUR SPINE. HOLD IT THERE...
NOW YOUR BELLY, YOUR HIPS, YOUR
THIGHS, KNEES, BACKS OF YOUR KNEES...
YOUR SHINS, CALVES, ANKLES, FEET, THE
SOLES OF YOUR FEET, YOUR TOES...
NOW YOUR UPPER ARMS, FOREARMS, YOUR WRISTS,
YOUR PALMS, YOUR FINGERS...

77

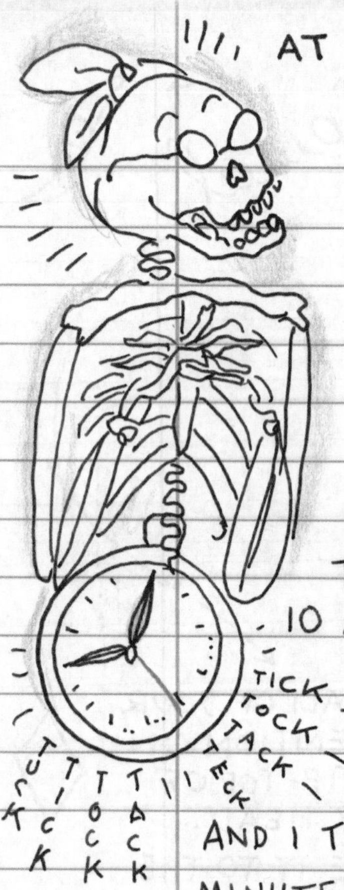
TICK — TOCK — TACK — TECK
TUCK TICK TOCK TACK

AT THIS POINT, WHEN I'M LEADING THIS EXERCISE, I RECITE A POEM, USUALLY RUMI'S "THE DIVER'S CLOTHES LYING EMPTY ON THE BEACH" (COLEMAN BARKS TRANSLATION)

AND THEN I ASK STUDENTS TO THINK BACK TO EARLY DAYS OF THEIR LIVES, TO JUST PICTURE SOMETHING FROM THAT TIME, AND THEN MOVE BACK THROUGH THEIR LIVES USING THE FIRST 10 MEMORIES ASSOCIATED WITH THE WORD I'M ABOUT TO SAY.

→ CAR (IT CAN BE ANY NOUN, BUT I USUALLY START WITH CAR)

AND I TELL THEM THEY HAVE ABOUT TWO MINUTES (I KEEP TIME) TO LIST THEM ON THE NUMBERED PAGE.

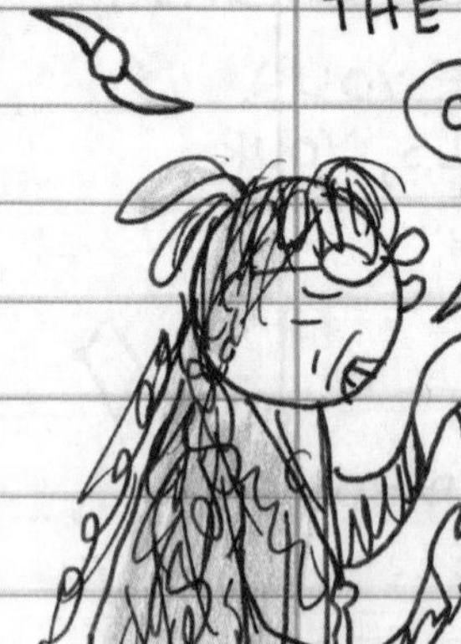
OK NOW READ OVER YOUR LIST AND PICK ONE THAT SEEMS VIVID TO YOU.
CIRCLE IT
THEN TURN THE PAGE AND WRITE IT AT THE TOP OF A CLEAN SHEET OF PAPER AS IF IT WERE THE TITLE OF A STORY.

1 RAMBLER W/ HUMAN TEETH MARKS IN THE DASHBOARD
2 RAYMOND'S CAR
3 CLEMENSON'S STATION WAGON
4 CAR THAT HIT QUEENIE
5 CAR THAT HIT RHONDA WHITE
6. DRIVER'S ED CAR
7. CONNIE'S MUSTANG
8. THAT DUDE'S VW IN PORTLAND
9. SCROUNGE'S DAD'S VOLARE
10. MY VALIENT

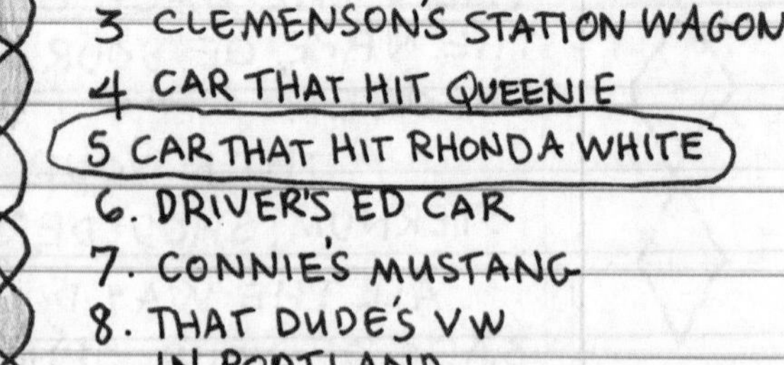

TITLE ← WRITE THE IMAGE FROM YOUR LIST AND DRAW A BIG 'X' ACROSS THE PAGE

THE 'X' PAGE IS OUR FIRST CONTACT WITH THE STORY WE ARE ABOUT TO WRITE.

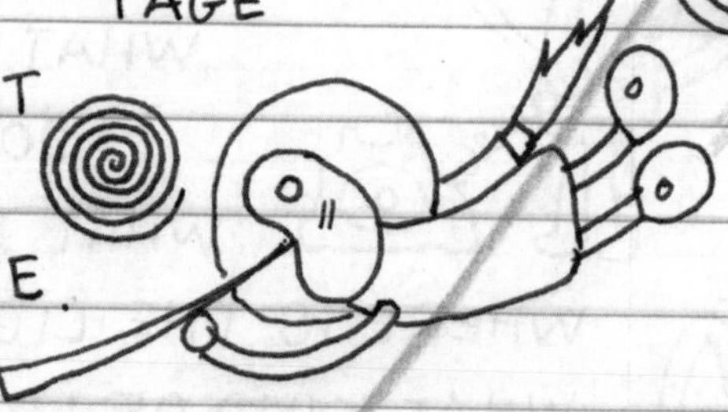

START BY PICTURING YOURSELF IN THE IMAGE.

PRETEND WE ARE ON THE TELEPHONE. YOU CAN SEE THE IMAGE BUT I CAN'T SO I'M GOING TO ASK YOU SOME QUESTIONS THAT WILL HELP ME 'SEE' IT TOO.

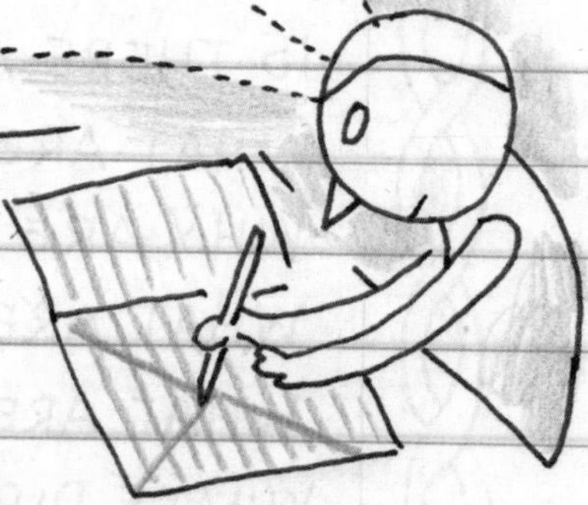

WRITE YOUR ANSWERS ANYWHERE ON THE 'X' PAGE. YOU'LL HAVE 10–20 SECONDS. KEEP WRITING UNTIL THE NEXT QUESTION IS ASKED.

NO DETAIL IS TOO SMALL OR UNIMPORTANT.

the questions →

THE QUESTIONS

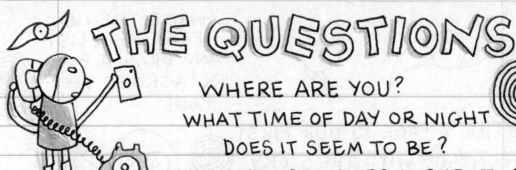

WHERE ARE YOU?

WHAT TIME OF DAY OR NIGHT DOES IT SEEM TO BE?

WHAT SEASON DOES IT SEEM TO BE?

WHERE IS THE LIGHT COMING FROM?

WHAT KIND OF LIGHT IS IT?

WHAT'S THE TEMPERATURE LIKE?

WHAT DOES THE AIR SMELL LIKE?

WHAT ARE YOU DOING?

IS THERE ANYONE ELSE IN THIS IMAGE WITH YOU?

WHAT ARE THEY DOING?

WHY ARE YOU THERE?

WHAT ARE SOME OF THE SOUNDS YOU CAN HEAR?

WHAT ARE SOME OF THE THINGS YOU CAN SEE?

WHAT'S DIRECTLY IN FRONT OF YOU?

IF YOU TURN YOUR HEAD TO YOUR RIGHT, WHAT'S THERE?

IF YOU TURN YOUR HEAD TO YOUR LEFT, WHAT DO YOU SEE?

WHAT'S BEHIND YOU?

WHAT'S BELOW AND AROUND YOUR FEET?

WHAT'S ABOVE YOUR HEAD?

 WHEN YOU ARE READY, TURN TO A CLEAN SHEET OF PAPER AND WRITE THIS IMAGE UP; STAY IN FIRST PERSON, PRESENT TENSE, WRITE FOR AT LEAST 8 MINUTES WITHOUT STOPPING.

2 ♥

GREEN carpet and pf fixg

HOT WHEELS

I'm looking down

NIGHT TIME,

SUMMER 87 DEGREES

OUTSIDE THE CAR

Green plastic covered living room light

CEILING/old light fixture

IT'S MY CAR

MOM COOKING + WEED)

THE TV (LOST in SPACE)

9 years old

A sliver's song

NOT IN THE IMAGE but NEARBY.

COFFEE TABLE

Lazy Susan with

BRAZIL NUTS

AND ALMONDS

COFFEE TABLE

SOFA and MOUNTAIN

Black VELVET OIL painting

TV and ENTRANCE to Kitchen

SISTER'S Shared Sleeping SPACE

WHAT IT IS STUDENT 'X' PAGE

WHAT IT IS SPRING 2012

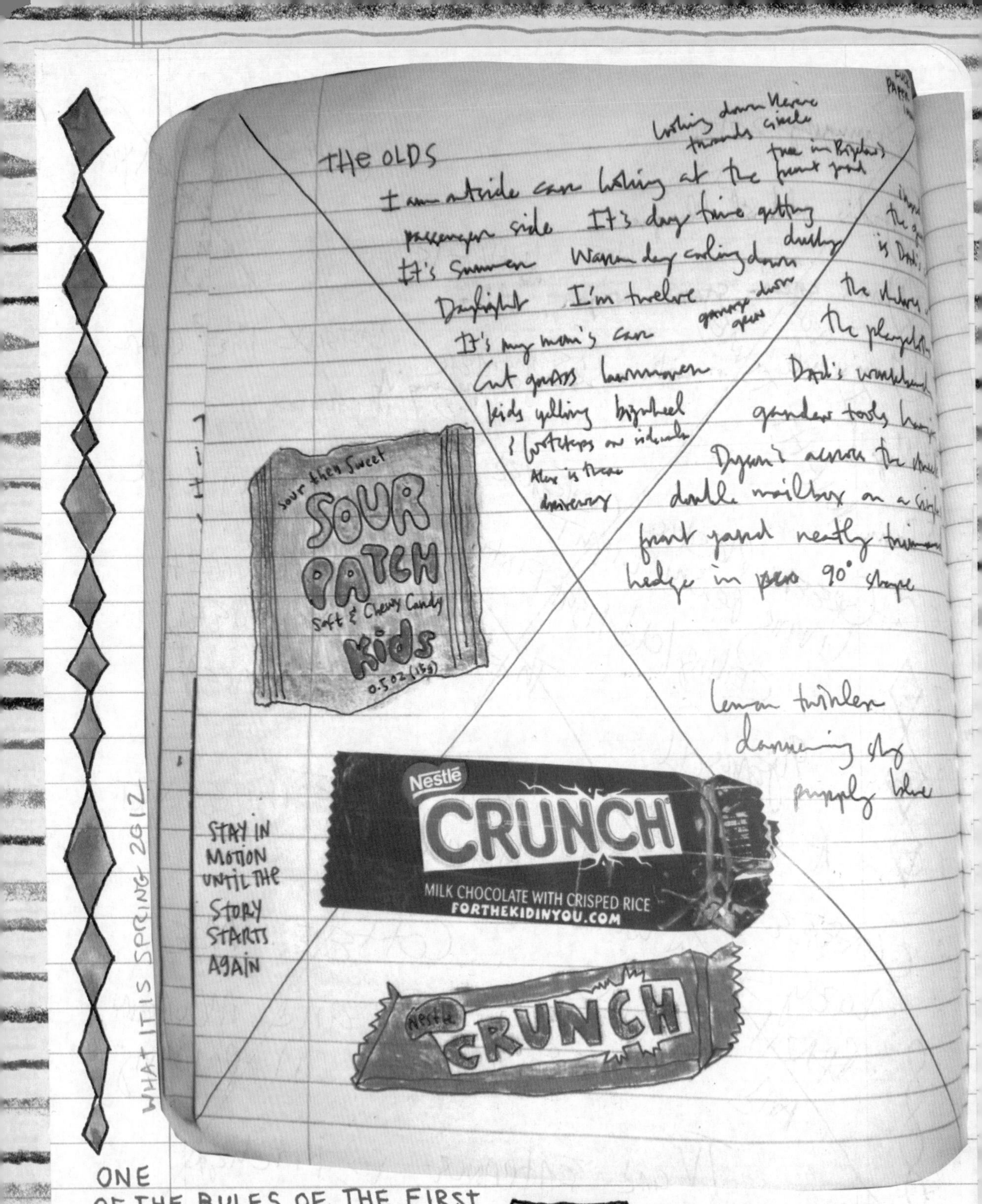
THE OLDS
It's summer
Daylight I'm twelve
It's my mom's car
kids yelling bigwheel
front yard neatly trimmed
hedge in perfect 90° shape
lemon twinkles
darkening sky
purply blue
sour then sweet
SOUR PATCH
Soft & Chewy Candy
Kids
STAY IN MOTION UNTIL THE STORY STARTS AGAIN
Nestlé
CRUNCH
MILK CHOCOLATE WITH CRISPED RICE
FORTHEKIDINYOU.COM
Nestlé
CRUNCH

ONE OF THE RULES OF THE FIRST CLASS IS YOU CAN HAVE ALL THE CANDY YOU WANT BUT YOU HAVE TO DRAW IT FIRST

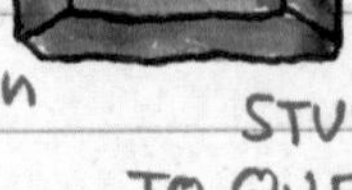

THIS IS AN EXAMPLE OF AN 'X' PAGE. STUDENTS WRITE ANSWERS TO QUESTIONS BEFORE WRITING

P.2: JAN 30 2012

HOMEWORK

PART of what we are doing in this class is NOTICING what we NOTICE and NOTICING MORE, but doing it in a natural way as we move through our day. Before our next class I'd like you to do ④ of these 'X' pages and I'd like you to do them when you are moving through your day, when you are bored or stuck somewhere. Each 'X' page takes 5 to 7 minutes.

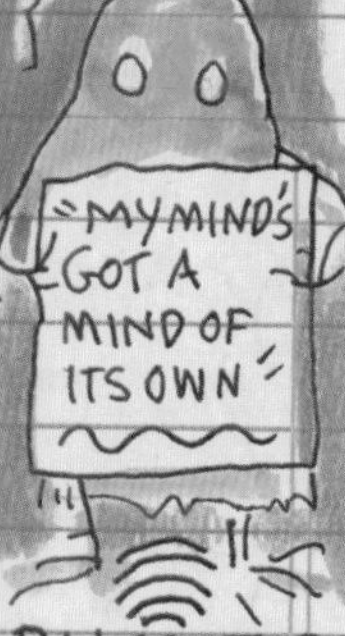
MY MIND'S GOT A MIND OF ITS OWN

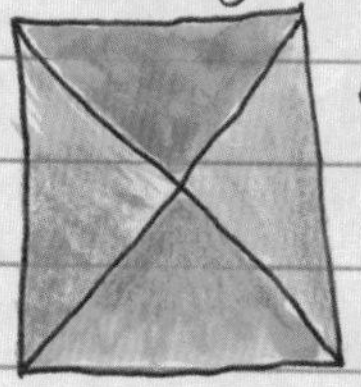

THE 'X' PAGE

¡PHONE CALL!

THE QUESTIONS

1. Where is the light coming from?
2. What time of day is it?
3. Season? and weather?
4. What's the temperature like?
5. What does the air smell like?
6. Where are you?
7. What are you doing?
8. Who else is there?
9. Why are you there?
10. What sounds can you hear?
11. What are some of the objects around you?
12. What's directly in front of you?
13. to your right? 14. Left?
15. Behind you? 16. Below?
17. Above? 18. There is something you haven't noticed yet. What is it? IT CAN BE VERY SMALL

I'd like you to color 2 pictures while doing something else.

① picture should be colored as we colored our last pages — with plenty of crayon.

① picture should be colored any way you like as long as you spend time on it.

AND I'd like you to practice looking at the TOPS of things. Remind yourself to lift your eyes and see what's there -

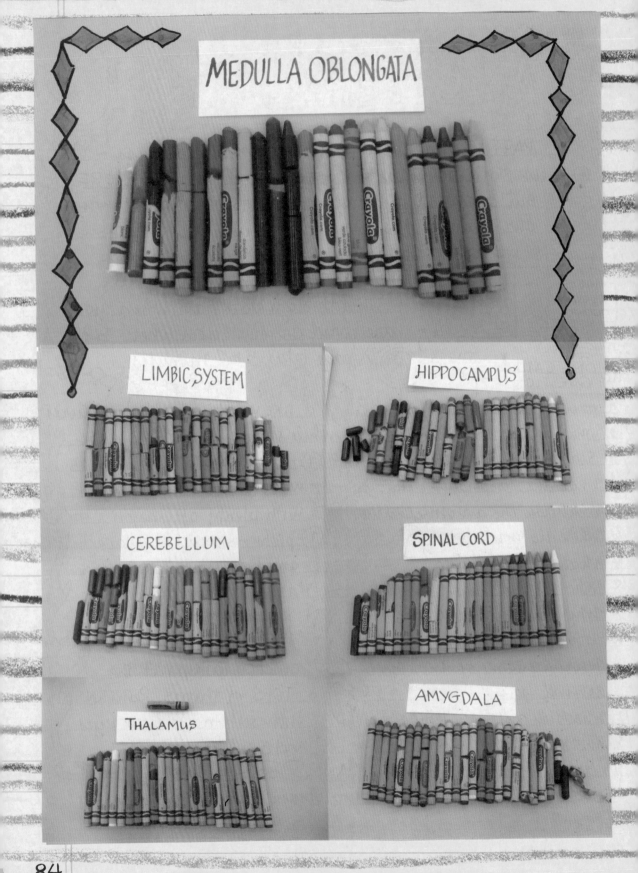

MEDULLA OBLONGATA

LIMBIC SYSTEM

HIPPOCAMPUS

CEREBELLUM

SPINAL CORD

THALAMUS

AMYGDALA

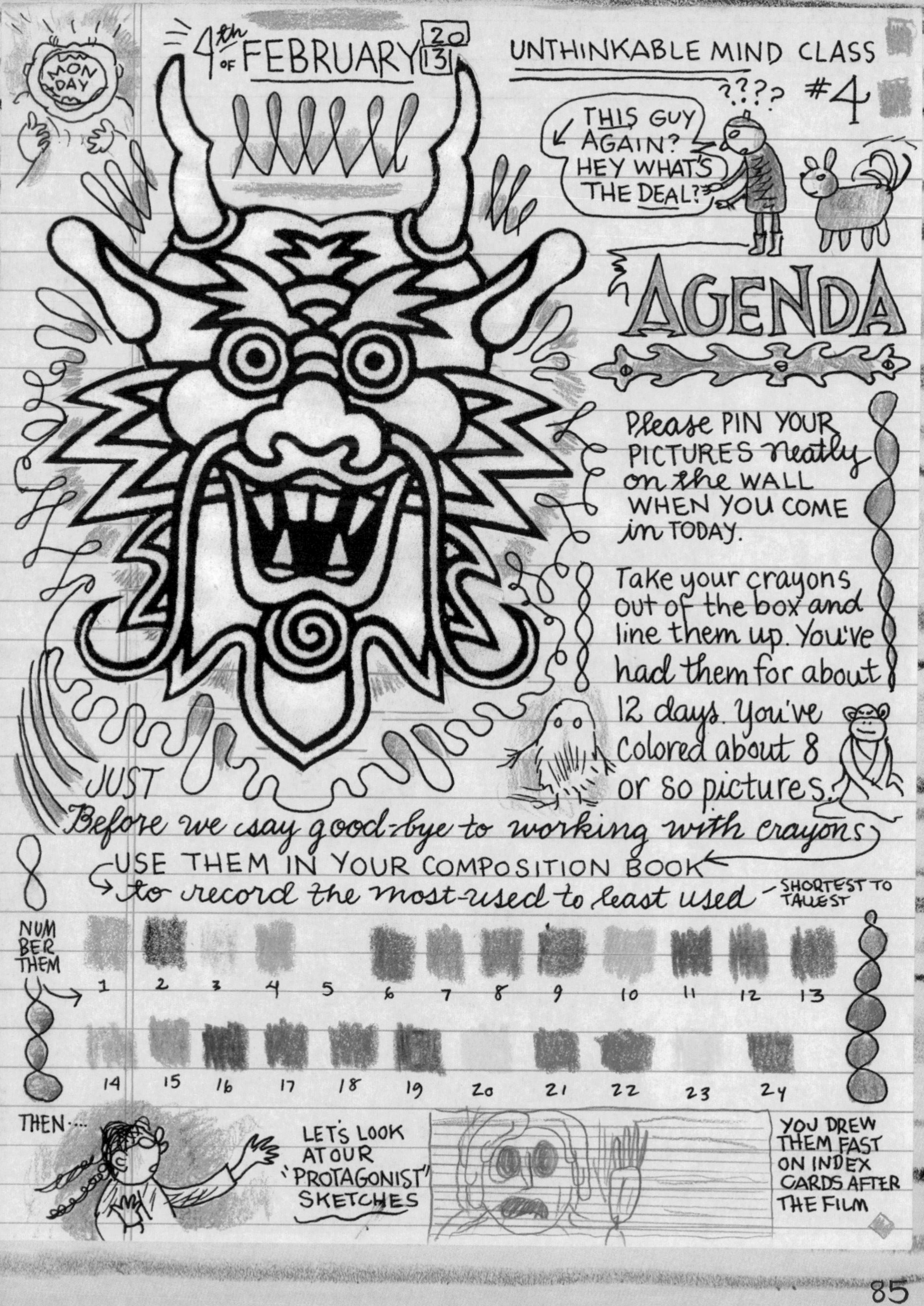
MON DAY
4th of FEBRUARY 2013
UNTHINKABLE MIND CLASS #4
????
THIS GUY AGAIN? HEY WHAT'S THE DEAL?
AGENDA
Please PIN YOUR PICTURES neatly on the WALL WHEN YOU COME in TODAY.
Take your crayons out of the box and line them up. You've had them for about 12 days. You've colored about 8 or so pictures.
JUST
Before we say good-bye to working with crayons
USE THEM IN YOUR COMPOSITION BOOK
to record the most-used to least used
SHORTEST TO TALLEST
NUMBER THEM
1 2 3 4 5 6 7 8 9 10 11 12 13
14 15 16 17 18 19 20 21 22 23 24
THEN....
LET'S LOOK AT OUR 'PROTAGONIST' SKETCHES
YOU DREW THEM FAST ON INDEX CARDS AFTER THE FILM

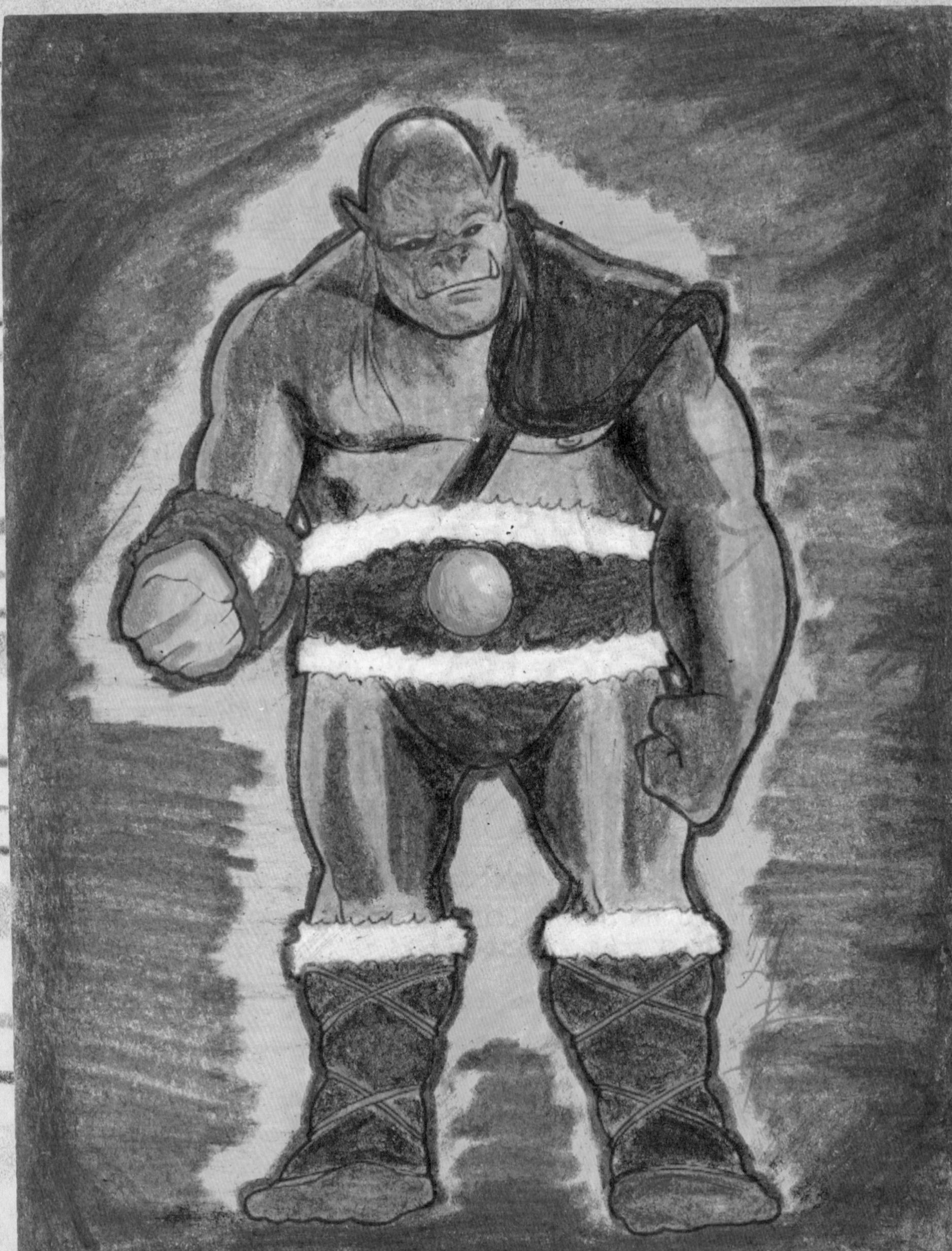

CRAYONS

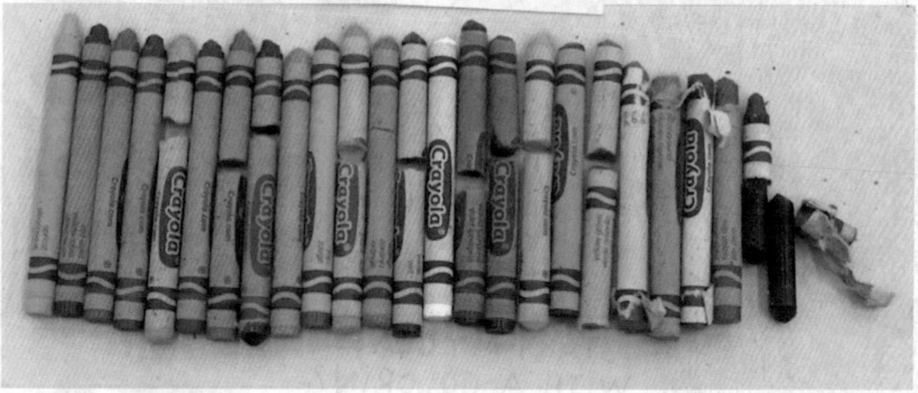

FROM LEAST USED TO MOST USED: 24 CRAYONS AFTER 3 PICTURES

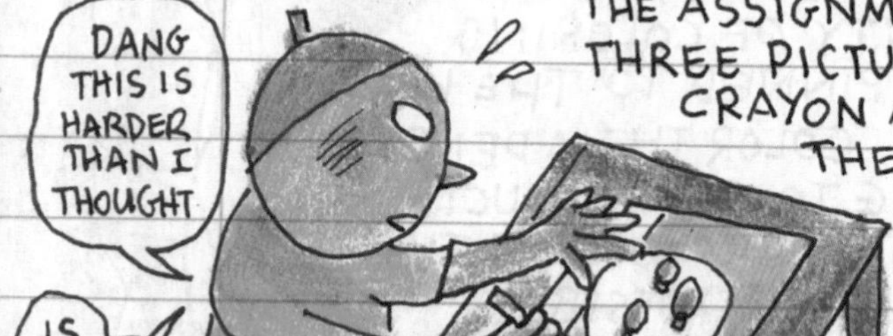
DANG THIS IS HARDER THAN I THOUGHT
IS THERE A SECRET?

THE ASSIGNMENT → TO COLOR THREE PICTURES, USING AS MUCH CRAYON AS POSSIBLE; TO COVER THE PAPER COMPLETELY SO NONE OF IT SHOWS THROUGH.

GETTING SOLID COLOR TAKES WORK. THE CRAYONS BREAK EASILY, THE WAX WON'T LAY ON THE PAPER EVENLY, AND YOUR FINGERS, HAND, AND ARM GET SORE. CRAYONS ARE A DRAG, MAN.

WHY USE THEM?

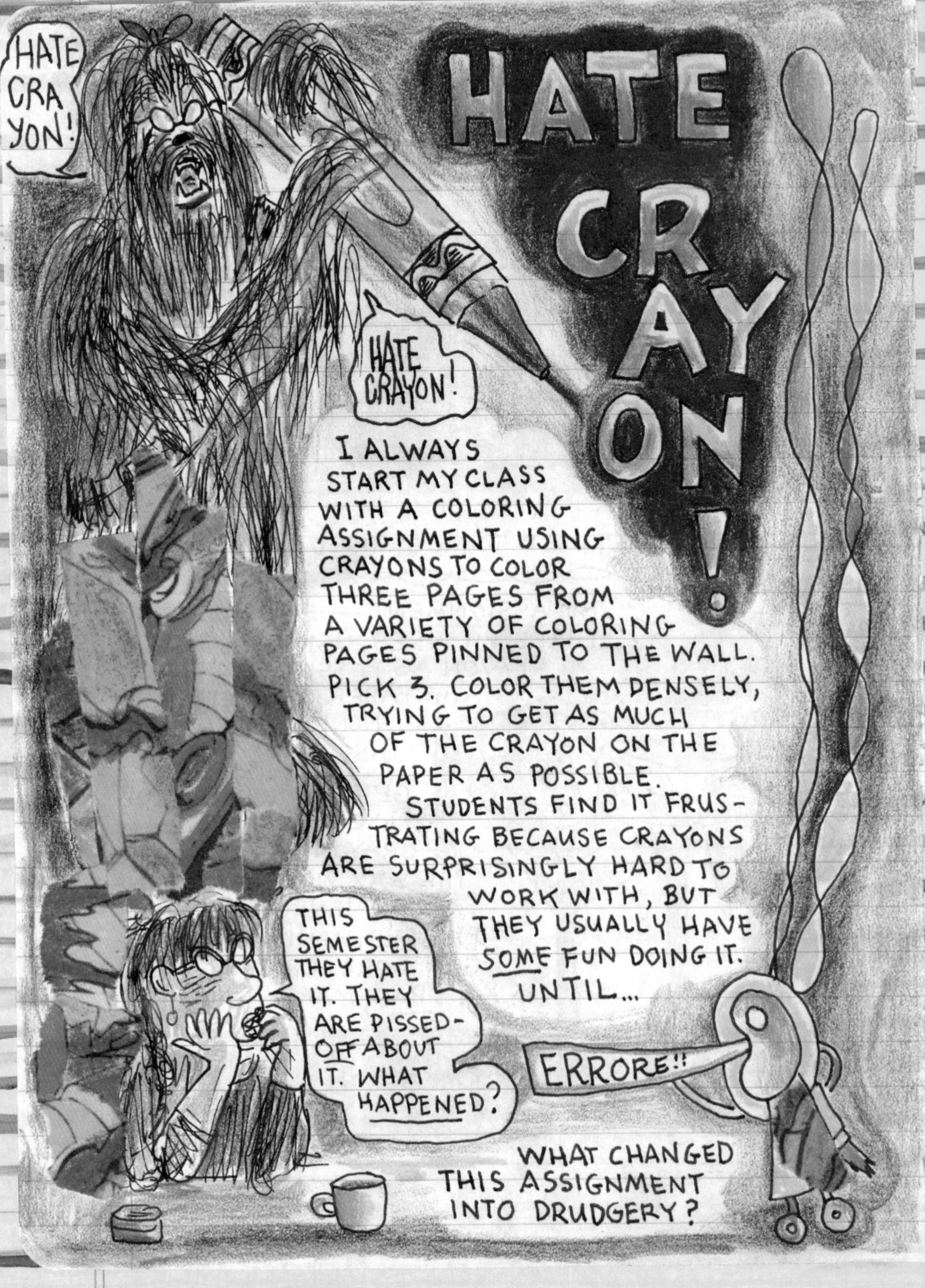
HATE CRAYON!
HATE CRA YON!
HATE CRAYON!
I ALWAYS START MY CLASS WITH A COLORING ASSIGNMENT USING CRAYONS TO COLOR THREE PAGES FROM A VARIETY OF COLORING PAGES PINNED TO THE WALL. PICK 3. COLOR THEM DENSELY, TRYING TO GET AS MUCH OF THE CRAYON ON THE PAPER AS POSSIBLE.
STUDENTS FIND IT FRUSTRATING BECAUSE CRAYONS ARE SURPRISINGLY HARD TO WORK WITH, BUT THEY USUALLY HAVE SOME FUN DOING IT. UNTIL...
THIS SEMESTER THEY HATE IT. THEY ARE PISSED-OFF ABOUT IT. WHAT HAPPENED?
ERRORE!!
WHAT CHANGED THIS ASSIGNMENT INTO DRUDGERY?

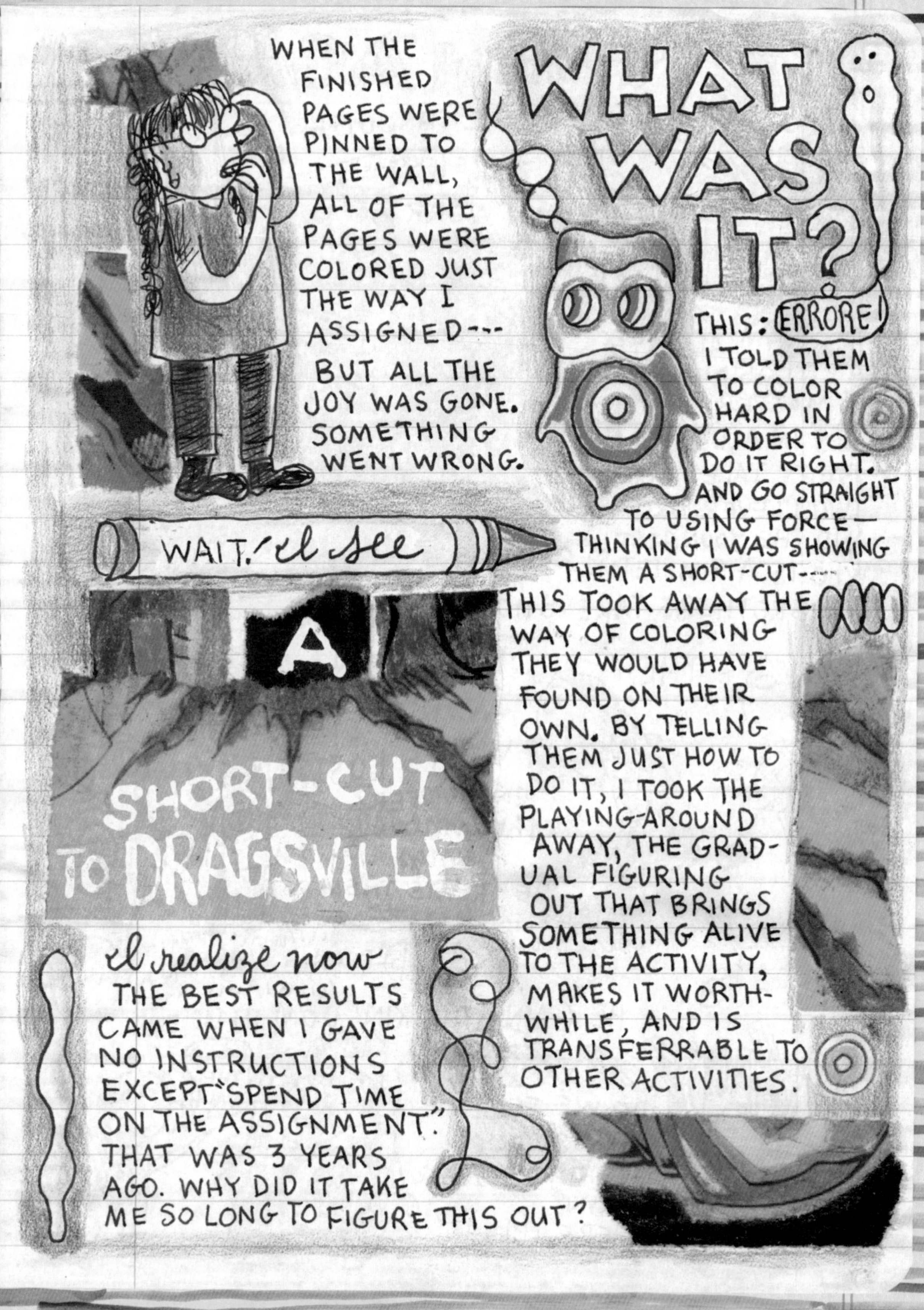
WHEN THE FINISHED PAGES WERE PINNED TO THE WALL, ALL OF THE PAGES WERE COLORED JUST THE WAY I ASSIGNED---
BUT ALL THE JOY WAS GONE. SOMETHING WENT WRONG.
WHAT WAS IT?
THIS: ERRORE!
I TOLD THEM TO COLOR HARD IN ORDER TO DO IT RIGHT. AND GO STRAIGHT TO USING FORCE— THINKING I WAS SHOWING THEM A SHORT-CUT----
WAIT! I see
A SHORT-CUT TO DRAGSVILLE
THIS TOOK AWAY THE WAY OF COLORING THEY WOULD HAVE FOUND ON THEIR OWN. BY TELLING THEM JUST HOW TO DO IT, I TOOK THE PLAYING-AROUND AWAY, THE GRADUAL FIGURING OUT THAT BRINGS SOMETHING ALIVE TO THE ACTIVITY, MAKES IT WORTHWHILE, AND IS TRANSFERRABLE TO OTHER ACTIVITIES.
I realize now
THE BEST RESULTS CAME WHEN I GAVE NO INSTRUCTIONS EXCEPT "SPEND TIME ON THE ASSIGNMENT." THAT WAS 3 YEARS AGO. WHY DID IT TAKE ME SO LONG TO FIGURE THIS OUT?

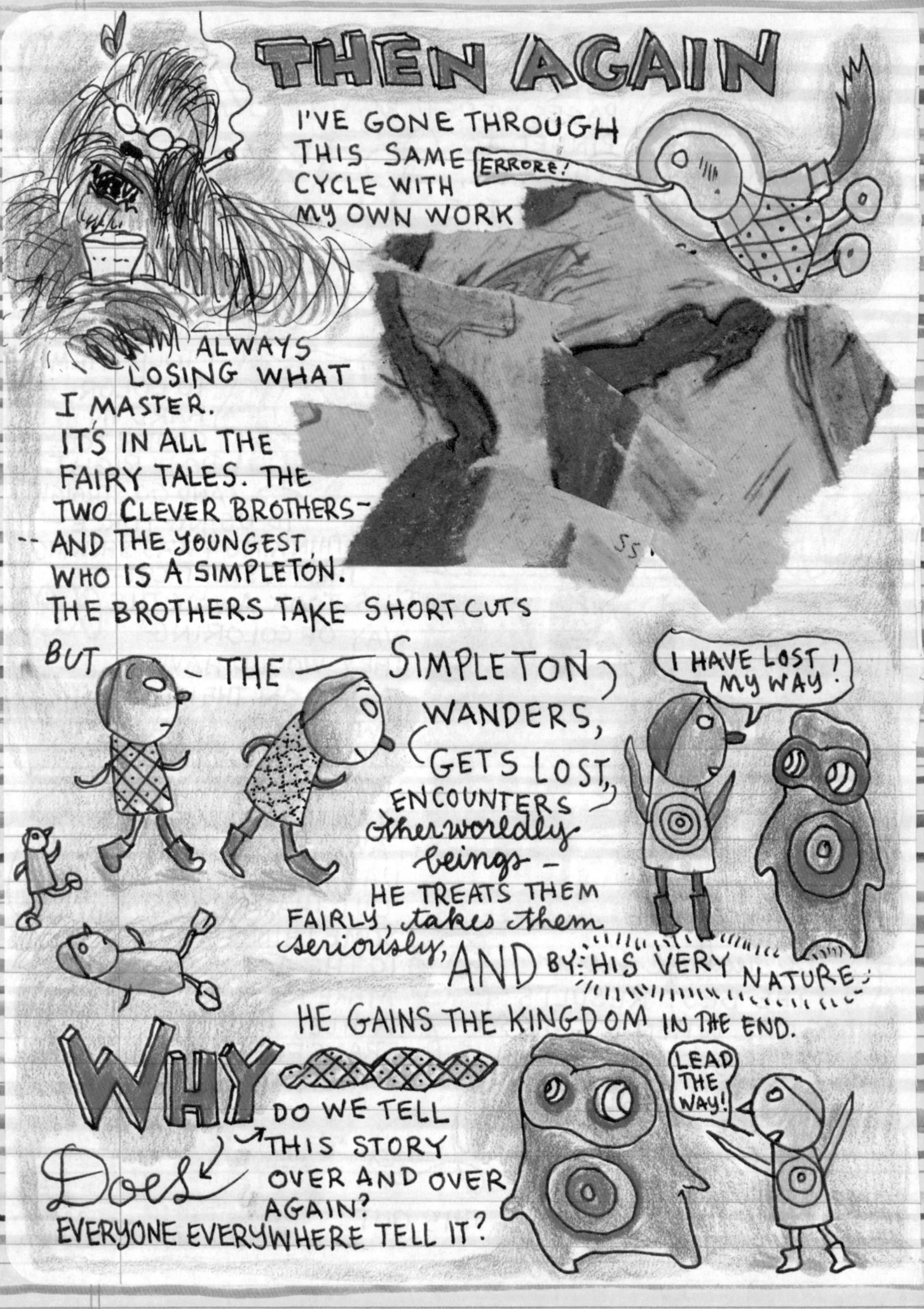
THEN AGAIN
I'VE GONE THROUGH THIS SAME CYCLE WITH MY OWN WORK
ERRORE!
ALWAYS LOSING WHAT I MASTER.
IT'S IN ALL THE FAIRY TALES. THE TWO CLEVER BROTHERS -- AND THE YOUNGEST WHO IS A SIMPLETON.
THE BROTHERS TAKE SHORT CUTS
BUT THE SIMPLETON WANDERS, GETS LOST, ENCOUNTERS otherworldly beings - HE TREATS THEM FAIRLY, takes them seriously, AND BY HIS VERY NATURE HE GAINS THE KINGDOM IN THE END.
I HAVE LOST MY WAY!
WHY DO WE TELL THIS STORY OVER AND OVER AGAIN?
Does EVERYONE EVERYWHERE TELL IT?
LEAD THE WAY!

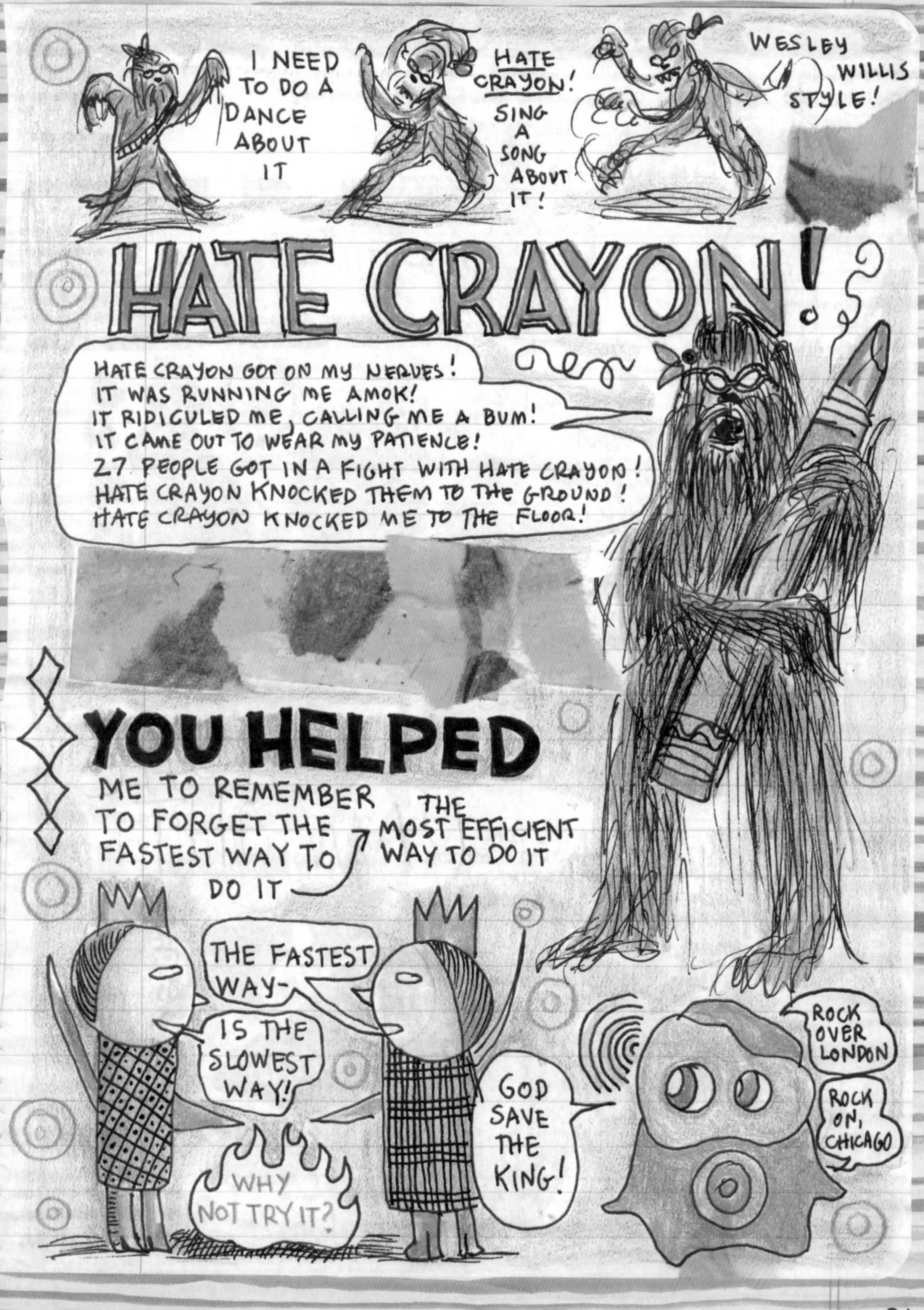
I NEED TO DO A DANCE ABOUT IT
HATE CRAYON! SING A SONG ABOUT IT!
WESLEY WILLIS STYLE!
HATE CRAYON!
HATE CRAYON GOT ON MY NERVES! IT WAS RUNNING ME AMOK! IT RIDICULED ME, CALLING ME A BUM! IT CAME OUT TO WEAR MY PATIENCE! 27 PEOPLE GOT IN A FIGHT WITH HATE CRAYON! HATE CRAYON KNOCKED THEM TO THE GROUND! HATE CRAYON KNOCKED ME TO THE FLOOR!
YOU HELPED ME TO REMEMBER TO FORGET THE FASTEST WAY TO DO IT
THE MOST EFFICIENT WAY TO DO IT
THE FASTEST WAY-
IS THE SLOWEST WAY!
WHY NOT TRY IT?
GOD SAVE THE KING!
ROCK OVER LONDON
ROCK ON, CHICAGO

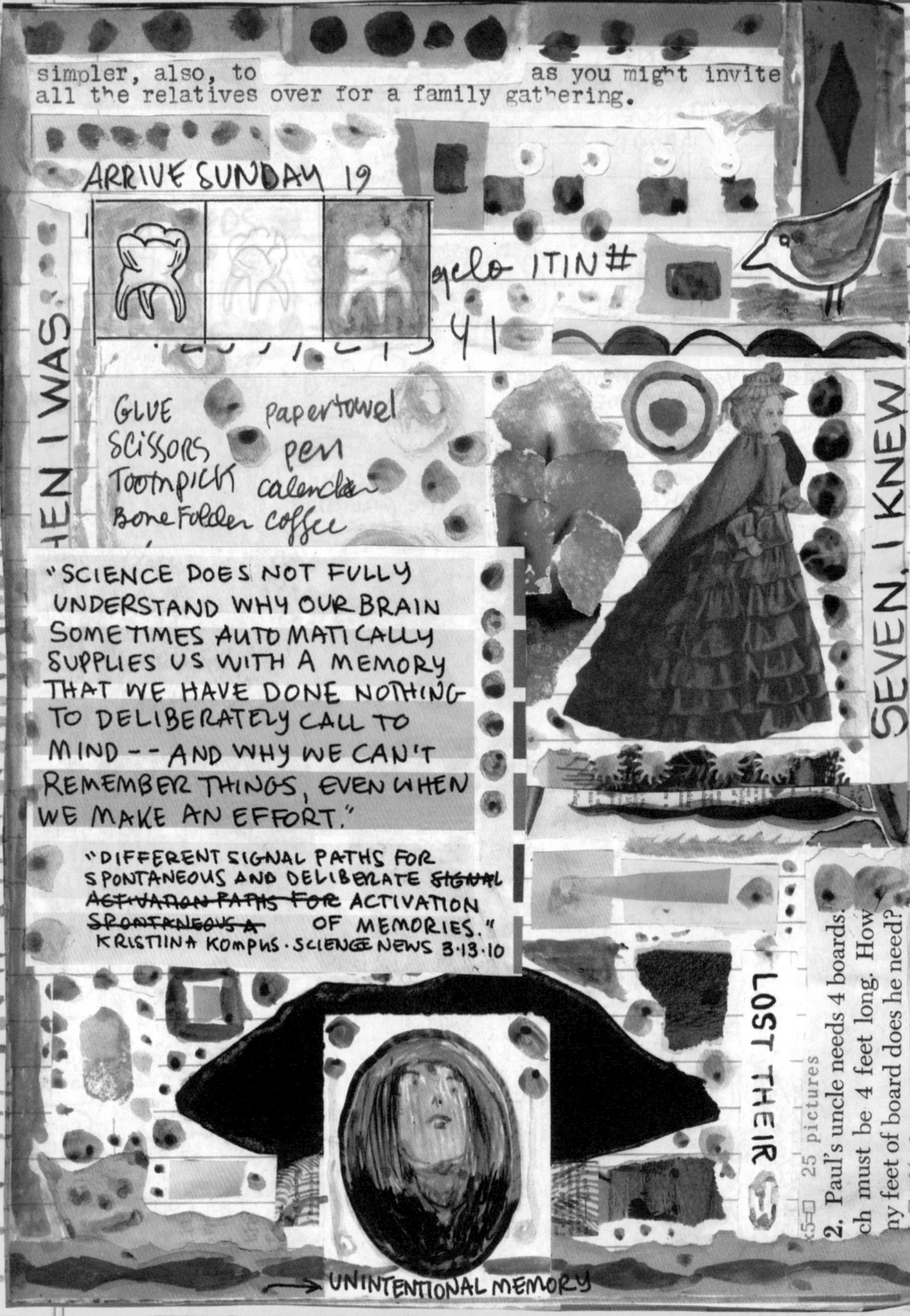
simpler, also, to as you might invite all the relatives over for a family gathering.
ARRIVE SUNDAY 19
gelo ITIN#
HEN I WAS
GLUE
SCISSORS
TOOTHPICK
Bone Folder
papertowel
pen
calendar
coffee
"SCIENCE DOES NOT FULLY UNDERSTAND WHY OUR BRAIN SOMETIMES AUTOMATICALLY SUPPLIES US WITH A MEMORY THAT WE HAVE DONE NOTHING TO DELIBERATELY CALL TO MIND -- AND WHY WE CAN'T REMEMBER THINGS, EVEN WHEN WE MAKE AN EFFORT."
"DIFFERENT SIGNAL PATHS FOR SPONTANEOUS AND DELIBERATE ~~SIGNAL ACTIVATION PATHS FOR~~ ACTIVATION ~~SPONTANEOUS A~~ OF MEMORIES."
KRISTIINA KOMPUS · SCIENCE NEWS 3·13·10
SEVEN, I KNEW
LOST THEIR
25 pictures
2. Paul's uncle needs 4 boards.
ch must be 4 feet long. How
ny feet of board does he need?
→ UNINTENTIONAL MEMORY

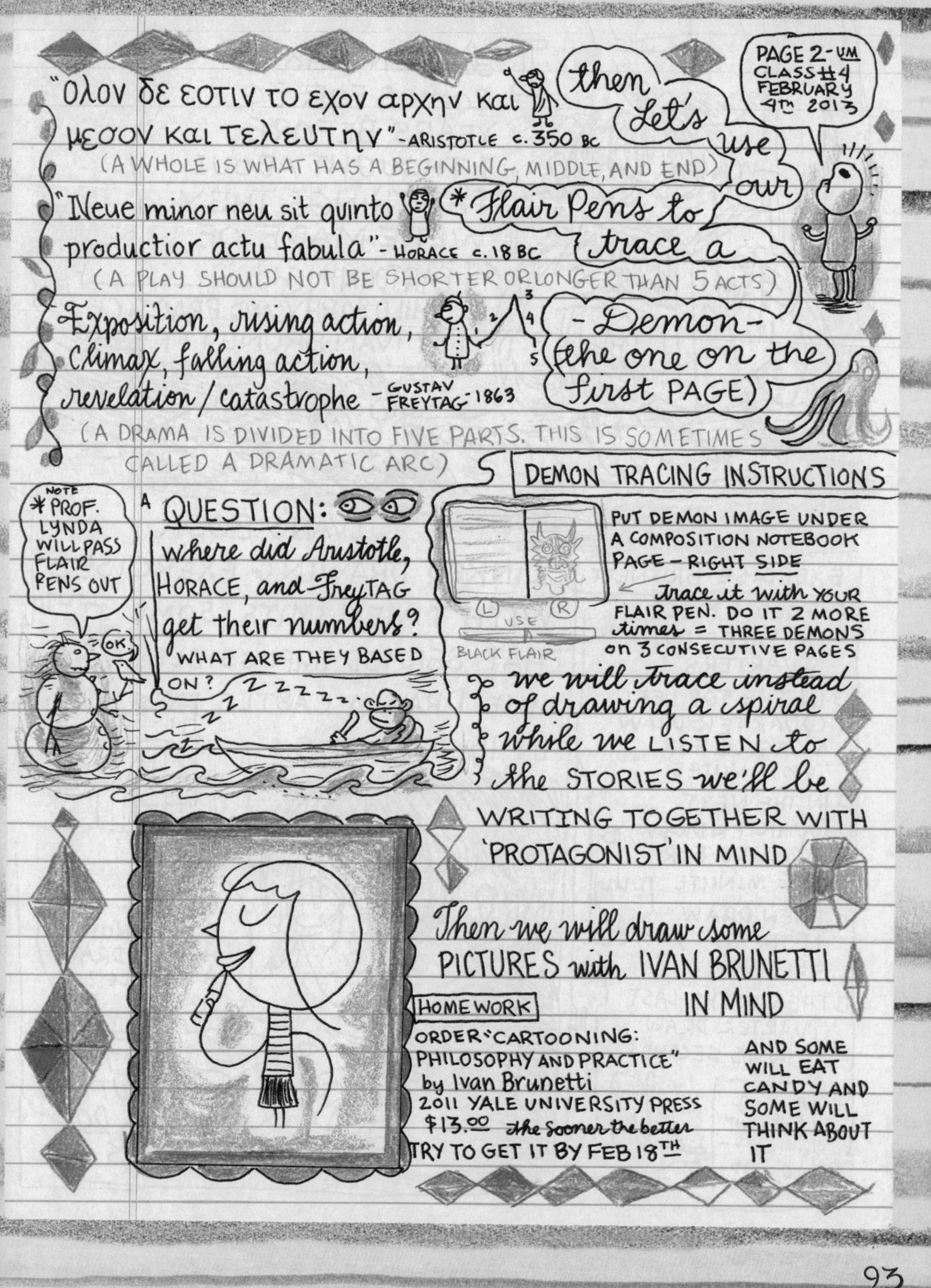
"Ολον δε εστιν το εχον αρχην και μεσον και τελευτην" - ARISTOTLE c. 350 BC
(A WHOLE IS WHAT HAS A BEGINNING, MIDDLE, AND END)
"Neue minor neu sit quinto productior actu fabula" - HORACE c. 18 BC
(A PLAY SHOULD NOT BE SHORTER OR LONGER THAN 5 ACTS)
Exposition, rising action, climax, falling action, revelation / catastrophe - GUSTAV FREYTAG - 1863
1 2 3 4 5
(A DRAMA IS DIVIDED INTO FIVE PARTS. THIS IS SOMETIMES CALLED A DRAMATIC ARC)
PAGE 2 - UM CLASS #4 FEBRUARY 4TH 2013
then Let's use our *Flair Pens to trace a - Demon - (the one on the first PAGE)
NOTE *PROF. LYNDA WILL PASS FLAIR PENS OUT
OK.
A QUESTION: where did Aristotle, HORACE, and Freytag get their numbers? WHAT ARE THEY BASED ON?
Z Z Z Z Z Z Z
DEMON TRACING INSTRUCTIONS
L R
USE
BLACK FLAIR
PUT DEMON IMAGE UNDER A COMPOSITION NOTEBOOK PAGE - RIGHT SIDE
Trace it with YOUR FLAIR PEN. DO IT 2 MORE times = THREE DEMONS on 3 CONSECUTIVE PAGES
we will trace instead of drawing a spiral while we LISTEN to the STORIES we'll be WRITING TOGETHER WITH 'PROTAGONIST' IN MIND
Then we will draw some PICTURES with IVAN BRUNETTI IN MIND
HOMEWORK
ORDER "CARTOONING: PHILOSOPHY AND PRACTICE" by Ivan Brunetti 2011 YALE UNIVERSITY PRESS $13.00 the sooner the better
TRY TO GET IT BY FEB 18TH
AND SOME WILL EAT CANDY AND SOME WILL THINK ABOUT IT

I'd BEEN MAKING COMICS FOR 30 YEARS BEFORE I THOUGHT ABOUT THE THINGS THEY WERE MADE OF.

CARTOONING: PHILOSOPHY AND PRACTICE BY IVAN BRUNETTI

IVAN'S BOOK LINKED DRAWING EXERCISES WITH TIME LIMITS, SOME THAT SEEMED IMPOSSIBLE, LIKE DRAW A CASTLE IN 15 SECONDS.

EXERCISE BRUNETTI
- ☐ FOLD A PIECE OF PAPER INTO QUARTERS.
- ☐ IN THE TOP LEFT QUARTER DRAW A CASTLE FOR TWO MINUTES
- ☐ IN THE NEXT QUARTER DRAW A CASTLE FOR ONE MINUTE
- ☐ THEN DRAW IT IN 30 SECONDS
- ☐ THEN IN THE LAST QUARTER DRAW IT IN 15 SECONDS

2 MINS	1 MIN
30 SECS	15 SECS

BUT WHAT IF YOU DON'T KNOW HOW TO DRAW A CASTLE? ...

IT TURNS OUT YOU DO

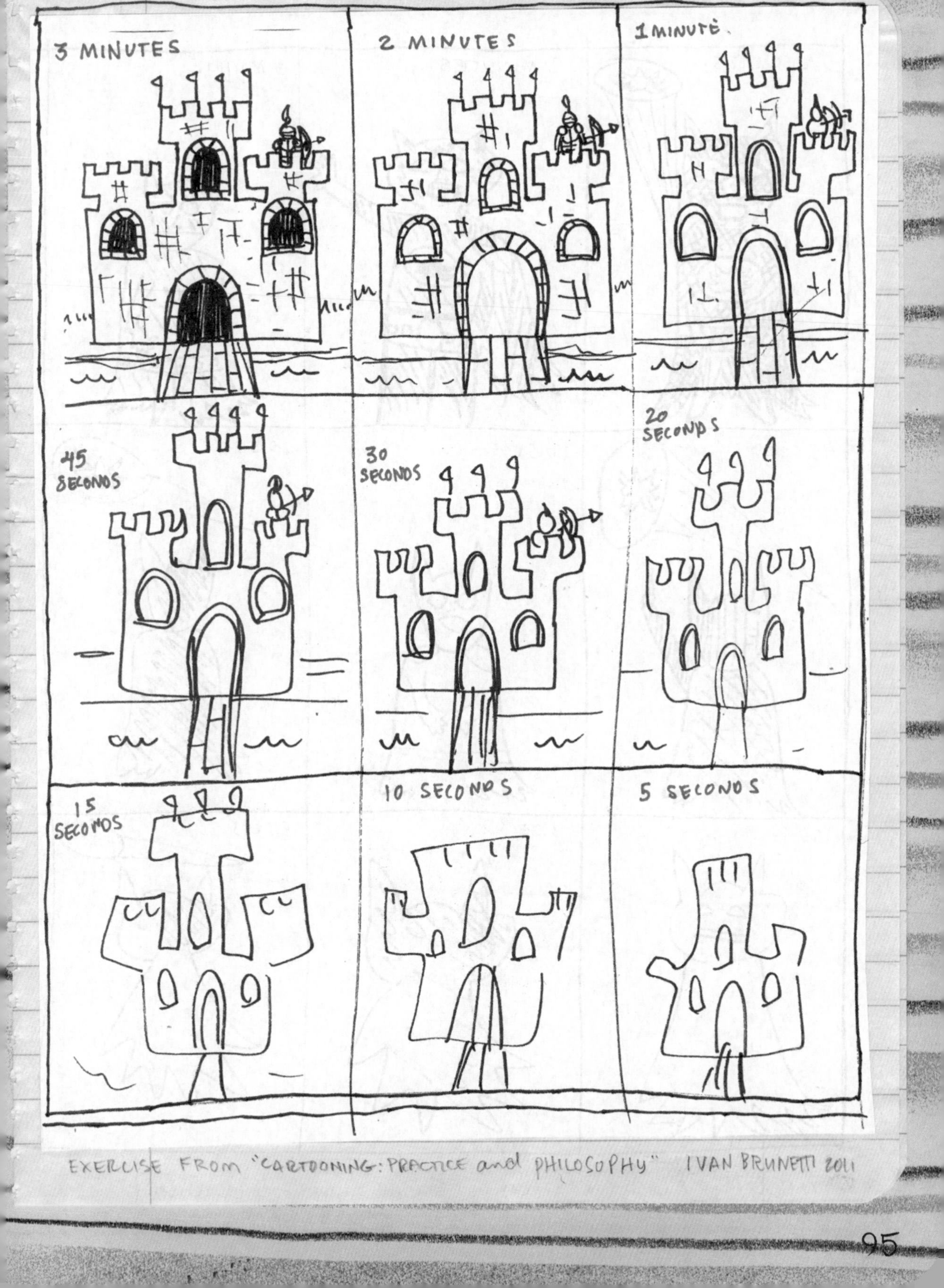
3 MINUTES
2 MINUTES
1 MINUTE
45 SECONDS
30 SECONDS
20 SECONDS
15 SECONDS
10 SECONDS
5 SECONDS

EXERCISE FROM "CARTOONING: PRACTICE and PHILOSOPHY" IVAN BRUNETTI 2011

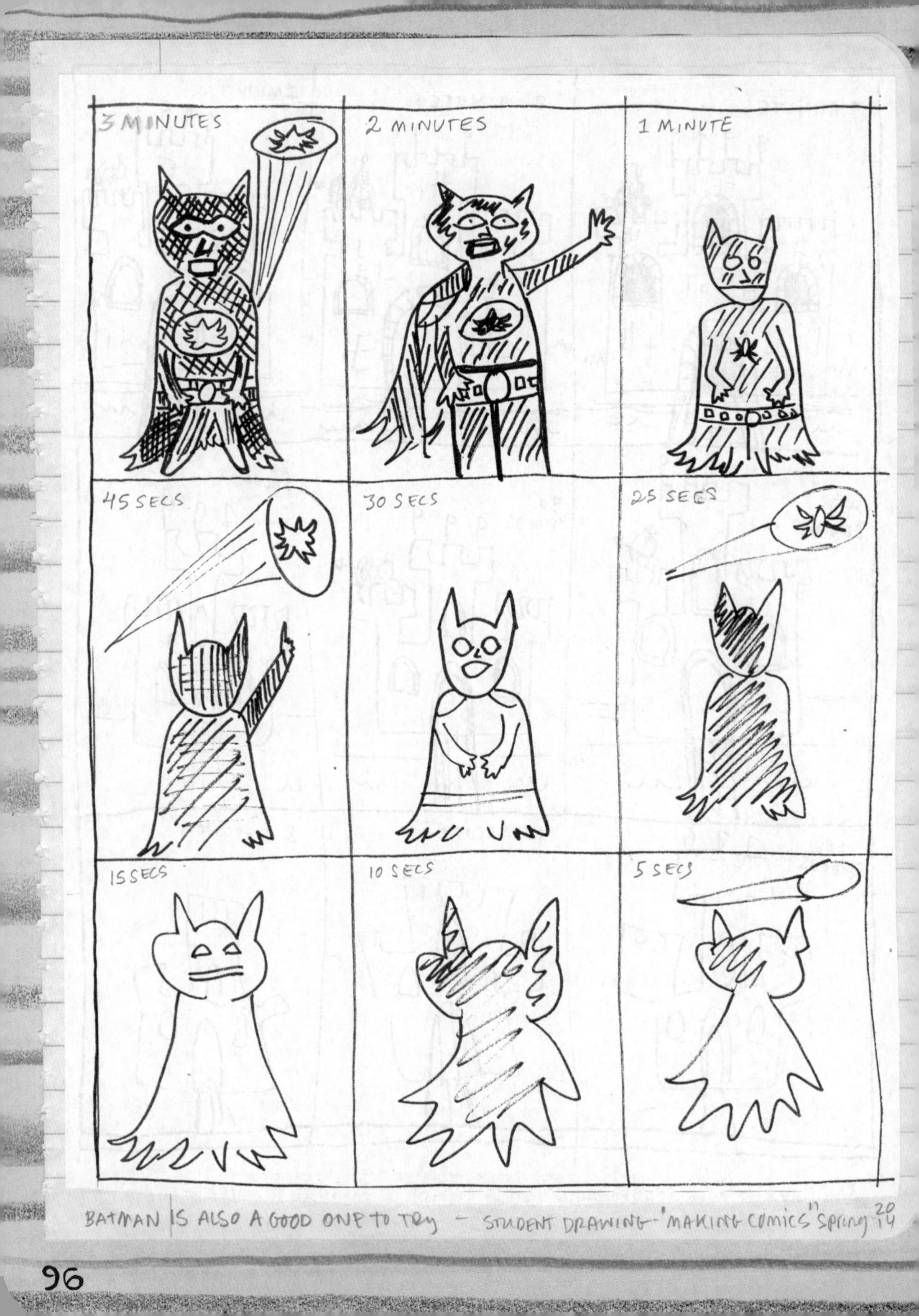
3 MINUTES
2 MINUTES
1 MINUTE
45 SECS
30 SECS
25 SECS
15 SECS
10 SECS
5 SECS

BATMAN IS ALSO A GOOD ONE TO TRY – STUDENT DRAWING – "MAKING COMICS" SPRING 2014

THAT IS TO SAY

THERE IS A KIND OF CALIBRATION OF WHAT TO INCLUDE GIVEN THE TIME CONSTRAINTS, AND TIME CONSTRAINTS ARE VITAL IN THE BEGINNING—

PRACTICE WITH A TIMER

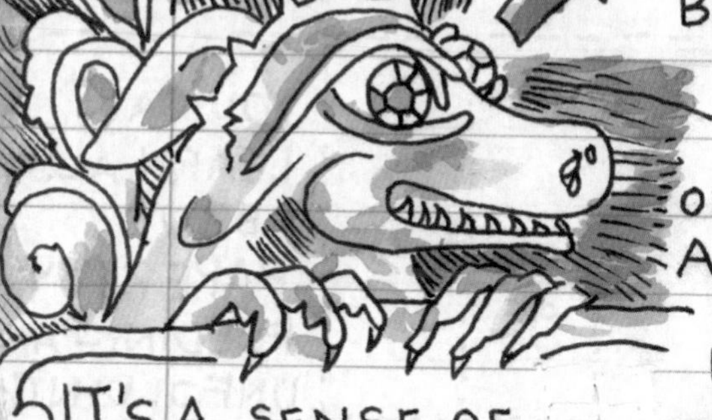

IF YOU HAD 10 MINUTES, FIVE MINUTES, TWO MINUTES, OR 45 SECONDS TO COPY A PHOTO, YOU'D SOMEHOW KNOW HOW TO FIT IT INTO THE TIME ALLOWED. BUT HOW ARE YOU DOING IT?

(HINT: IT'S NOT THINKING IT ALL OUT FIRST—)

IT'S A SENSE OF WHAT NEEDS TO BE THERE IF YOU ONLY HAVE A MINUTE TO COPY A FAMILY PORTRAIT OR SIX MINUTES TO COPY A WANTED POSTER. COPYING HELPS YOU WITH TIMING OUT THE PACE AND RHYTHM OF MOVING YOUR HANDS AND FINGERS IN A WAY THAT LEAVES LINES AND SHAPES

MAR GIN ALIA IS GOOD

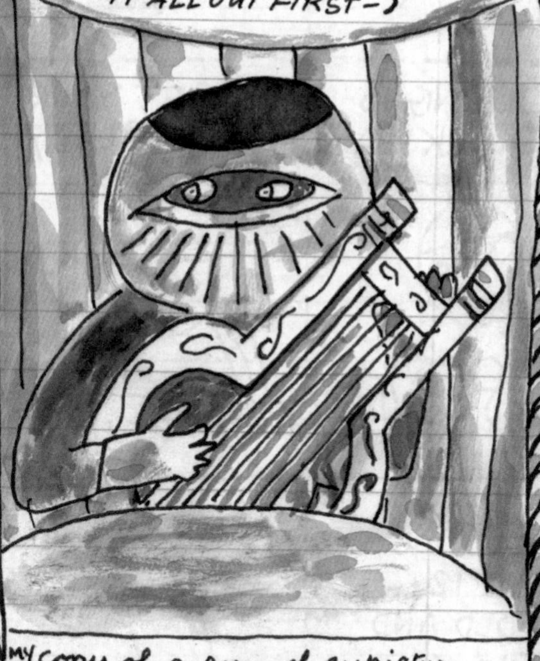

my copy of a copy of a picture by my student, G.K.

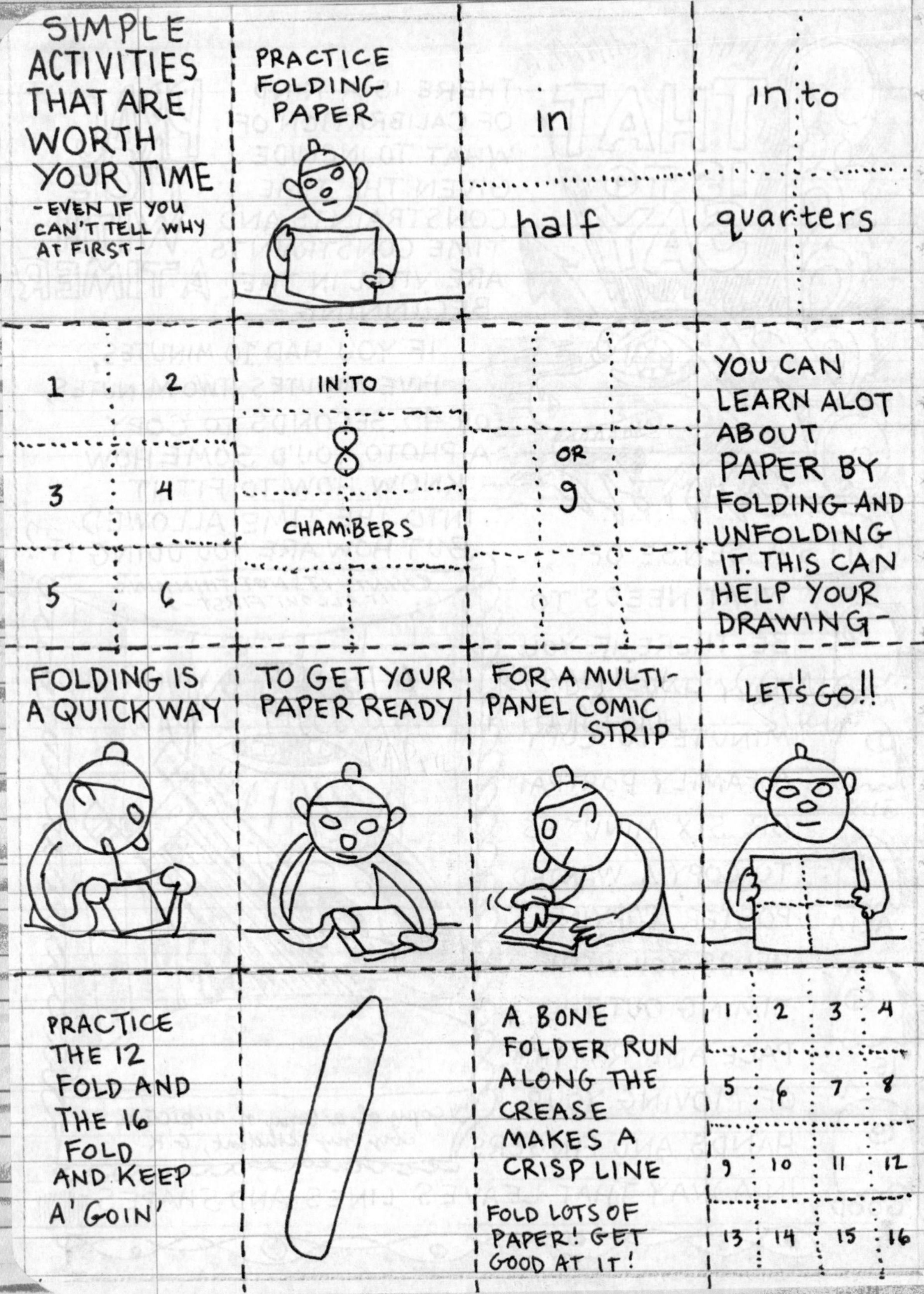

SIMPLE ACTIVITIES THAT ARE WORTH YOUR TIME

-EVEN IF YOU CAN'T TELL WHY AT FIRST-

PRACTICE FOLDING PAPER

in ..... into

half ..... quarters

1	2
3	4
5	6

INTO

8

CHAMBERS

or

9

YOU CAN LEARN ALOT ABOUT PAPER BY FOLDING AND UNFOLDING IT. THIS CAN HELP YOUR DRAWING-

FOLDING IS A QUICK WAY

TO GET YOUR PAPER READY

FOR A MULTI-PANEL COMIC STRIP

LET'S GO!!

PRACTICE THE 12 FOLD AND THE 16 FOLD AND KEEP A' GOIN'

A BONE FOLDER RUN ALONG THE CREASE MAKES A CRISP LINE

FOLD LOTS OF PAPER! GET GOOD AT IT!

1	2	3	4
5	6	7	8
9	10	11	12
13	14	15	16

WORTH your TIME Activities

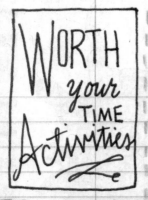

IT IS WORTH YOUR TIME TO FOLD A PAGE INTO 16

CHAMBERS AND HAND-DRAW A FRAME-LINE INSIDE EACH BOX

EVEN THOUGH AT FIRST YOU GO A LITTLE CRAZY. THE LINE WON'T REALLY OBEY

IT'S ALL MESSED UP BUT THEN IT STEADIES— THEN YOU START TO GET SOMEWHERE. AND THEN— YOUR HAND—

YOUR OWN HAND-LEAPS WIDE OF THE LINE YOU AIMED TO DRAW

RUINED!

STILL GOT IT!

ALTHOUGH IN THIS CASE, THERE IS NOTHING TO RUIN EXCEPT BY STOPPING.

WHAT HAPPENS WHEN YOU DRAW THE LINE MORE SLOWLY?

WHAT HAPPENS IF YOU KEEP YOUR EYE ON THE CREASE AS YOU DRAW? YOUR PEN ALONG IT

OR DRAW LINES IN PARALLEL

DOING SUCH ORDINARY THINGS WITH PAPER, FOLDED AND INKED—

CAN MAKE A DIFFERENCE TO YOUR WAY OF MAKING IMAGES

IF YOU RELAX YOUR FINGERS WHAT CHANGES? IF YOU TRY A LOOSER GRIP

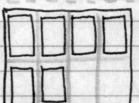

AND WHAT ABOUT WHEN YOU GET BORED WITH MAKING SO MANY LINES?

STOP! YOU WILL ONLY LEARN THAT SECRET WHEN YOU NEED IT.

what is the SECRET??

(HINT:)
(INK IS CRAZY AND PAPER IS STRONGER THAN YOU REALIZE)

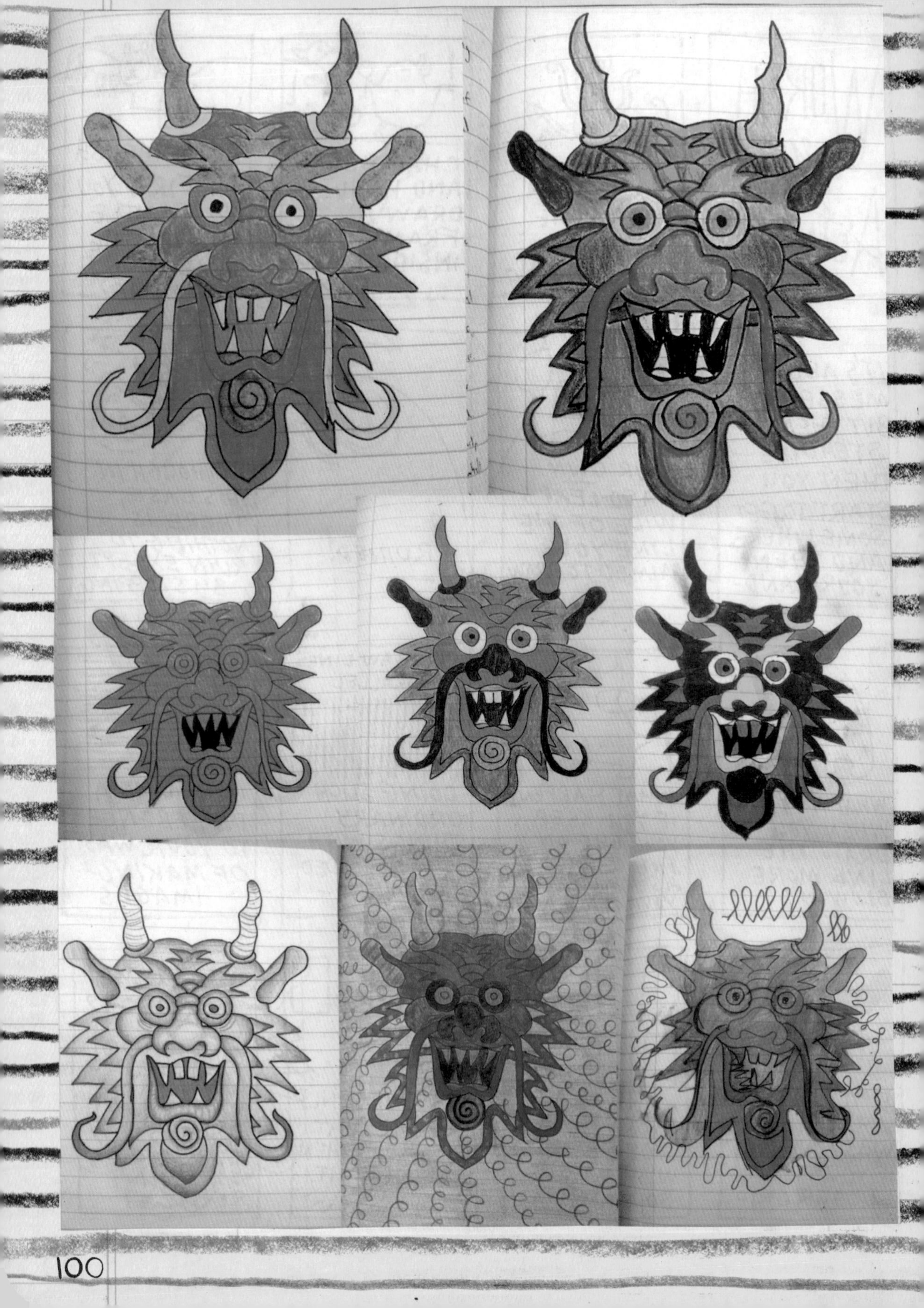

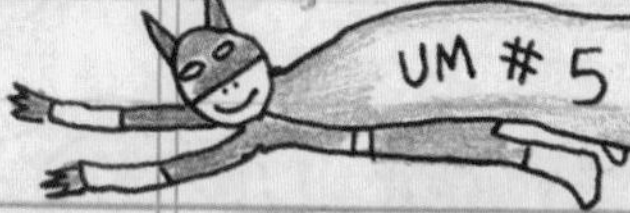

UM # 5 February 6, 2013 ← FUTURE PAST → and ONCE UPON A TIME CALLED NOW!

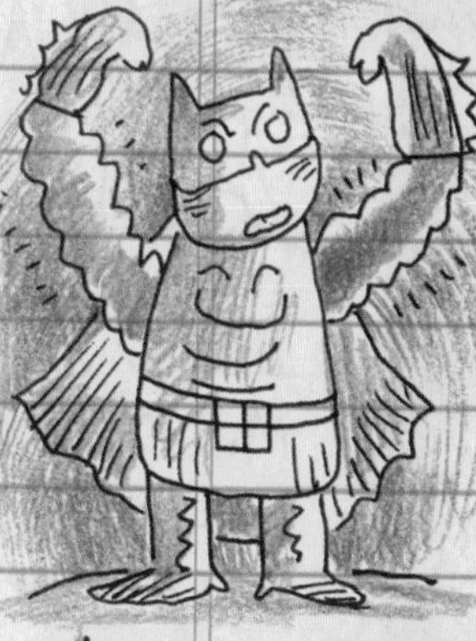

Dear Unthinkable Mind Class,

NOW YOUR HANDS ARE READY TO GO!!

YOU WILL NEED:

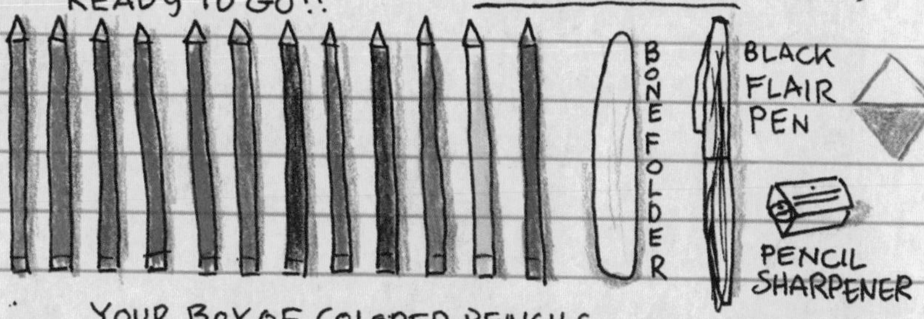
BONE FOLDER
BLACK FLAIR PEN
PENCIL SHARPENER

YOUR BOX OF COLORED PENCILS

AGENDA

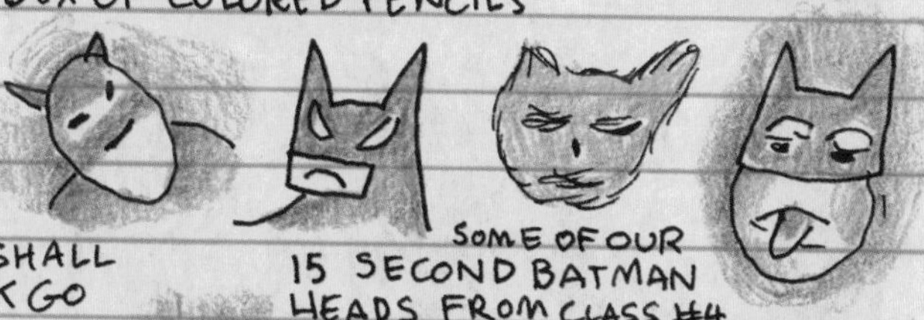

① SONG OF THE DAY: "THIS TOO SHALL PASS" by OK GO

SOME OF OUR 15 SECOND BATMAN HEADS FROM CLASS #4

② ~~DISCUSSION~~ WRITING RIGHT AWAY!

WE WILL WRITE MORE STORIES TOGETHER AND COLOR ONE OF THE DEMON HEADS WE TRACED ON MONDAY WHILE WE LISTEN. FOR THE FIRST DEMON WE WILL USE JUST ONE COLORED PENCIL

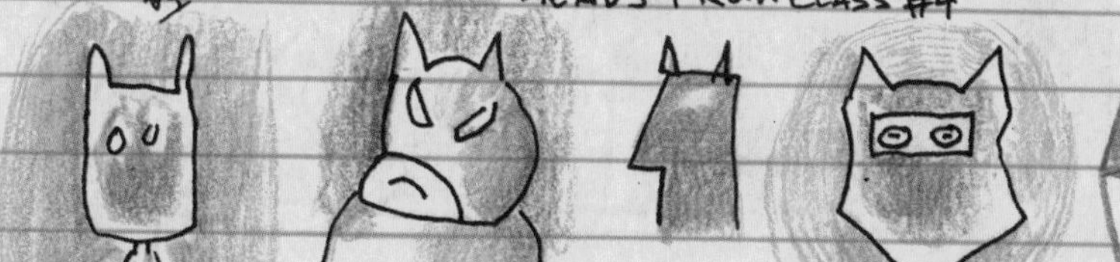

③ WE WILL HAVE A 10 minute break AT ABOUT 2:30

④ 2:40–3:50 DRAWING TIME AND GRIMMS' FAIRYTALE TIME

TRACED FROM YOUR ORIGINALS

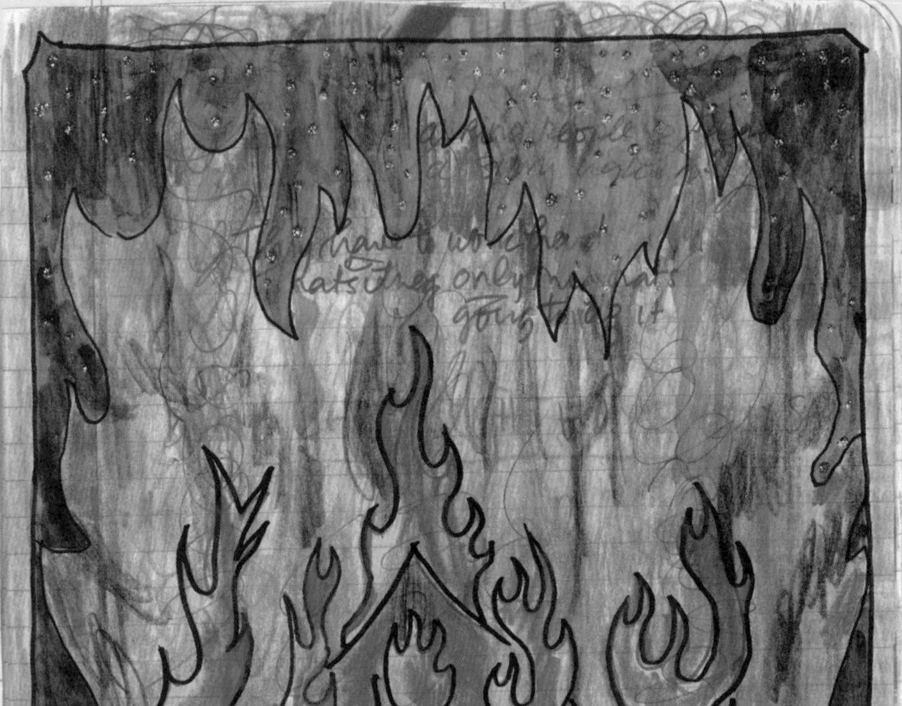
6 11 13 19 21 24 26 30 33 36 38 45 45 48 50 51 53 56 59 62 64 67

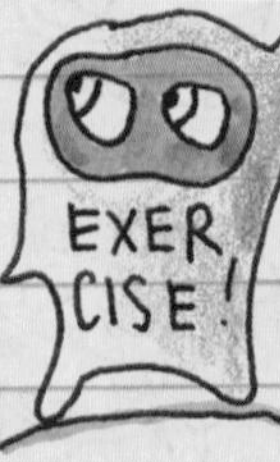
EXER CISE!

SPEND 3 MINUTES DRAWING A HOUSE ON FIRE IN NON-PHOTO BLUE PENCIL. USE A WHOLE COMP BOOK PAGE WITH A HAND-DRAWN BORDER. COLOR IT WITH YOUR COLOR PENCILS AFTER YOU INK IT IN.

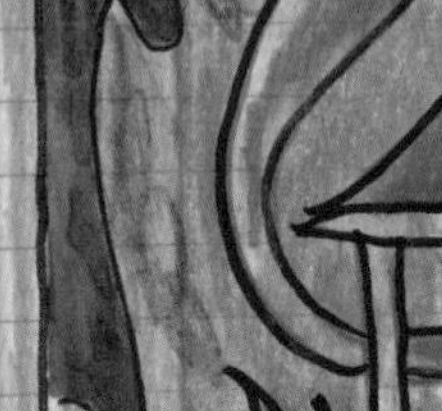

THERE ARE A LOT OF WAYS TO DRAW A BURNING HOUSE... DON'T THINK ABOUT IT TOO HARD.

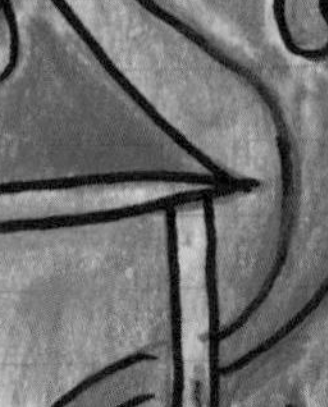

SPEND TIME ON THE COLORING PART. WHAT HAPPENS WHEN YOU LAYER ONE COLOR UPON ANOTHER?

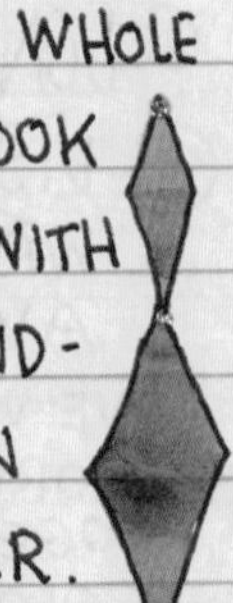

PAGE 2
CLASS #5
FEB 6
2013

HOMEWORK FOR MON FEB 11th 2013

- ☐ FIGURE OUT WHICH OF YOUR CLASSMATES ARE YOUR TWO NEIGHBORS IN THE BRAIN
- ☐ COLOR THE 'SURPRISE PICTURE' USING YOUR COLOR PENCILS
- ☐ DO ONE FULL WRITING EXERCISE IN YOUR COMP BOOKS EVERY DAY (about 20 MINUTES)
- ☐ CONTINUE 4 MINUTE DIARY EVERY DAY
- ☐ 3 DEMON HEADS FULLY COLORED IN (JUST HEADS - NOT BACKGROUND)
  1. USING ONLY ONE COLORED PENCIL (WE'LL START THIS IN CLASS TODAY)
  2. USING THE UGLIEST COLORS YOU CAN - UGLY COLOR COMBOS - BUT COLOR CAREFULLY even when USING UGLY COLORS
  3. COLOR ANY WAY YOU LIKE. MAKE SURE YOU'RE REALLY GETTING THE PIGMENT DOWN: <u>DENSE</u> COLOR
- ☐ CHECK TUMBLR PAGE FOR 1 HOUR PODCAST TO LISTEN TO WHILE COLORING (POSTED THURSDAY)
- ☐ Be prepared to TURN IN YOUR COMP BOOKS ON MONDAY
  I will look them over and return them on WEDS FEB 13th

- ☐ FINISH THE 16 PANEL DRAWINGS WE STARTED IN CLASS

SOME OF OUR "SOUR FACES" FROM CLASS #4

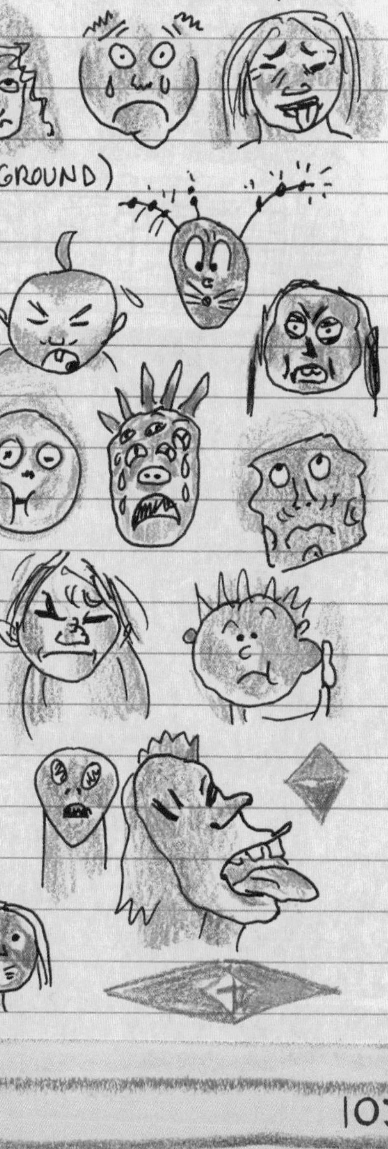

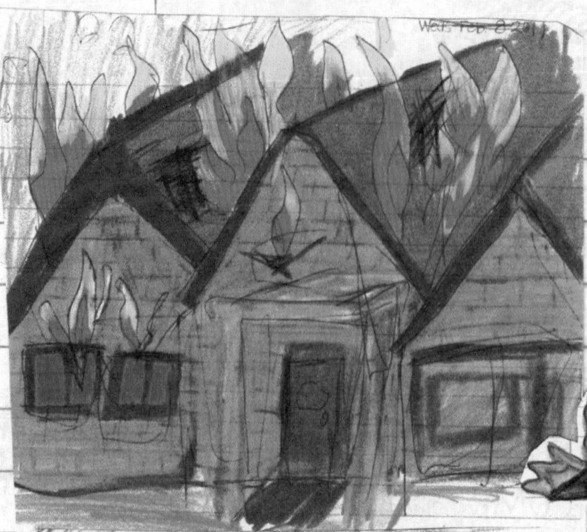

IVAN BRUNETTI POINTED OUT THAT THERE ARE THINGS ALL OF US CAN DRAW IN A WAY THAT IS RECOGNIZABLE: A CAR, A CASTLE, A CAT. A HOUSE ON FIRE IS ONE OF THESE THINGS.

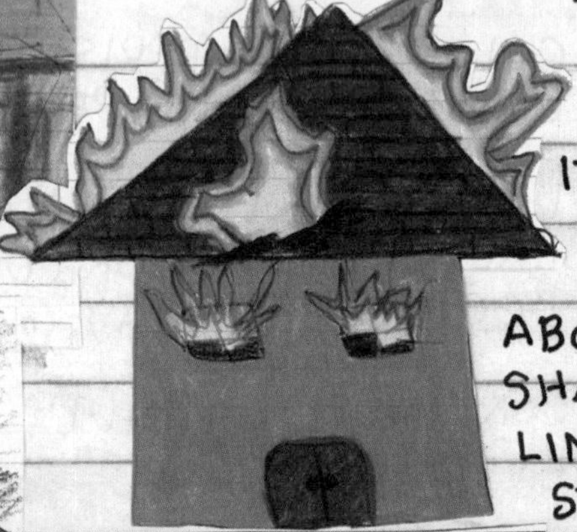

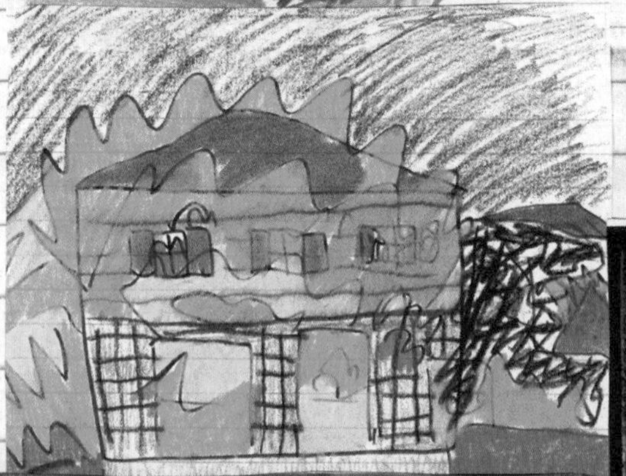

WITHOUT KNOWING IT CONCIOUSLY, WE ALL HAVE IDEAS ABOUT DOOR SHAPES, ROOF-LINES, WINDOW STYLES, AND THE COLOR AND NATURE OF FIRE. THERE IS ALSO THE MATTER OF WHERE THE VIEWER IS STANDING: POINT OF VIEW. ALL OF THESE THINGS SHOW UP WITHOUT EFFORT— THEY ARE ALREADY IN US.

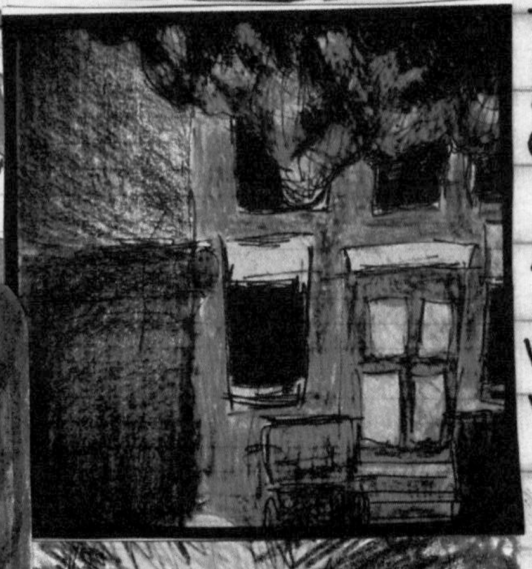

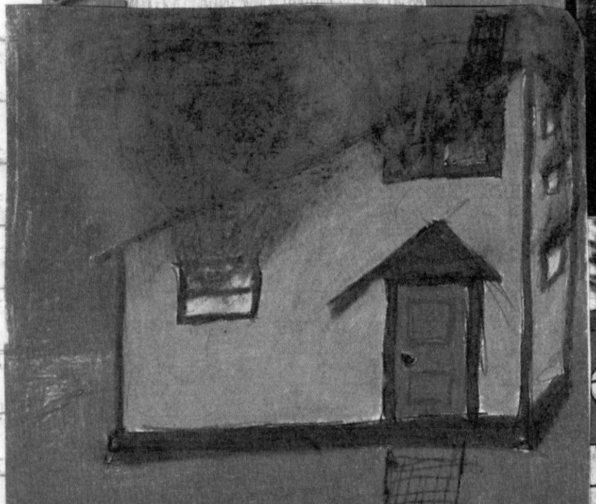

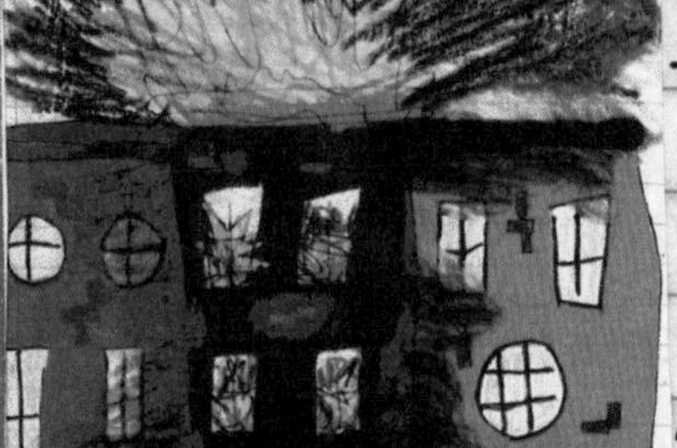

HOUSE ON FIRE DRAWINGS BY "WHAT IT IS" CLASS, SPRING 2012

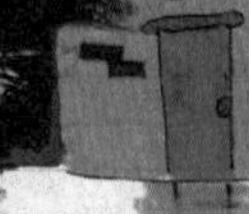
Shit House on fire!!

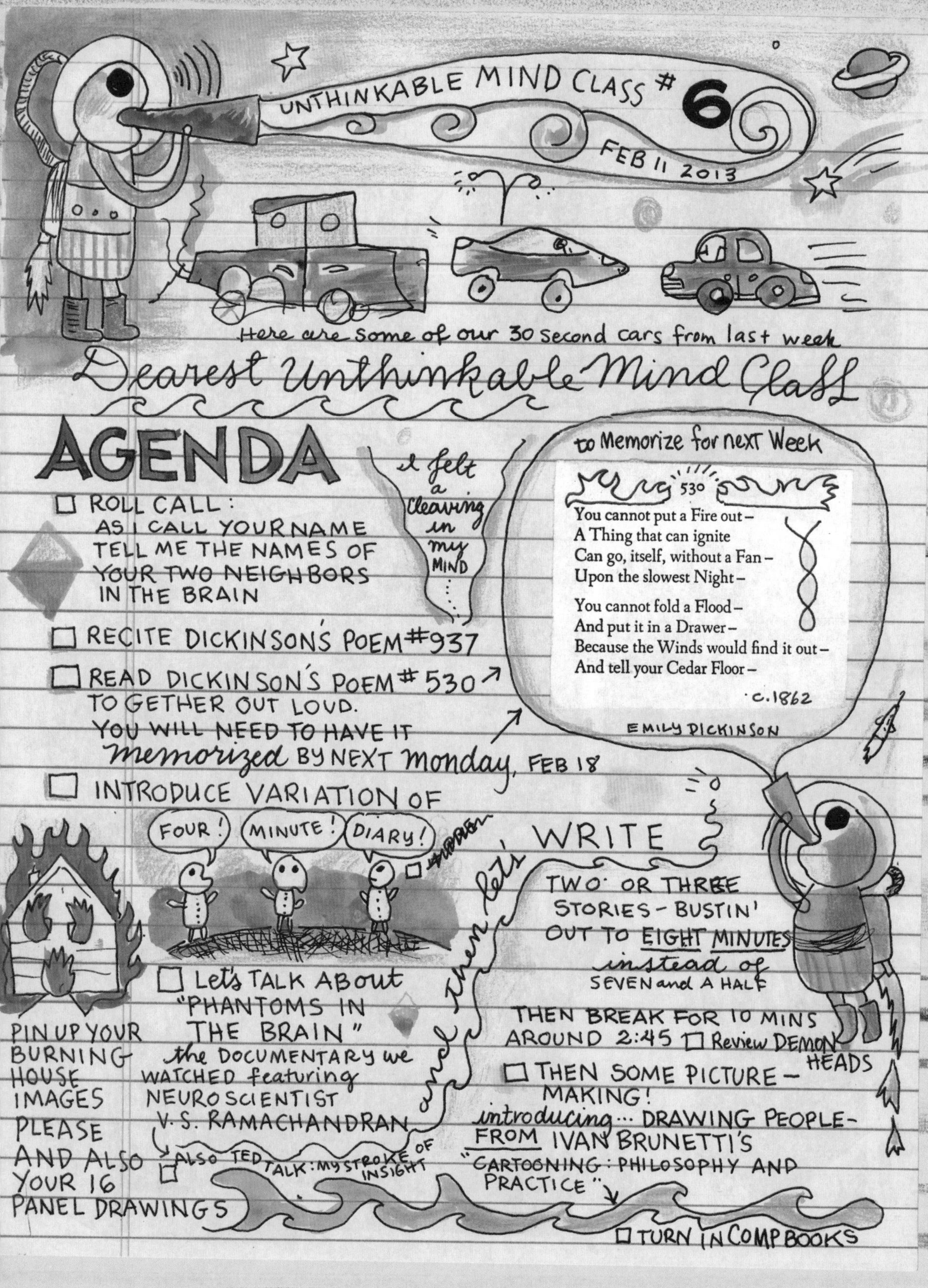
UNTHINKABLE MIND CLASS #6
FEB 11 2013
Here are some of our 30 second cars from last week
Dearest Unthinkable Mind Class
AGENDA
☐ ROLL CALL: AS I CALL YOUR NAME TELL ME THE NAMES OF YOUR TWO NEIGHBORS IN THE BRAIN
I felt a Cleaving in my MIND
☐ RECITE DICKINSON'S POEM #937
☐ READ DICKINSON'S POEM #530 TOGETHER OUT LOUD. YOU WILL NEED TO HAVE IT memorized BY NEXT monday, FEB 18
to Memorize for next Week
530
You cannot put a Fire out –
A Thing that can ignite
Can go, itself, without a Fan –
Upon the slowest Night –
You cannot fold a Flood –
And put it in a Drawer –
Because the Winds would find it out –
And tell your Cedar Floor –
· c. 1862
EMILY DICKINSON
☐ INTRODUCE VARIATION OF
FOUR!
MINUTE!
DIARY!
and then let's WRITE
TWO OR THREE STORIES – BUSTIN' OUT TO EIGHT MINUTES instead of SEVEN and A HALF
☐ Let's TALK ABOUT "PHANTOMS IN THE BRAIN" the DOCUMENTARY we WATCHED featuring NEUROSCIENTIST V.S. RAMACHANDRAN
☐ ALSO TED TALK: MY STROKE OF INSIGHT
PIN UP YOUR BURNING HOUSE IMAGES PLEASE AND ALSO YOUR 16 PANEL DRAWINGS
THEN BREAK FOR 10 MINS AROUND 2:45 ☐ Review DEMON HEADS
☐ THEN SOME PICTURE-MAKING!
introducing... DRAWING PEOPLE FROM IVAN BRUNETTI'S "CARTOONING: PHILOSOPHY AND PRACTICE"
☐ TURN IN COMP BOOKS

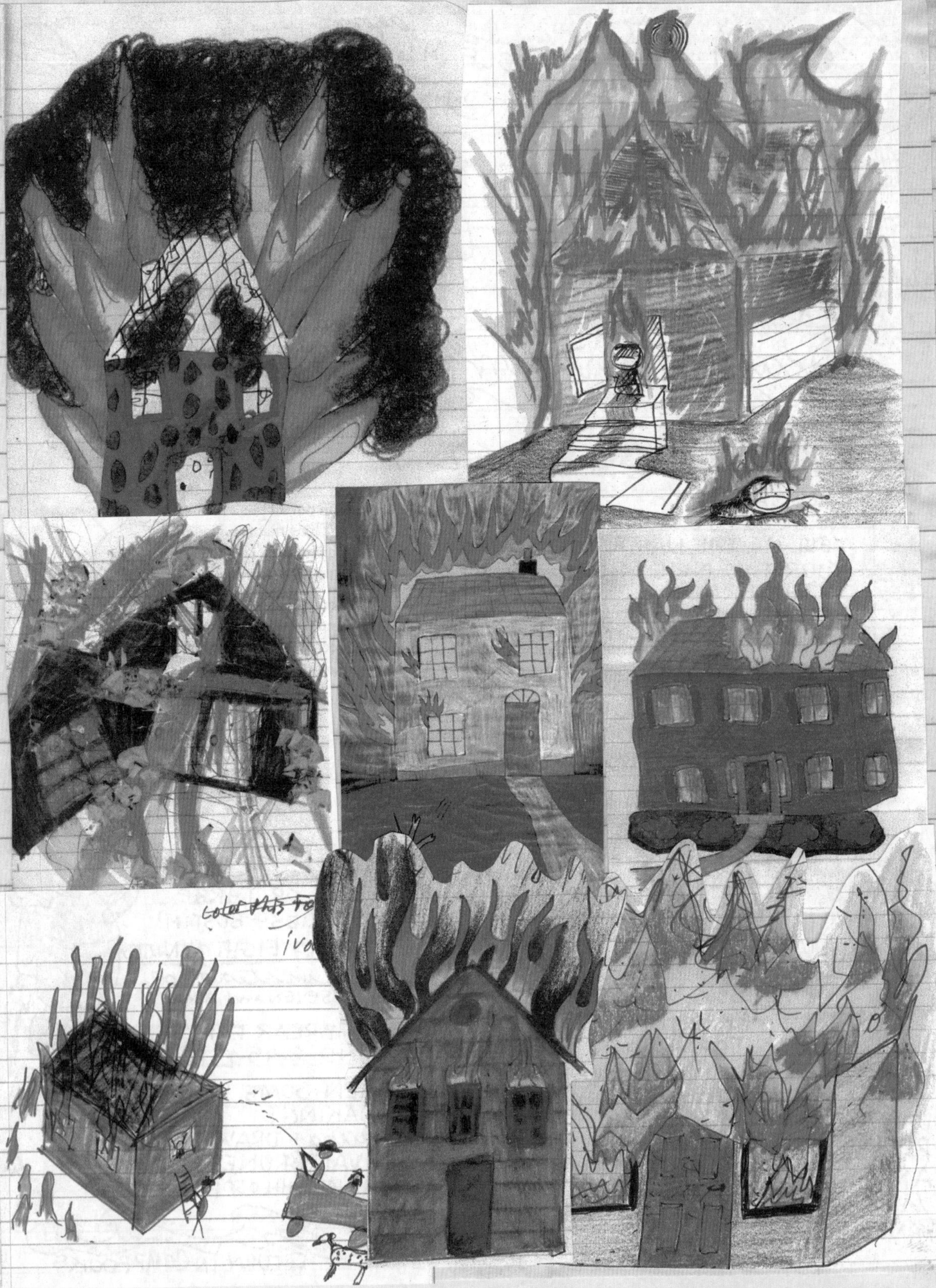

UM#6

HOMEWORK!!!

UM#6th CLASS
FEB 11 2013

FOR WEDS FEB 13

- ☐ Read the Iain McGilchrist handout
- ☐ WORK on COLORING ASSIGNMENT
- ☐ Read the new Dickinson poem BEFORE Going to SLEEP TONIGHT and TUESDAY night, saying the words out loud
- ☐ Keep up YOUR 4-minute diary using the NEW VARIATION. use ½ of Paper → SO YOU CAN GLUE it INTO YOUR comp. books WHEN I RETURN THEM to YOU ON WEDS. FEB 13

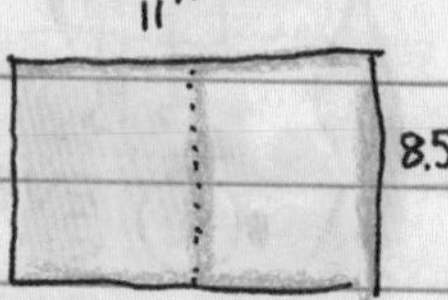

11"
8.5"

FOLD → and do your DIARY ON ½ PAGE OR it will be too large to glue into YOUR comp Book

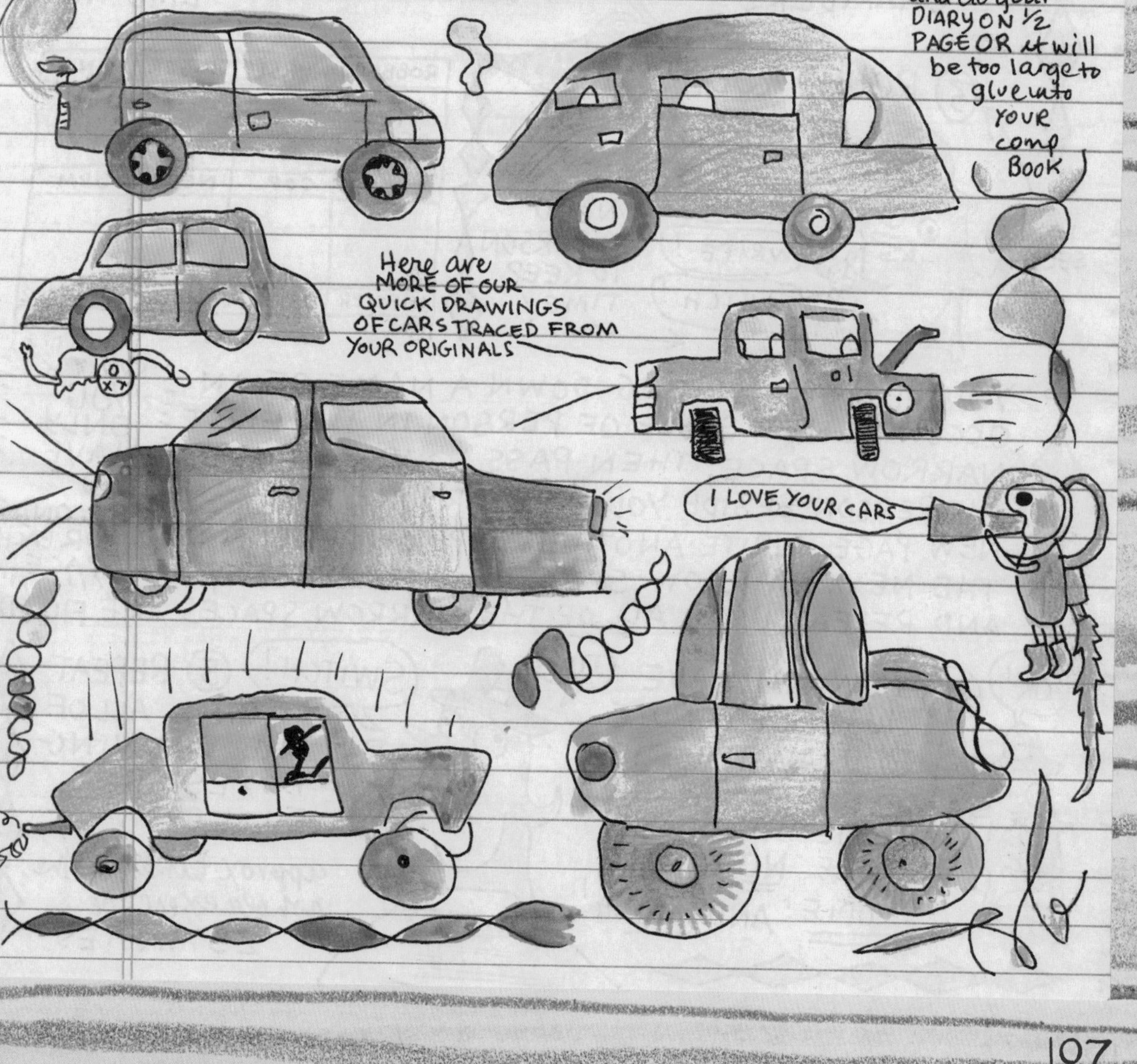

Here are MORE OF OUR QUICK DRAWINGS OF CARS TRACED FROM YOUR ORIGINALS
I LOVE YOUR CARS

EXERCISE: *the basic*

DRAWING JAM!

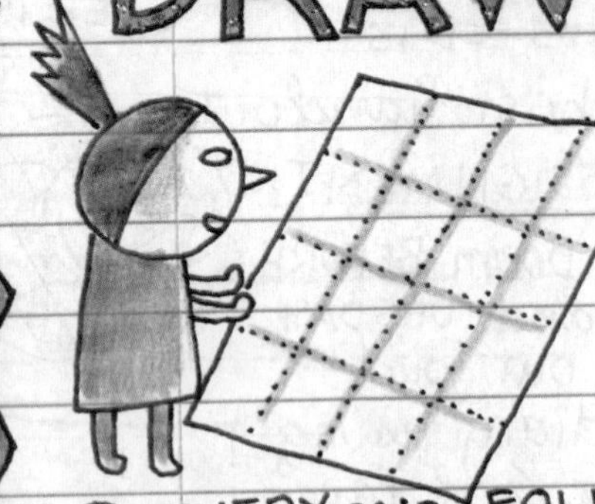

① EVERYONE FOLDS A SHEET OF 8.5" x 11" PAPER INTO 16 CHAMBERS

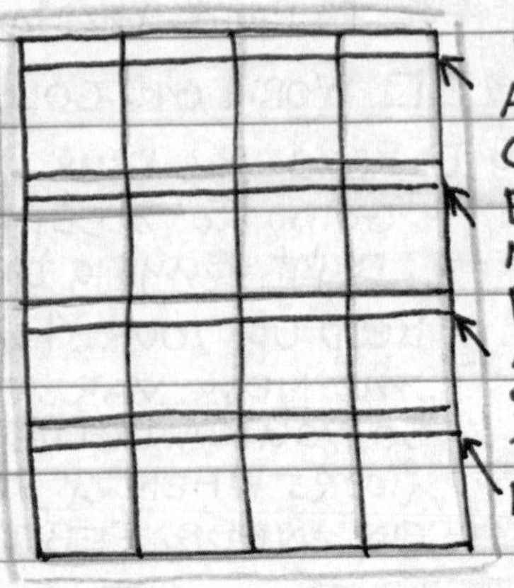

② DRAW LINES ALONG THE CREASES AND EDGES TO MAKE QUICK BORDERS AND ANOTHER SET OF LINES TO MAKE A NARROW ROW LIKE THIS

③ ROUND ROBIN!

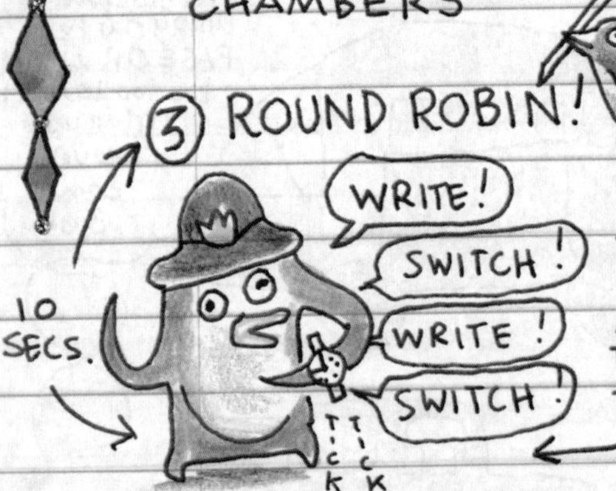
WRITE!
SWITCH!
WRITE!
SWITCH!
10 SECS.
TICK

YOU WILL NEED A PERSON TO KEEP TIME!

ROBBER	NURSE	SINGER	KING
PLAYBOY	COP	NERD	BUM
HIPSTER	DETECTIVE	JOCK	STRIPPER

→ YOU BEGIN BY WRITING DOWN A NAME OF AN OCCUPATION OR STYLE OF PERSON IN THE FIRST NARROW SPACE, THEN PASS YOUR PAPER TO THE PERSON BESIDE YOU SO EVERYONE HAS A NEW PAGE. WRITE ANOTHER TYPE OF PERSON IN THE NEXT NARROW SPACE, SWITCH PAGES, AND REPEAT UNTIL ALL OF THE NARROW SPACES ARE FILLED

QUICK! YOU ONLY HAVE 10 SECONDS FOR EACH SPACE

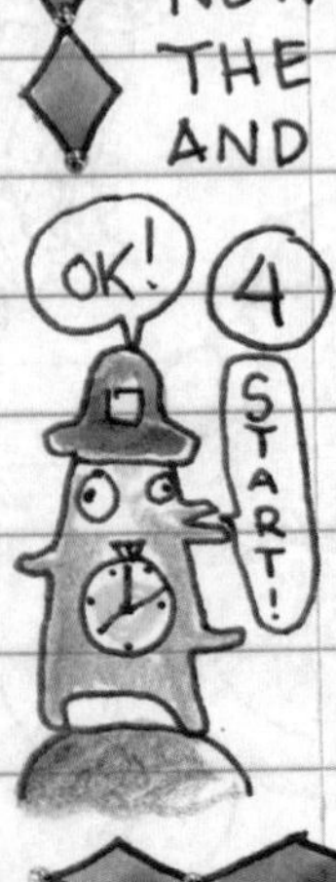
OK!
START!

④ NOW YOU HAVE JUST ONE MINUTE TO DRAW THE TYPE OF PERSON WRITTEN ABOVE THE BLANK SPACE. NO STICK-PEOPLE! AND SWITCH!

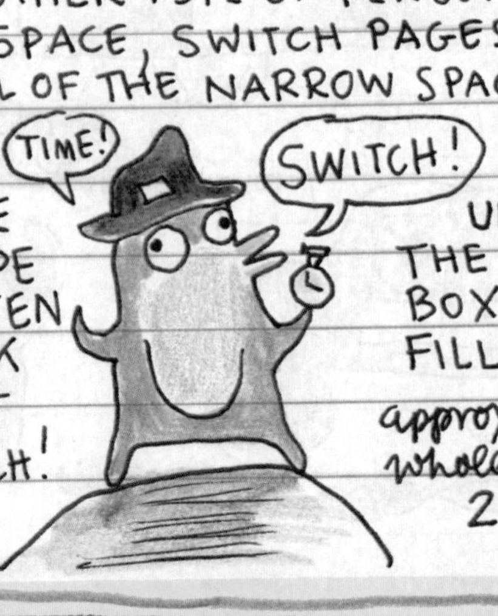
TIME!
SWITCH!

⑤ REPEAT UNTIL ALL OF THE DRAWING BOXES ARE FILLED.

approx time for the whole exercise: 25 MINUTES

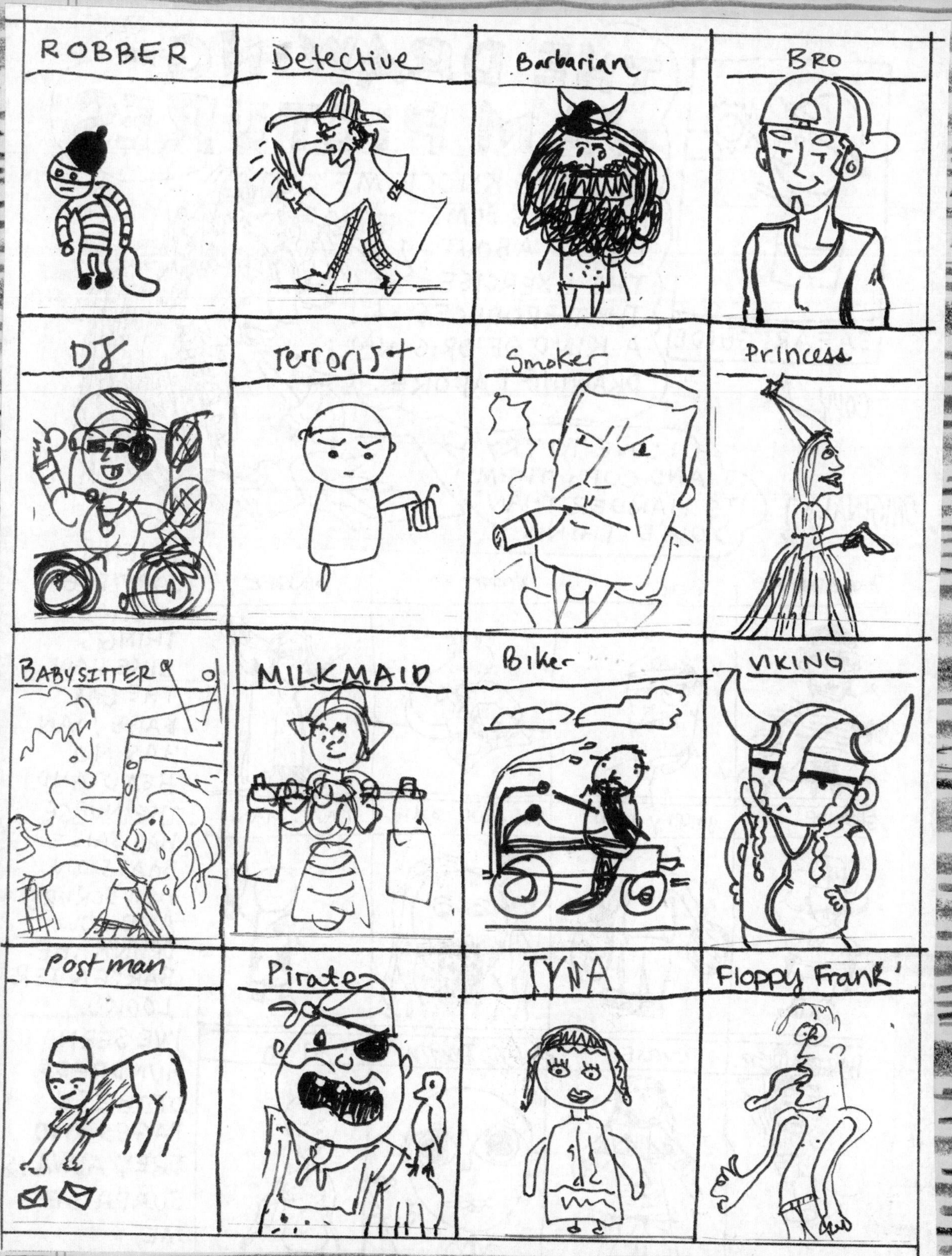
ROBBER
Detective
Barbarian
BRO
DJ
Terrorist
Smoker
Princess
BABYSITTER
MILKMAID
Biker
VIKING
Post man
Pirate
TYNA
Floppy Frank'

ACH PAGE HAS DRAWINGS AND NEW CHARACTERS CREATED BY DIFFERENT PEOPLE

THE DRAWING-JAM PICTURES

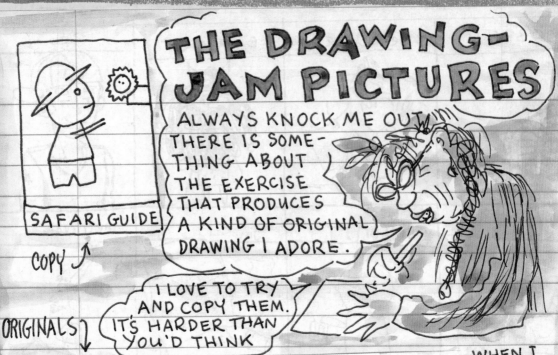

SAFARI GUIDE

COPY ↗

ALWAYS KNOCK ME OUT! THERE IS SOMETHING ABOUT THE EXERCISE THAT PRODUCES A KIND OF ORIGINAL DRAWING I ADORE.

ORIGINALS ↓

I LOVE TO TRY AND COPY THEM. IT'S HARDER THAN YOU'D THINK

ROBBER	COP	Writer	SINGER
SHERIFF	GARBAGE MAN	Bearded Lady	CAVE MAN
BARTENDER	NURSE	Evil Doctor	Alien

WHEN I COPY THEM I NOTICE THINGS LIKE HOW THE GARBAGE MAN HAS NO HEAD AND THE NURSE HAS SAILBOATS ON HER SCRUBS AND HOW DRUNK THE BARTENDER LOOKS.

I'VE SEEN HUNDREDS OF THESE PAGES AND THEY ALWAYS SURPRISE ME.

110

DRAWN IN ONE MINUTE

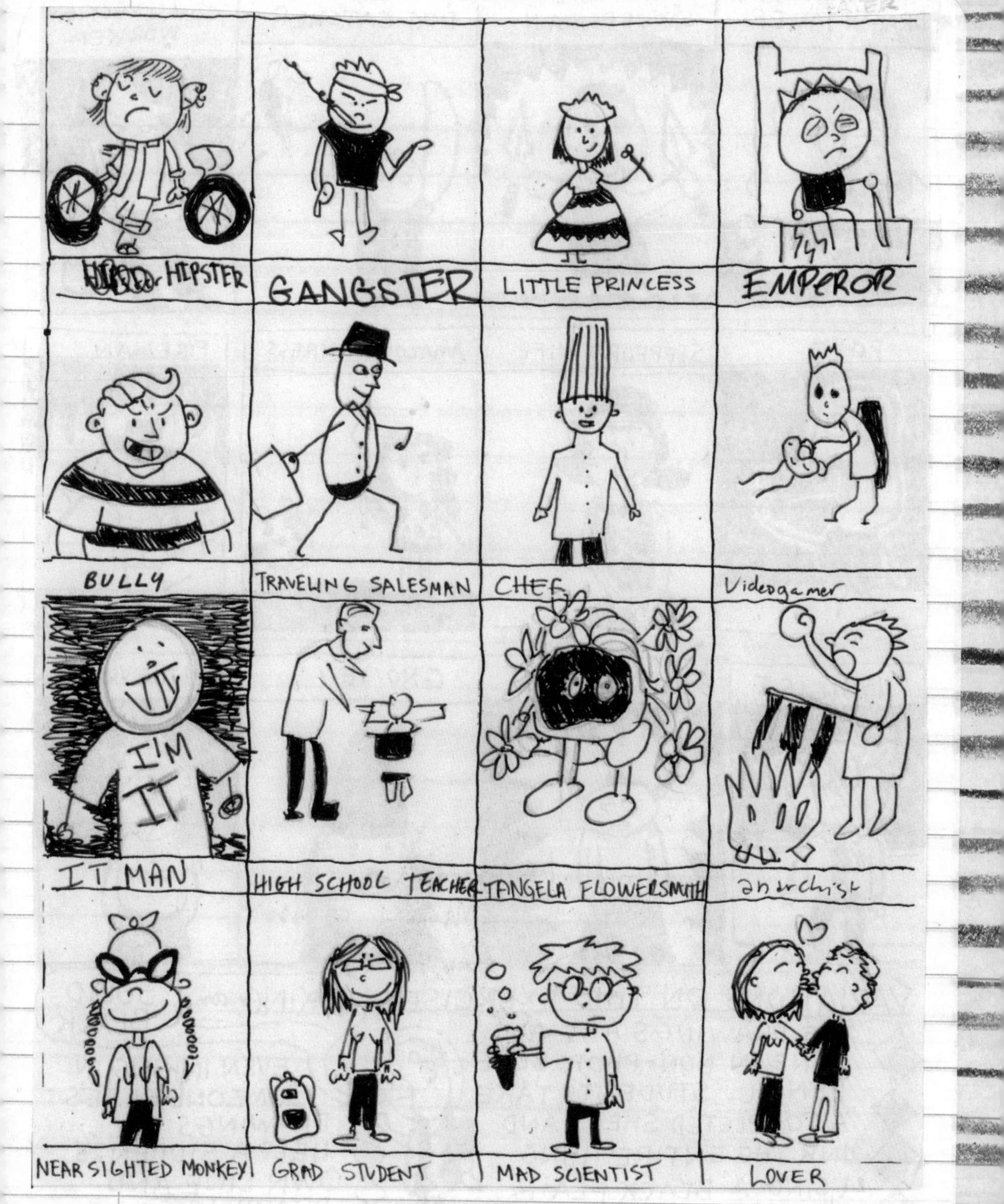
HIPSTER
GANGSTER
LITTLE PRINCESS
EMPEROR
BULLY
TRAVELING SALESMAN
CHEF
Videogamer
I'M IT
IT MAN
HIGH SCHOOL TEACHER
TANGELA FLOWERSMITH
anarchist
NEAR SIGHTED MONKEY
GRAD STUDENT
MAD SCIENTIST
LOVER

DRAWING JAM IN NON-PHOTO BLUE, INKED IN BY PREFRONTAL CORTEX

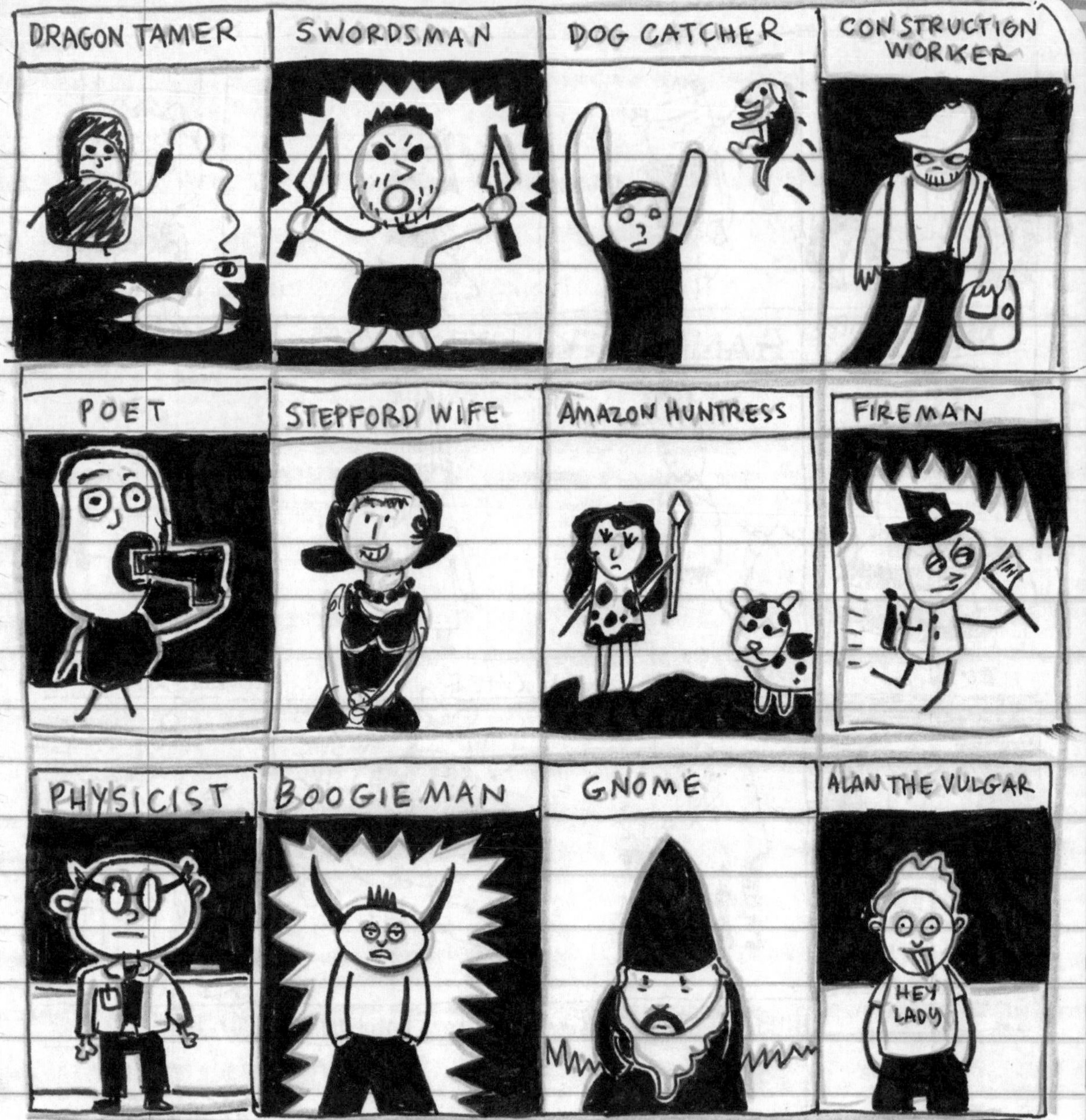
DRAGON TAMER
SWORDSMAN
DOG CATCHER
CONSTRUCTION WORKER
POET
STEPFORD WIFE
AMAZON HUNTRESS
FIREMAN
PHYSICIST
BOOGIE MAN
GNOME
ALAN THE VULGAR
HEY LADY

VARIATIONS ON THIS EXERCISE: INKING and SOLID BLACK

THE DRAWINGS ARE ALL DONE IN NON-PHOTO BLUE PENCIL. STUDENTS TAKE A COMPLETED SHEET AND INK THE ENTIRE THING USING A BLACK FLAIR PEN, MAKING SURE THERE IS SOLID BLACK IN EACH FRAME

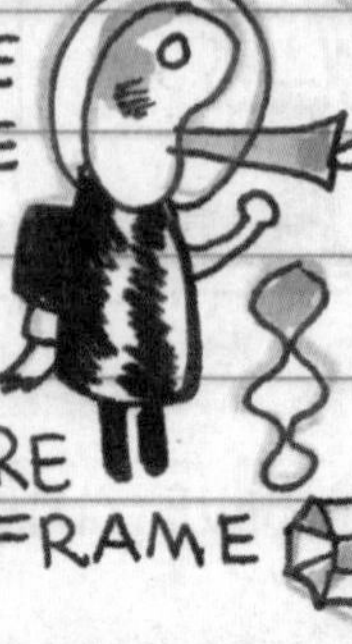

EVEN INKING IN SOMEONE ELSE'S DRAWINGS WILL HELP A STUDENT'S OWN LINE AND DRAWING STYLE DEVELOP.

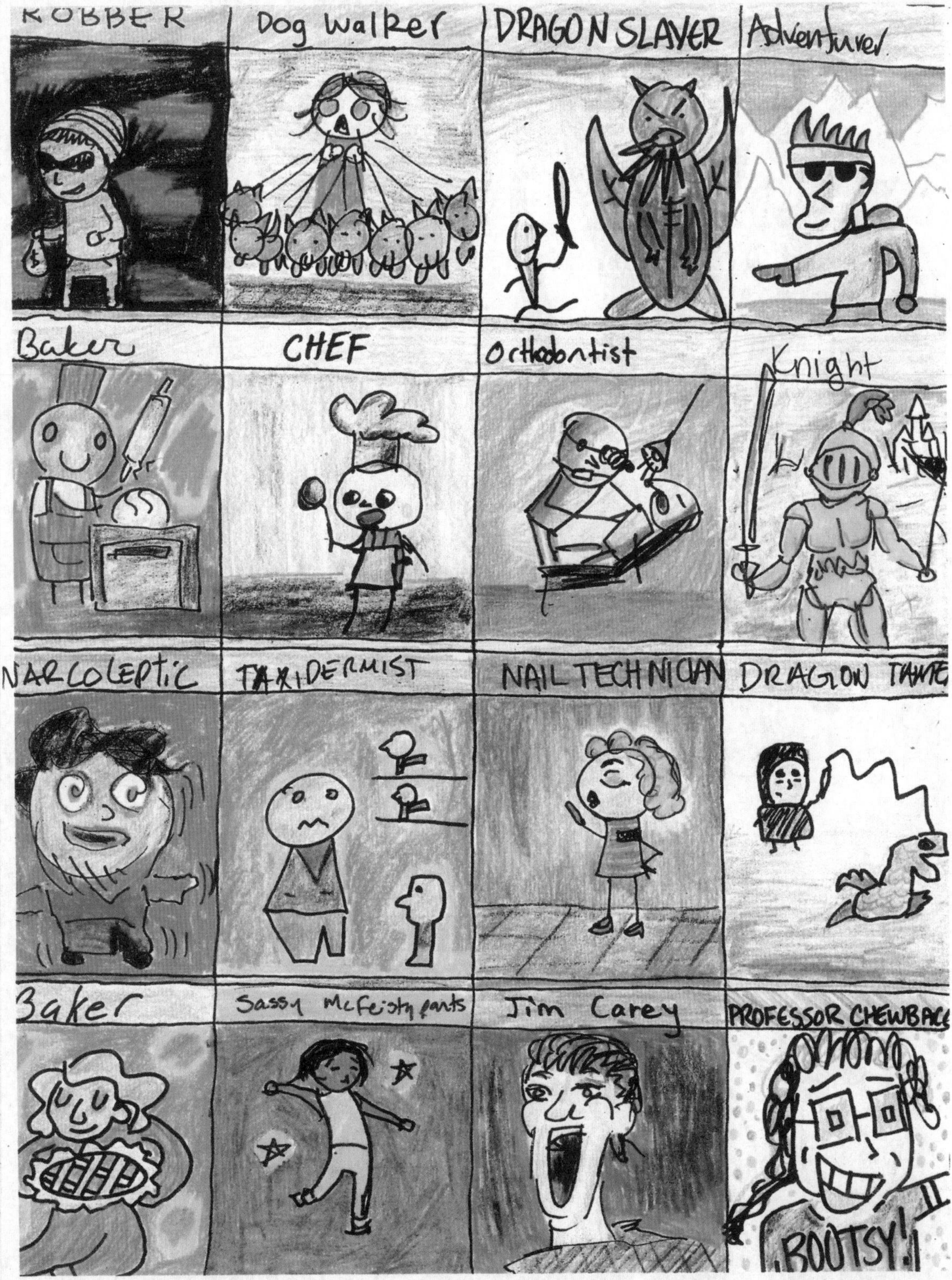

ROBBER
Dog walker
DRAGON SLAYER
Adventurer
Baker
CHEF
Orthodontist
Knight
NARCOLEPTIC
TAXIDERMIST
NAIL TECHNICIAN
DRAGON TAME
Baker
Sassy McFeistypants
Jim Carey
PROFESSOR CHEWBACC
BOOTSY!

STUDENT COLORING PAGE - MAYBE CAPTAIN UNDERPANTS - COMICS SPRING 2017

YOU CAN PRACTICE YOUR COLOR PENCIL WORK ON DRAWING JAM PAGES

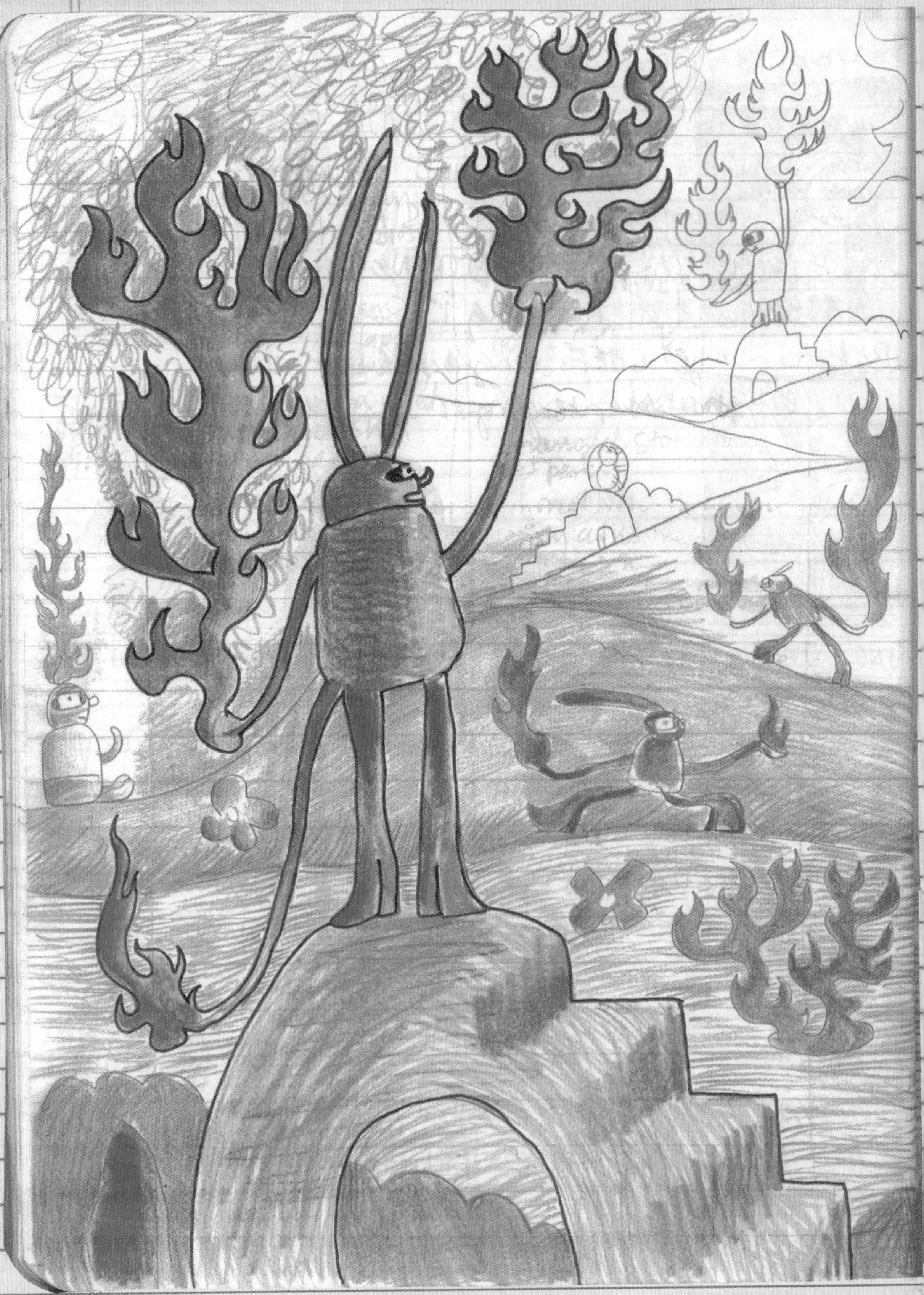

Dear Unthinkable Mind Class,

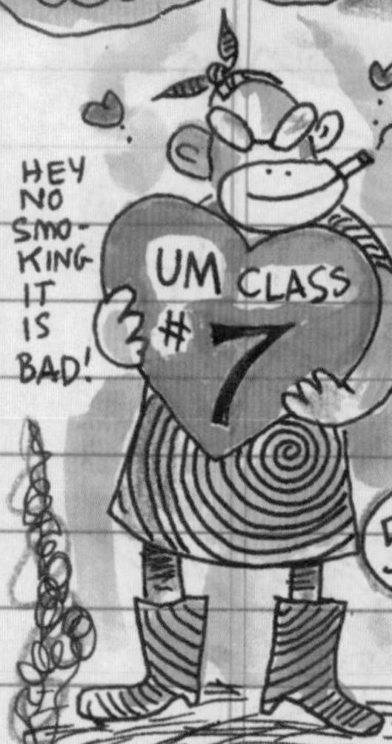
HEY NO SMO-KING IT IS BAD!
UM CLASS #7

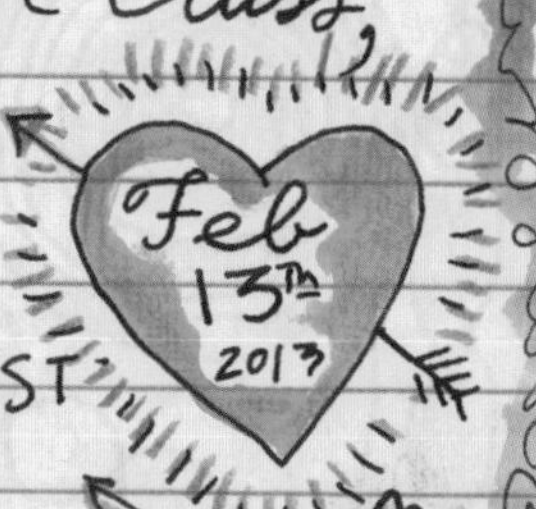
Feb 13th 2013

YOU'VE KEPT A DIARY FOR 21 days AND written 14 STORIES AND COLORED 8 PICTURES AND MADE ALMOST 56 ~~40~~ LITTLE DRAWINGS ~~AD~~ AND LISTENED TO, READ, WATCHED Brain-related material THROUGH MUCH OF IT.

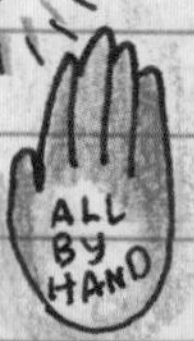
ALL BY HAND

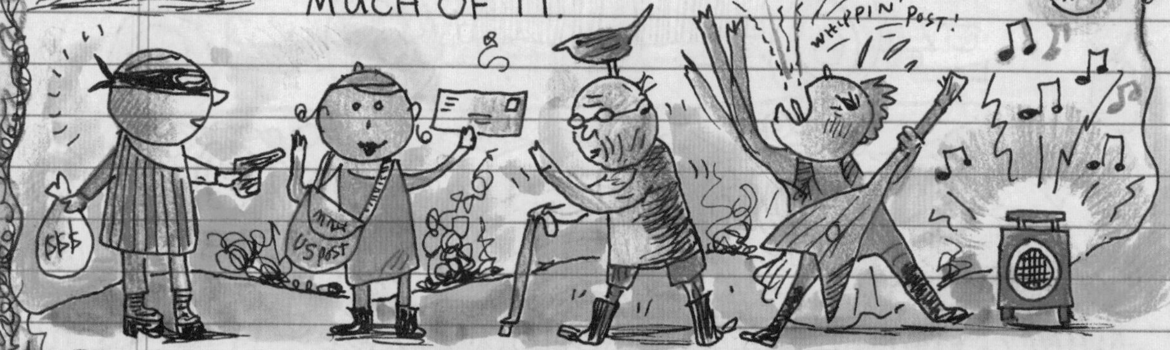
$$$
US post
WHIPPIN' POST!

DAILY PRACTICE WITH IMAGES BOTH WRITTEN AND DRAWN is RARE once WE have LOST OUR baby teeth AND begin TO THINK of OURSELVES AS good AT SOMETHINGS AND bad AT OTHER things. IT'S not that this isn't TRUE... BUT the SIDE EFFECTS ARE profound once WE ABANDON a certain ACTIVITY like DRAWING BECAUSE WE are BAD at IT. A certain STATE of MIND — (what McGilchrist might CALL "ATTENTION") is ALSO LOST. A certain CAPACITY of THE mind IS SHUTTERED AND FOR most people, IT STAYS THAT WAY for life →

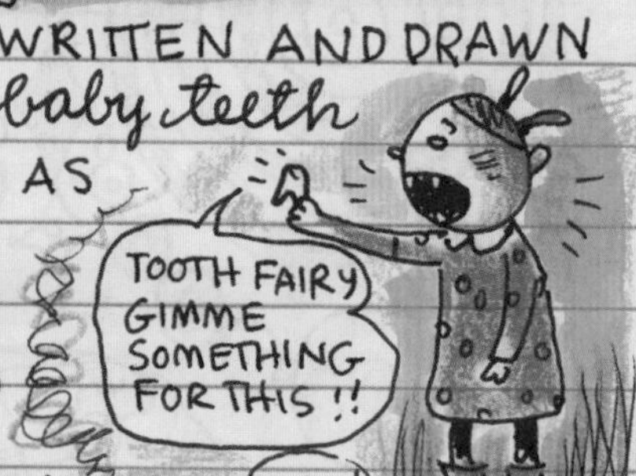
TOOTH FAIRY GIMME SOMETHING FOR THIS!!
SURE!

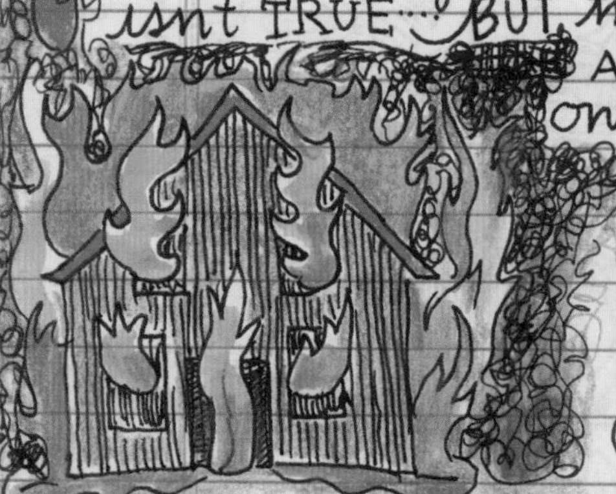

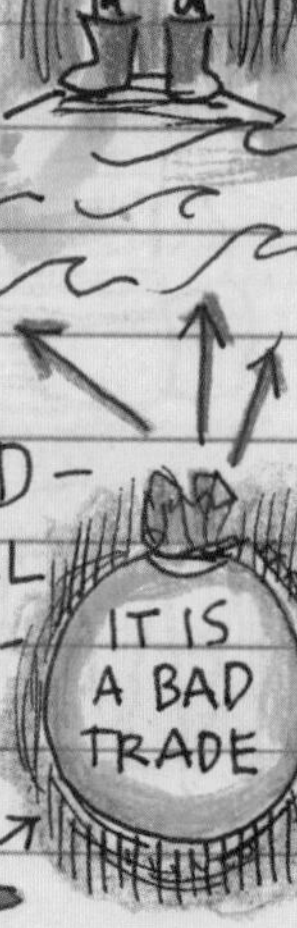
IT IS A BAD TRADE

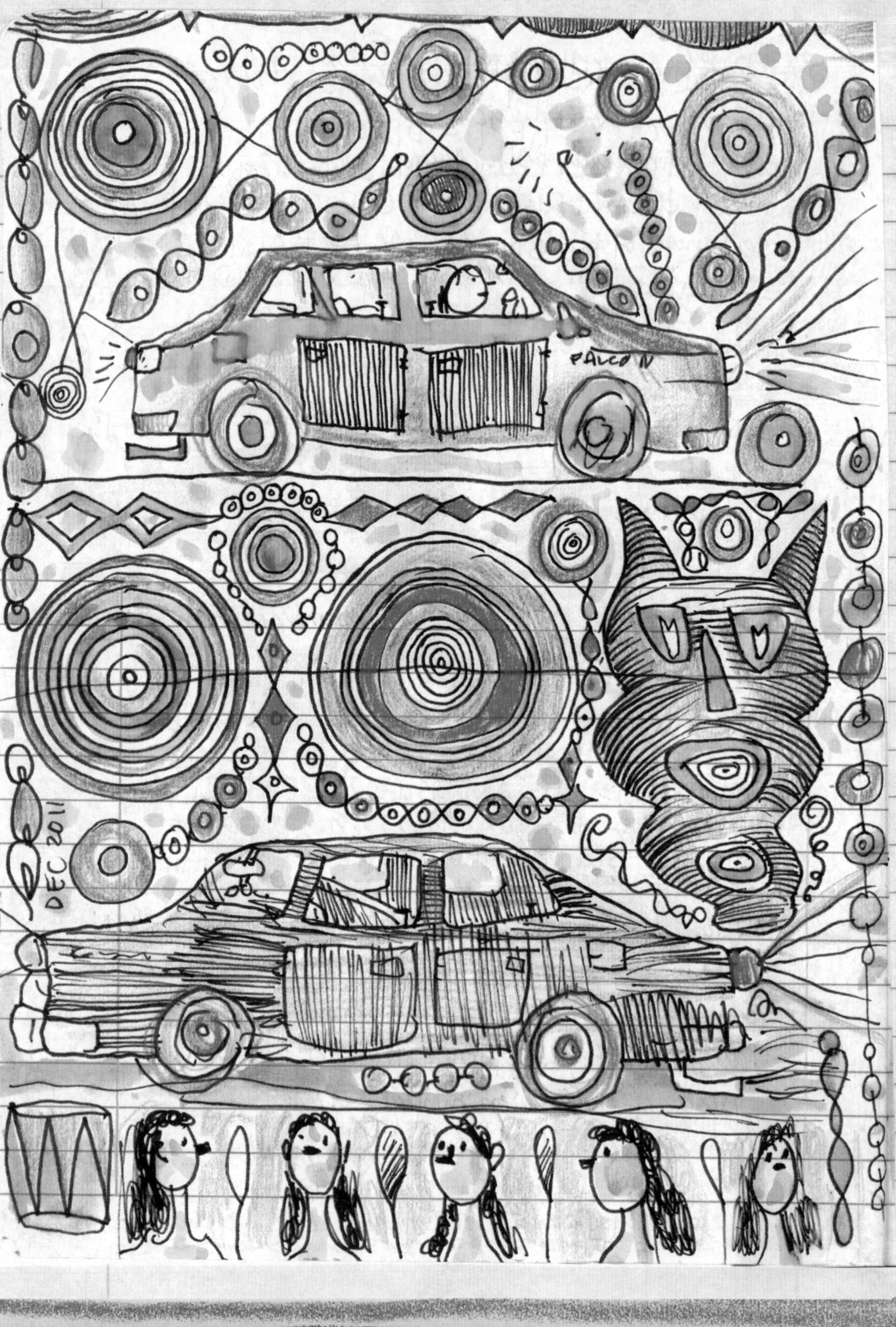
FALCON
DEC 2011

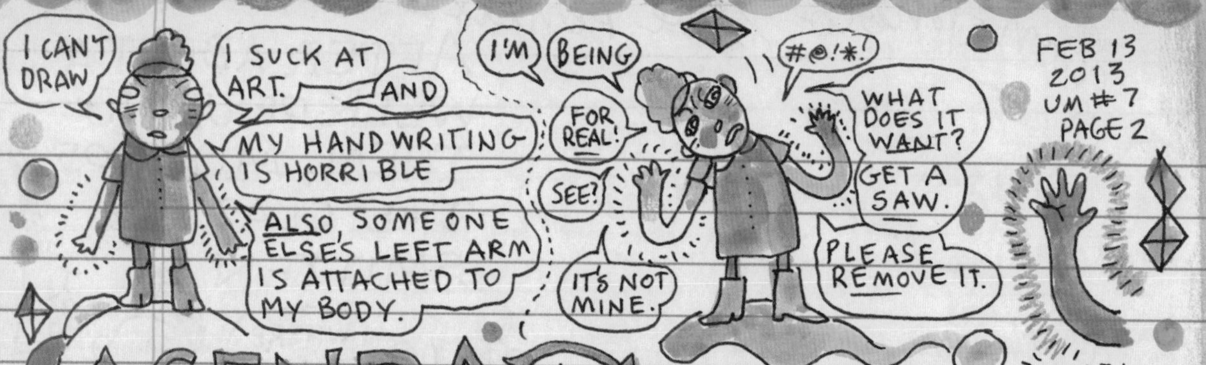
I CAN'T DRAW
I SUCK AT ART. AND
MY HANDWRITING IS HORRIBLE
ALSO, SOMEONE ELSE'S LEFT ARM IS ATTACHED TO MY BODY.
I'M BEING
FOR REAL!
SEE?
IT'S NOT MINE.
#@!*!
WHAT DOES IT WANT?
GET A SAW.
PLEASE REMOVE IT.

FEB 13 2013
UM #7
PAGE 2

WHAT DOES IT WANT?

AGENDA

NOW GET YOUR SPACE BOOTS ON

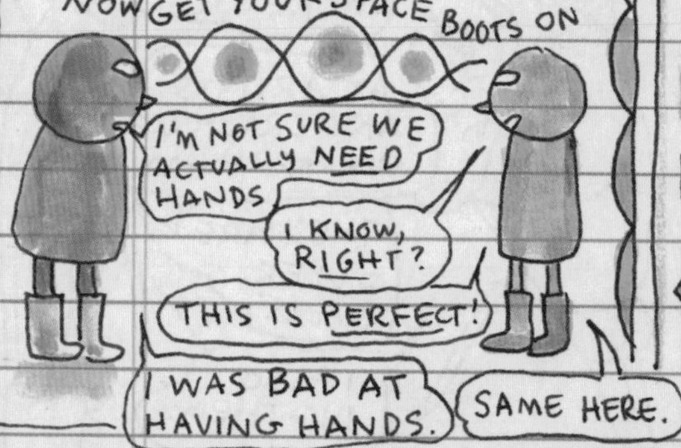
I'M NOT SURE WE ACTUALLY NEED HANDS
I KNOW, RIGHT?
THIS IS PERFECT!
I WAS BAD AT HAVING HANDS.
SAME HERE.

- VALENTINE ROLL CALL
- PUT UP A SHOW OF OUR CRAYON IMAGES AND CRAYON PHOTOS IN the HALL
- WRITING EXERCISES:
  1: TITLES OF STORIES WE HAVE WRITTEN IN ALL CAPITAL LETTERS
  2: POEMS + JINGLES
- INTRO TO NON-PHOTO BLUE PENCIL
- new Brunetti assignment
- FILM: "OFF THE CHARTS"

HOMEWORK

- DAILY STORY WRITING: CHECK TUMBLR PAGE
- TYPE UP ALL YOUR STORIES TO HAND IN ON MONDAY. STAY TRUE TO FIRST DRAFT. (YOU CAN WRITE A 2nd VERSION IF YOU WANT, BUT INCLUDE FIRST DRAFT)
- READ HANDOUTS:
  GARY PANTER ON KEEPING A SKETCHBOOK
  SHERMAN ALEXIE WHAT YOU PAWN I WILL REDEEM
- FINISH BRUNETTI PAGES WE STARTED IN CLASS

one-on-one MEETINGS WITH Prof. LYNDA AT WID

MEET ME ON FIRST FLOOR BY THE ELEVATORS. BRING YOUR COMP BOOK

Thursday	Friday
10:00 CEREBELLUM	10:00 AUDITORY CORTEX
10:45 LIMBIC SYSTEM	10:45 Hypothalamus
11:30 CORPUS CALLOSUM	11:30 AMYGDALA
12:15 Prefrontal cortex	12:15 THALAMUS
1:00 SPINAL CORD	1:00 Medulla oblongata!
1:45 OCCIPITAL LOBE	1:45 PARIETAL LOBE
2:30 BASAL GANGLIA	2:30 HIPPOCAMPUS
3:15 BRAIN STEM	OTHER BRAIN PARTS... IF WE DON'T HAVE A DATE YET PLEASE SEE ME AND LET'S MAKE ONE.

FREE ASSOCIATION ISN'T FREE.
☐ TRUE ☐ FALSE

non-photo blue pencils

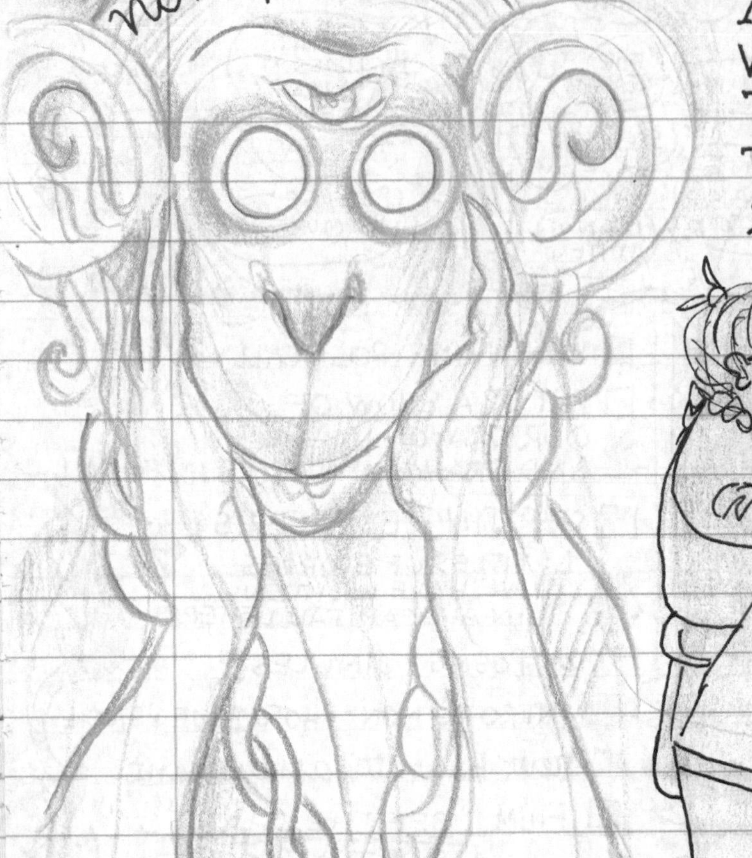

AFTER ABOUT A WEEK OF USING THEM, MOST OF THE CLASS IS SMITTEN

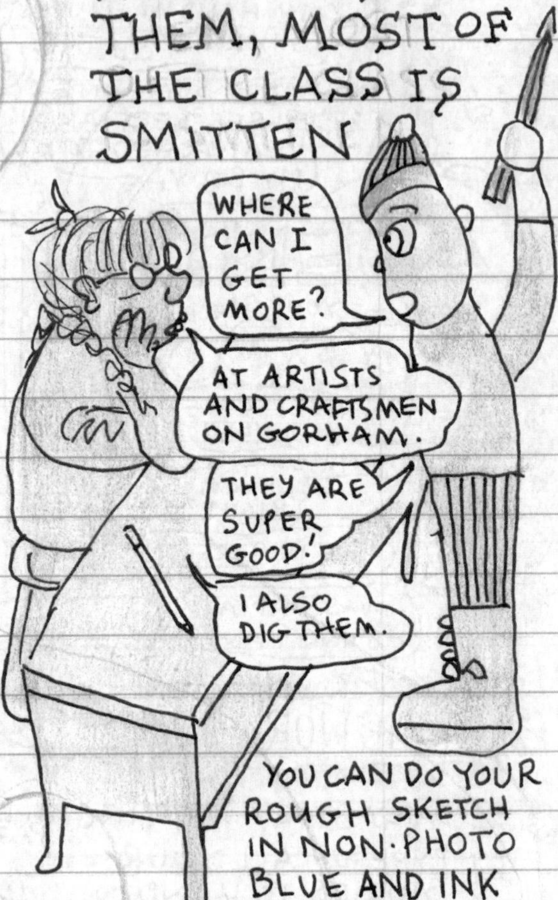
WHERE CAN I GET MORE?
AT ARTISTS AND CRAFTSMEN ON GORHAM.
THEY ARE SUPER GOOD!
I ALSO DIG THEM.

YOU CAN DO YOUR ROUGH SKETCH IN NON·PHOTO BLUE AND INK RIGHT ON TOP OF IT. WHEN YOU RUN IT THROUGH A BLACK + WHITE PHOTO-COPIER, THE BLUE DISAPPEARS, LEAVING ONLY THE BLACK.

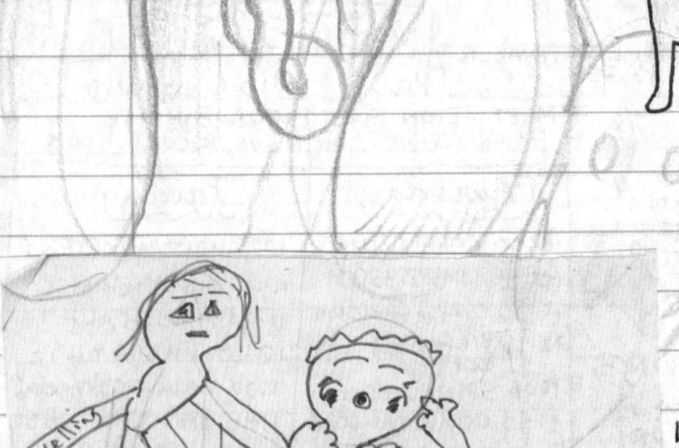
ARM 4 YELLING
TIMMY STAY OUT OF THE HOUSE!

IT'S NOT USED AS MUCH AS IT WAS IN THE OLD DAYS BUT THERE IS SOMETHING ABOUT IT THAT CAN MAKE DRAWING SOMETHING EASIER AND MORE SPONTANEOUS. I'M NOT SURE WHY, BUT IT'S SO.

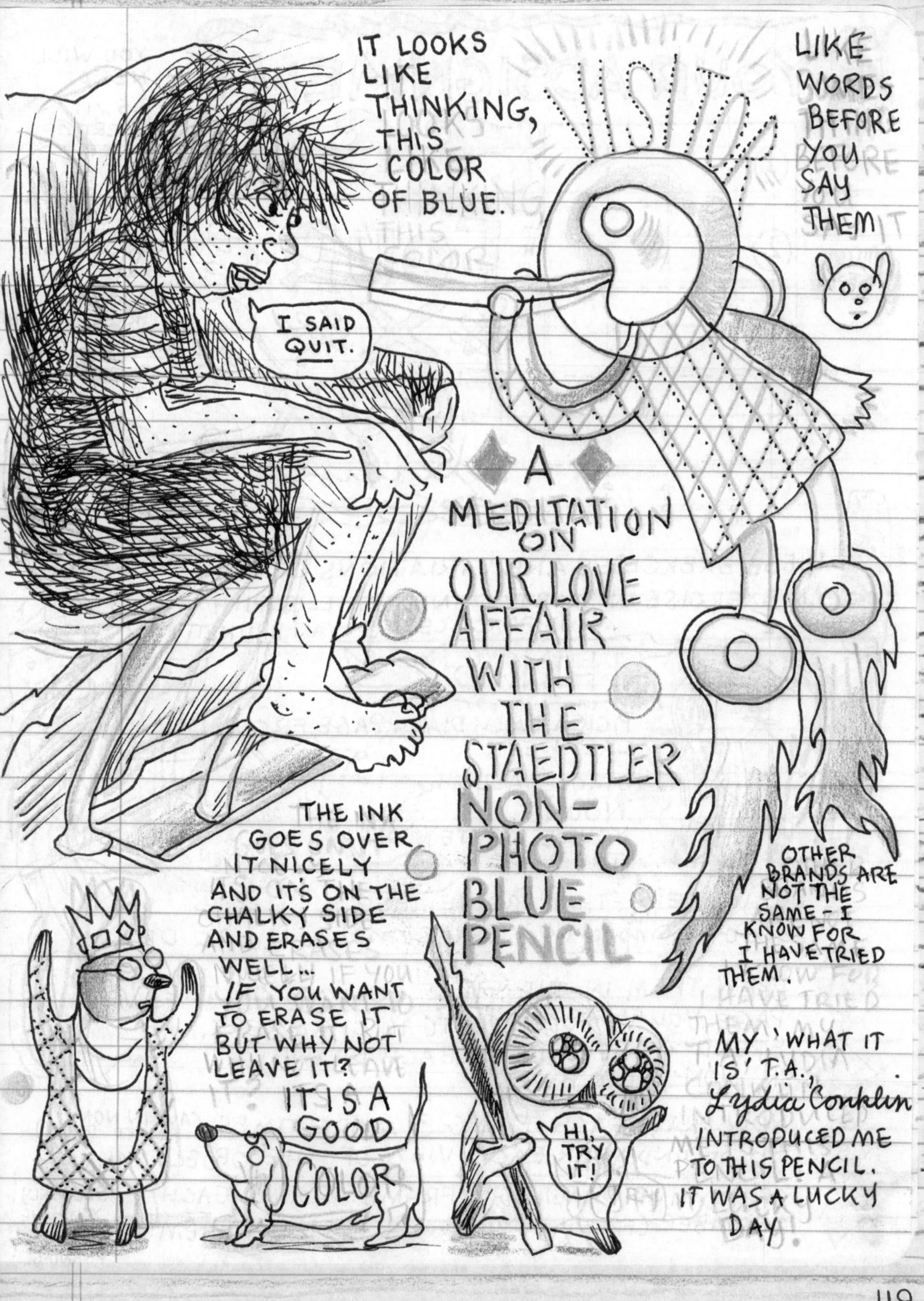
IT LOOKS LIKE THINKING, THIS COLOR OF BLUE.
VISITOR
LIKE WORDS BEFORE YOU SAY THEM
I SAID QUIT.
A MEDITATION ON OUR LOVE AFFAIR WITH THE STAEDTLER NON-PHOTO BLUE PENCIL
THE INK GOES OVER IT NICELY AND IT'S ON THE CHALKY SIDE AND ERASES WELL... IF YOU WANT TO ERASE IT BUT WHY NOT LEAVE IT?
OTHER BRANDS ARE NOT THE SAME - I KNOW FOR I HAVE TRIED THEM.
IT IS A GOOD COLOR
HI, TRY IT!
MY 'WHAT IT IS' T.A., Lydia Conklin INTRODUCED ME TO THIS PENCIL. IT WAS A LUCKY DAY

YOUR ASSIGNMENT:

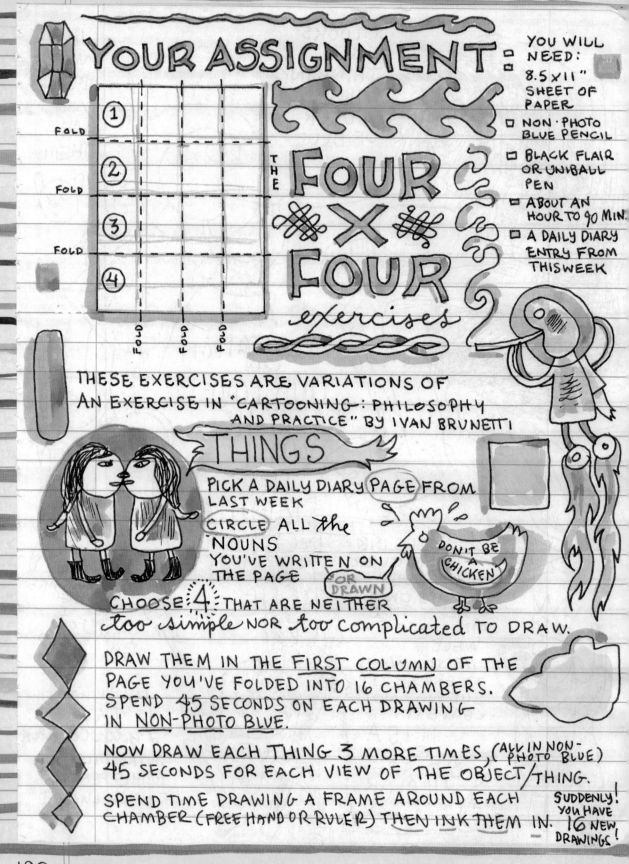

FOLD — FOLD — FOLD

① ② ③ ④

FOLD FOLD FOLD

THE FOUR X FOUR exercises

YOU WILL NEED:

- 8.5 x 11" SHEET OF PAPER
- NON·PHOTO BLUE PENCIL
- BLACK FLAIR OR UNIBALL PEN
- ABOUT AN HOUR TO 90 MIN.
- A DAILY DIARY ENTRY FROM THIS WEEK

THESE EXERCISES ARE VARIATIONS OF AN EXERCISE IN "CARTOONING: PHILOSOPHY AND PRACTICE" BY IVAN BRUNETTI

THINGS

PICK A DAILY DIARY PAGE FROM LAST WEEK

CIRCLE ALL the NOUNS YOU'VE WRITTEN ON THE PAGE (OR DRAWN)

CHOOSE 4 THAT ARE NEITHER too simple NOR too complicated TO DRAW.

DON'T BE A CHICKEN

DRAW THEM IN THE FIRST COLUMN OF THE PAGE YOU'VE FOLDED INTO 16 CHAMBERS. SPEND 45 SECONDS ON EACH DRAWING IN NON-PHOTO BLUE.

NOW DRAW EACH THING 3 MORE TIMES, (ALL IN NON-PHOTO BLUE) 45 SECONDS FOR EACH VIEW OF THE OBJECT/THING.

SPEND TIME DRAWING A FRAME AROUND EACH CHAMBER (FREE HAND OR RULER) THEN INK THEM IN. SUDDENLY! YOU HAVE 16 NEW DRAWINGS!

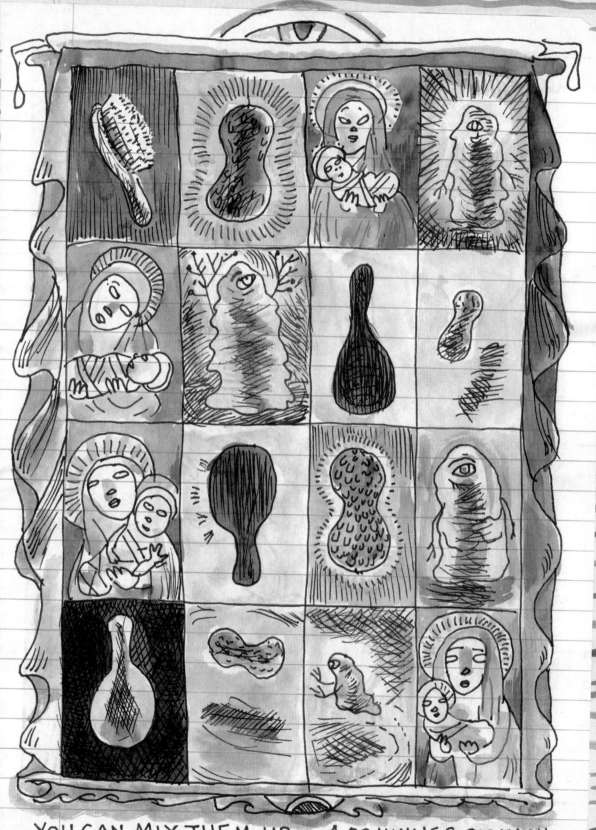

YOU CAN MIX THEM UP — 4 DRAWINGS OF EACH

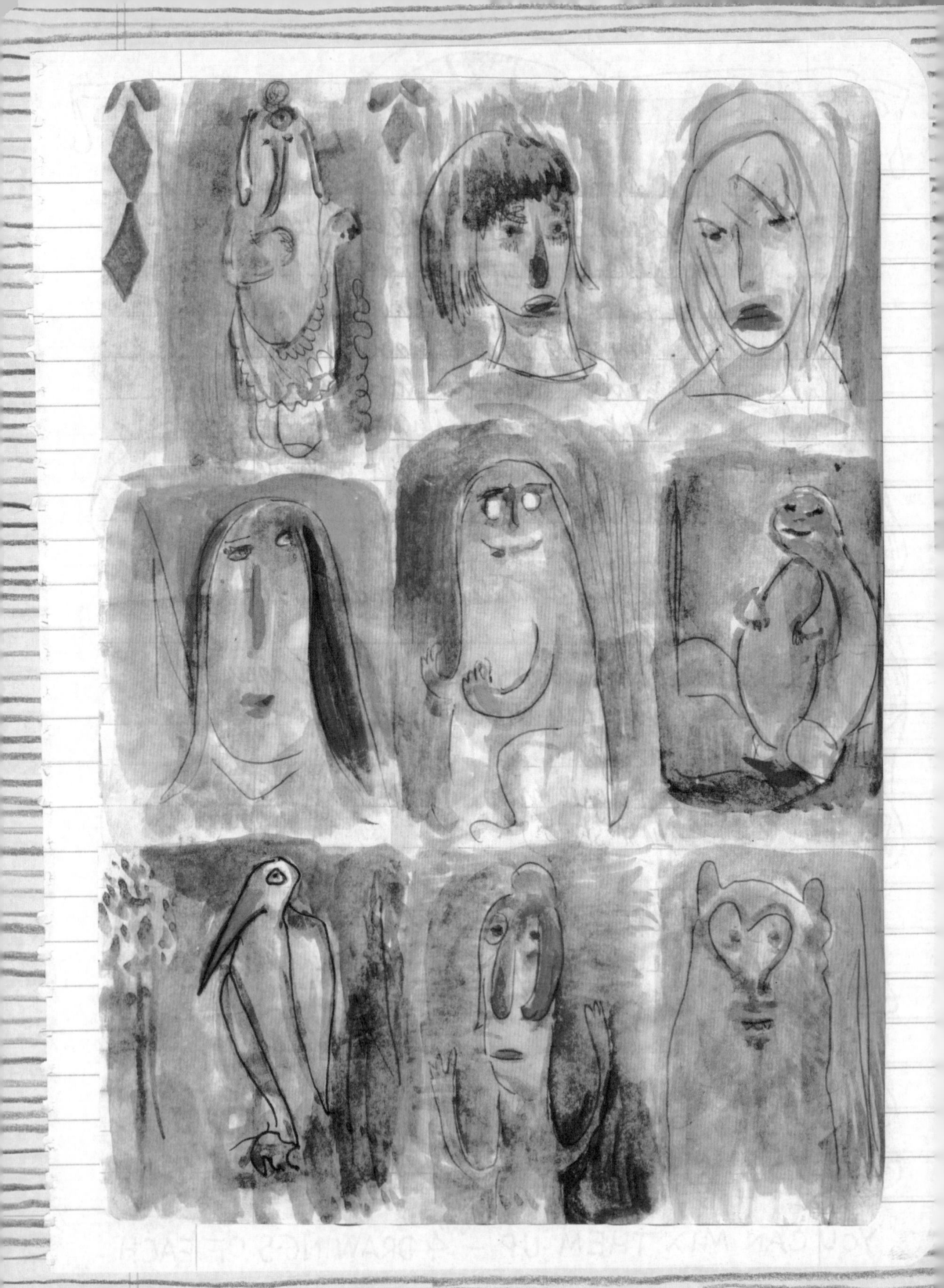

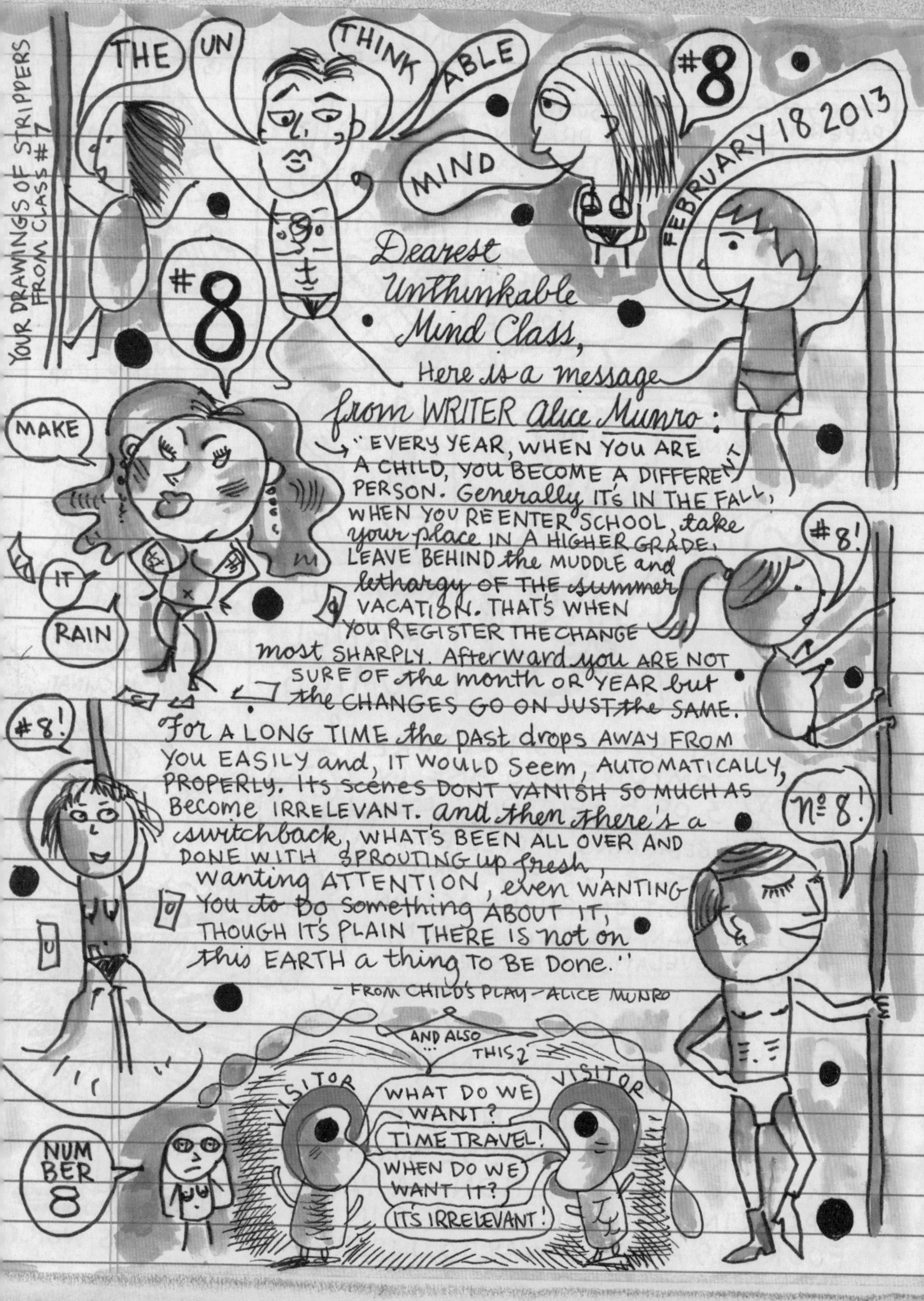
YOUR DRAWINGS OF STRIPPERS FROM CLASS #7
THE
UN
THINK
ABLE
MIND
#8
FEBRUARY 18 2013
#8
Dearest Unthinkable Mind Class,
Here is a message from WRITER Alice Munro:
"EVERY YEAR, WHEN YOU ARE A CHILD, YOU BECOME A DIFFERENT PERSON. Generally IT'S IN THE FALL, WHEN YOU REENTER SCHOOL, take your place IN A HIGHER GRADE, LEAVE BEHIND the MUDDLE and lethargy OF THE summer VACATION. THAT'S WHEN YOU REGISTER THE CHANGE most SHARPLY. AfterWard you ARE NOT SURE OF the month OR YEAR but the CHANGES GO ON JUST the SAME. For A LONG TIME the past drops AWAY FROM YOU EASILY and, IT WOULD Seem, AUTOMATICALLY, PROPERLY. Its scenes DONT VANISH SO MUCH AS Become IRRELEVANT. and then there's a switchback, WHAT'S BEEN ALL OVER AND DONE WITH SPROUTING up fresh, wanting ATTENTION, even WANTING You to Do something ABOUT IT, THOUGH IT'S PLAIN THERE IS not on this EARTH a thing TO BE Done."
- FROM CHILD'S PLAY - ALICE MUNRO
MAKE
IT
RAIN
#8!
#8!
Nº 8!
NUMBER 8
AND ALSO ... THIS
VISITOR
VISITOR
WHAT DO WE WANT?
TIME TRAVEL!
WHEN DO WE WANT IT?
IT'S IRRELEVANT!

DRAWING JAM VARIATIONS

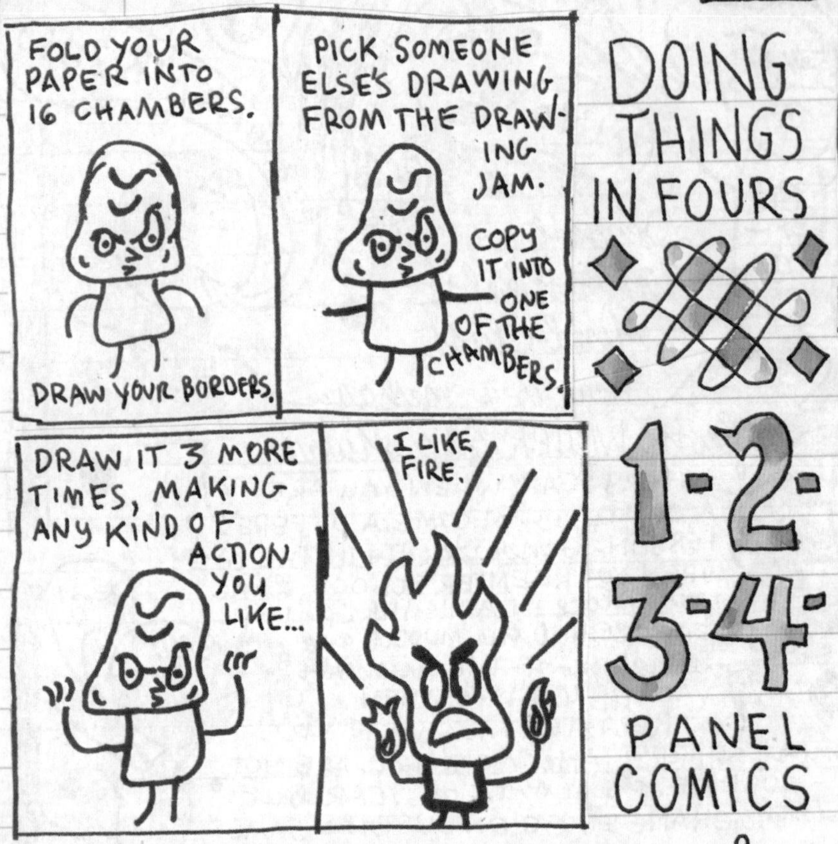

FOLD YOUR PAPER INTO 16 CHAMBERS.
DRAW YOUR BORDERS.
PICK SOMEONE ELSE'S DRAWING FROM THE DRAWING JAM.
COPY IT INTO ONE OF THE CHAMBERS.
DRAW IT 3 MORE TIMES, MAKING ANY KIND OF ACTION YOU LIKE...
I LIKE FIRE.

DOING THINGS IN FOURS

1-2-3-4- PANEL COMICS

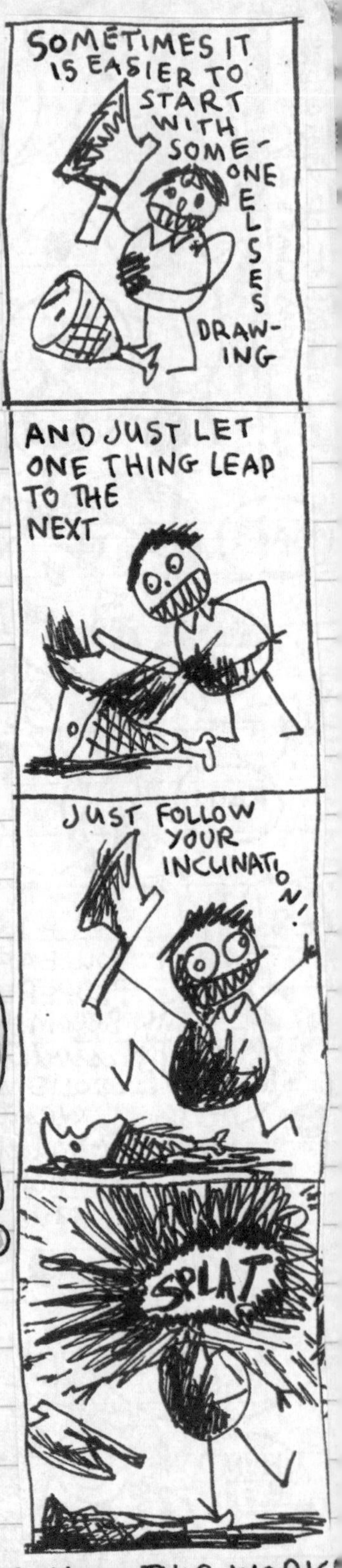

SOMETIMES IT IS EASIER TO START WITH SOMEONE ELSES DRAWING
AND JUST LET ONE THING LEAP TO THE NEXT
JUST FOLLOW YOUR INCLINATION!
SPLAT

Notice MOST STORY STRUCTURE COMPONENTS ARE IN 3 OR 5 SECTIONS

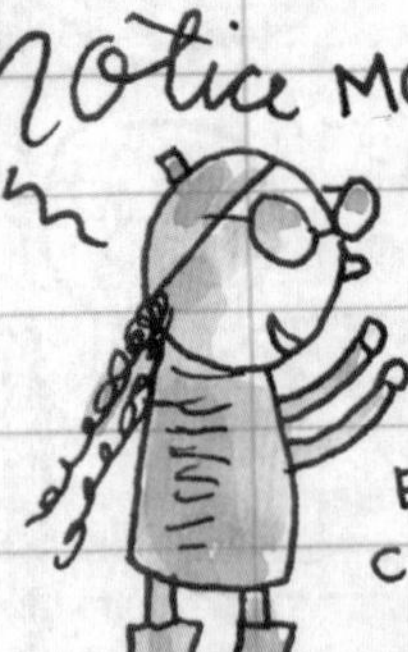

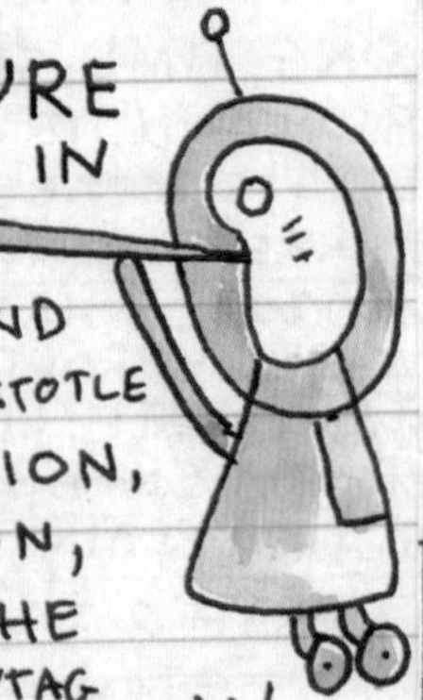

BEGINNING, MIDDLE, END
- ARISTOTLE

OR

EXPOSITION, RISING ACTION, CLIMAX, FALLING ACTION, REVELATION/CATASTROPHE
- FREYTAG

- BUT COMICS SOMEHOW FIT COMFORTABLY IN 4 PANELS
- THERE SEEMS TO BE A NEED FOR AN EXTRA BEAT - MAYBE SOMETHING LIKE A NO-ACTION ACTION - A PAUSE.
- PRACTICING DRAWING THINGS IN FOURS IS A GOOD WAY TO UNDERSTAND HOW THIS WORKS.

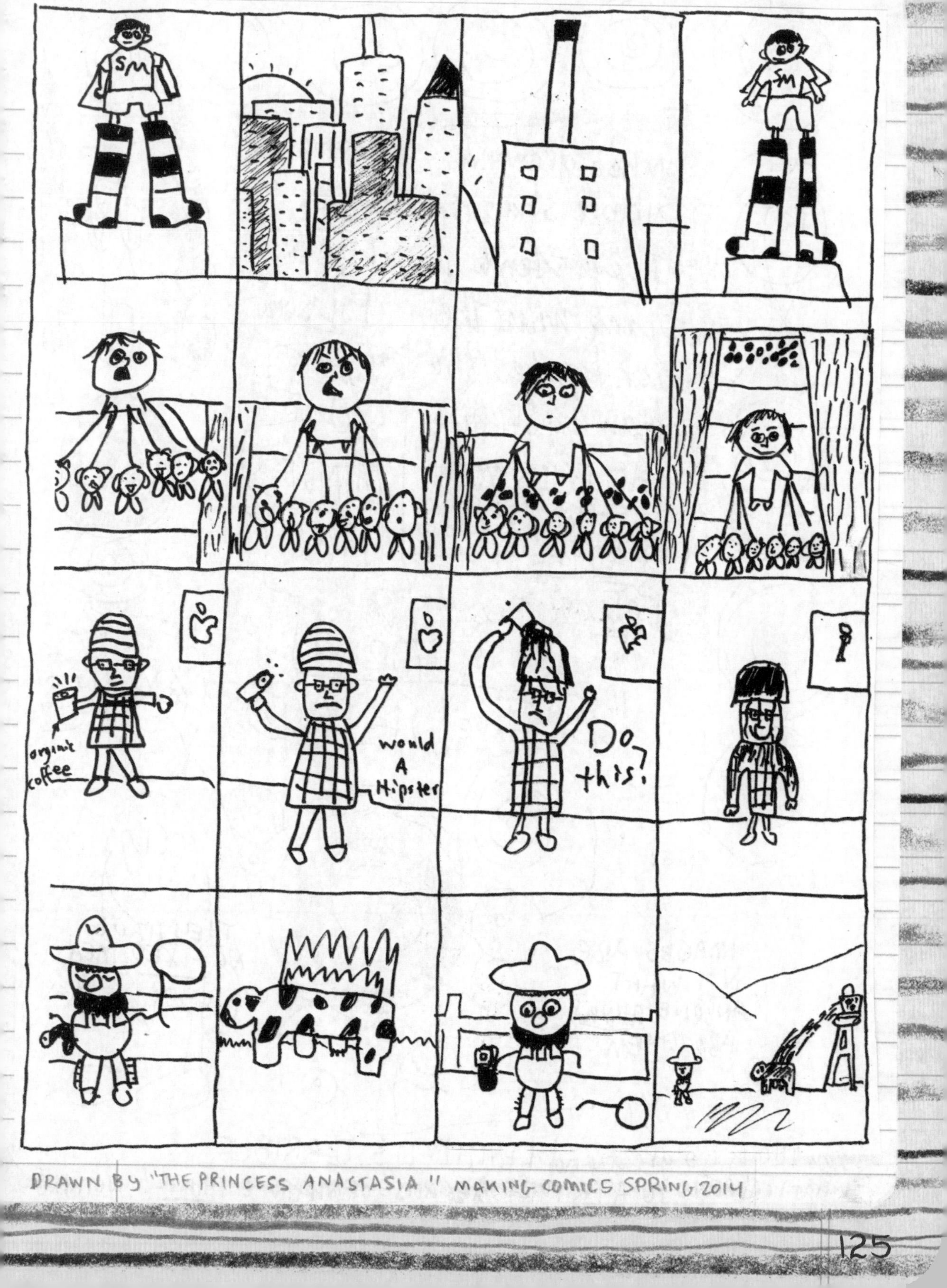
SM
SM
orginic coffee
would A Hipster
Do this!

DRAWN BY "THE PRINCESS ANASTASIA" MAKING COMICS SPRING 2014

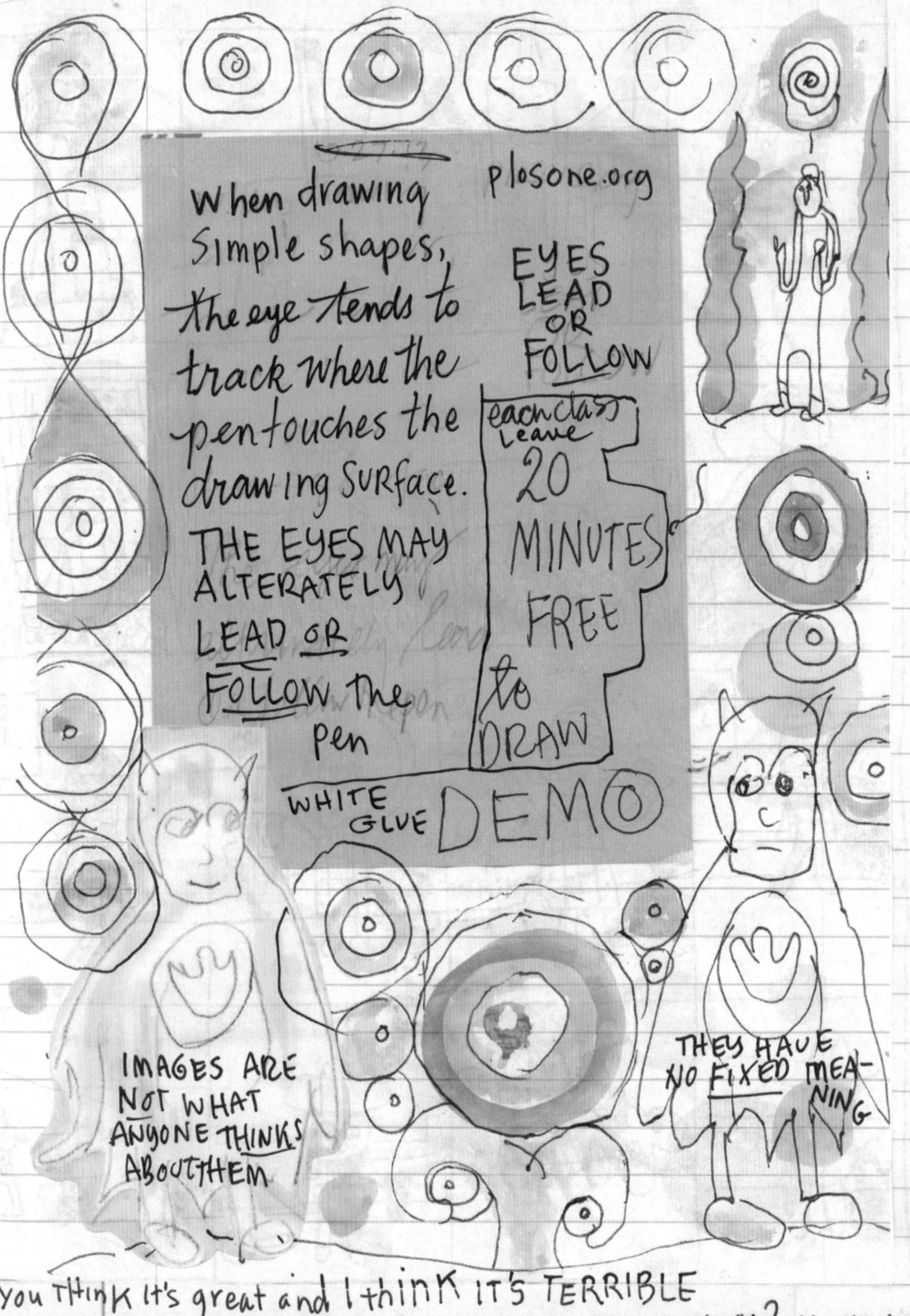
plosone.org
When drawing simple shapes, the eye tends to track where the pen touches the drawing surface.
THE EYES MAY ALTERATELY LEAD OR FOLLOW the pen
EYES LEAD OR FOLLOW
each class leave 20 MINUTES FREE to DRAW
WHITE GLUE
DEMO
IMAGES ARE NOT WHAT ANYONE THINKS ABOUT THEM
THEY HAVE NO FIXED MEANING

You think it's great and I think it's TERRIBLE
- WHAT HAPPENS TO A PICTURE BECAUSE OF WHAT WE THINK? NOTHING.

DIG IT, MAN

AGENDA!

P. 2. UM#8 FEB 18 2013

- ☐ UNFANCY ROLL CALL ☐ RECITE #530
- ☐ EMILY DICKINSON ACTION MOVIE TRAILER
- ☐ TITLES VID ☐ PREMATURE MEMORIZATON VID
- ☐ DEMON HEADS VID ☐ RECITE #530 AGAIN

Please pin up your finished Brunetti Pages + Turn in Manuscripts

- ☐ INTRODUCE NEW DIARY FORMAT FOR THIS WEEK
- ☐ ~~one~~ WRITING EXERCISE
  - ☐ ~~INTRODUCTION TO WATERCOLOR~~
  - ☐ ~~PRACTICE WATERCOLOR~~

WHILE LISTENING TO *"The Fourth State of Matter"* by Jo Ann Beard – READ ALOUD TO YOU BY

ROCK AND ROLL

SOME OF YOUR PICTURES OF PICTURES OF PROF. OLD SKULL

HOMEWORK

- ☐ KEEP YOUR DIARY PRACTICE GOING W/ NEW FORMAT:
  - ONE "X" PAGE PER DAY and NOTICE (10) ROUND THINGS AND LIST THEM WITH THE 'X' PAGE
- ☐ LOOK AT the TOPS of things
- ☐ CONTINUE WATERCOLOR PAGES
- ☐ LOOK AROUND YOU
- ☐ Get Started on Reading the IVAN BRUNETTI BOOK – intro + syllabus :-) – IT'S FOR NEXT WEEK

LOOK UP!

OLD SKULL

WHAT IS THE DIFFERENCE BETWEEN LOOKING AND GAZING??

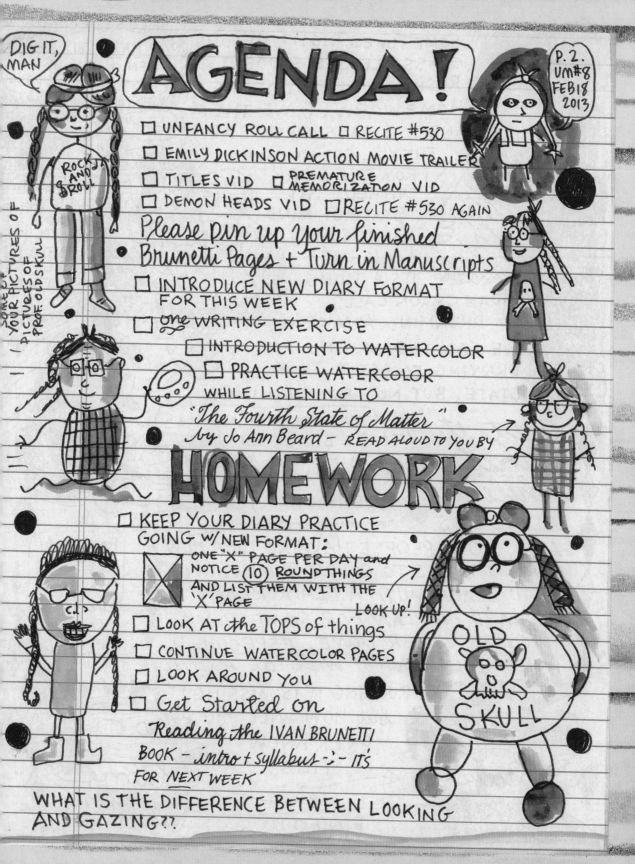

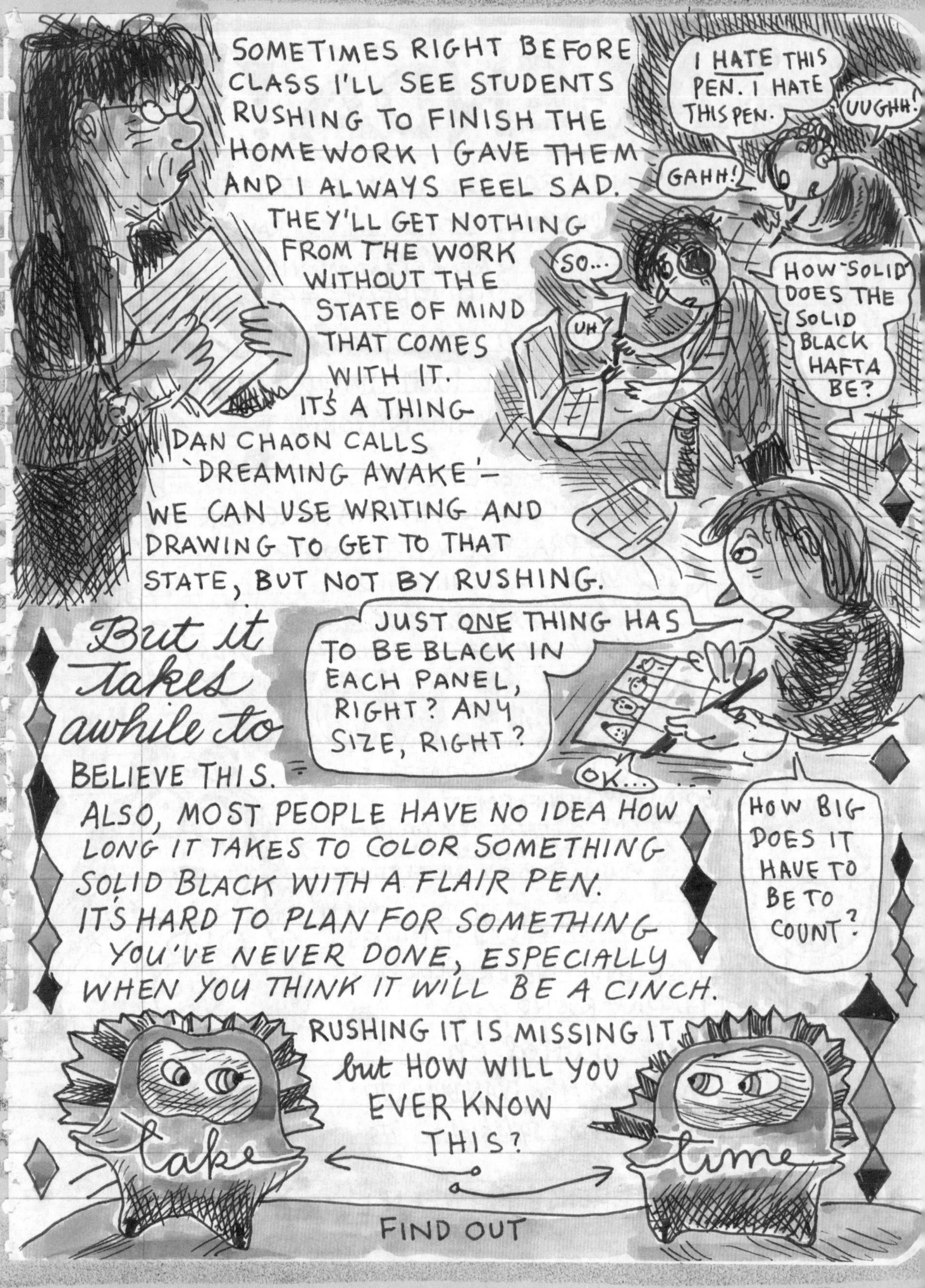
SOMETIMES RIGHT BEFORE CLASS I'LL SEE STUDENTS RUSHING TO FINISH THE HOMEWORK I GAVE THEM AND I ALWAYS FEEL SAD.
I HATE THIS PEN. I HATE THIS PEN.
UUGHH!
GAHH!
THEY'LL GET NOTHING FROM THE WORK WITHOUT THE STATE OF MIND THAT COMES WITH IT.
SO...
UH
HOW "SOLID" DOES THE SOLID BLACK HAFTA BE?
IT'S A THING DAN CHAON CALLS 'DREAMING AWAKE'— WE CAN USE WRITING AND DRAWING TO GET TO THAT STATE, BUT NOT BY RUSHING.
But it takes awhile to BELIEVE THIS.
JUST ONE THING HAS TO BE BLACK IN EACH PANEL, RIGHT? ANY SIZE, RIGHT?
OK...
ALSO, MOST PEOPLE HAVE NO IDEA HOW LONG IT TAKES TO COLOR SOMETHING SOLID BLACK WITH A FLAIR PEN. IT'S HARD TO PLAN FOR SOMETHING YOU'VE NEVER DONE, ESPECIALLY WHEN YOU THINK IT WILL BE A CINCH.
HOW BIG DOES IT HAVE TO BE TO COUNT?
RUSHING IT IS MISSING IT but HOW WILL YOU EVER KNOW THIS?
take
time
FIND OUT

EXERCISE IN TIMING

CAN DRAWING CHANGE OUR SENSE of TIME?

YOU WILL NEED: A CLOCK, YOUR COMP BOOK, NON-PHOTO BLUE PENCIL A PHOTOGRAPH OF A GROUP OF PEOPLE POSING FOR A PHOTO - AT LEAST FIVE PEOPLE, NO MORE THAN TEN YOUR UNIBALL PEN SOME UNINTERRUPTED TIME

HOW LONG DOES IT TAKE TO DRAW A PICTURE?

THIS IS SOMETHING TO FIND OUT —

IT'S BOTH FASTER AND SLOWER THAN YOU'D EXPECT AND ALSO

DIFFERENT EACH TIME

YOU'D THINK THAT AFTER SPENDING SO MANY YEARS MAKING COMICS, I COULD ANSWER THIS QUESTION, BUT THE ANSWER ISN'T FIXED. VARIABLES INCLUDE:

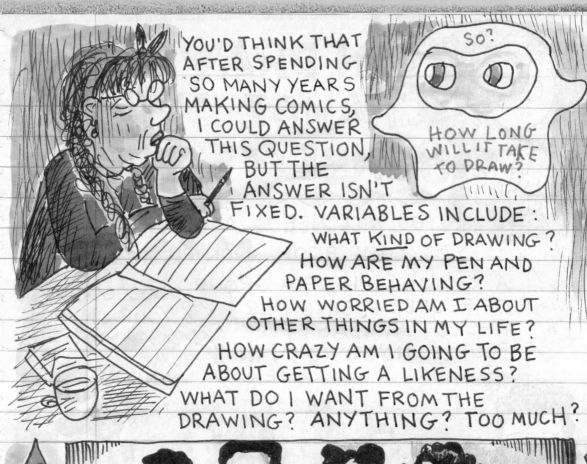

SO?

HOW LONG WILL IT TAKE TO DRAW?

WHAT KIND OF DRAWING?
HOW ARE MY PEN AND PAPER BEHAVING?
HOW WORRIED AM I ABOUT OTHER THINGS IN MY LIFE?
HOW CRAZY AM I GOING TO BE ABOUT GETTING A LIKENESS?
WHAT DO I WANT FROM THE DRAWING? ANYTHING? TOO MUCH?

Here is HOW LONG IT took me to draw that photo:
START TIME 2:49 PM   FINISH TIME : 3:05 PM
(ABOUT 15 MINUTES FOR THE MOST BASIC LINE DRAWING)
ADDING SOLID BLACK: START 3:08, END 3:17
ADDING BLUE COLOR PENCIL START 3:18 END 3:27
TOTAL: 33 MINUTES

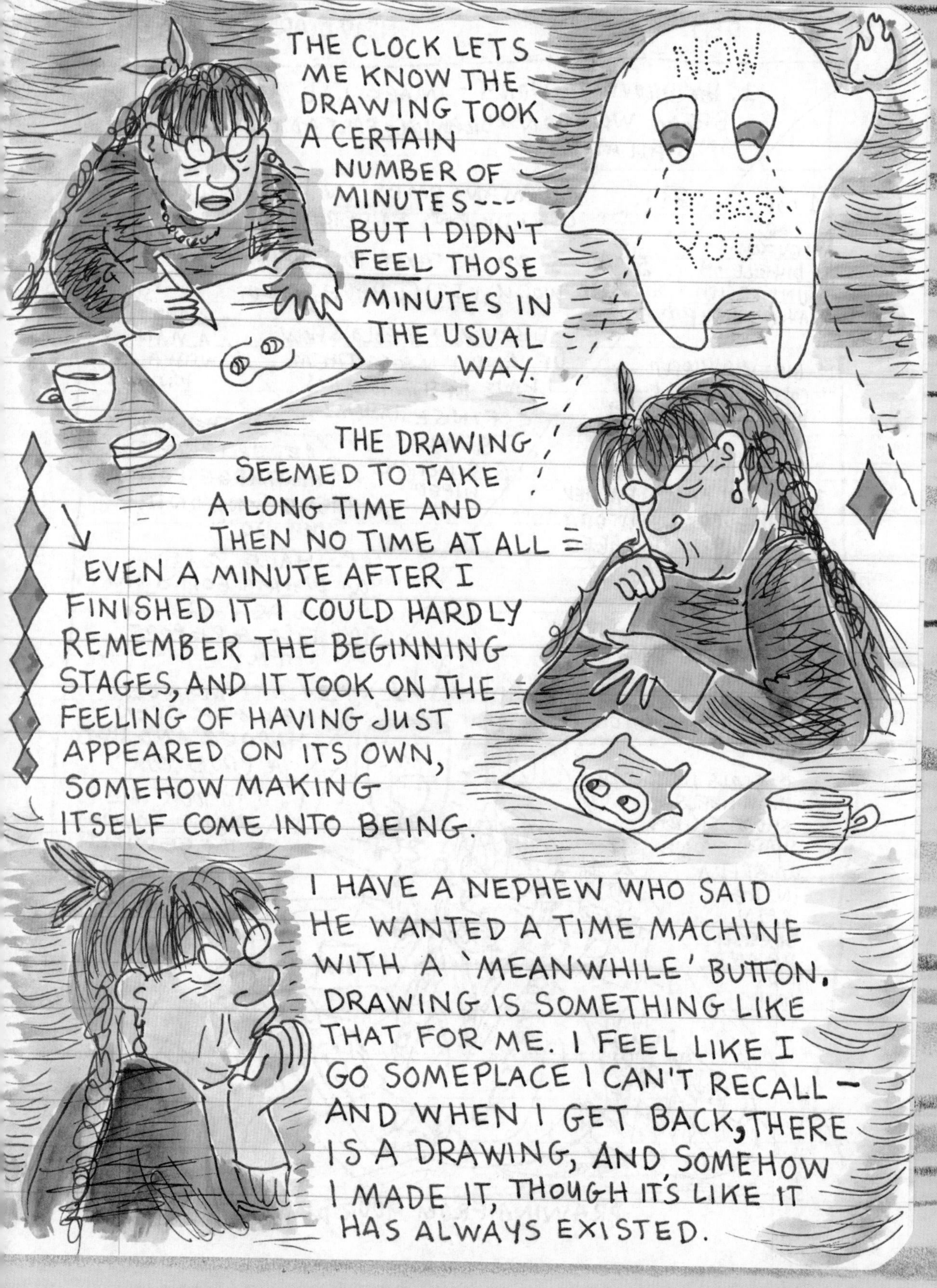
THE CLOCK LETS ME KNOW THE DRAWING TOOK A CERTAIN NUMBER OF MINUTES--- BUT I DIDN'T FEEL THOSE MINUTES IN THE USUAL WAY.
NOW
IT HAS YOU
THE DRAWING SEEMED TO TAKE A LONG TIME AND THEN NO TIME AT ALL
EVEN A MINUTE AFTER I FINISHED IT I COULD HARDLY REMEMBER THE BEGINNING STAGES, AND IT TOOK ON THE FEELING OF HAVING JUST APPEARED ON ITS OWN, SOMEHOW MAKING ITSELF COME INTO BEING.
I HAVE A NEPHEW WHO SAID HE WANTED A TIME MACHINE WITH A 'MEANWHILE' BUTTON. DRAWING IS SOMETHING LIKE THAT FOR ME. I FEEL LIKE I GO SOMEPLACE I CAN'T RECALL - AND WHEN I GET BACK, THERE IS A DRAWING, AND SOMEHOW I MADE IT, THOUGH IT'S LIKE IT HAS ALWAYS EXISTED.

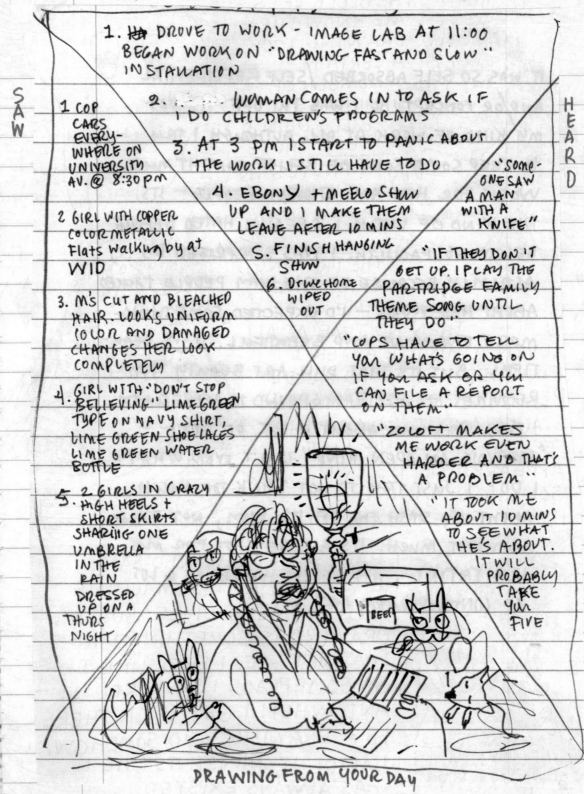

SAW

HEARD

1. ~~HA~~ DROVE TO WORK - IMAGE LAB AT 11:00
BEGAN WORK ON "DRAWING FAST AND SLOW"
INSTALLATION

2. ~~F.S.~~ WOMAN COMES IN TO ASK IF
I DO CHILDREN'S PROGRAMS

3. AT 3 PM I START TO PANIC ABOUT
THE WORK I STILL HAVE TO DO

4. EBONY + MEELO SHOW
UP AND I MAKE THEM
LEAVE AFTER 10 MINS

5. FINISH HANGING
SHOW

6. DRIVE HOME
WIPED
OUT

1 COP
CARS EVERY-
WHERE ON
UNIVERSITY
AV. @ 8:30 PM

2 GIRL WITH COPPER
COLOR METALLIC
FLATS WALKING BY AT
WID

3. M's CUT AND BLEACHED
HAIR. LOOKS UNIFORM
COLOR AND DAMAGED
CHANGES HER LOOK
COMPLETELY

4. GIRL WITH "DON'T STOP
BELIEVING" LIME GREEN
TYPE ON NAVY SHIRT,
LIME GREEN SHOE LACES
LIME GREEN WATER
BOTTLE

5. 2 GIRLS IN CRAZY
HIGH HEELS +
SHORT SKIRTS
SHARING ONE
UMBRELLA
IN THE
RAIN

DRESSED
UP ON A
THURS
NIGHT

"SOME-
ONE SAW
A MAN
WITH A
KNIFE"

"IF THEY DON'T
GET UP, I PLAY THE
PARTRIDGE FAMILY
THEME SONG UNTIL
THEY DO"

"COPS HAVE TO TELL
YOU WHAT'S GOING ON
IF YOU ASK OR YOU
CAN FILE A REPORT
ON THEM"

"ZOLOFT MAKES
ME WORK EVEN
HARDER AND THAT'S
A PROBLEM"

"IT TOOK ME
ABOUT 10 MINS
TO SEE WHAT
HE'S ABOUT.
IT WILL
PROBABLY
TAKE
YOU
FIVE

DRAWING FROM YOUR DAY

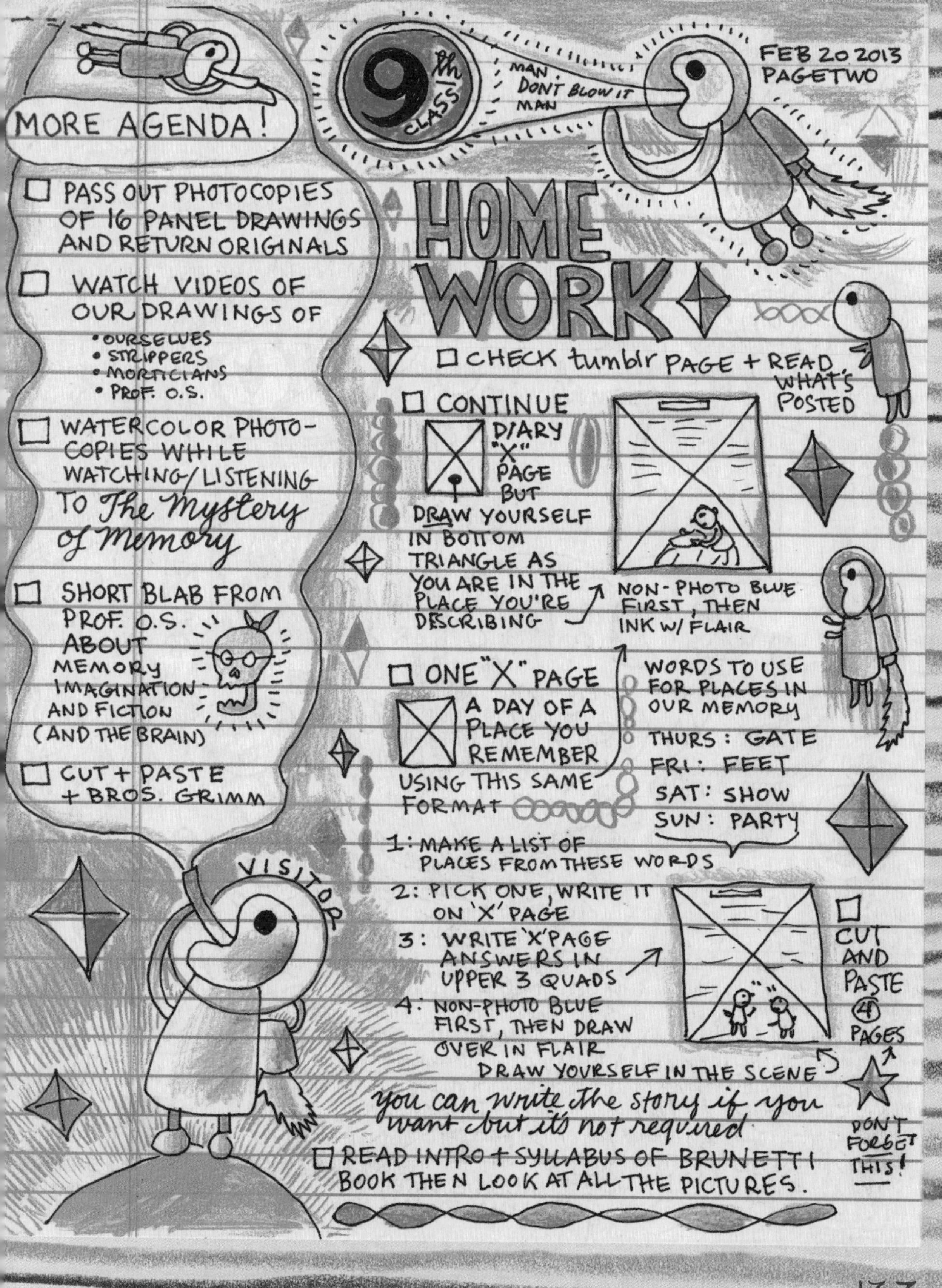
MORE AGENDA!
☐ PASS OUT PHOTOCOPIES OF 16 PANEL DRAWINGS AND RETURN ORIGINALS
☐ WATCH VIDEOS OF OUR DRAWINGS OF
• OURSELVES
• STRIPPERS
• MORTICIANS
• PROF. O.S.
☐ WATERCOLOR PHOTOCOPIES WHILE WATCHING/LISTENING TO The Mystery of Memory
☐ SHORT BLAB FROM PROF. O.S. ABOUT MEMORY IMAGINATION AND FICTION (AND THE BRAIN)
☐ CUT + PASTE + BROS. GRIMM
VISITOR
9th CLASS
MAN, DON'T BLOW IT MAN
FEB 20 2013
PAGETWO
HOME WORK
☐ CHECK tumblr PAGE + READ WHAT'S POSTED
☐ CONTINUE DIARY "X" PAGE BUT DRAW YOURSELF IN BOTTOM TRIANGLE AS YOU ARE IN THE PLACE YOU'RE DESCRIBING
NON-PHOTO BLUE FIRST, THEN INK W/ FLAIR
☐ ONE "X" PAGE
A DAY OF A PLACE YOU REMEMBER USING THIS SAME FORMAT
WORDS TO USE FOR PLACES IN OUR MEMORY
THURS: GATE
FRI: FEET
SAT: SHOW
SUN: PARTY
1: MAKE A LIST OF PLACES FROM THESE WORDS
2: PICK ONE, WRITE IT ON 'X' PAGE
3: WRITE 'X' PAGE ANSWERS IN UPPER 3 QUADS
4: NON-PHOTO BLUE FIRST, THEN DRAW OVER IN FLAIR
DRAW YOURSELF IN THE SCENE
☐ CUT AND PASTE 4 PAGES
DON'T FORGET THIS!
you can write the story if you want but it's not required
☐ READ INTRO + SYLLABUS OF BRUNETTI BOOK THEN LOOK AT ALL THE PICTURES.

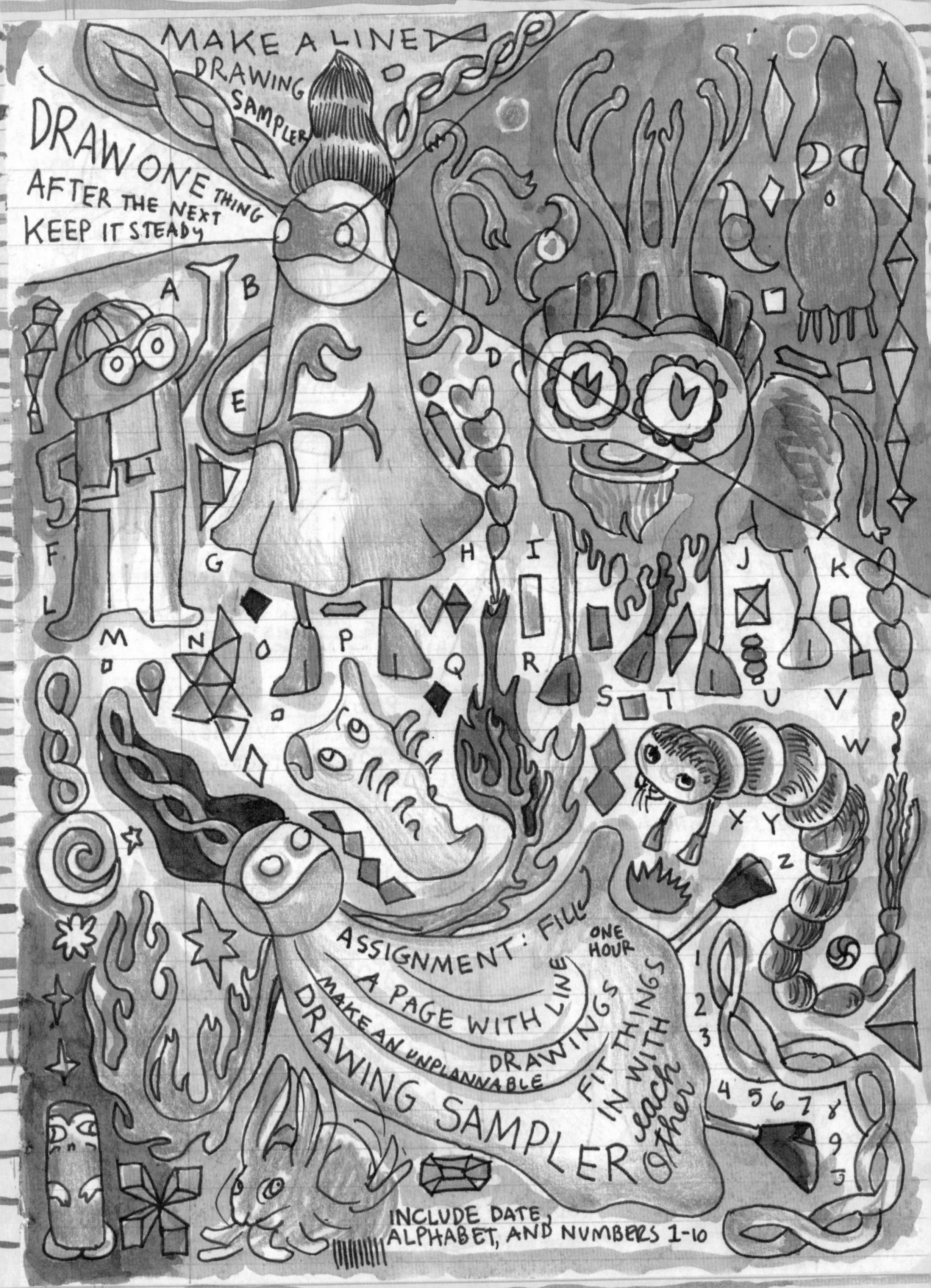
MAKE A LINE
DRAWING
SAMPLER
DRAW ONE THING
AFTER THE NEXT
KEEP IT STEADY
ASSIGNMENT: FILL
A PAGE WITH LINE
DRAWINGS
ONE HOUR
MAKE AN UNPLANNABLE
DRAWING SAMPLER
FIT THINGS IN WITH each other
INCLUDE DATE,
ALPHABET, AND NUMBERS 1-10

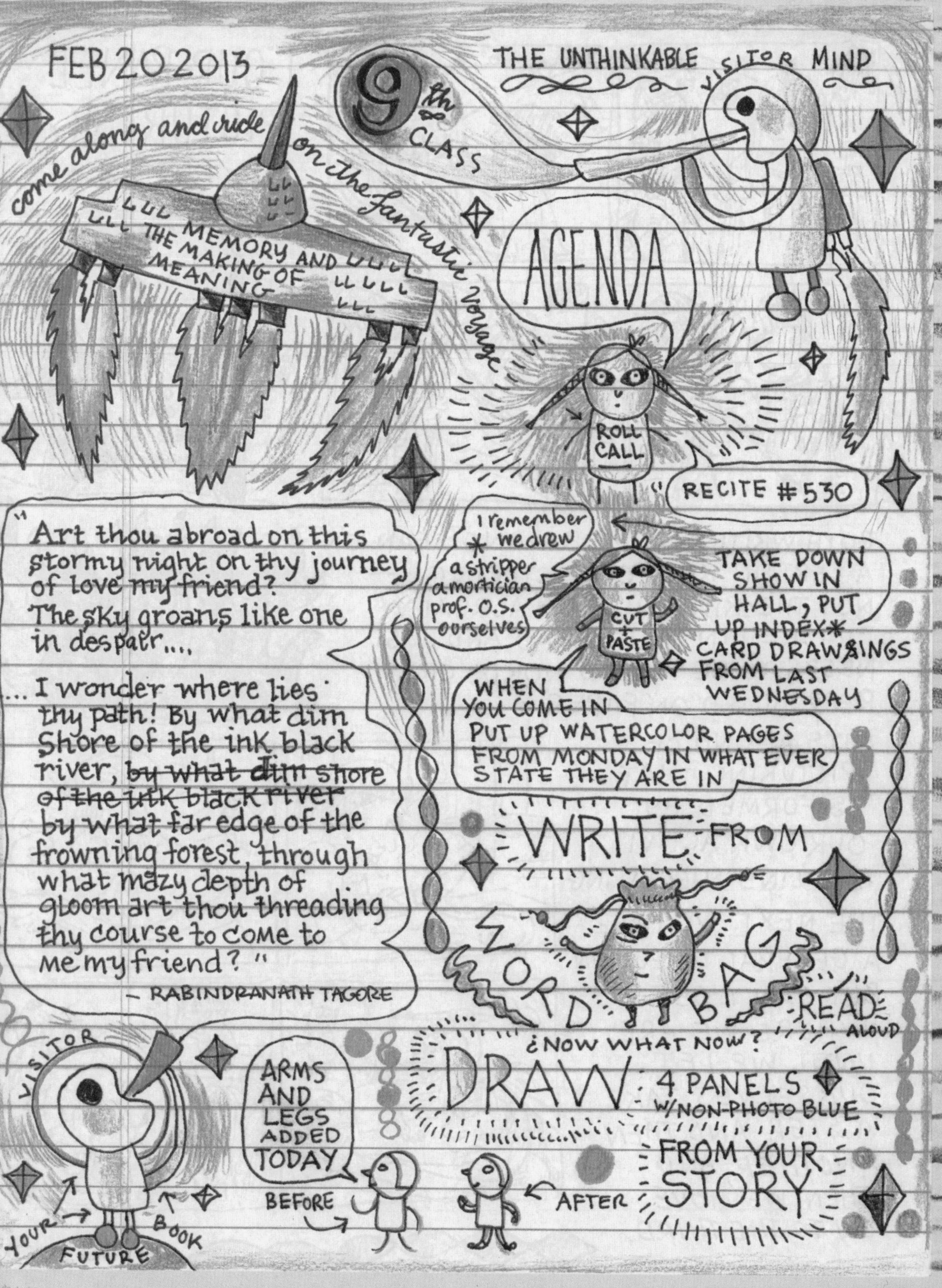
FEB 20 2013
9th CLASS
THE UNTHINKABLE VISITOR MIND
come along and ride on the fantastic voyage
MEMORY AND THE MAKING OF MEANING
AGENDA
ROLL CALL
RECITE #530
"Art thou abroad on this stormy night on thy journey of love my friend? The sky groans like one in despair....
... I wonder where lies thy path! By what dim Shore of the ink black river, by what dim shore of the ink black river by what far edge of the frowning forest, through what mazy depth of gloom art thou threading thy course to come to me my friend?"
– RABINDRANATH TAGORE
I remember * we drew a stripper a mortician prof. O.S. ourselves
CUT + PASTE
TAKE DOWN SHOW IN HALL, PUT UP INDEX* CARD DRAWINGS FROM LAST WEDNESDAY
WHEN YOU COME IN PUT UP WATERCOLOR PAGES FROM MONDAY IN WHAT EVER STATE THEY ARE IN
WRITE FROM WORD BAG
READ ALOUD
¿NOW WHAT NOW?
DRAW 4 PANELS W/NON-PHOTO BLUE FROM YOUR STORY
VISITOR
YOUR FUTURE BOOK
ARMS AND LEGS ADDED TODAY
BEFORE
AFTER

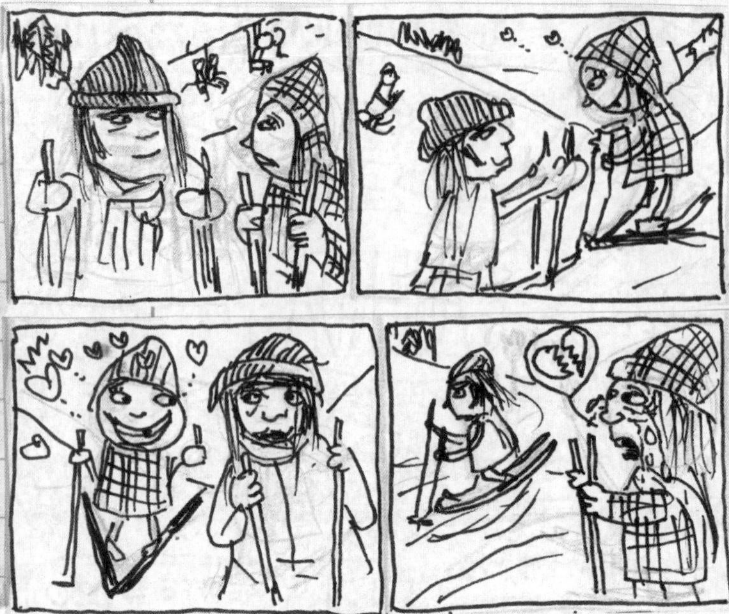

FOUR PANEL PICTURING *exercise.*

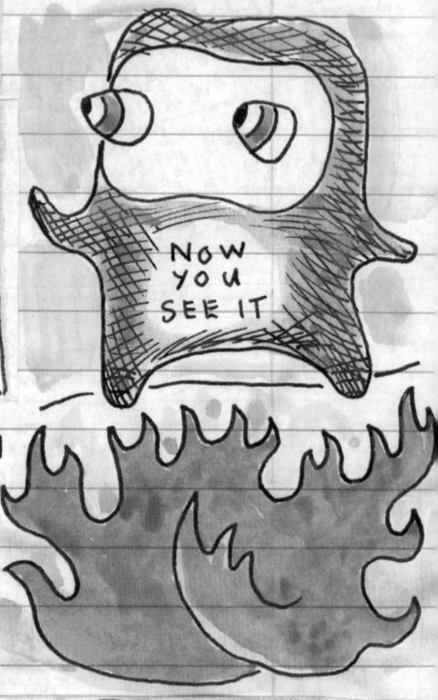
NOW YOU SEE IT

BOTH WRITING AND DRAWING LEAN ON A CERTAIN KIND OF PICTURING --- NOT THE KIND THAT IS ALREADY FINISHED IN YOUR HEAD AND JUST NEEDS TO BE PUT TO WORDS OR REPRODUCED ON PAPER - IT'S A KIND OF PICTURING THAT IS FORMED BY OUR OWN ACTIVITY, ONE LINE SUGGESTING THE NEXT. WE HAVE A GENERAL DIRECTION BUT CAN'T SEE WHERE WE ARE UNTIL WE LET OURSELVES TAKE A STEP, AND THEN ANOTHER, AND THEN WE MOVE ON TO THE THIRD.

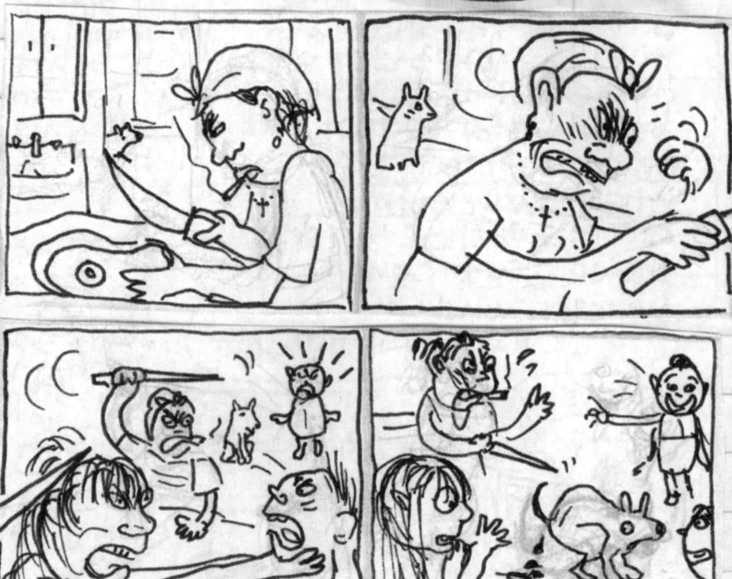

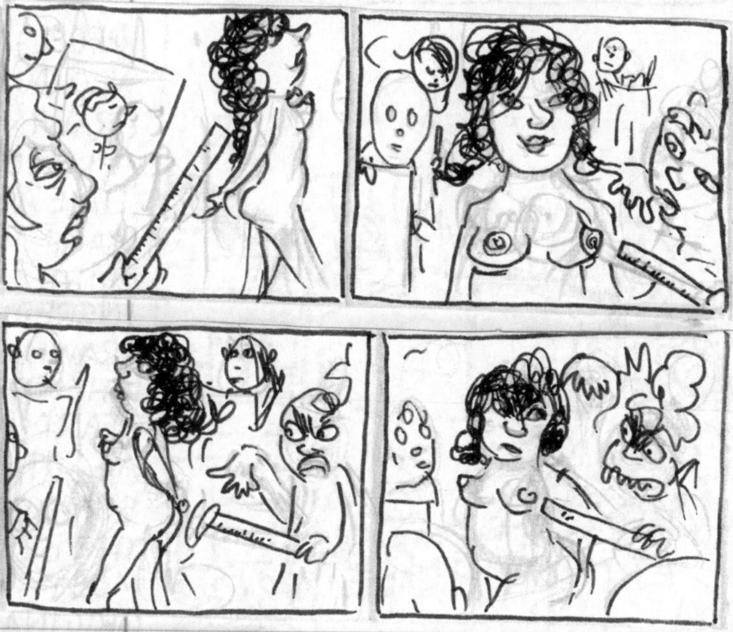

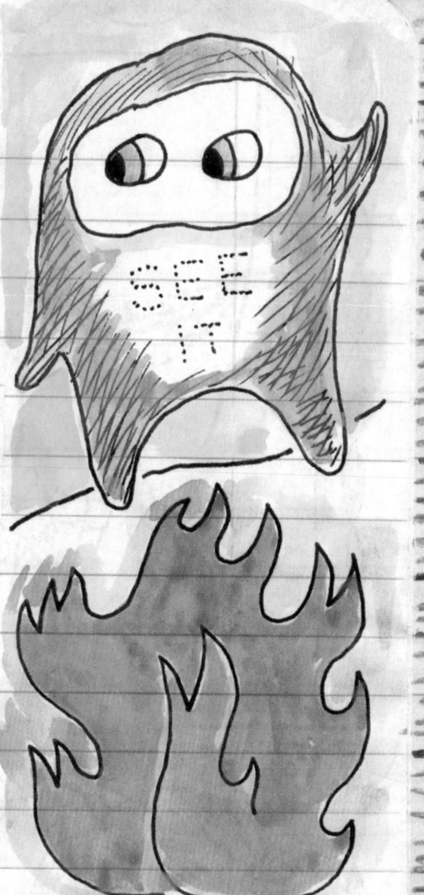
SEE IT

WHEN YOU ARE WORKING FROM ONE OF YOUR 'X' PAGE STORIES TO MAKE SOME DRAWINGS, YOU KNOW WHERE THE STORY BEGINS AND ENDS-AND YOU KNOW TWO THINGS HAPPEN IN THE MIDDLE= IF YOU ARE DRAWING IT IN FOUR PANELS. BUT YOU DON'T KNOW WHAT YOUR DRAWINGS WILL BE LIKE UNTIL YOU DRAW THEM WITH THIS KIND OF PICTURING IN YOUR MIND THAT MOVES YOUR HAND.

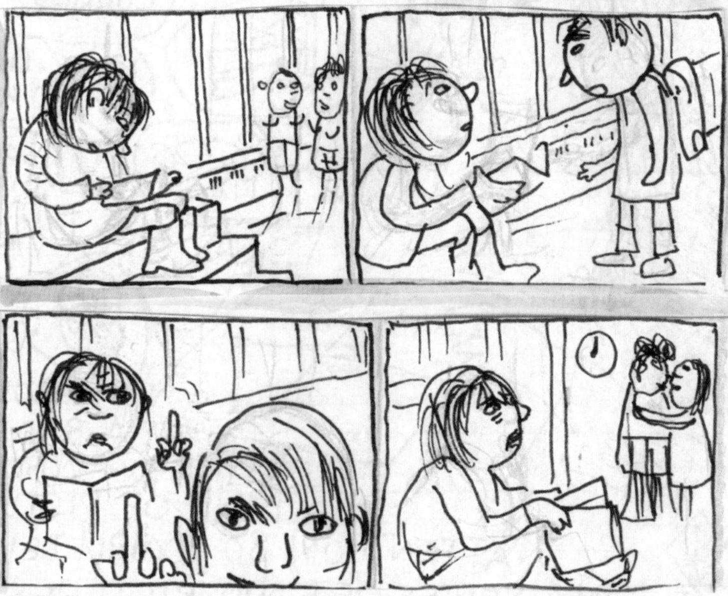

≍THE TRICK IS JUST THAT: LET IT MOVE YOUR HAND.

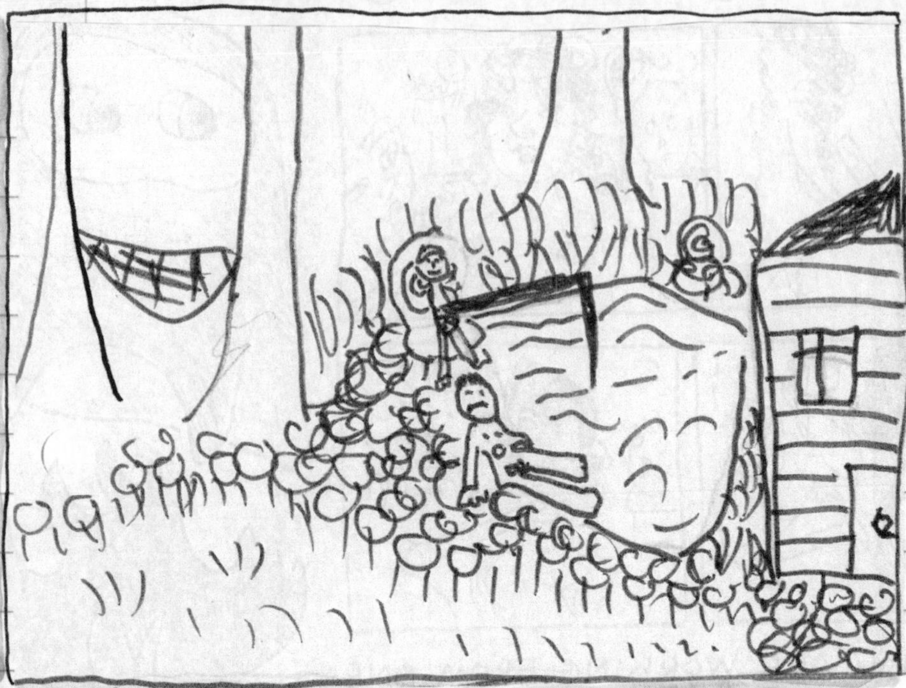

PEOPLE WHO QUIT DRAWING A LONG TIME AGO MAKE THE MOST INCREDIBLE DRAWINGS WHEN THEY START UP AGAIN. SOME OF THE BEST, MOST ORIGINAL WORK I'VE SEEN SINCE I'VE STARTED TEACHING WAS MADE BY STUDENTS WHO HADN'T DRAWN SINCE THEY WERE KIDS. I HAVE A HARD TIME EXPLAINING WHAT IT IS I FIND SO COMPELLING ABOUT WHAT FEELS LIKE A BAD DRAWING TO THE PERSON WHO MADE IT AND WHY THIS KIND OF PICTURE HOLDS MY ATTENTION SO COMPLETELY. THIS IS THE FIRST IN A SERIES OF FOUR PICTURES DRAWN BY A STUDENT IN MY "WHAT IT IS" CLASS.

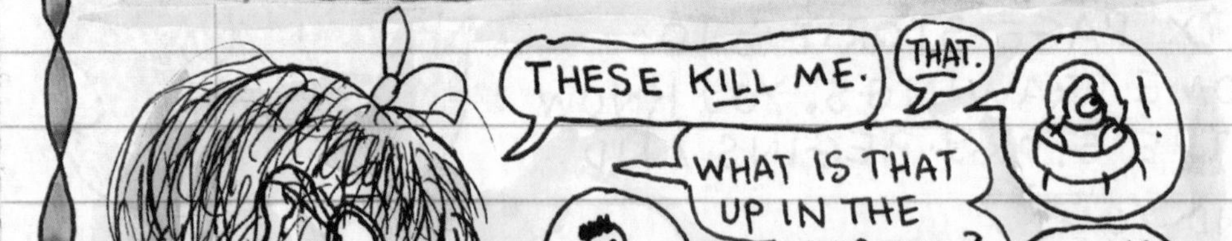
THESE KILL ME.
THAT.
WHAT IS THAT UP IN THE CORNER?
LOOKS LIKE A LITTLE SPACE MAN.
BARBEQUE. THAT'S MAYBE IT. OR LAWN CHAIR.

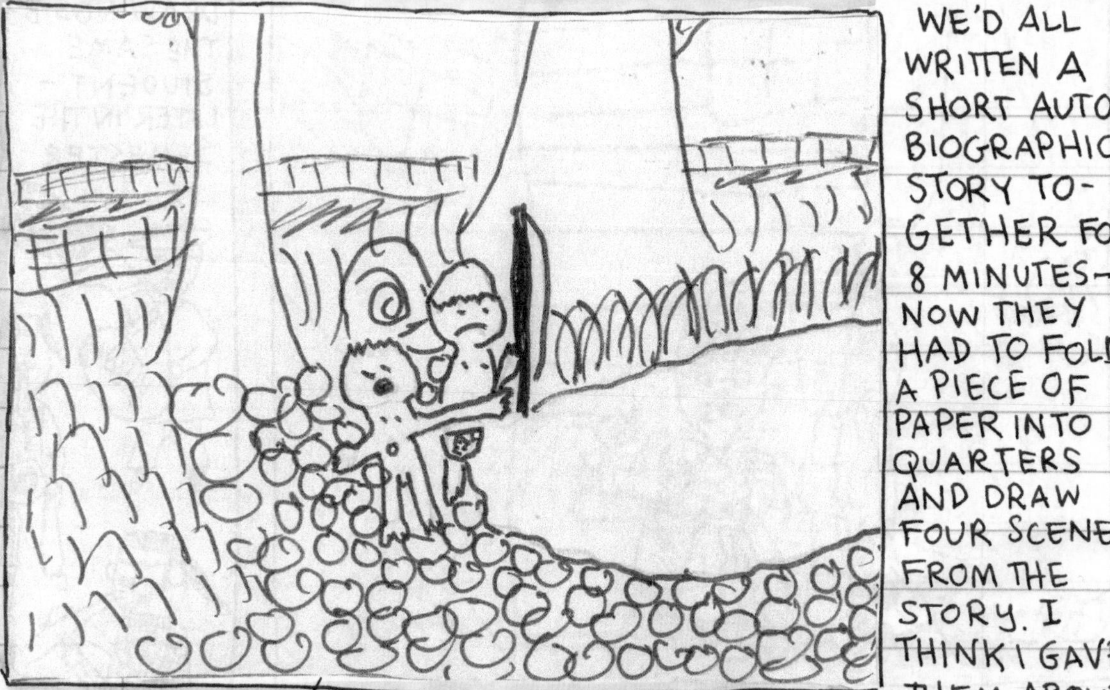

WE'D ALL WRITTEN A SHORT AUTO-BIOGRAPHICAL STORY TO-GETHER FOR 8 MINUTES—— NOW THEY HAD TO FOLD A PIECE OF PAPER INTO QUARTERS AND DRAW FOUR SCENES FROM THE STORY. I THINK I GAVE THEM ABOUT 2 MINUTES TO DO A NON-PHOTO BLUE SKETCH FOR EACH PANEL AND ABOUT 4 MINUTES TO INK THEM IN. ABOUT 20 MINUTES FOR ALL OF IT

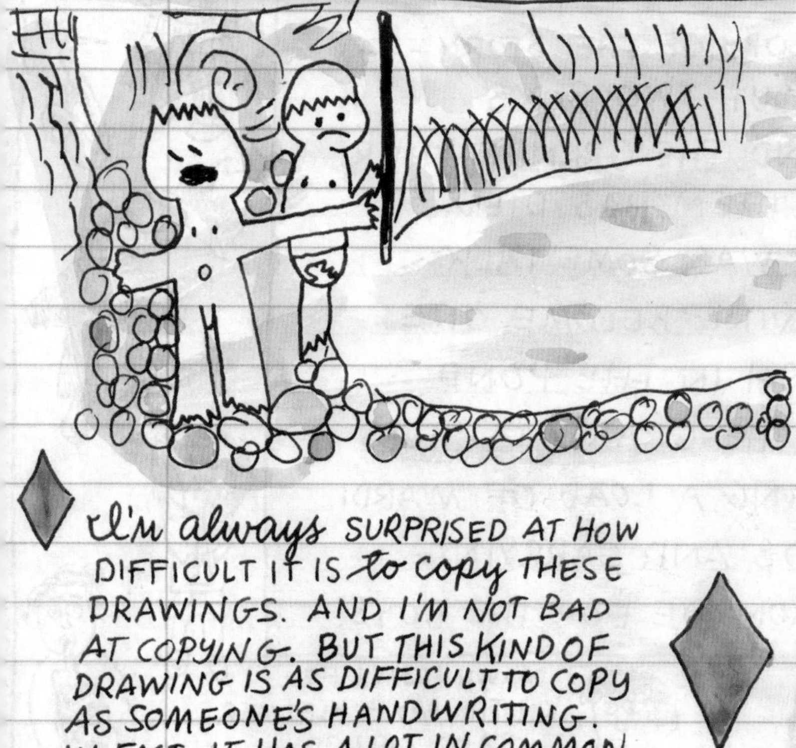

I'M *always* SURPRISED AT HOW DIFFICULT IT IS *to copy* THESE DRAWINGS. AND I'M NOT BAD AT COPYING. BUT THIS KIND OF DRAWING IS AS DIFFICULT TO COPY AS SOMEONE'S HANDWRITING. IN FACT, IT HAS A LOT IN COMMON WITH HANDWRITING, TO MY EYE

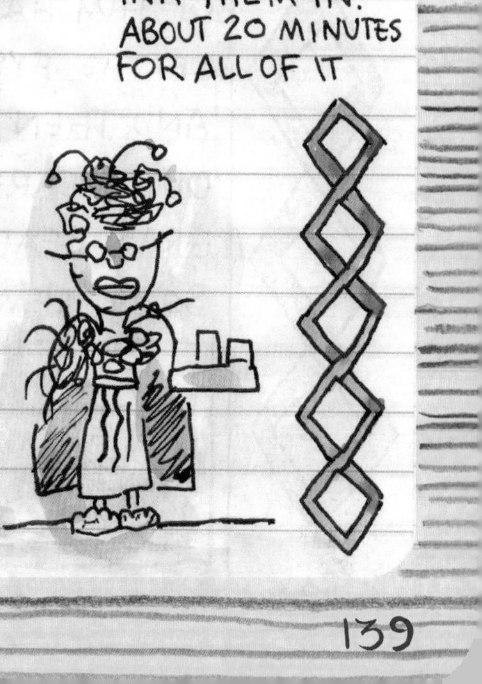

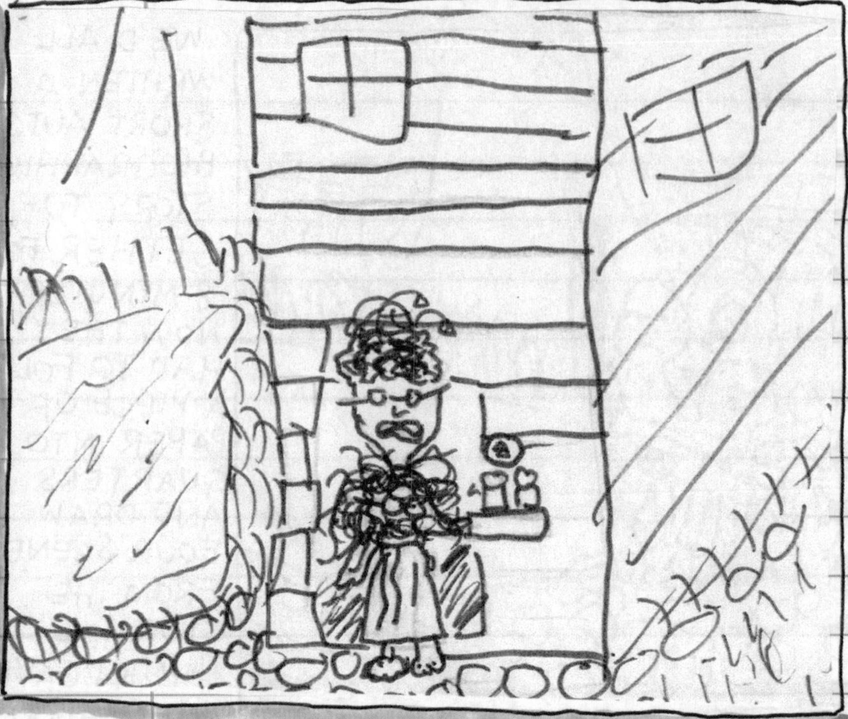

DRAWINGS BY THE SAME STUDENT — LATER IN THE SEMESTER —

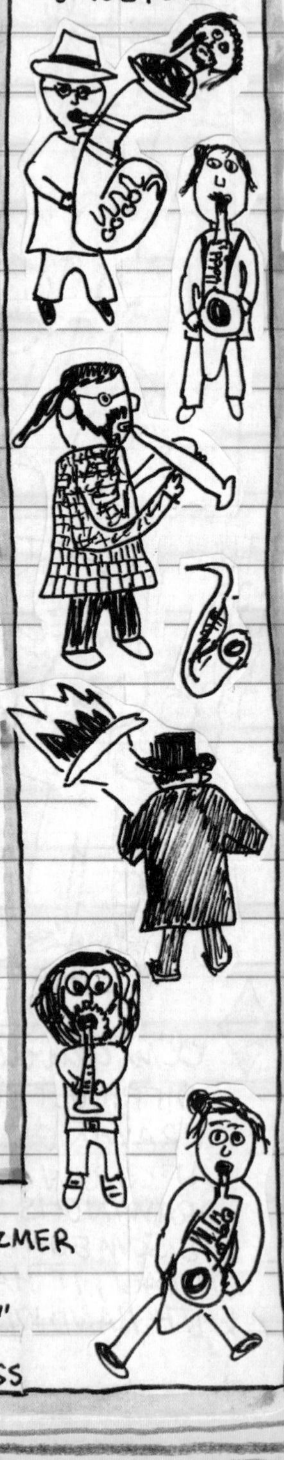

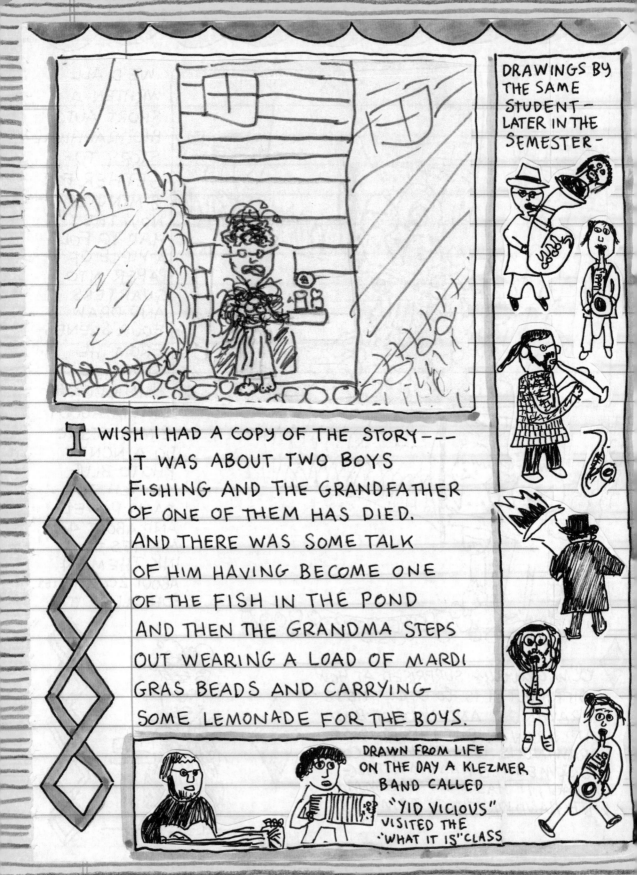

I WISH I HAD A COPY OF THE STORY——— IT WAS ABOUT TWO BOYS FISHING AND THE GRANDFATHER OF ONE OF THEM HAS DIED. AND THERE WAS SOME TALK OF HIM HAVING BECOME ONE OF THE FISH IN THE POND AND THEN THE GRANDMA STEPS OUT WEARING A LOAD OF MARDI GRAS BEADS AND CARRYING SOME LEMONADE FOR THE BOYS.

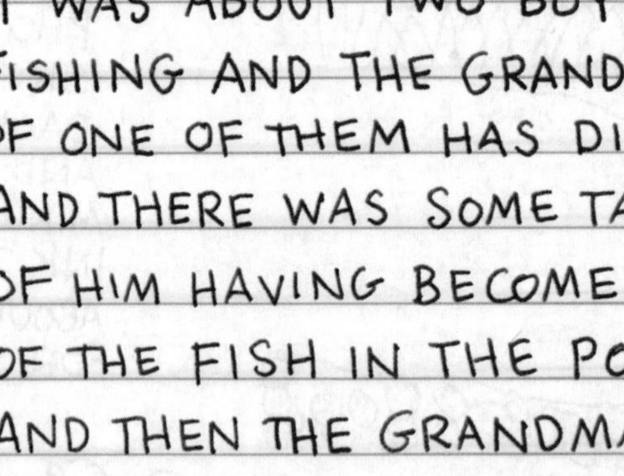

DRAWN FROM LIFE ON THE DAY A KLEZMER BAND CALLED "YID VICIOUS" VISITED THE "WHAT IT IS" CLASS

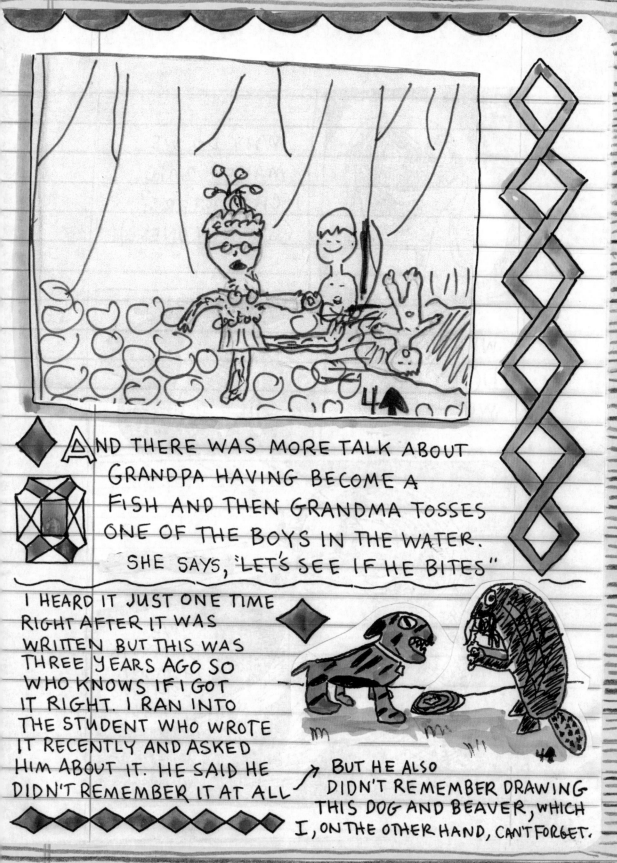

AND THERE WAS MORE TALK ABOUT
GRANDPA HAVING BECOME A
FISH AND THEN GRANDMA TOSSES
ONE OF THE BOYS IN THE WATER.
SHE SAYS, "LET'S SEE IF HE BITES"

I HEARD IT JUST ONE TIME
RIGHT AFTER IT WAS
WRITTEN BUT THIS WAS
THREE YEARS AGO SO
WHO KNOWS IF I GOT
IT RIGHT. I RAN INTO
THE STUDENT WHO WROTE
IT RECENTLY AND ASKED
HIM ABOUT IT. HE SAID HE
DIDN'T REMEMBER IT AT ALL → BUT HE ALSO
DIDN'T REMEMBER DRAWING
THIS DOG AND BEAVER, WHICH
I, ON THE OTHER HAND, CAN'T FORGET.

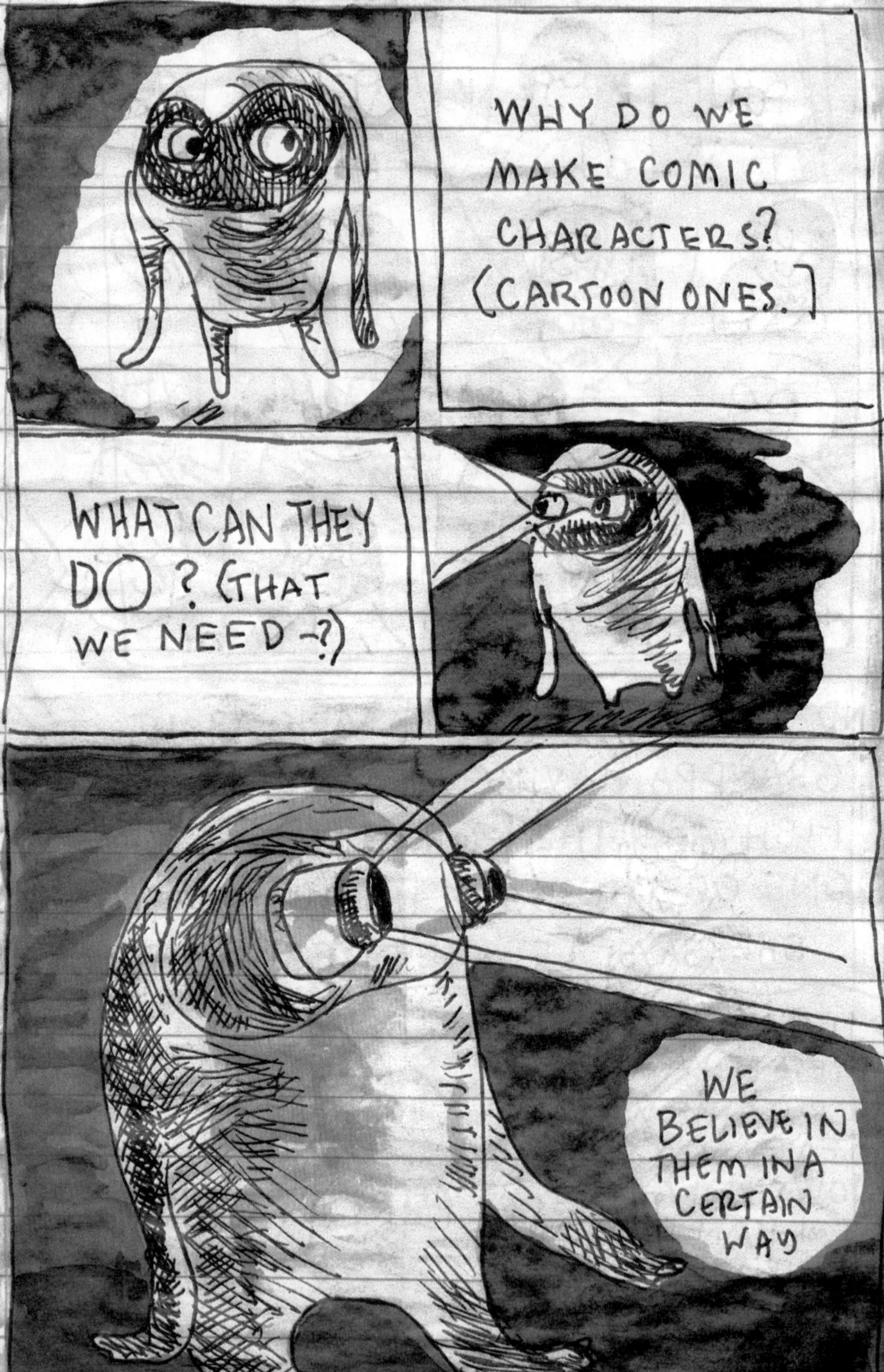
WHY DO WE MAKE COMIC CHARACTERS? (CARTOON ONES.)
WHAT CAN THEY DO? (THAT WE NEED-?)
WE BELIEVE IN THEM IN A CERTAIN WAY

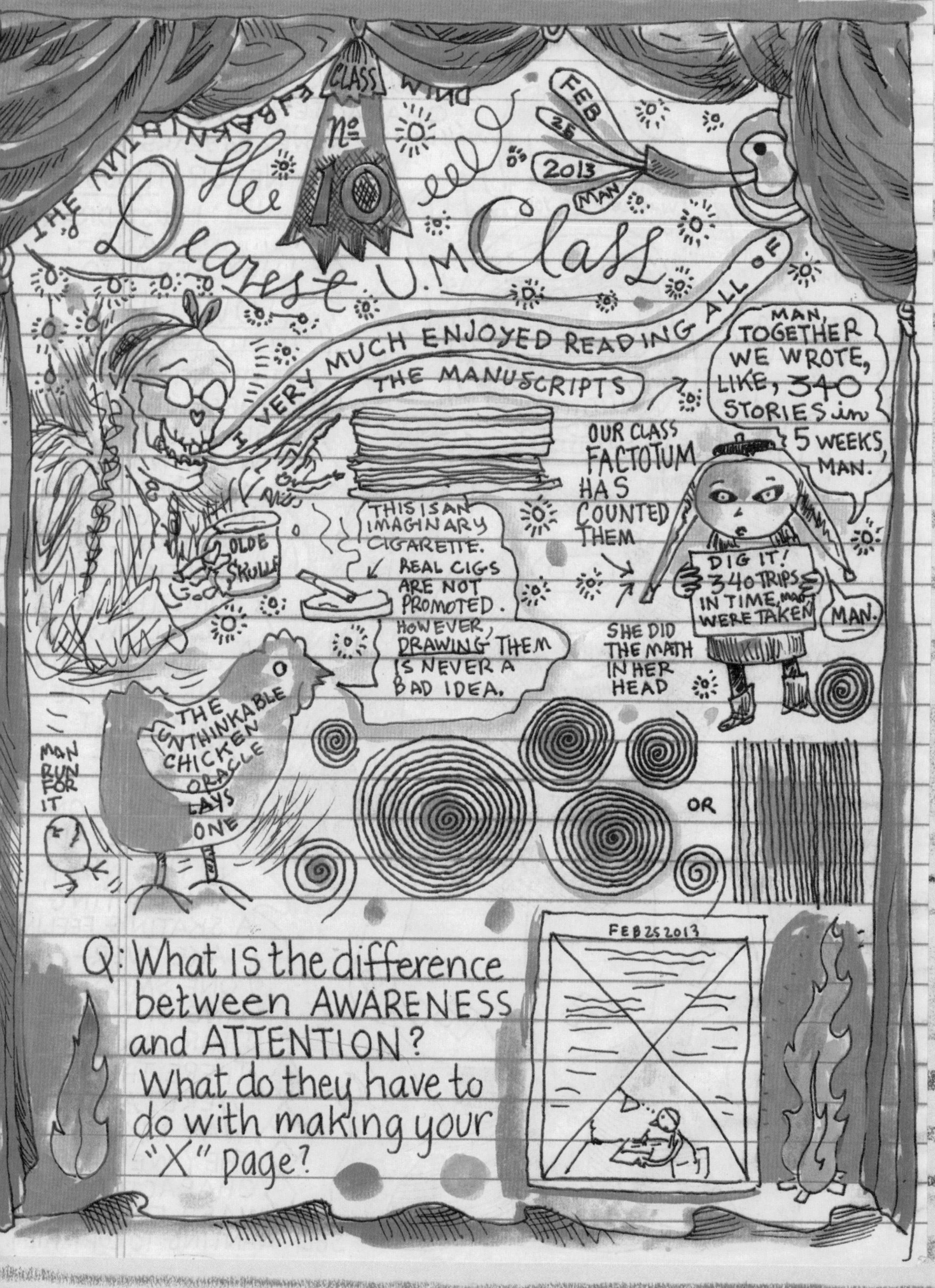
CLASS
№ 10
Dearest U.M. Class
FEB 25 2013
MAN
I VERY MUCH ENJOYED READING ALL OF THE MANUSCRIPTS
MAN, TOGETHER WE WROTE, LIKE, 340 STORIES in 5 WEEKS, MAN.
OUR CLASS FACTOTUM HAS COUNTED THEM
SHE DID THE MATH IN HER HEAD
DIG IT! 340 TRIPS IN TIME, MAN WERE TAKEN
MAN.
OLDE SKULL
THIS IS AN IMAGINARY CIGARETTE. REAL CIGS ARE NOT PROMOTED. HOWEVER, DRAWING THEM IS NEVER A BAD IDEA.
THE UNTHINKABLE CHICKEN ORACLE LAYS ONE
MAN RUN FOR IT
OR
FEB 25 2013
Q: What is the difference between AWARENESS and ATTENTION? What do they have to do with making your "X" page?

QUESTION!

Where DO cartoon CHARACTERS COME FROM?

IN OVER 30 YEARS OF DRAWING I'VE NEVER THOUGHT ONE UP.. I JUST DRAW —AND— THEY SEEM TO SHOW UP

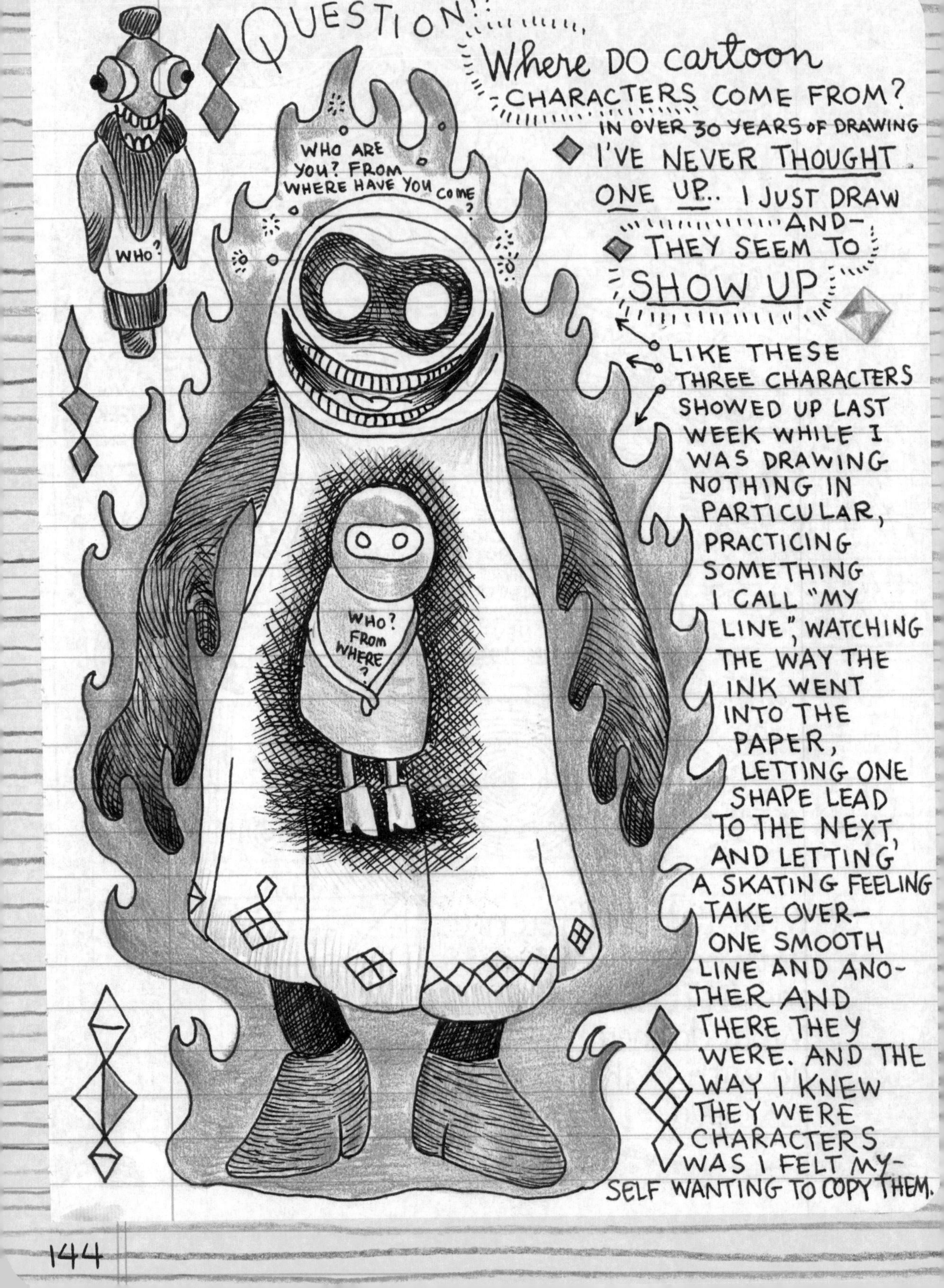
WHO ARE YOU? FROM WHERE HAVE YOU COME?
WHO?
WHO? FROM WHERE?

LIKE THESE THREE CHARACTERS SHOWED UP LAST WEEK WHILE I WAS DRAWING NOTHING IN PARTICULAR, PRACTICING SOMETHING I CALL "MY LINE", WATCHING THE WAY THE INK WENT INTO THE PAPER, LETTING ONE SHAPE LEAD TO THE NEXT, AND LETTING A SKATING FEELING TAKE OVER— ONE SMOOTH LINE AND ANOTHER AND THERE THEY WERE. AND THE WAY I KNEW THEY WERE CHARACTERS WAS I FELT MYSELF WANTING TO COPY THEM.

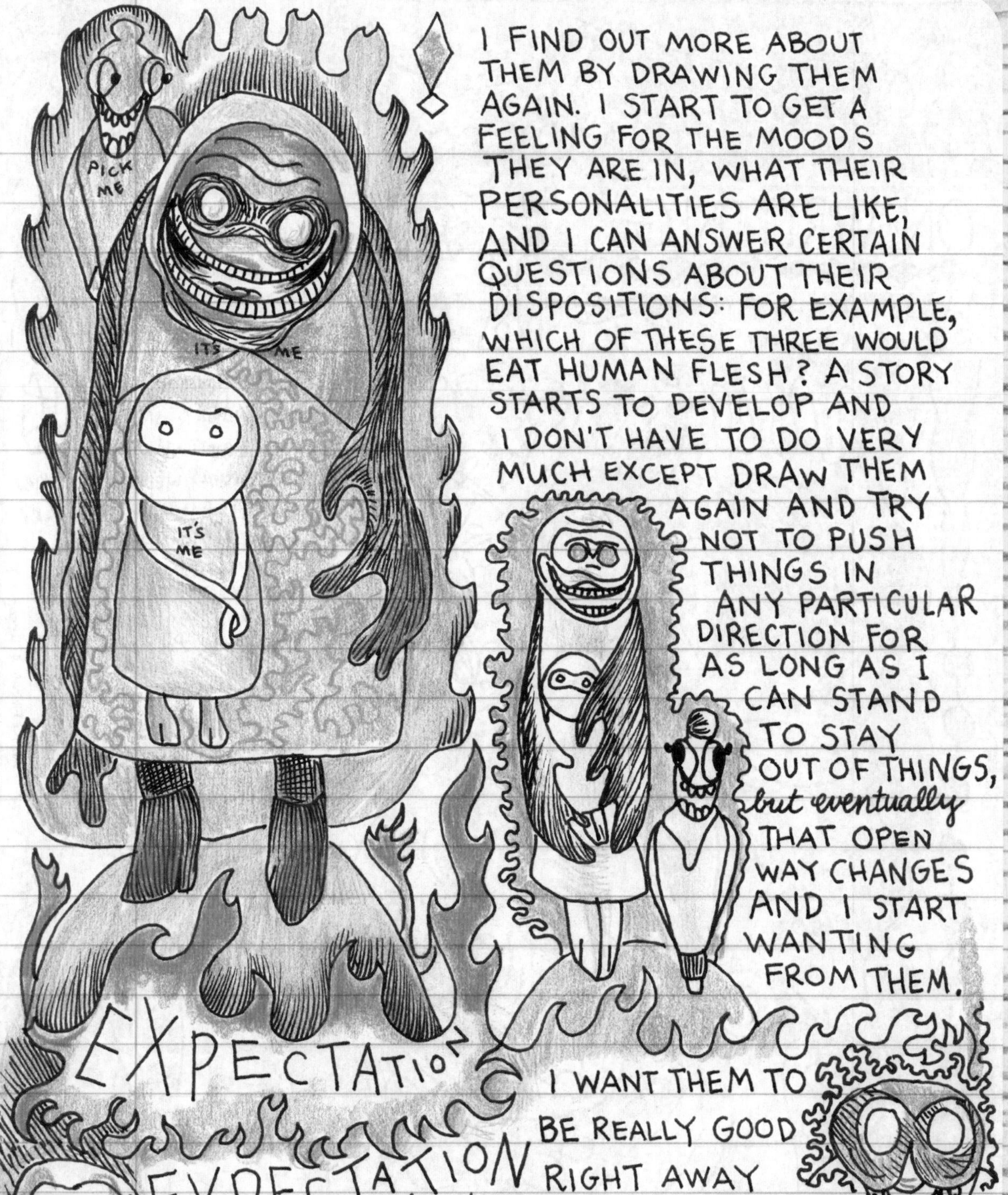
PICK ME
IT'S ME
IT'S ME
I FIND OUT MORE ABOUT THEM BY DRAWING THEM AGAIN. I START TO GET A FEELING FOR THE MOODS THEY ARE IN, WHAT THEIR PERSONALITIES ARE LIKE, AND I CAN ANSWER CERTAIN QUESTIONS ABOUT THEIR DISPOSITIONS: FOR EXAMPLE, WHICH OF THESE THREE WOULD EAT HUMAN FLESH? A STORY STARTS TO DEVELOP AND I DON'T HAVE TO DO VERY MUCH EXCEPT DRAW THEM AGAIN AND TRY NOT TO PUSH THINGS IN ANY PARTICULAR DIRECTION FOR AS LONG AS I CAN STAND TO STAY OUT OF THINGS, but eventually THAT OPEN WAY CHANGES AND I START WANTING FROM THEM.
EXPECTATION
I WANT THEM TO BE REALLY GOOD RIGHT AWAY
EXPECTATION
and this stops the natural pace of discovery and replaces it with an objective. THIS CAN'T BE HELPED.

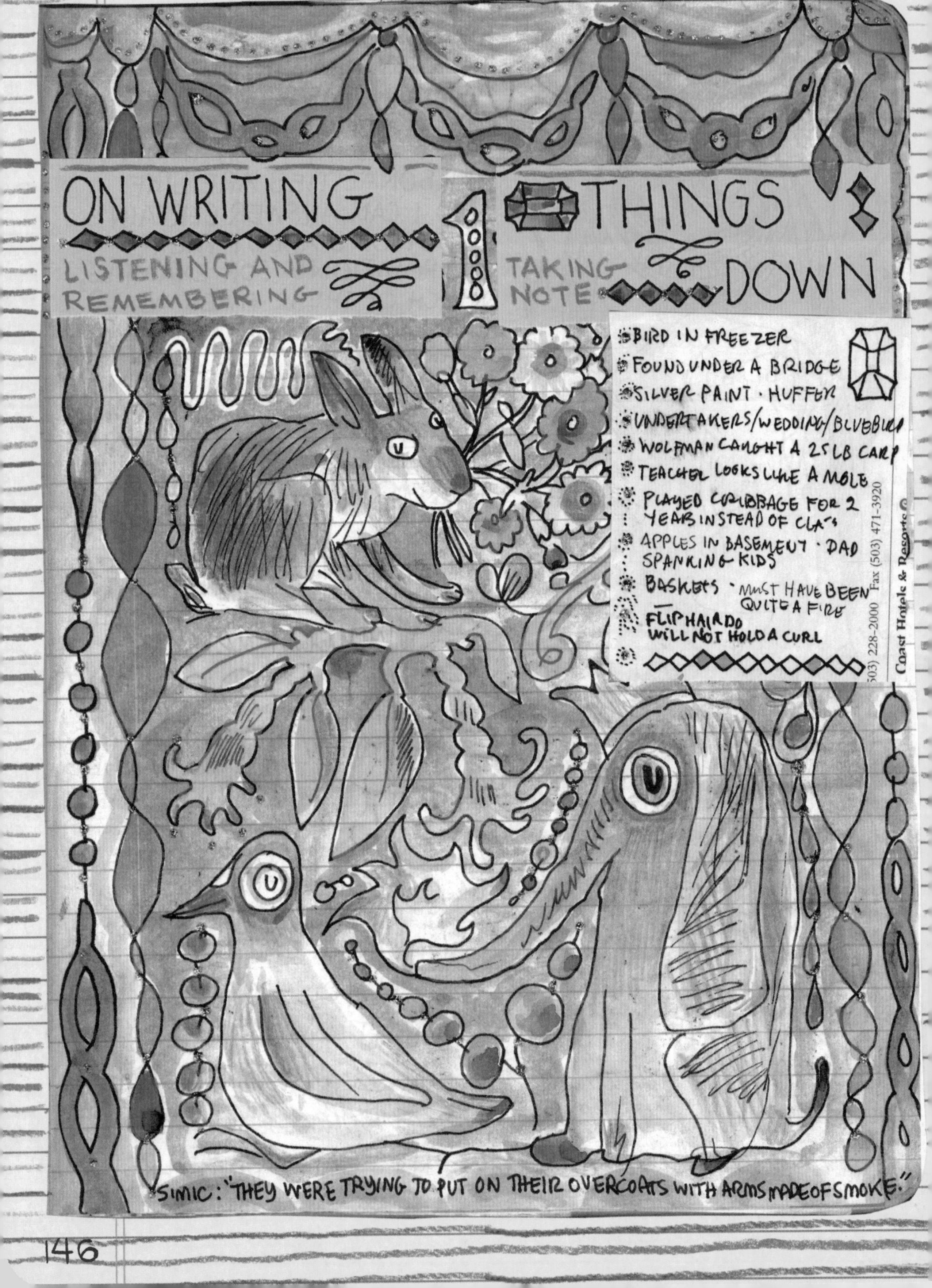
ON WRITING
LISTENING AND REMEMBERING
1
THINGS
TAKING NOTE
DOWN
BIRD IN FREEZER
FOUND UNDER A BRIDGE
SILVER PAINT · HUFFER
UNDERTAKERS/WEDDING/BLUEBIRD
WOLFMAN CAUGHT A 25 LB CARP
TEACHER LOOKS LIKE A MOLE
PLAYED CRIBBAGE FOR 2 YEARS INSTEAD OF CLASS
APPLES IN BASEMENT · DAD SPANKING KIDS
BASKETS · MUST HAVE BEEN QUITE A FIRE
FLIP HAIRDO WILL NOT HOLD A CURL
(503) 228-2000 Fax (503) 471-3920
Coast Hotels & Resorts
SIMIC: "THEY WERE TRYING TO PUT ON THEIR OVERCOATS WITH ARMS MADE OF SMOKE."

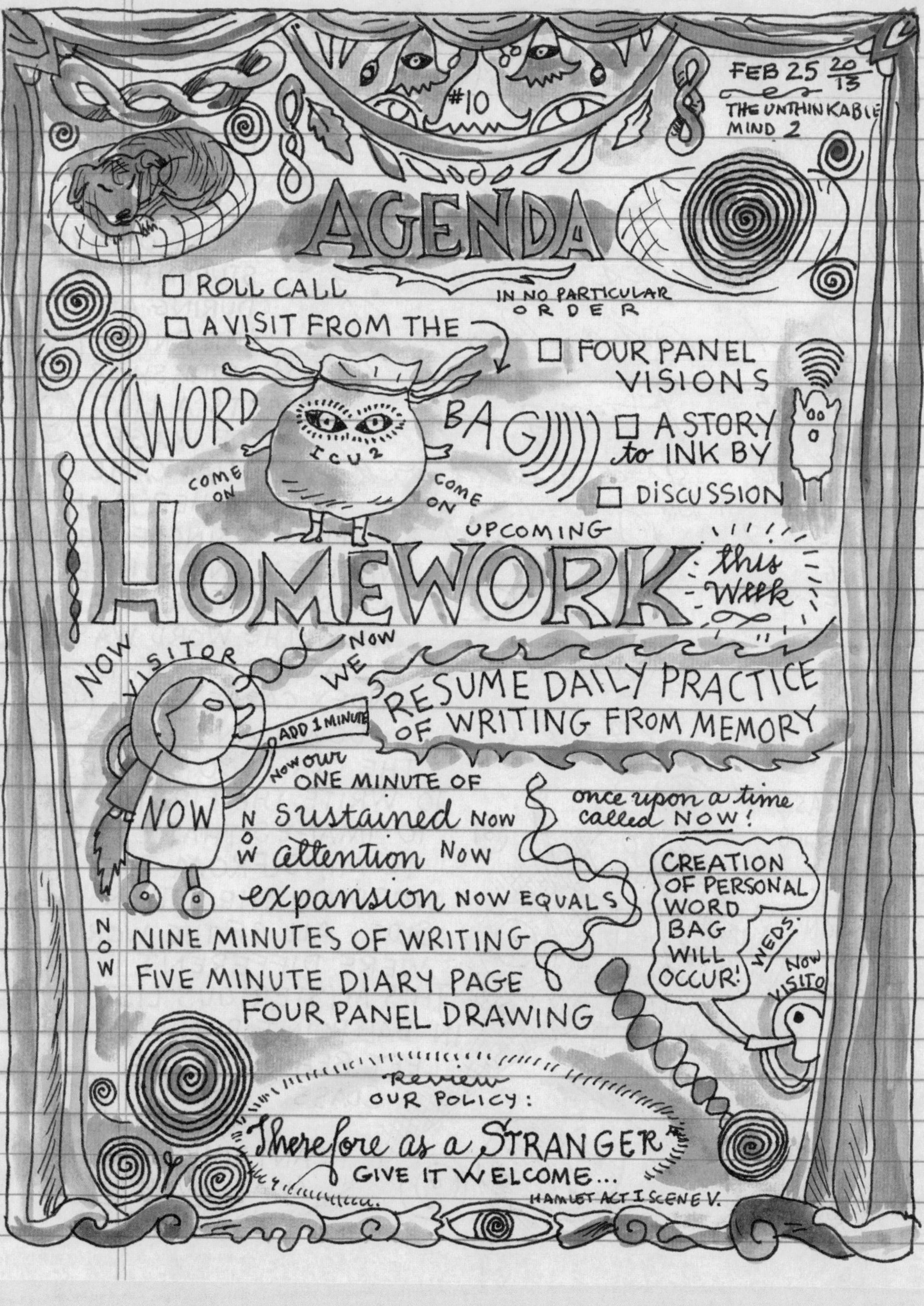
#10
FEB 25 2013
THE UNTHINKABLE MIND 2
AGENDA
IN NO PARTICULAR ORDER
☐ ROLL CALL
☐ A VISIT FROM THE WORD BAG
ICU2
COME ON
COME ON
☐ FOUR PANEL VISIONS
☐ A STORY to INK BY
☐ DISCUSSION
UPCOMING
HOMEWORK this week
NOW VISITOR
NOW WE
RESUME DAILY PRACTICE OF WRITING FROM MEMORY
ADD 1 MINUTE
NOW our ONE MINUTE OF
NOW
NOW sustained NOW
attention NOW
expansion NOW EQUALS
NOW
NINE MINUTES OF WRITING
FIVE MINUTE DIARY PAGE
FOUR PANEL DRAWING
once upon a time called NOW!
CREATION OF PERSONAL WORD BAG WILL OCCUR!
WEDS.
NOW VISITO
Review OUR POLICY:
"Therefore as a STRANGER GIVE IT WELCOME..."
HAMLET ACT I SCENE V.

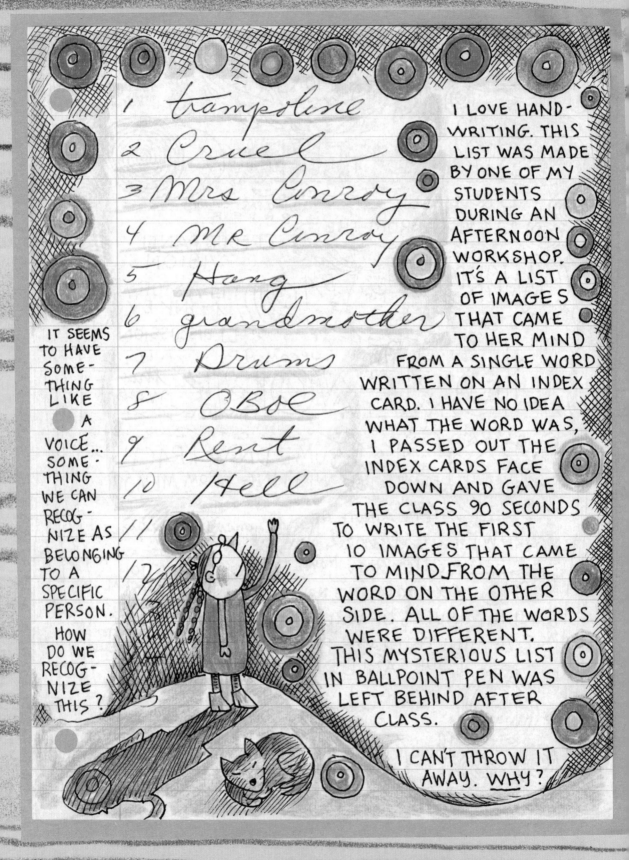

1 trampoline
2 Cruel
3 Mrs Conroy
4 Mr Conroy
5 Hong
6 grandmother
7 Drums
8 Oboe
9 Rent
10 Hell
11
12

IT SEEMS TO HAVE SOMETHING LIKE A VOICE... SOMETHING WE CAN RECOGNIZE AS BELONGING TO A SPECIFIC PERSON.

HOW DO WE RECOGNIZE THIS?

I LOVE HANDWRITING. THIS LIST WAS MADE BY ONE OF MY STUDENTS DURING AN AFTERNOON WORKSHOP. IT'S A LIST OF IMAGES THAT CAME TO HER MIND FROM A SINGLE WORD WRITTEN ON AN INDEX CARD. I HAVE NO IDEA WHAT THE WORD WAS, I PASSED OUT THE INDEX CARDS FACE DOWN AND GAVE THE CLASS 90 SECONDS TO WRITE THE FIRST 10 IMAGES THAT CAME TO MIND FROM THE WORD ON THE OTHER SIDE. ALL OF THE WORDS WERE DIFFERENT. THIS MYSTERIOUS LIST IN BALLPOINT PEN WAS LEFT BEHIND AFTER CLASS.

I CAN'T THROW IT AWAY. WHY?

The UNTHINKABLE MIND

FEB 27 2013

VISITOR

NEW POEM FROM Emily Dickinson

#764

Presentiment – is that long Shadow – on the Lawn –
Indicatives that Suns go down –
The Notice to the startled Grass
That Darkness – is about to pass

> **PLEASE MEMORIZE BY WEDS, MARCH 6**

Dear Unthinkable Mind Class

| FIXED |
| CREEPY |
| DISTANCE |
| SATURDAY |

☐ PLEASE use these words to write 4, 9 minute pieces: one word a day.

☐ PLEASE draw one four-panel page in non-photo blue and ink it ──→

CHOOSE ONE OF THE 4 STORIES TO ILLUSTRATE

USE NO WORDS IN THE ILLUSTRATIONS

HOME WORK

PLEASE
☐ CONTINUE YOUR DAILY DIARY PRACTICE
☐ PLEASE DRAW ONE 4-PANEL PAGE from the class story I gave you, first in non-photo blue, then ink it
☐ check our Tumblr Page

☐ PLEASE START TO FILL IN WORDS FOR YOUR WORD BAG on the back side OF THIS page

AGENDA

☐ ROLL! ☐ PIN UP WORK! ☐ DRAWING JAM!
☐ READINGS FROM CLASS MANUSCRIPT

EXERCISE: 4-PANEL DAILY DIARY (THE SILENT TYPE)

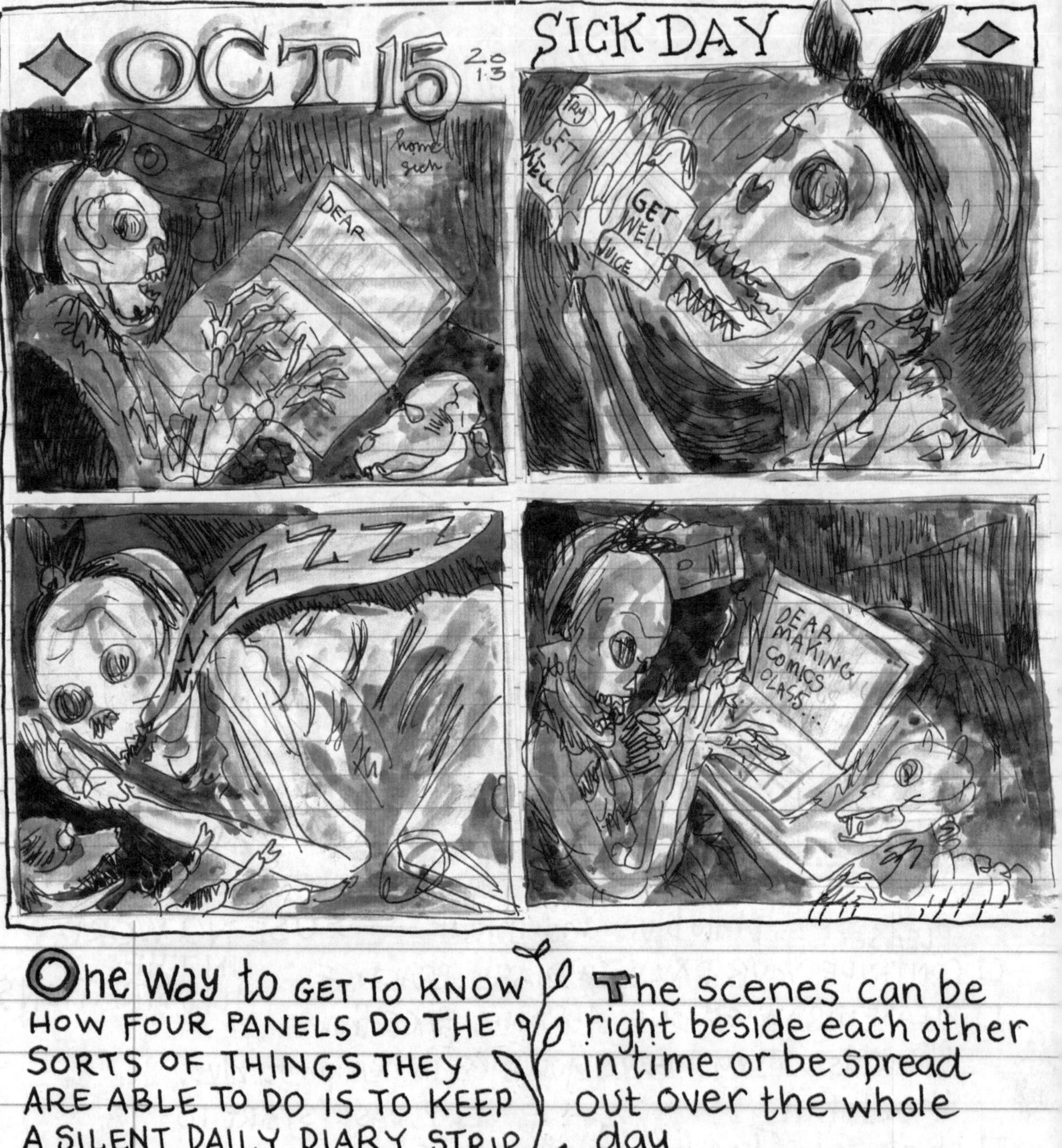
OCT 15 2013
SICK DAY
home sick
DEAR
TRY GET WELL
GET WELL JUICE
ZZZZZZ
DEAR MAKING COMICS CLASS...

One way to get to know how four panels do the sorts of things they are able to do is to keep a silent daily diary strip for 14 days.

Just draw 4 scenes from your day, spend at <u>least</u> a minute on each panel – more if you like

The scenes can be right beside each other in time or be spread out over the whole day

Include the daily sorts of things – pouring milk on cereal, waiting in line – along with things that stand out – a fight, a kiss, a crazy neighbor.

HOMEWORK! Due MON

PICTURE YOUR-SELF IN THIS IMAGE

① Keep Daily Diary as **4-PANEL SILENT COMIC STRIP** in your comp book about your day

DAY + DATE — DRAW YOUR FRAME

MONDAY FEB 24 '14	
YOU	MUST
DRAW	YOUR-SELF

IT CAN BE 4 DIFFERENT SCENES OR 4 CONSECUTIVE IMAGES.

1. NON-PHOTO BLUE 1 MIN. PER PANEL ... AT LEAST
2. UNIBALL FOR 3 MINS PER PANEL - DRAW FOR THE ENTIRE TIME.

FOUR NINE MINUTE X-PAGE EXERCISE START IS

② Create a word bag USING **50 INDEX CARDS** cut in HALF AND **WORDS** FROM YOUR STORIES, NOTES, AND DIARIES in YOUR COMP BOOKS

WORKING THROUGH YOUR WORD BAG, THE GOAL IS TO 'SEE' WHATS THERE - NOT BEAUTIFUL WRITING THOUGH THAT

a ① CUT INDEX CARDS IN HALF - WRITE WORDS FROM...

② WORD HUNT: DON'T BE TOO PICKY! THE BACK OF THE MIND IS VERY FLEXIBLE. MOST NOUNS WORK. ALSO "ING" WORDS (GERUNDS)

③ WRAP IT UP WITH A RUBBER BAND

④ READY WHEN YOU ARE!

MAY JUST HAP PEN !!!

(MORE→)

TRY TO LIMIT THE STRIPS ABOUT HOW TIRED AND STRESSED YOU ARE OR HOW BORING YOUR DAY WAS TO ONE PER WEEK. THESE STRIPS GIVE VERY LITTLE BACK TO US. DRAWING CAN GIVE OFF A KIND OF ENERGY. COMPARE MY COMIC STRIP ABOUT BEING EXHAUSTED →
WITH THE STRIP ABOUT A BARBARIAN STICKING HIS BUTT OUT. WHICH MAKES YOU FEEL MORE ALIVE? ↓

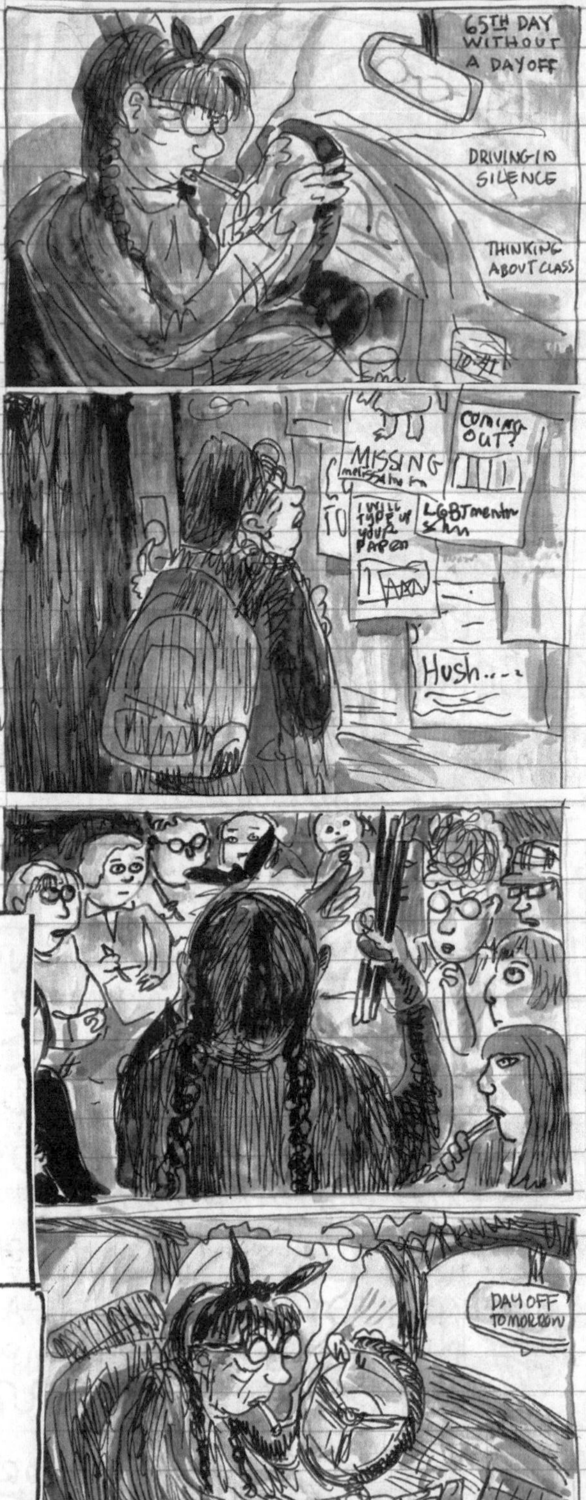
65TH DAY WITHOUT A DAYOFF
DRIVING IN SILENCE
THINKING ABOUT CLASS
COMING OUT?
MISSING
Hush....
DAY OFF TOMORROW

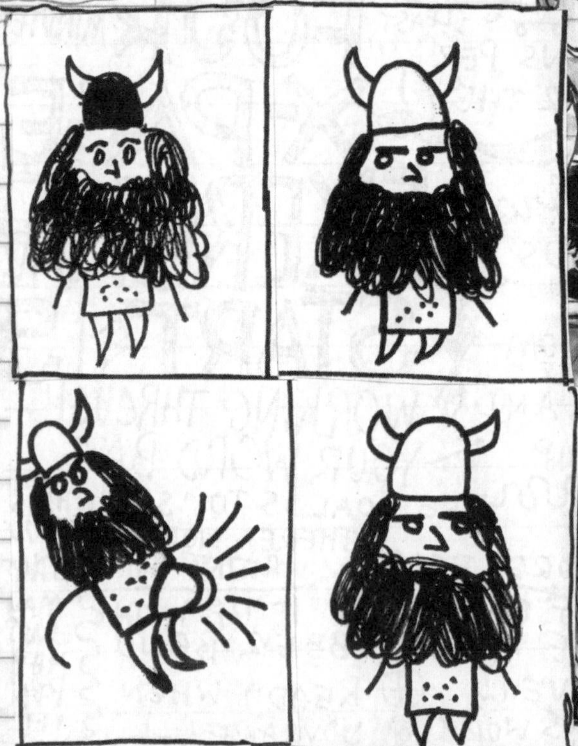

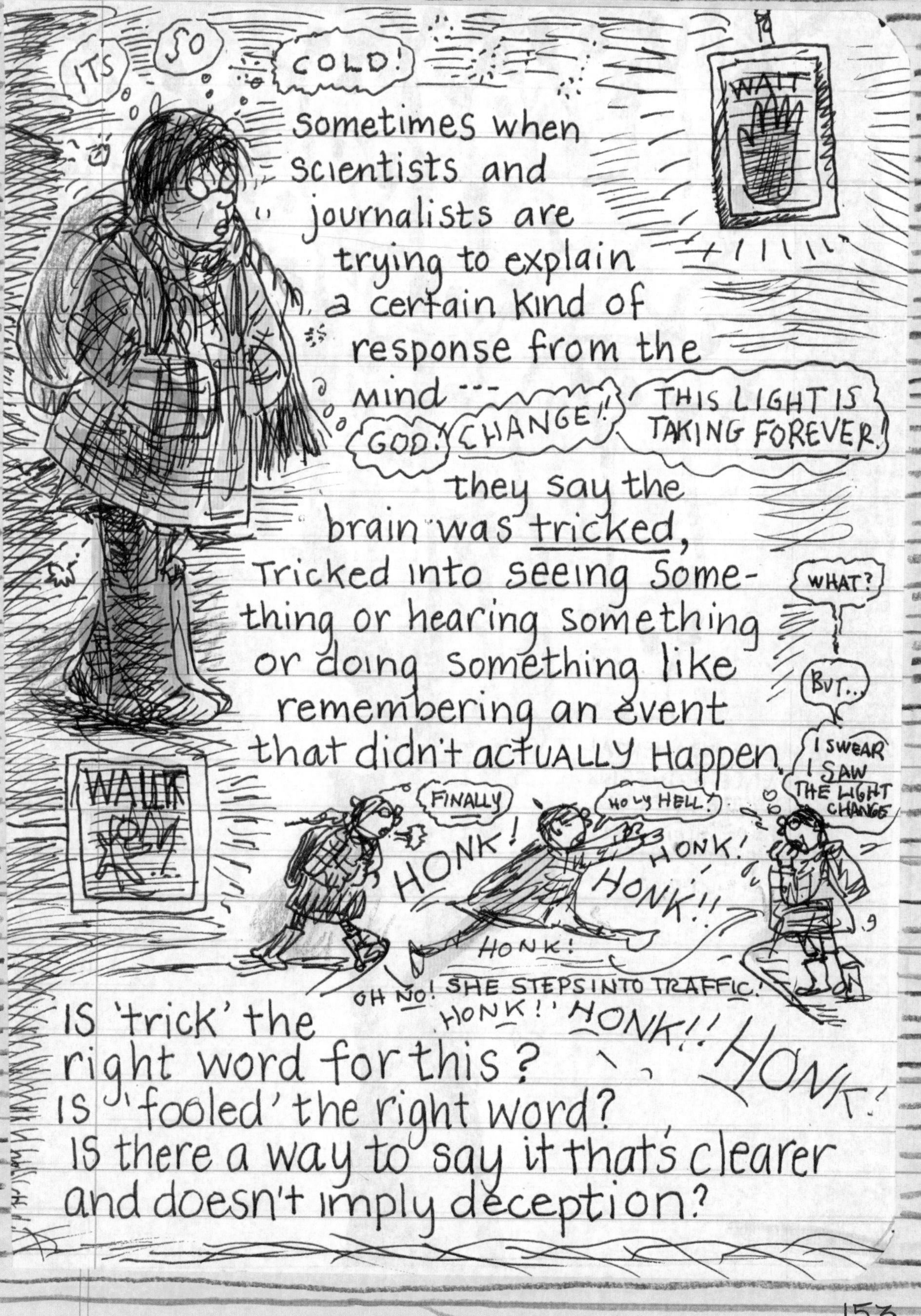
ITS
SO
COLD!
WALT
sometimes when scientists and journalists are trying to explain a certain kind of response from the mind---
GOD!
CHANGE!!
THIS LIGHT IS TAKING FOREVER!
they say the brain was tricked,
Tricked into seeing Something or hearing something or doing something like remembering an event that didn't actually Happen.
WHAT?
BUT...
I SWEAR I SAW THE LIGHT CHANGE
WALK
FINALLY
HOLY HELL!
HONK!
HONK!
HONK!!
HONK!
OH NO! SHE STEPS INTO TRAFFIC!
HONK!!
HONK!!
HONK!
IS 'trick' the right word for this?
IS 'fooled' the right word?
IS there a way to say it that's clearer and doesn't imply deception?

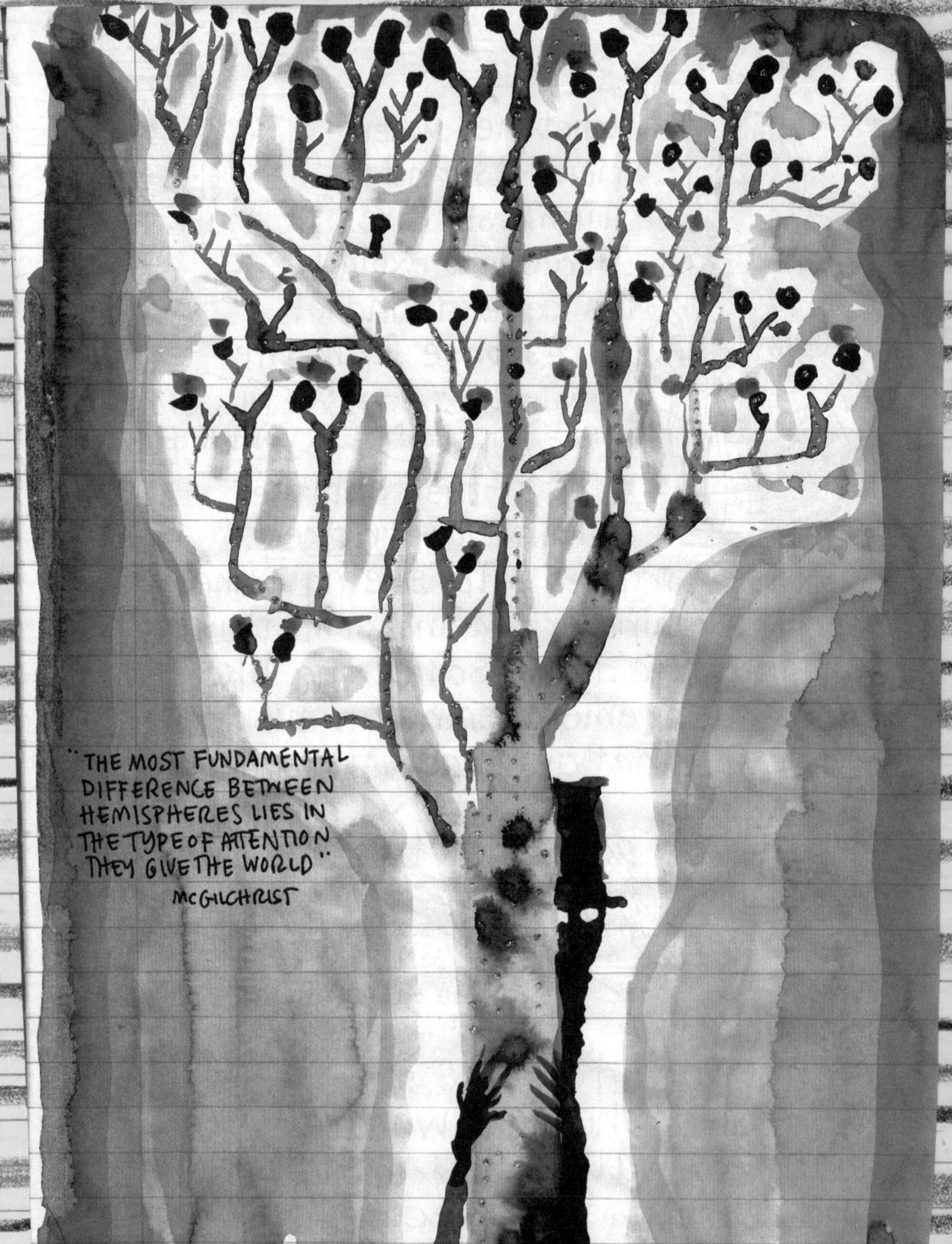
"THE MOST FUNDAMENTAL DIFFERENCE BETWEEN HEMISPHERES LIES IN THE TYPE OF ATTENTION THEY GIVE THE WORLD"
MCGILCHRIST

NEW PEN

IT'S UNI·BALL! TIME!

ROLLER
BALLIN'

IT'S DIFFERENT FROM

- THE FLAIR IN INK:
  - the uniball ink is WATERPROOF
- IN PRESSURE REQUIRED-
  - pushing harder doesn't make a stronger line after a certain point
- IN FAMILIARITY
  - THE metal tip may feel strange at first. It moves across the paper with a different speed. Give it some time. It can do certain things that a FLAIR can't.

PATTERN PRACTICE

COPY THIS

DRAW A SET OF VERTICAL LINES; VARY THE PRESSURE AS YOU GO

PAY ATTENTION TO YOUR BREATH

DO IT AGAIN, NOW - CLOSER - EACH LINE IS AN ACT

DRAW ON THE EXHALE · TIME IT TO THE LINE

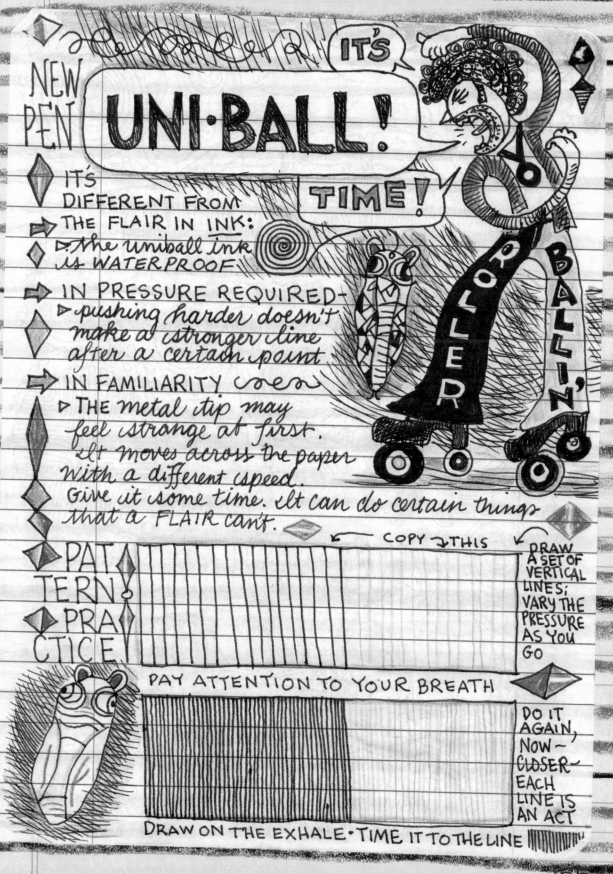

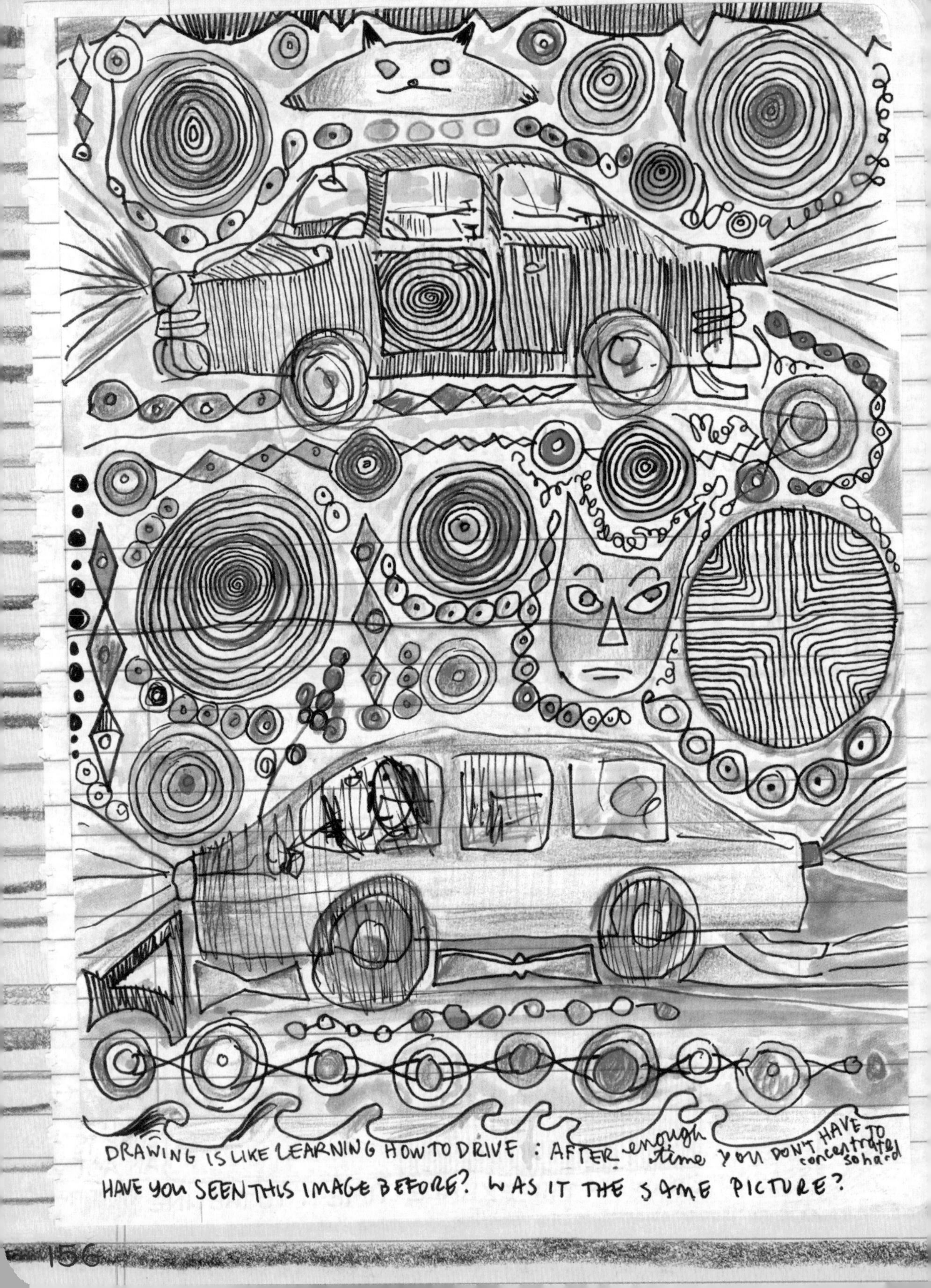

DRAWING IS LIKE LEARNING HOW TO DRIVE : AFTER enough time YOU DON'T HAVE TO concentrate so hard

HAVE YOU SEEN THIS IMAGE BEFORE? WAS IT THE SAME PICTURE?

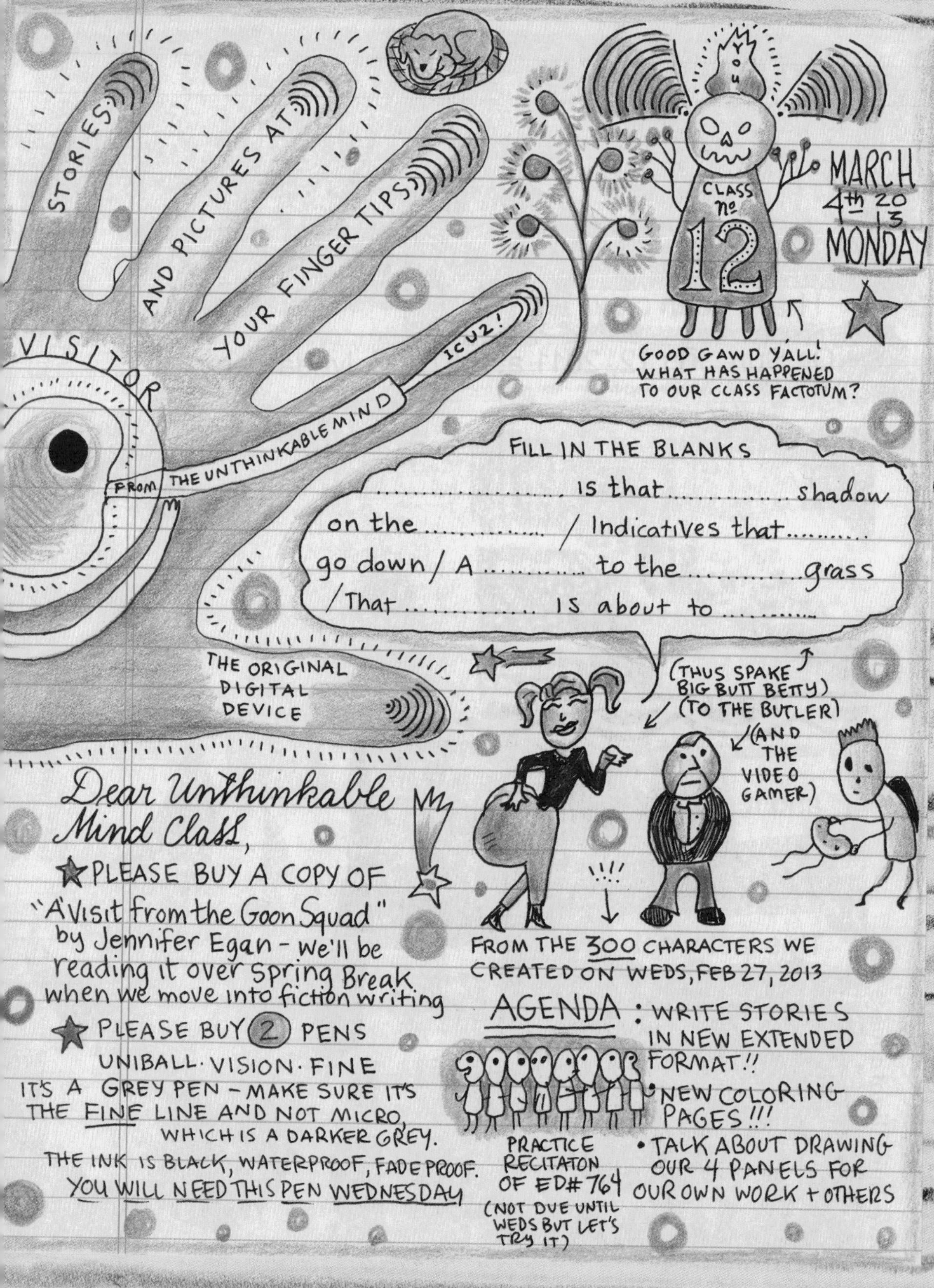
STORIES AND PICTURES AT YOUR FINGER TIPS
VISITOR
FROM THE UNTHINKABLE MIND
ICU2!
YOU
CLASS № 12
MARCH 4th 2013 MONDAY
GOOD GAWD Y'ALL! WHAT HAS HAPPENED TO OUR CLASS FACTOTUM?
FILL IN THE BLANKS
.... is that .... shadow on the .... / Indicatives that .... go down / A .... to the .... grass / That .... is about to ....
THE ORIGINAL DIGITAL DEVICE
(THUS SPAKE BIG BUTT BETTY)
(TO THE BUTLER)
(AND THE VIDEO GAMER)
!!!!
FROM THE 300 CHARACTERS WE CREATED ON WEDS, FEB 27, 2013
Dear Unthinkable Mind Class,
★ PLEASE BUY A COPY OF "A Visit from the Goon Squad" by Jennifer Egan - we'll be reading it over Spring Break when we move into fiction writing
★ PLEASE BUY 2 PENS
UNIBALL · VISION · FINE
IT'S A GREY PEN - MAKE SURE IT'S THE FINE LINE AND NOT MICRO, WHICH IS A DARKER GREY.
THE INK IS BLACK, WATERPROOF, FADEPROOF.
YOU WILL NEED THIS PEN WEDNESDAY
AGENDA: WRITE STORIES IN NEW EXTENDED FORMAT!!
• NEW COLORING PAGES!!!
• TALK ABOUT DRAWING OUR 4 PANELS FOR OUR OWN WORK + OTHERS
PRACTICE RECITATON OF ED# 764
(NOT DUE UNTIL WEDS BUT LET'S TRY IT)

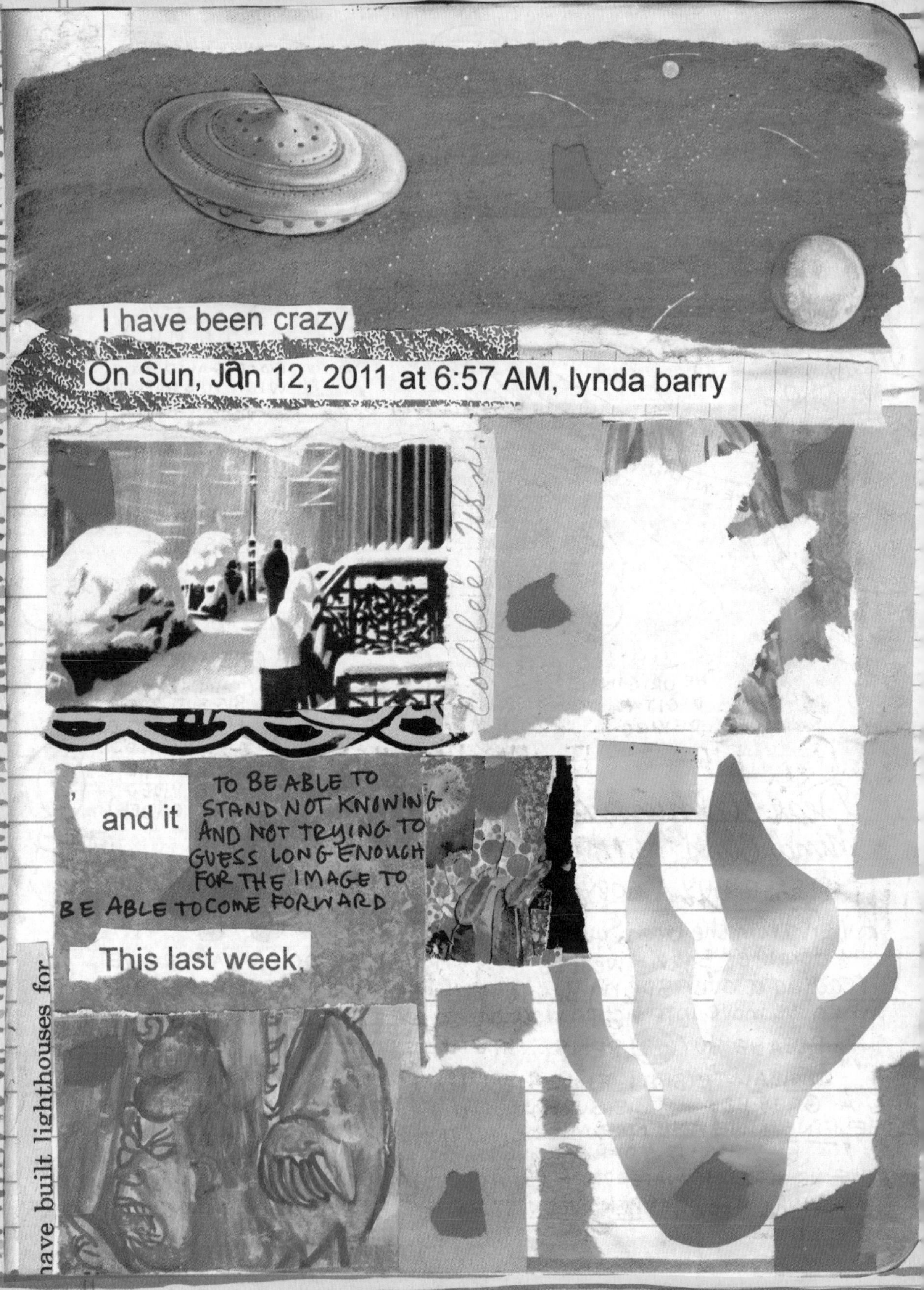
I have been crazy
On Sun, Jan 12, 2011 at 6:57 AM, lynda barry
, and it
TO BE ABLE TO STAND NOT KNOWING AND NOT TRYING TO GUESS LONG ENOUGH FOR THE IMAGE TO BE ABLE TO COME FORWARD
This last week,
have built lighthouses for

CLASS# 13 THE UNTHINKABLE MIND

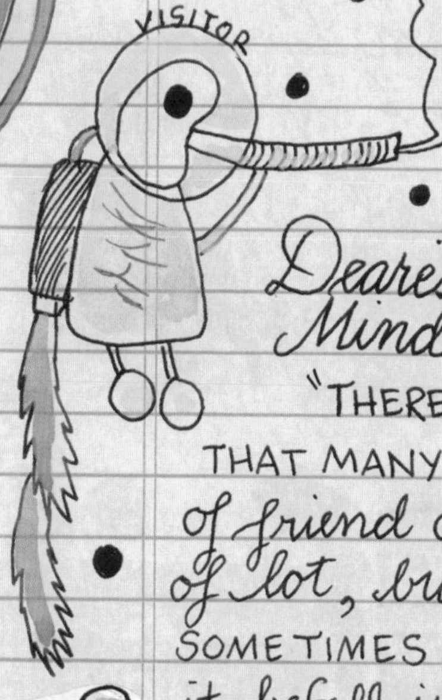
VISITOR

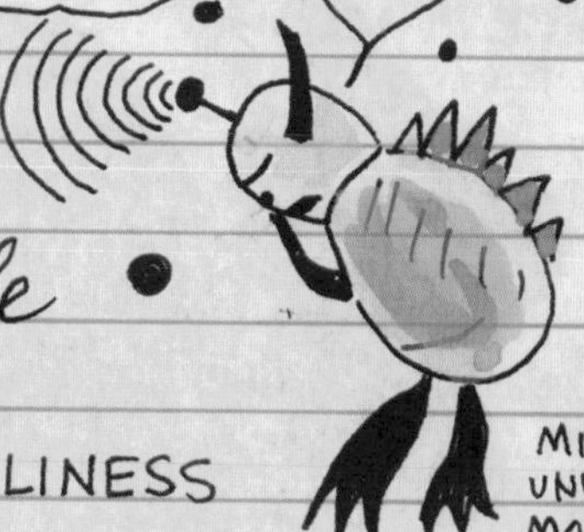
MIS-
UNDERSTOOD
MONSTER

MARCH 6, 2013

Dearest Unthinkable Mind Students,

"THERE IS ANOTHER LONELINESS THAT MANY DIE WITHOUT. not want of friend occasions it, or circumstances of lot, but NATURE sometimes, SOMETIMES THOUGHT, and who so it befall is RICHER than can be revealed by mortal numeral. ALSO, WHEN IN THE COURSE OF HUMAN EVENTS IT BECOMES NECESSARY to ASK about EXPERIENCES we've had with HIPPIES, vet techs, HIGH SCHOOL TEACHERS, Big Butt Betty, THE 'IT' MAN, DORKS, DICKS, vegans, dead people, gamblers, ARTISTS, DENTISTS, People named 'ALEX', MOTHERS, Priests, DOCTORS, LIBRARIANS, ghosts, KINGS, Gassy Lassy, Cops, FLIRTS, Jackasses, FRENCH PEOPLE, or any of the 300 characters CREATED DURING OUR 150 MINUTES together on FEB 27, 2013, We must also ASK OURSELVES about the STORIES these EXPERIENCES have left behind..."

EMILY DICKINSON #1116

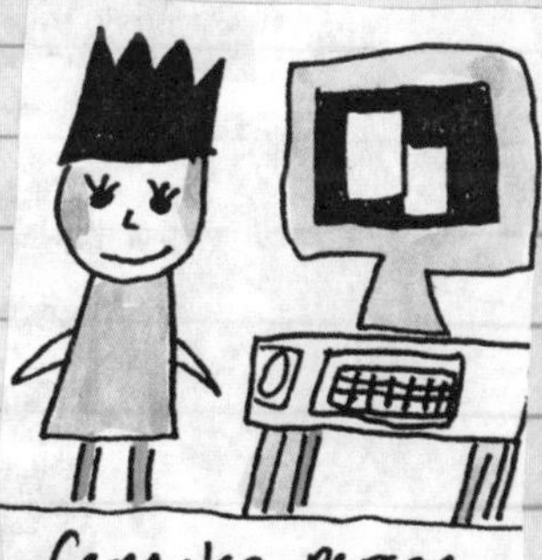
Computer person

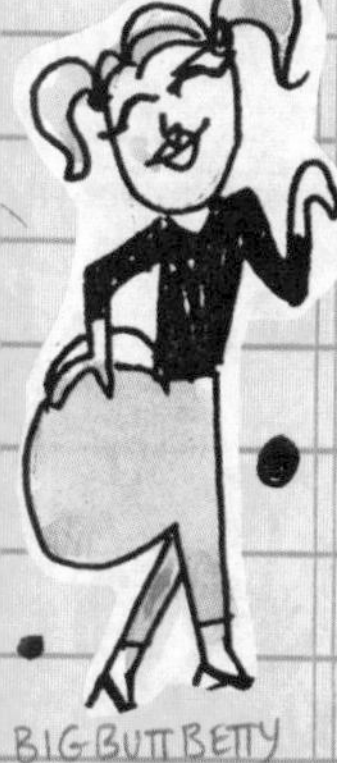
BIG BUTT BETTY

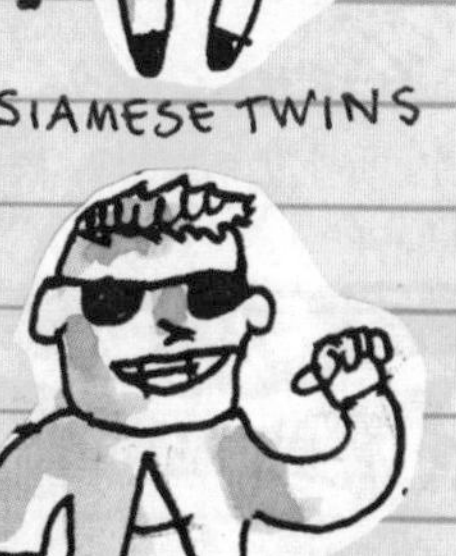
SIAMESE TWINS

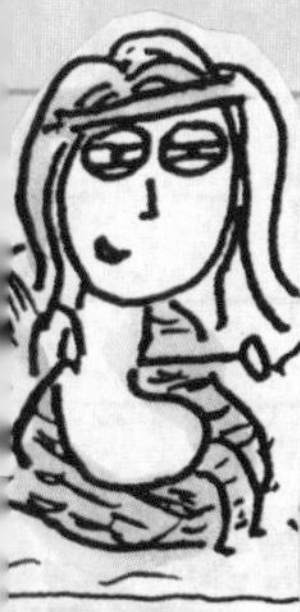
STONER

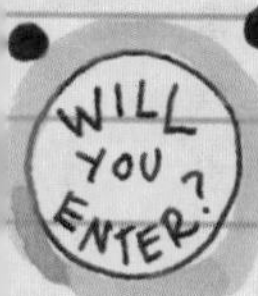
WILL YOU ENTER?

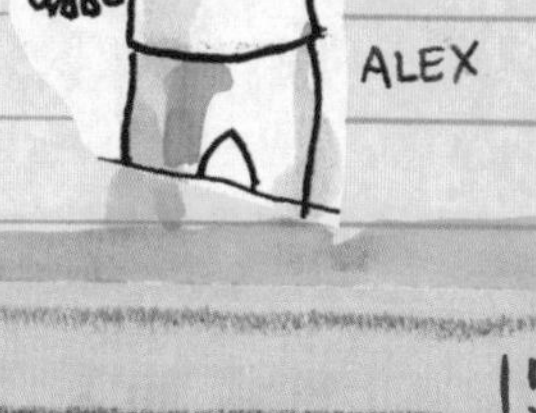
ALEX

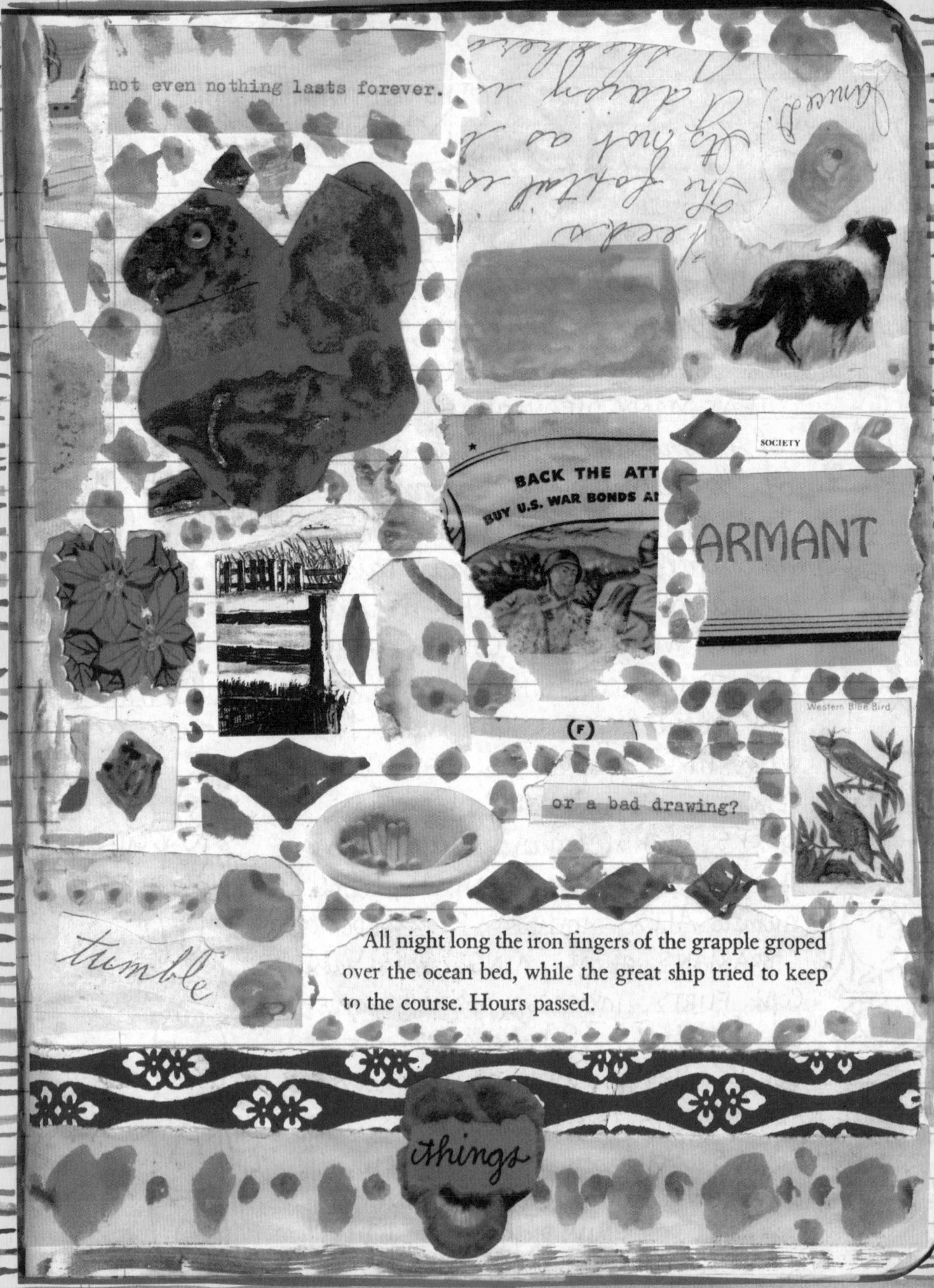
not even nothing lasts forever.
BACK THE ATT
BUY U.S. WAR BONDS A
SOCIETY
ARMANT
Western Blue Bird
or a bad drawing?
tumble
All night long the iron fingers of the grapple groped over the ocean bed, while the great ship tried to keep to the course. Hours passed.
things

UM #13
PAGE 2
MAR 6 2013

HOME WORK DUE MONDAY

- CONTINUE DAILY DIARY PRACTICE
- FOUR 9-MINUTE STORIES *in the* 3rd PERSON, USING CHARACTERS *on* THE HANDOUT *of* IMAGES I GAVE YOU:

  STEP ONE: NUMBER PAGE FROM 1-10

  STEP TWO: PICK A CHARACTER FROM ONE OF THE PAGES, LIKE "DENTIST"

  STEP THREE: WRITE THE FIRST TEN MEMORIES THAT COME TO YOU ABOUT ENCOUNTERS YOU'VE HAD WITH THIS TYPE OF PERSON

  STEP FOUR: CHOOSE ONE, DO YOUR [X] page, WRITE FOR 9 MINUTES IN THE 3RD PERSON, REFERRING TO YOURSELF AS "X"

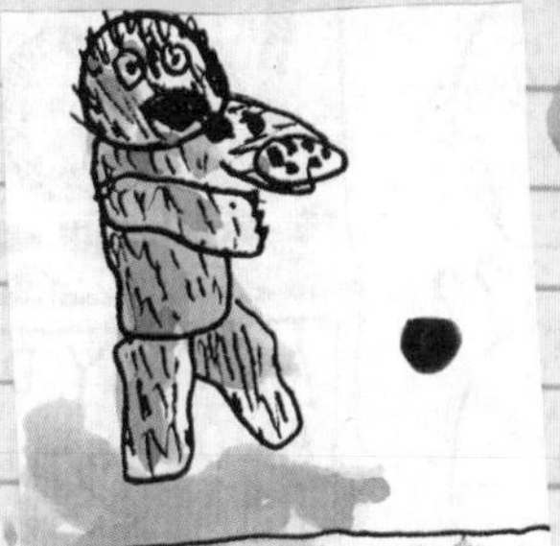
Cookie Monster

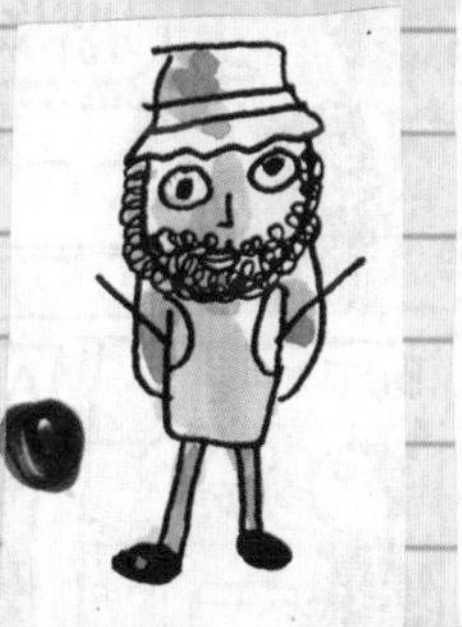
BACKPACKER

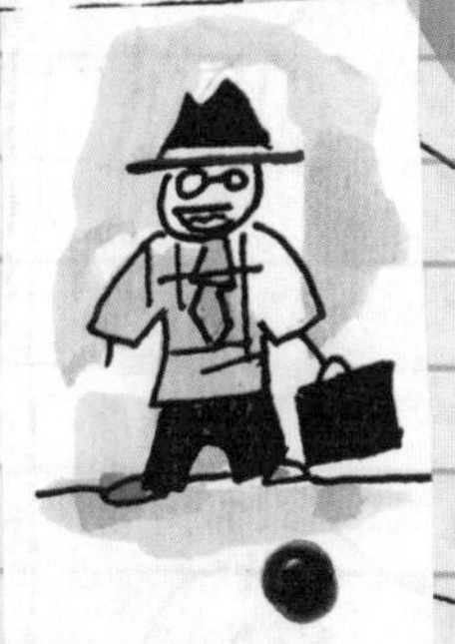
Salesman

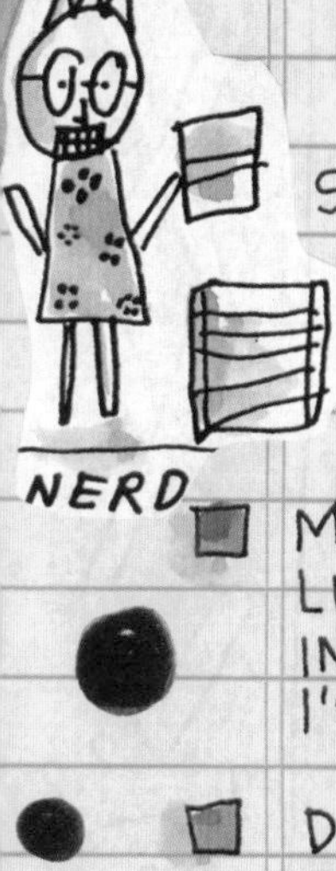
NERD

- MAKE YOUR "WORD BAG" OF AT LEAST 100 WORDS USING THE INDEX CARDS AND ENVELOPES I'VE GIVEN YOU

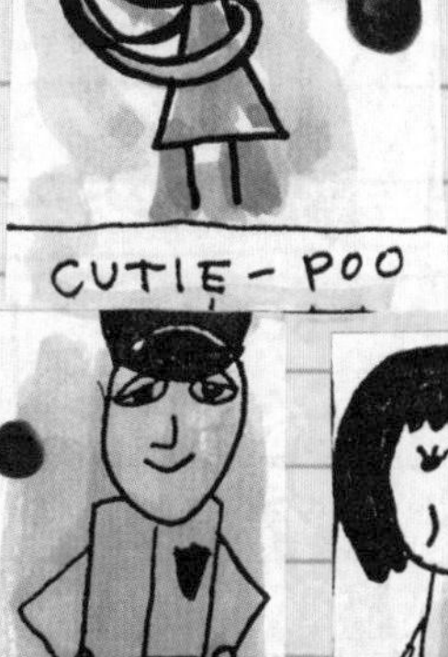
CUTIE-POO

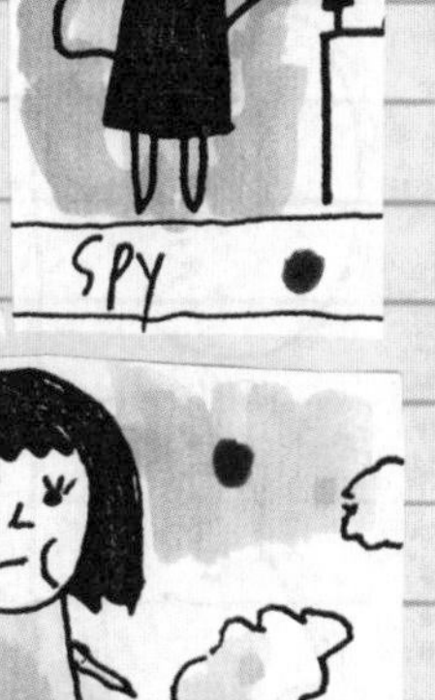
SPY

- DO EXERCISE # 3.1 IN THE BRUNETTI BOOK (PAGE 37) USE NON-PHOTO BLUE FIRST, THEN INK THEM IN, BRING THEM TO CLASS, PUT THEM UP. INSTEAD OF INDEX CARDS, USE 8.5 X 11 PAPER FOLDED TO MAKE 12 PANELS. FILL SOMETHING IN EACH PANEL W/ BLACK

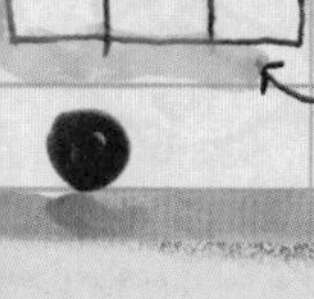

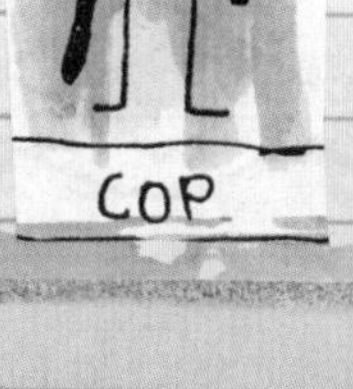
COP

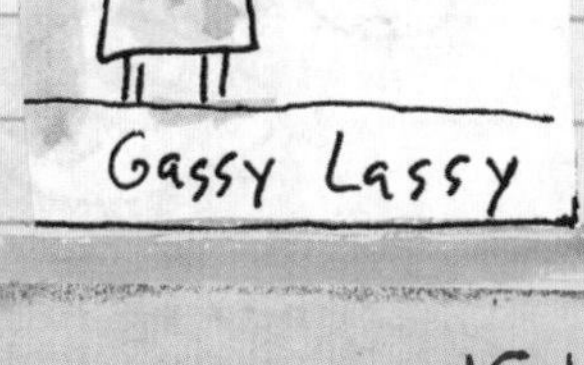
Gassy Lassy

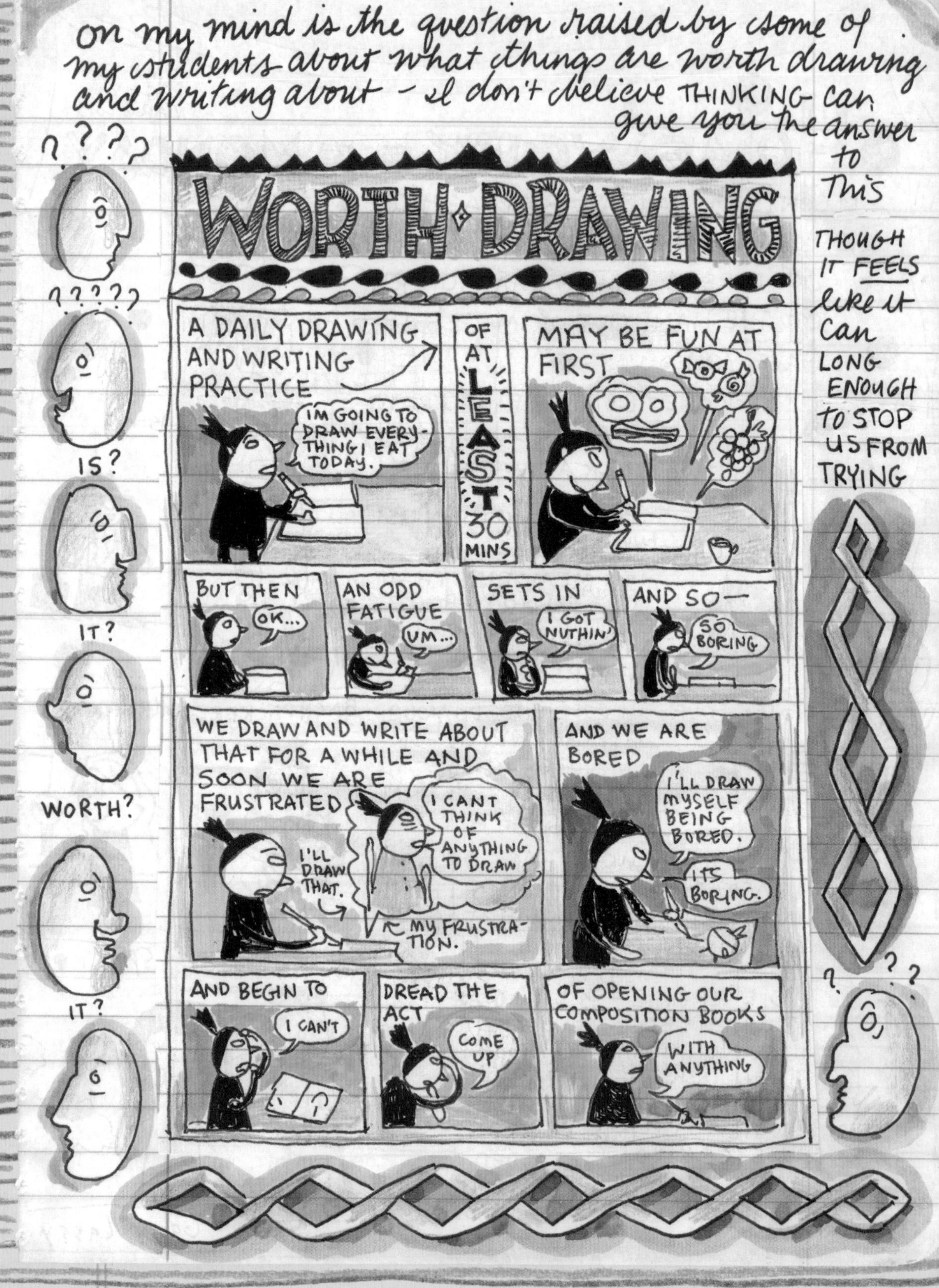

on my mind is the question raised by some of my students about what things are worth drawing and writing about - I don't believe THINKING can give you the answer to this
THOUGH IT FEELS like it can LONG ENOUGH TO STOP US FROM TRYING
??? ?
?????
IS?
IT?
WORTH?
IT?
? ? ?
WORTH DRAWING
A DAILY DRAWING AND WRITING PRACTICE
I'M GOING TO DRAW EVERYTHING I EAT TODAY.
OF AT LEAST 30 MINS
MAY BE FUN AT FIRST
BUT THEN
OK...
AN ODD FATIGUE
UM...
SETS IN
I GOT NUTHIN'
AND SO—
SO BORING
WE DRAW AND WRITE ABOUT THAT FOR A WHILE AND SOON WE ARE FRUSTRATED
I CANT THINK OF ANYTHING TO DRAW
I'LL DRAW THAT.
MY FRUSTRATION.
AND WE ARE BORED
I'LL DRAW MYSELF BEING BORED.
ITS BORING.
AND BEGIN TO
I CAN'T
DREAD THE ACT
COME UP
OF OPENING OUR COMPOSITION BOOKS
WITH ANYTHING

we know that athletes, musicians, and actors all have to practice, rehearse, repeat things until it gets into the body, the 'muscle memory', but for some reason, writers and visual artists think they have

to be INSPIRED before they make something. not suspecting the PHYSICAL ACT of writing or drawing is what brings that INSPIRATION about.

WORRYING ABOUT ITS WORTH and VALUE to others BEFORE it exists can keep us IMMOBILIZED forever.

NOTHING IN OUR LIVES

IS WORTH DRAWING A COMIC ABOUT

OR AT LEAST IT FEELS THIS WAY

I GIVE UP

UNTIL

THE MOMENT WHEN WE REALIZE

THERE ARE MITES IN OUR EYEBROWS LAYING EGGS IN THE FOLLICLES

AND A STORY ABOUT A MURDER ON THE NEWS

AND A PERSON PASSING BY WITH A RASPBERRY BIRTHMARK THAT

COVERS HALF THEIR FACE—

AND WE ARE AWAKENED AGAIN TO WHAT IS THERE AND EVER-THERE.

I WANNA DO IT, BUT WHO WILL WANNA READ IT?

ANY STORY WE WRITE OR PICTURE WE MAKE CANNOT DEMONSTRATE ITS WORTH UNTIL WE WRITE IT OR DRAW IT. the answer can't come to us any other way.

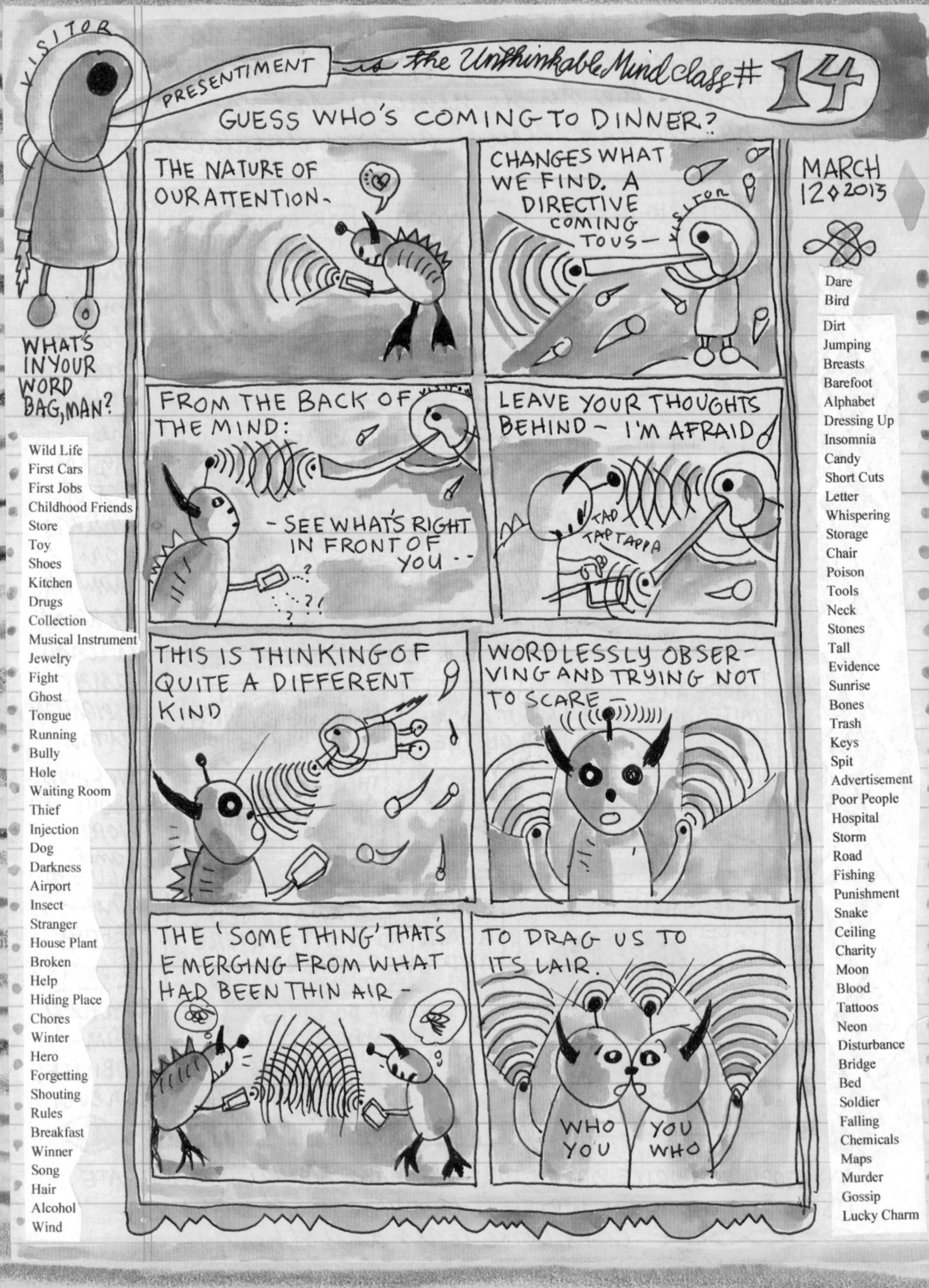
VISITOR
PRESENTIMENT
is the Unthinkable Mind class # 14
GUESS WHO'S COMING TO DINNER?
WHAT'S IN YOUR WORD BAG, MAN?
Wild Life
First Cars
First Jobs
Childhood Friends
Store
Toy
Shoes
Kitchen
Drugs
Collection
Musical Instrument
Jewelry
Fight
Ghost
Tongue
Running
Bully
Hole
Waiting Room
Thief
Injection
Dog
Darkness
Airport
Insect
Stranger
House Plant
Broken
Help
Hiding Place
Chores
Winter
Hero
Forgetting
Shouting
Rules
Breakfast
Winner
Song
Hair
Alcohol
Wind
THE NATURE OF OUR ATTENTION-
CHANGES WHAT WE FIND. A DIRECTIVE COMING TO US-
VISITOR
FROM THE BACK OF THE MIND:
- SEE WHAT'S RIGHT IN FRONT OF YOU - -
LEAVE YOUR THOUGHTS BEHIND - I'M AFRAID
TAP TAP TAPPA
THIS IS THINKING OF QUITE A DIFFERENT KIND
WORDLESSLY OBSERVING AND TRYING NOT TO SCARE -
THE 'SOMETHING' THAT'S EMERGING FROM WHAT HAD BEEN THIN AIR -
TO DRAG US TO ITS LAIR.
WHO YOU
YOU WHO
MARCH 12 ◊ 2013
Dare
Bird
Dirt
Jumping
Breasts
Barefoot
Alphabet
Dressing Up
Insomnia
Candy
Short Cuts
Letter
Whispering
Storage
Chair
Poison
Tools
Neck
Stones
Tall
Evidence
Sunrise
Bones
Trash
Keys
Spit
Advertisement
Poor People
Hospital
Storm
Road
Fishing
Punishment
Snake
Ceiling
Charity
Moon
Blood
Tattoos
Neon
Disturbance
Bridge
Bed
Soldier
Falling
Chemicals
Maps
Murder
Gossip
Lucky Charm

Silence
Warmth
Departure
Big Sister
Vandalism
Teacher
Tree
Underwear
Club
Revenge
Church
Thumbprint
Visitor
Fat
Digging
Fire
Wild Animal
Cigarette
Skin
Misfit
Park
Tourist
Stench
Stubborn
Cat
Curled Up
Staircase
Card Game
Secret
Washing
Monster
Wallet
Abandoned
Window
Puddle
Cooking
Names
Kiss
Criticism
Gardening
Gun
Blanket
Fixing
Rain
Injury
Questions
Scars
Vacation

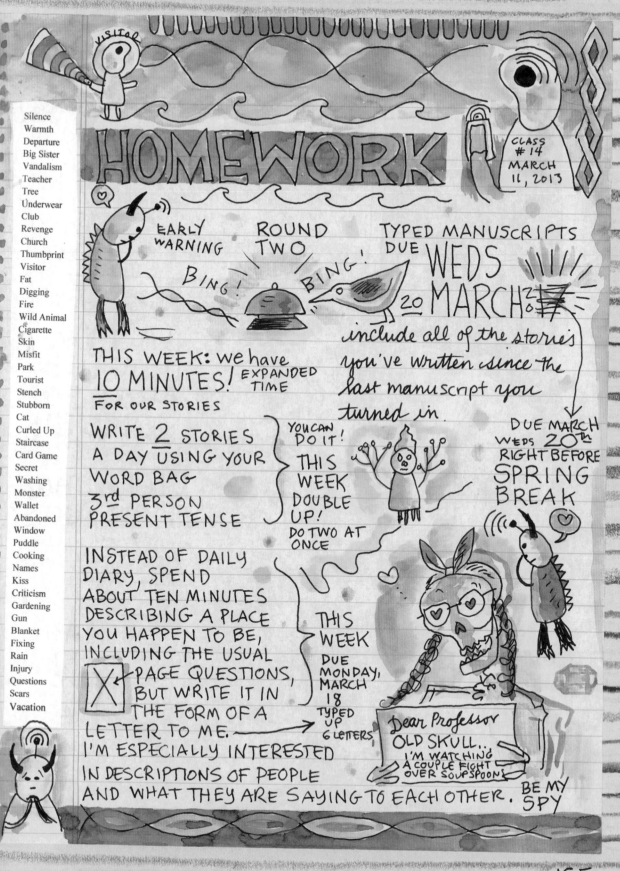

VISITOR

HOMEWORK

CLASS #14
MARCH 11, 2013

EARLY WARNING ROUND TWO

BING! BING!

TYPED MANUSCRIPTS DUE WEDS 20 MARCH 2013

include all of the stories you've written since the last manuscript you turned in.

DUE MARCH WEDS 20th RIGHT BEFORE SPRING BREAK

THIS WEEK: we have 10 MINUTES! EXPANDED TIME FOR OUR STORIES

WRITE 2 STORIES A DAY USING YOUR WORD BAG
3rd PERSON PRESENT TENSE

YOU CAN DO IT!
THIS WEEK DOUBLE UP!
DO TWO AT ONCE

INSTEAD OF DAILY DIARY, SPEND ABOUT TEN MINUTES DESCRIBING A PLACE YOU HAPPEN TO BE, INCLUDING THE USUAL X PAGE QUESTIONS, BUT WRITE IT IN THE FORM OF A LETTER TO ME.

THIS WEEK
DUE MONDAY, MARCH 18
TYPED UP 6 LETTERS

I'M ESPECIALLY INTERESTED IN DESCRIPTIONS OF PEOPLE AND WHAT THEY ARE SAYING TO EACH OTHER.

Dear Professor OLD SKULL.. I'M WATCHING A COUPLE FIGHT OVER SOUPSPOONS

BE MY SPY

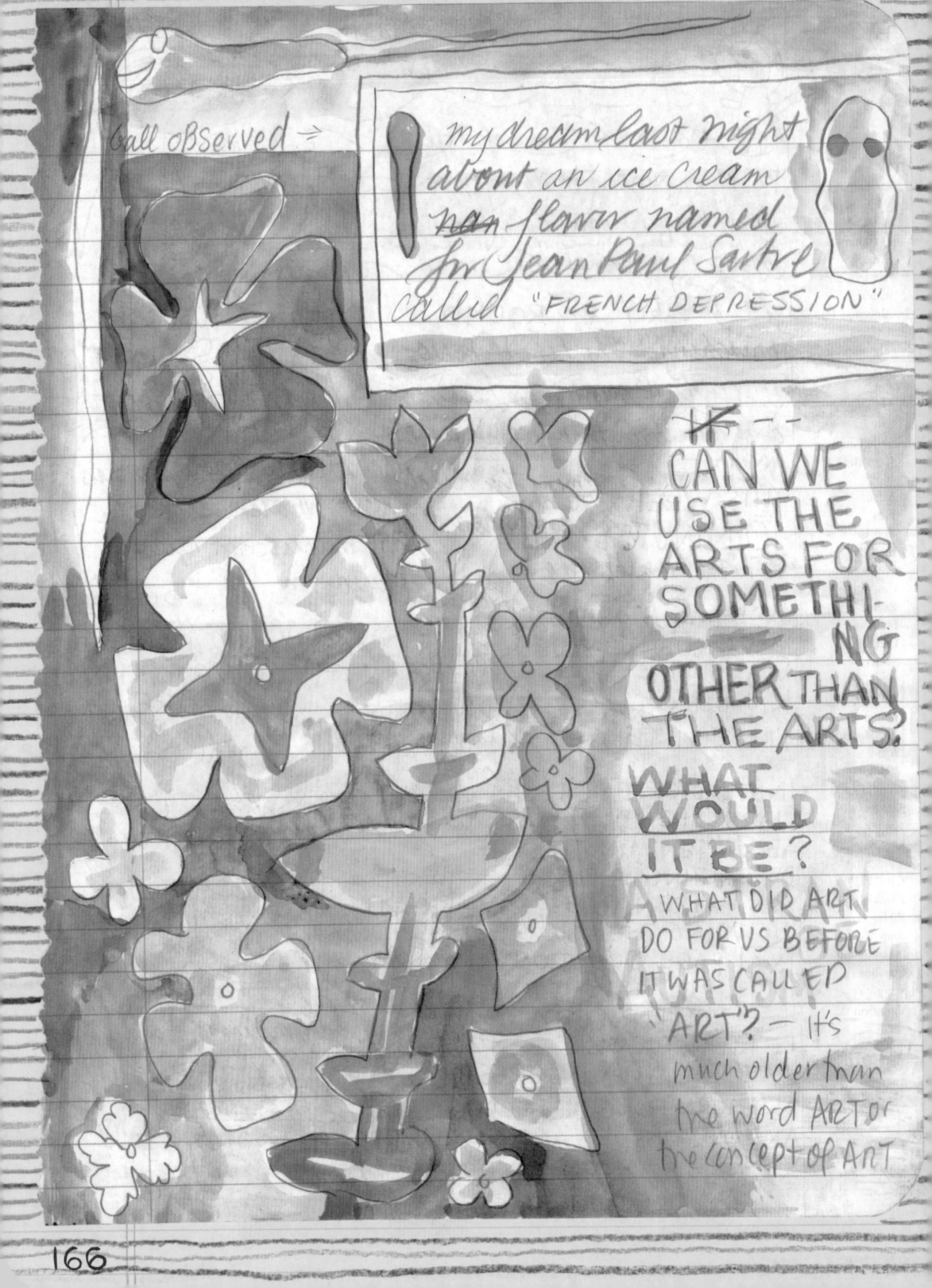
ball observed ⇒
my dream last night about an ice cream ~~nan~~ flavor named for Jean Paul Sartre called "FRENCH DEPRESSION"
~~IF~~ --
CAN WE USE THE ARTS FOR SOMETHI-NG OTHER THAN THE ARTS?
WHAT WOULD IT BE?
WHAT DID ART DO FOR US BEFORE IT WAS CALLED 'ART'? — It's much older than the word ART or the concept of ART

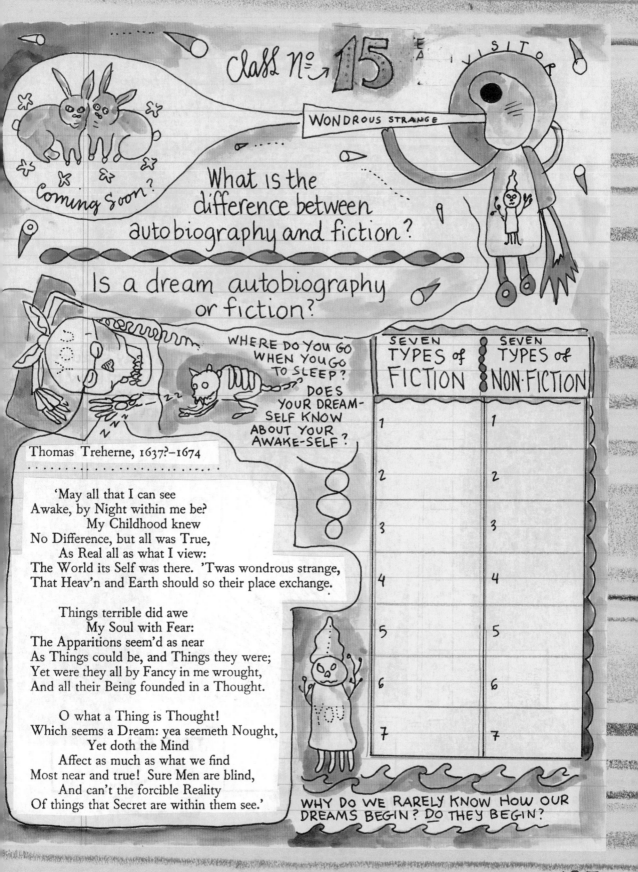

Class No. 15

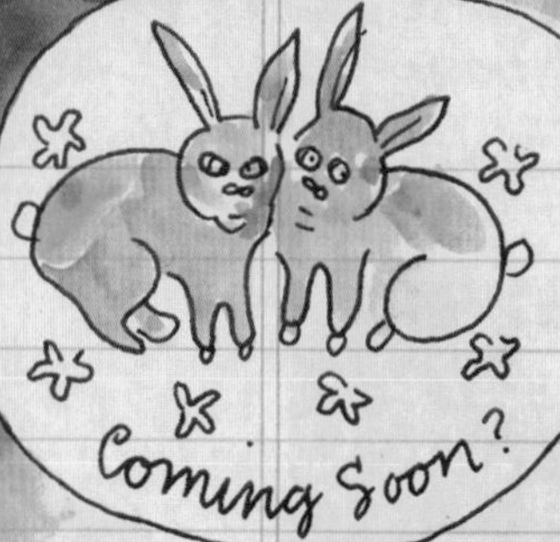
Coming Soon?

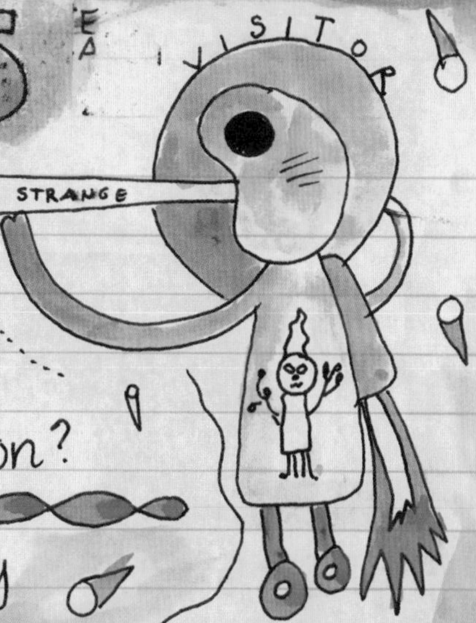
WONDROUS STRANGE

What is the difference between autobiography and fiction?

Is a dream autobiography or fiction?

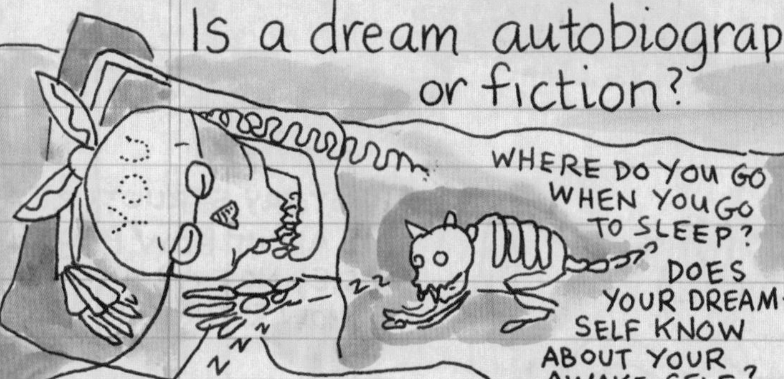
YOU

WHERE DO YOU GO WHEN YOU GO TO SLEEP?

DOES YOUR DREAM-SELF KNOW ABOUT YOUR AWAKE-SELF?

Thomas Treherne, 1637?–1674

'May all that I can see
Awake, by Night within me be?
My Childhood knew
No Difference, but all was True,
As Real all as what I view:
The World its Self was there. 'Twas wondrous strange,
That Heav'n and Earth should so their place exchange.

Things terrible did awe
My Soul with Fear:
The Apparitions seem'd as near
As Things could be, and Things they were;
Yet were they all by Fancy in me wrought,
And all their Being founded in a Thought.

O what a Thing is Thought!
Which seems a Dream: yea seemeth Nought,
Yet doth the Mind
Affect as much as what we find
Most near and true! Sure Men are blind,
And can't the forcible Reality
Of things that Secret are within them see.'

SEVEN TYPES of FICTION	SEVEN TYPES of NON-FICTION
1	1
2	2
3	3
4	4
5	5
6	6
7	7

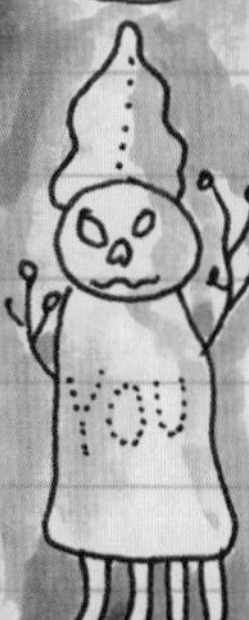
YOU

WHY DO WE RARELY KNOW HOW OUR DREAMS BEGIN? DO THEY BEGIN?

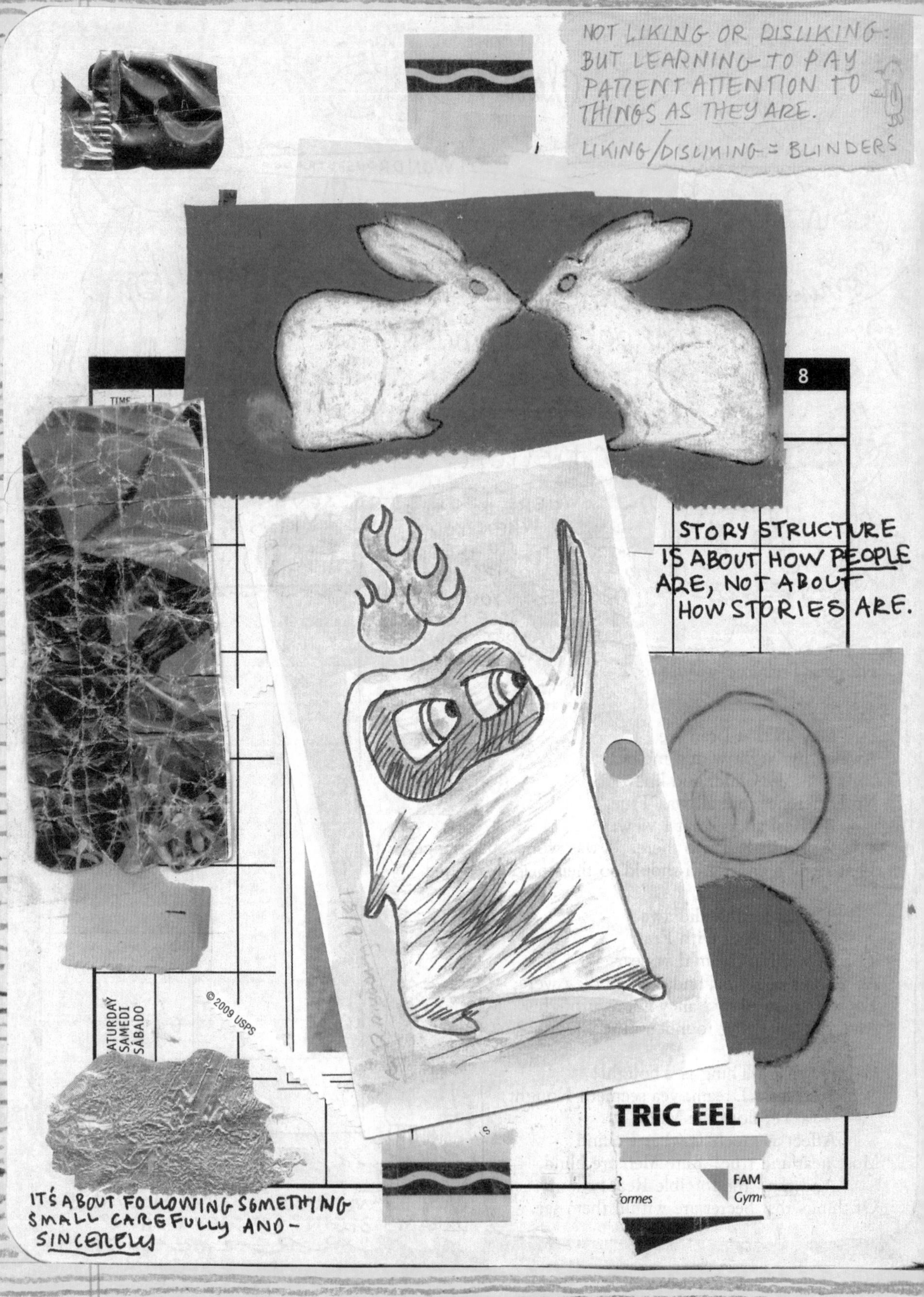
NOT LIKING OR DISLIKING: BUT LEARNING TO PAY PATIENT ATTENTION TO THINGS AS THEY ARE.
LIKING/DISLIKING = BLINDERS
8
TIME
STORY STRUCTURE IS ABOUT HOW PEOPLE ARE, NOT ABOUT HOW STORIES ARE.
SATURDAY
SAMEDI
SÁBADO
© 2009 USPS
TRIC EEL
FAM
Gymn
formes
IT'S ABOUT FOLLOWING SOMETHING SMALL CAREFULLY AND - SINCERELY

UM
#15
PAGE 2

HOMEWORK

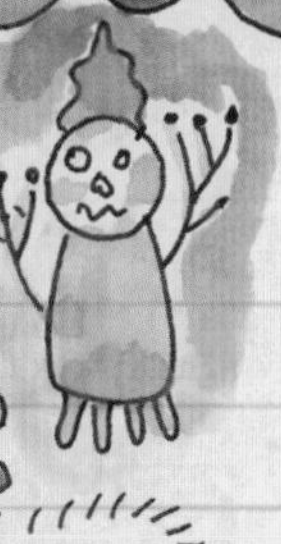

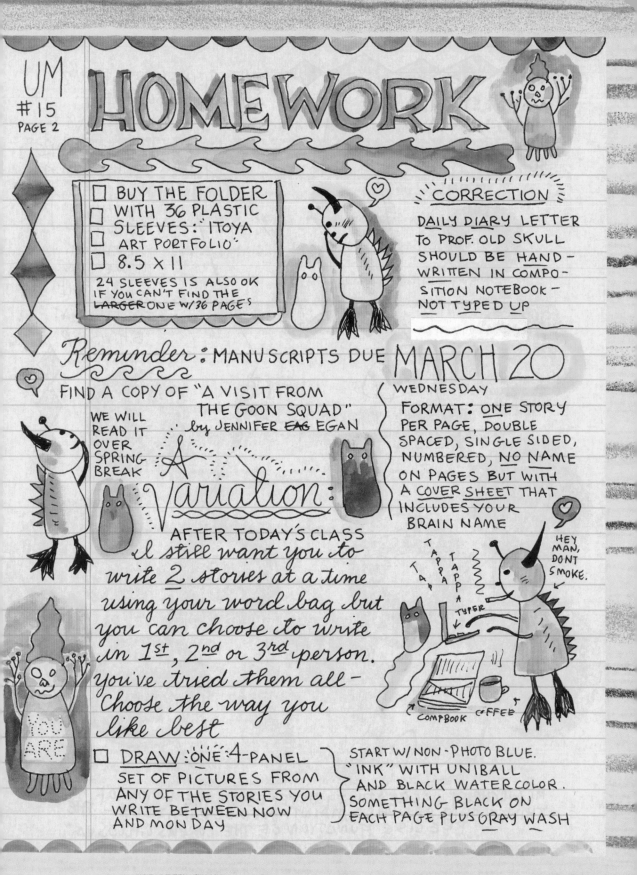

- ☐ BUY THE FOLDER
- ☐ WITH 36 PLASTIC SLEEVES: "ITOYA
- ☐ ART PORTFOLIO"
- ☐ 8.5 x 11

24 SLEEVES IS ALSO OK IF YOU CAN'T FIND THE ~~LARGER~~ ONE W/36 PAGES

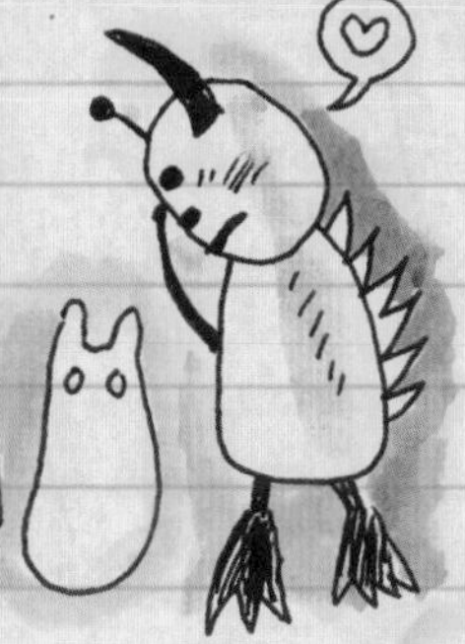

CORRECTION

DAILY DIARY LETTER TO PROF. OLD SKULL SHOULD BE HAND-WRITTEN IN COMPOSITION NOTEBOOK - NOT TYPED UP

Reminder: MANUSCRIPTS DUE MARCH 20 WEDNESDAY

FIND A COPY OF "A VISIT FROM THE GOON SQUAD" by JENNIFER ~~EAG~~ EGAN

WE WILL READ IT OVER SPRING BREAK

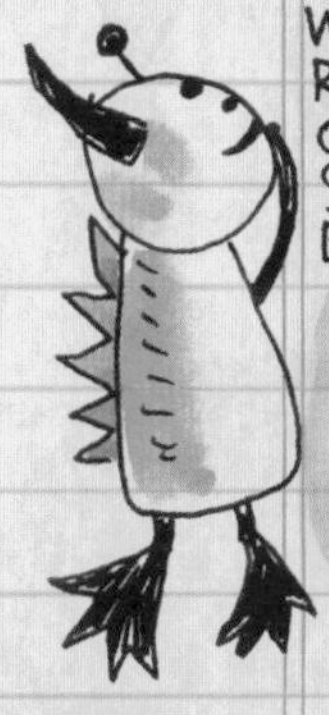

FORMAT: ONE STORY PER PAGE, DOUBLE SPACED, SINGLE SIDED, NUMBERED, NO NAME ON PAGES BUT WITH A COVER SHEET THAT INCLUDES YOUR BRAIN NAME

A Variation:

AFTER TODAY'S CLASS

I still want you to write 2 stories at a time using your word bag but you can choose to write in 1st, 2nd or 3rd person. you've tried them all - Choose the way you like best

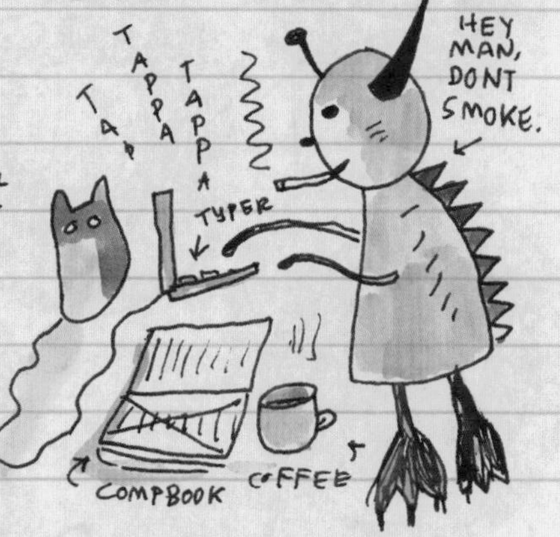

HEY MAN, DONT SMOKE.
TAP
TAPPA
TAPPA
TYPER
COMPBOOK
COFFEE

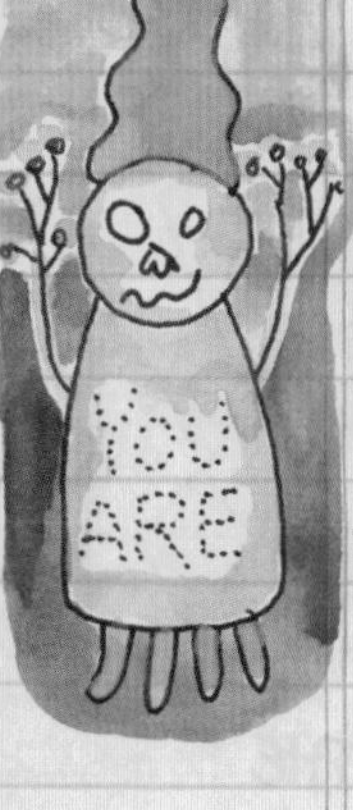

YOU ARE

☐ DRAW: ONE 4-PANEL SET OF PICTURES FROM ANY OF THE STORIES YOU WRITE BETWEEN NOW AND MONDAY

START W/ NON-PHOTO BLUE. "INK" WITH UNIBALL AND BLACK WATERCOLOR. SOMETHING BLACK ON EACH PAGE PLUS GRAY WASH

'WE MEET OUR DESTINY IN THE ROAD WE TAKE TO AVOID IT. "
—JUNG

" ART BRINGS INTO BEING A TRUTH ABOUT THE WORLD THAT WAS NOT THERE BEFORE "
—McGILCHRIST

WRITING + DRAWING CAN DO THIS IF WE CAN TAKE THE TRUTH THAT SHOWS UP.

MCGILCHRIST: "CREATIVITY DEPENDS ON THE UNION OF THINGS THAT ARE ALSO MAINTAINED SEPARATELY — THE PRECISE FUNCTION OF THE CORPUS CALLOSUM"

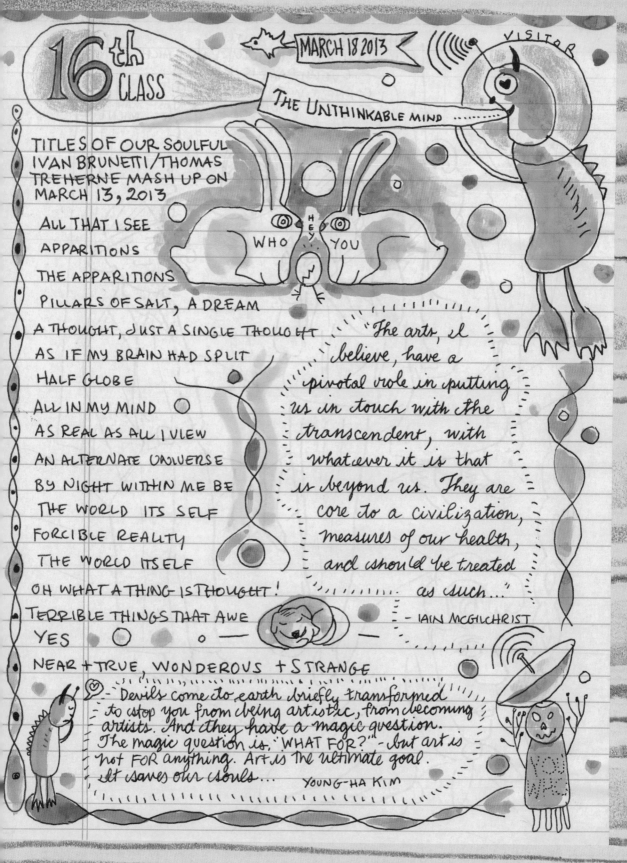

16th CLASS

MARCH 18 2013

THE UNTHINKABLE MIND

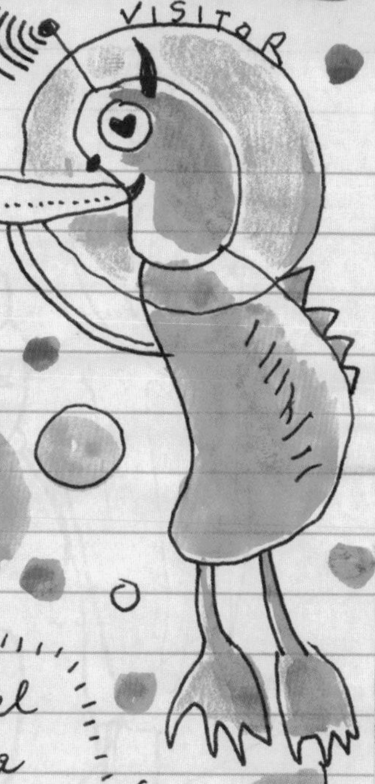
VISITOR

TITLES OF OUR SOULFUL IVAN BRUNETTI/THOMAS TREHERNE MASH UP ON MARCH 13, 2013

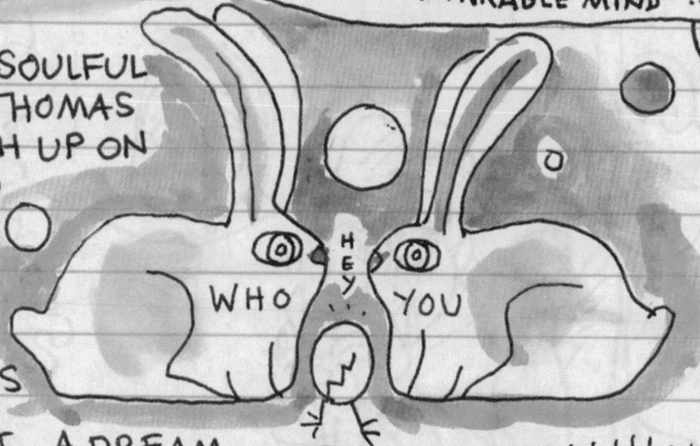
WHO
HEY
YOU

ALL THAT I SEE
APPARITIONS
THE APPARITIONS
PILLARS OF SALT, A DREAM
A THOUGHT, JUST A SINGLE THOUGHT
AS IF MY BRAIN HAD SPLIT
HALF GLOBE
ALL IN MY MIND
AS REAL AS ALL I VIEW
AN ALTERNATE UNIVERSE
BY NIGHT WITHIN ME BE
THE WORLD ITS SELF
FORCIBLE REALITY
THE WORLD ITSELF
OH WHAT A THING IS THOUGHT!
TERRIBLE THINGS THAT AWE
YES
NEAR + TRUE, WONDEROUS + STRANGE

"The arts, I believe, have a pivotal role in putting us in touch with the transcendent, with whatever it is that is beyond us. They are core to a civilization, measures of our health, and should be treated as such..."
— IAIN MCGILCHRIST

"Devils come to earth briefly transformed to stop you from being artistic, from becoming artists. And they have a magic question. The magic question is, "WHAT FOR?" — but art is not FOR anything. Art is the ultimate goal. It saves our souls...
YOUNG-HA KIM

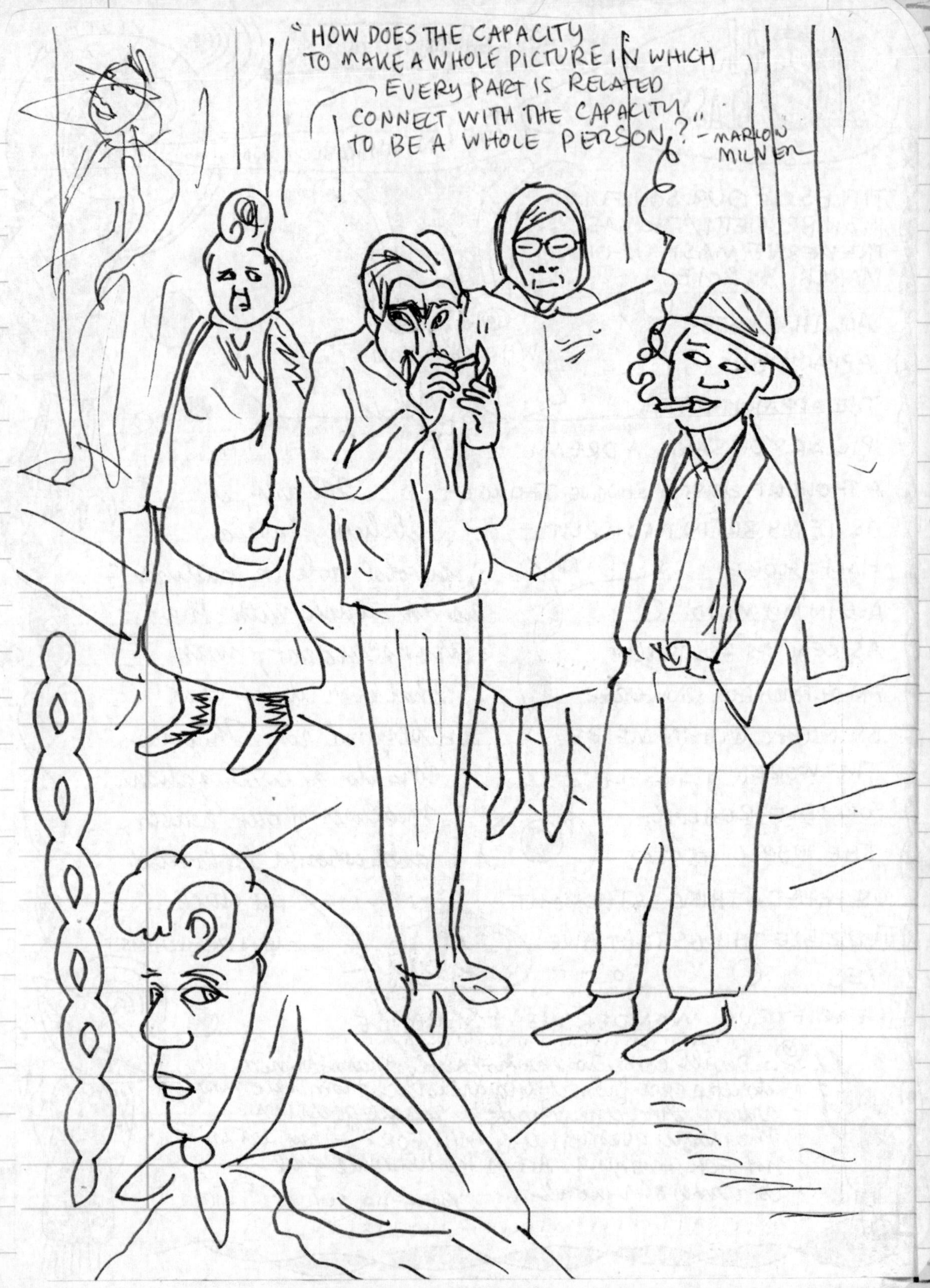
"HOW DOES THE CAPACITY
TO MAKE A WHOLE PICTURE IN WHICH
EVERY PART IS RELATED
CONNECT WITH THE CAPACITY
TO BE A WHOLE PERSON?" - MARION MILNER

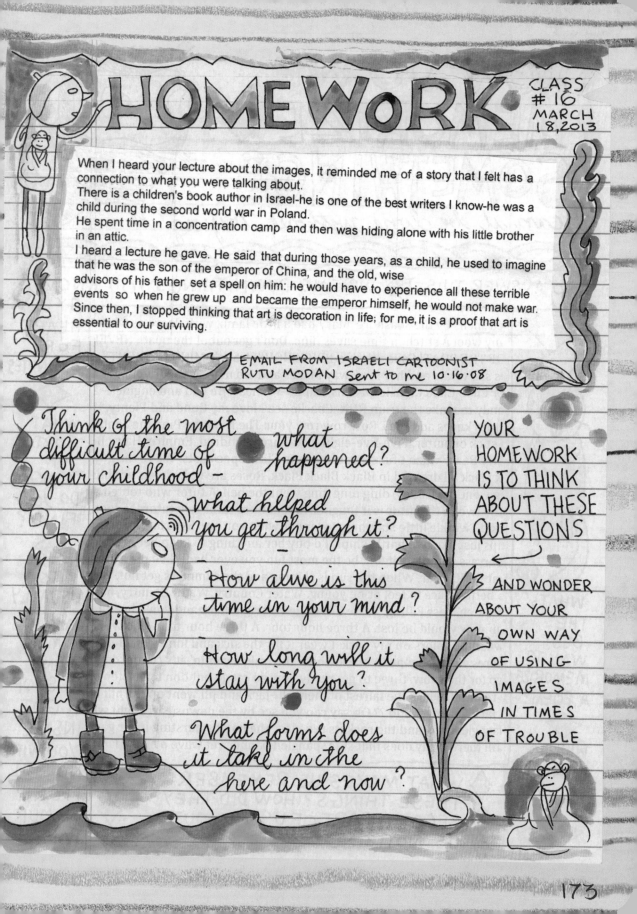

HOMEWORK

When I heard your lecture about the images, it reminded me of a story that I felt has a connection to what you were talking about.

There is a children's book author in Israel-he is one of the best writers I know-he was a child during the second world war in Poland.

He spent time in a concentration camp and then was hiding alone with his little brother in an attic.

I heard a lecture he gave. He said that during those years, as a child, he used to imagine that he was the son of the emperor of China, and the old, wise advisors of his father set a spell on him: he would have to experience all these terrible events so when he grew up and became the emperor himself, he would not make war. Since then, I stopped thinking that art is decoration in life; for me, it is a proof that art is essential to our surviving.

EMAIL FROM ISRAELI CARTOONIST
RUTU MODAN sent to me 10·16·08

Think of the most difficult time of your childhood —

what happened?

what helped you get through it?

How alive is this time in your mind?

How long will it stay with you?

What forms does it take in the here and now?

YOUR HOMEWORK IS TO THINK ABOUT THESE QUESTIONS

AND WONDER ABOUT YOUR OWN WAY OF USING IMAGES IN TIMES OF TROUBLE

HOW DO WE MEMORIZE SOMETHING?

can it be done without trying?

TO ANSWER THIS, TRY WRITING DOWN THINGS YOU KNOW BY HEART FOR 3 MINUTES

ea shells by the seashore. Mary had a little lamb, with fleece as white any wool A stitch in time saves nine. Don't get out of the boat! NEVEF OF THE BOAT! Cause she's a BRICK HOUSE! She's MIGHTY MIGHTY.. s she wears and her sexy way Makes and old man wish for younger er Choo Choo Charlie was his name—we hear. He had and engine— andy to make the train RUN. Charlie sez I love my Good and Plenty. H toes knees and toes. Row row row your The Nina the Pina the Santa stick of butter. Five-five-eight-two- three hundred, Empire! Hairy Be airy Beary wazn't fuzzy was he? Auto Glass Specialists. We're the guy k Mack all dressed in Black Black Black. Roses are red, violets are blu g went the trolley, ding ding ding went the bell. A tutor who tooted a the two to the tutor is it tougher to toot or to tutor two tutors to toot kle Twinkle little star, how I wonder what you are. Sky rockets in flip ips just like two battle ships. I'd buy her anything to keep her in style barrass your dad, it will be the most fun you ever had! Give me a brea at Kit Kat Bar. When the sun is shining and the summers get hot, Wa better place to feel or be young. Water Country, Water Country, hav ite Hen. Less Filling. Taste Great! Just sit right back and you'll hear a minnow would be lost. A three hour tour. A three hour tour. You won wear the colors on my back. I wear it for the sick and lonely old, for th eres always a man in black. I hear the train a comin', it's comin' dow o for the show, three to get ready now go cat go but don't you step o the wall, who's the fairest of them all? Jack and Jill went up the hill to Jack fell down and ?? Oh say can you see by the dawns early light wl last gleaming and the rockets red glare the bombs bursting in air gav till there O say does that star spangled banner yet wave o'er the land

WHAT SORTS OF THINGS DO YOU FIND?

IT'S USUALLY QUITE A MIX AND MOST OF IT GOT INSIDE YOU WITH NO REAL EFFORT ON YOUR PART

WHAT'S THE BEST WAY TO MEMORIZE A POEM?

WHY DO IT AT ALL??

WHAT MAKES US REMEMBER THESE THINGS? HOW DID THEY BECOME PART OF US WITHOUT US NOTICING?

HOMEWORK

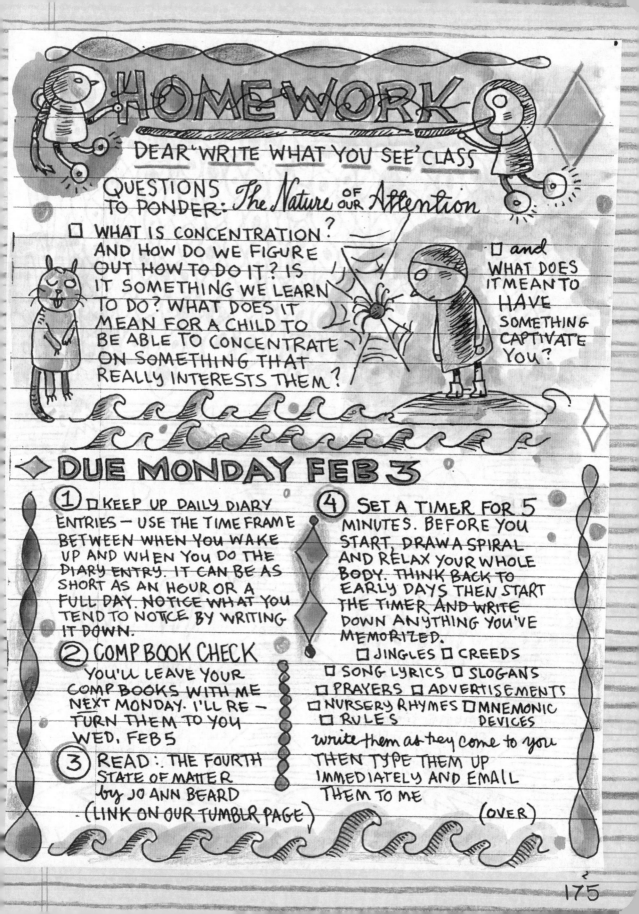

DEAR "WRITE WHAT YOU SEE" CLASS

QUESTIONS TO PONDER: *The Nature of our Attention*

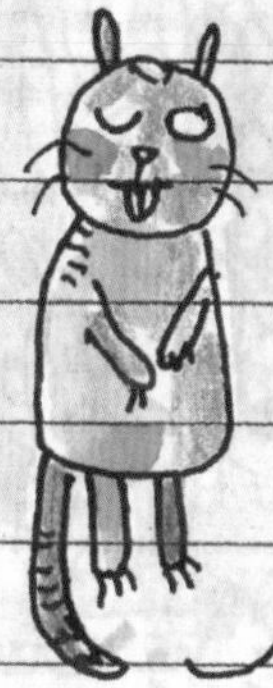

☐ WHAT IS CONCENTRATION? AND HOW DO WE FIGURE OUT HOW TO DO IT? IS IT SOMETHING WE LEARN TO DO? WHAT DOES IT MEAN FOR A CHILD TO BE ABLE TO CONCENTRATE ON SOMETHING THAT REALLY INTERESTS THEM?

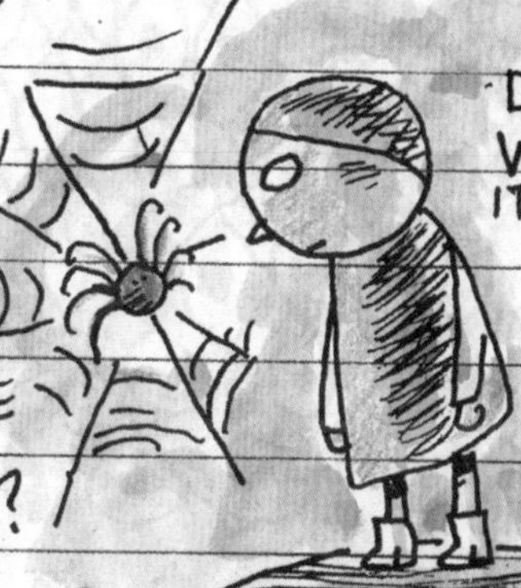

☐ *and* WHAT DOES IT MEAN TO HAVE SOMETHING CAPTIVATE YOU?

DUE MONDAY FEB 3

① ☐ KEEP UP DAILY DIARY ENTRIES — USE THE TIME FRAME BETWEEN WHEN YOU WAKE UP AND WHEN YOU DO THE DIARY ENTRY. IT CAN BE AS SHORT AS AN HOUR OR A FULL DAY. NOTICE WHAT YOU TEND TO NOTICE BY WRITING IT DOWN.

② COMP BOOK CHECK
YOU'LL LEAVE YOUR COMP BOOKS WITH ME NEXT MONDAY. I'LL RETURN THEM TO YOU WED, FEB 5

③ READ: THE FOURTH STATE OF MATTER *by* JO ANN BEARD (LINK ON OUR TUMBLR PAGE)

④ SET A TIMER FOR 5 MINUTES. BEFORE YOU START, DRAW A SPIRAL AND RELAX YOUR WHOLE BODY. THINK BACK TO EARLY DAYS THEN START THE TIMER AND WRITE DOWN ANYTHING YOU'VE MEMORIZED.

☐ JINGLES ☐ CREEDS
☐ SONG LYRICS ☐ SLOGANS
☐ PRAYERS ☐ ADVERTISEMENTS
☐ NURSERY RHYMES ☐ MNEMONIC DEVICES
☐ RULES

write them as they come to you THEN TYPE THEM UP IMMEDIATELY AND EMAIL THEM TO ME

(OVER)

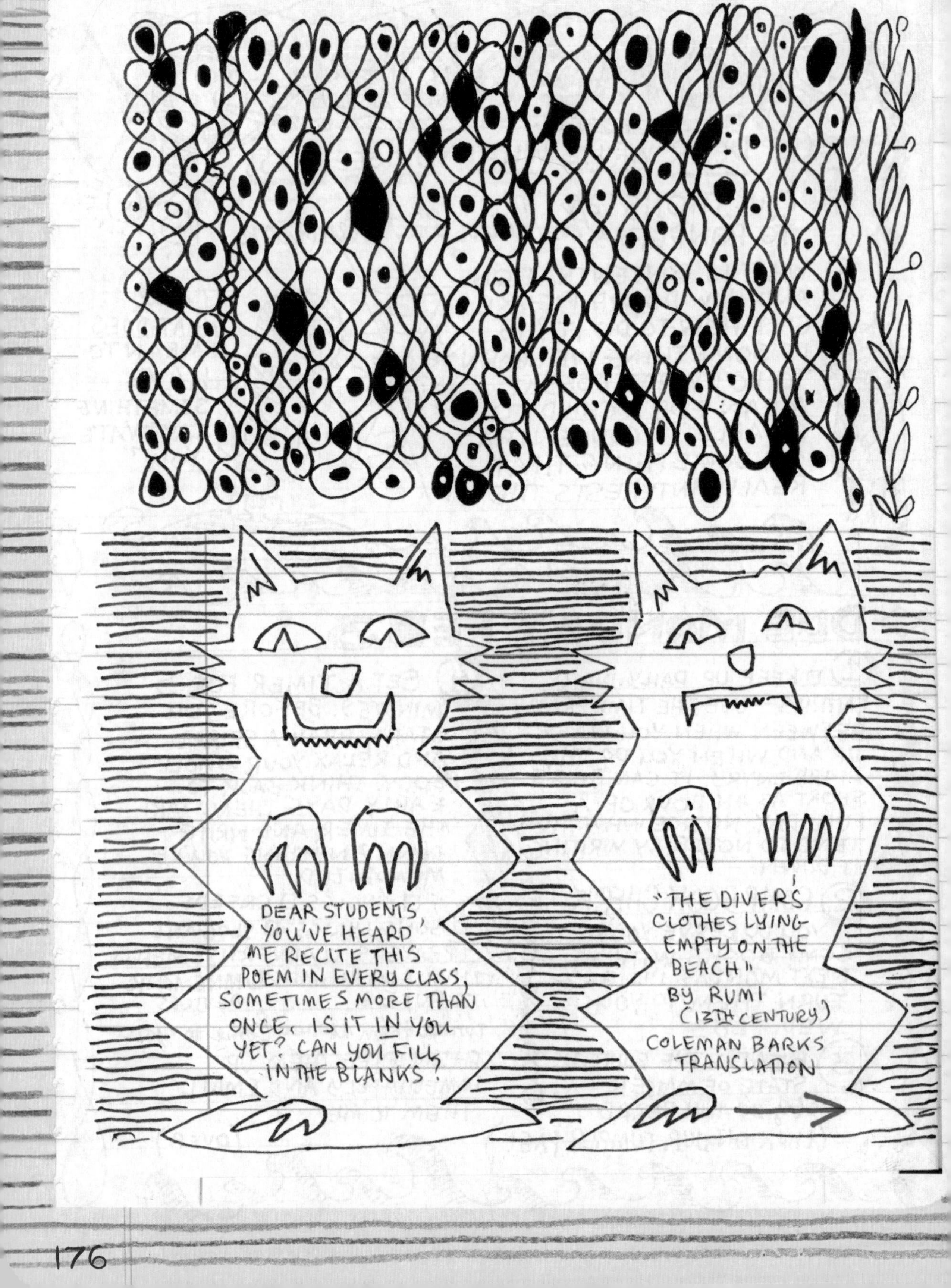
DEAR STUDENTS, YOU'VE HEARD ME RECITE THIS POEM IN EVERY CLASS, SOMETIMES MORE THAN ONCE. IS IT IN YOU YET? CAN YOU FILL IN THE BLANKS?
"THE DIVER'S CLOTHES LYING EMPTY ON THE BEACH" BY RUMI (13TH CENTURY) COLEMAN BARKS TRANSLATION

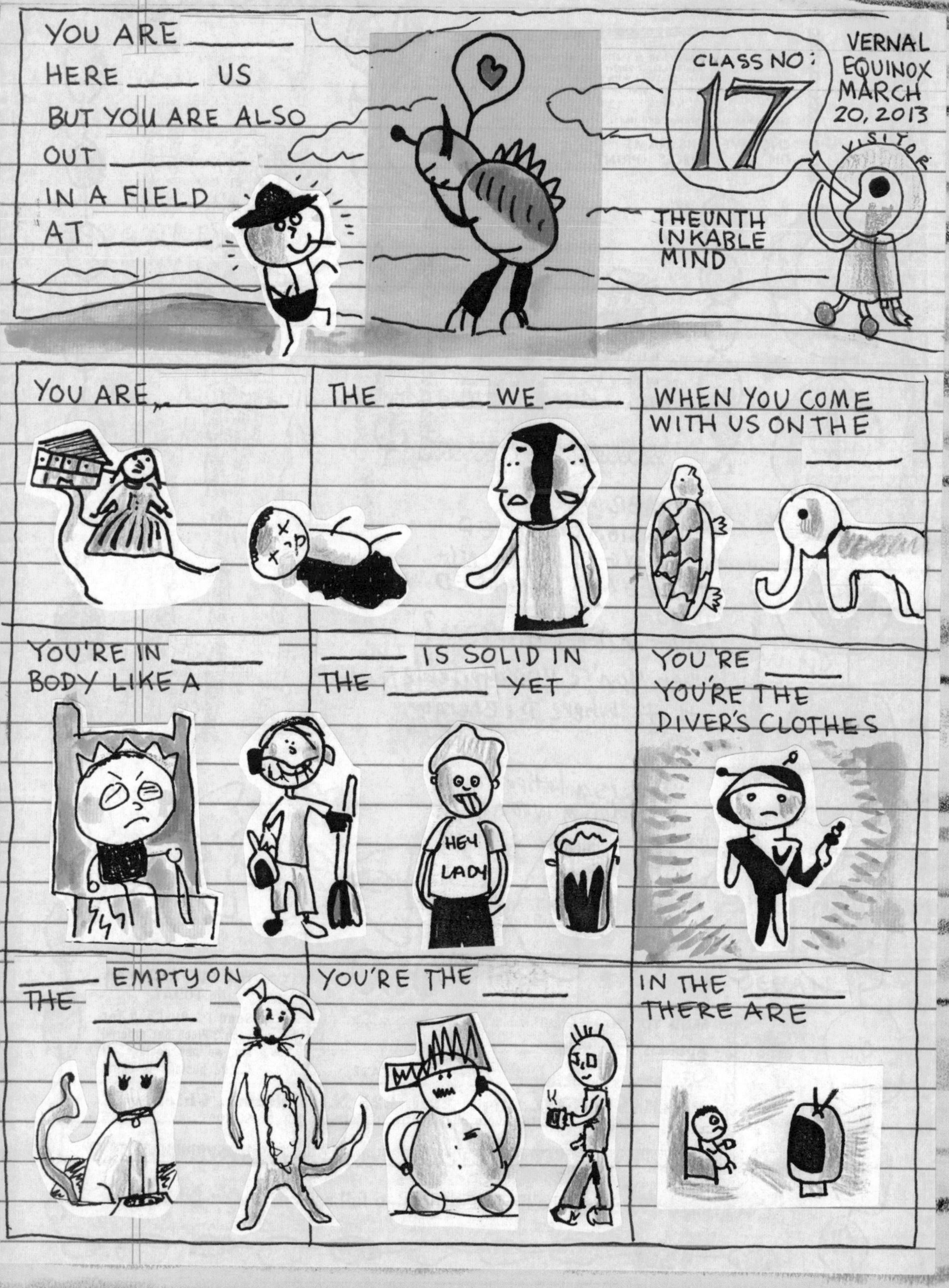
YOU ARE ____
HERE ____ US
BUT YOU ARE ALSO
OUT ____
IN A FIELD
AT ____
CLASS NO: 17
VERNAL EQUINOX MARCH 20, 2013
THEUNTH INKABLE MIND
VISITOR
YOU ARE ____
THE ____ WE ____
WHEN YOU COME WITH US ON THE ____
YOU'RE IN ____ BODY LIKE A
____ IS SOLID IN THE ____ YET
YOU'RE ____ YOU'RE THE DIVER'S CLOTHES
HEY LADY
____ EMPTY ON THE ____
YOU'RE THE ____
IN THE ____ THERE ARE

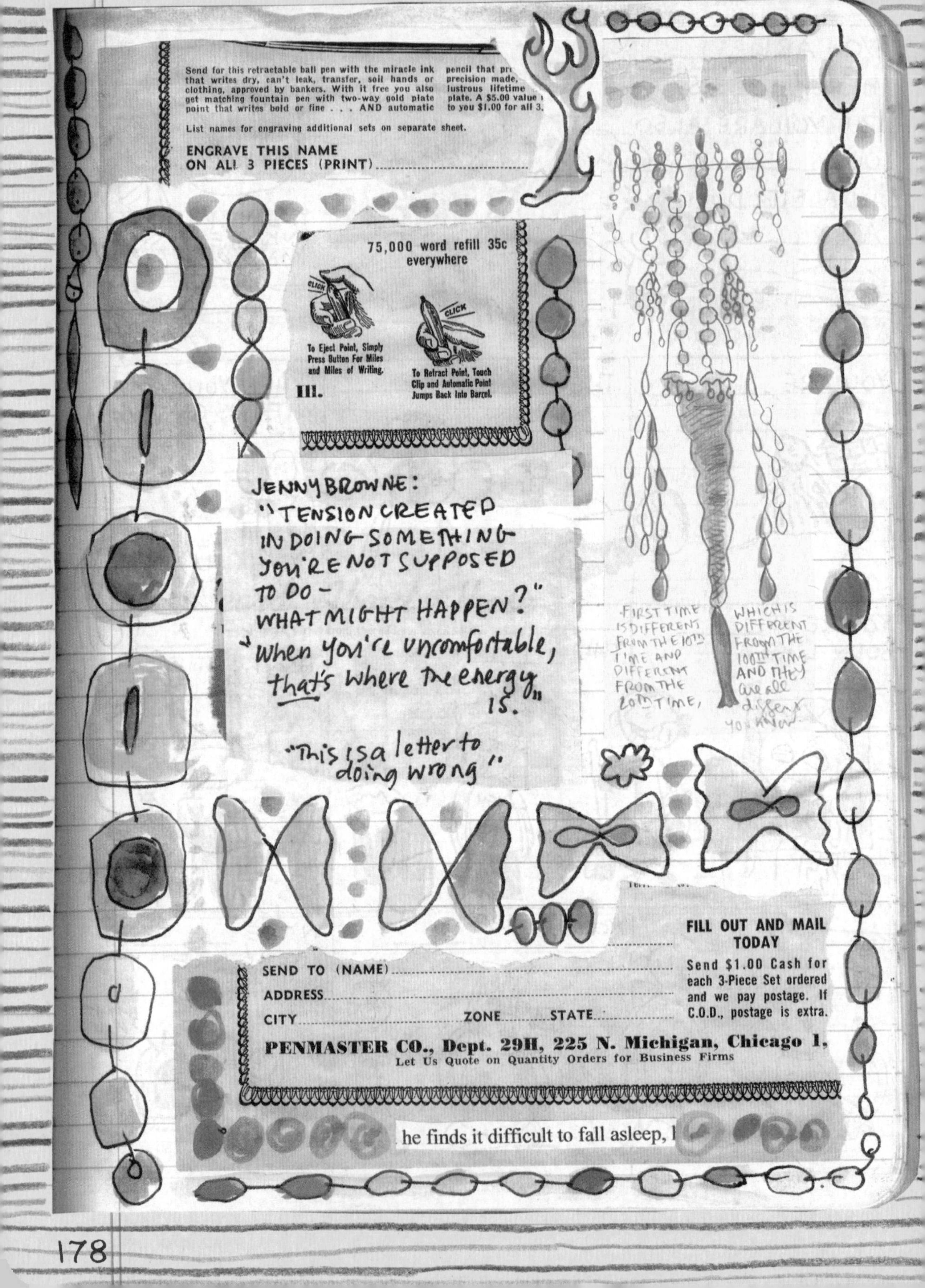

Send for this retractable ball pen with the miracle ink that writes dry, can't leak, transfer, soil hands or clothing, approved by bankers. With it free you also get matching fountain pen with two-way gold plate point that writes bold or fine . . . AND automatic
pencil that pr precision made, lustrous lifetime plate. A $5.00 value to you $1.00 for all 3.
List names for engraving additional sets on separate sheet.
ENGRAVE THIS NAME ON ALL 3 PIECES (PRINT)
75,000 word refill 35c everywhere
CLICK
To Eject Point, Simply Press Button For Miles and Miles of Writing.
CLICK
To Retract Point, Touch Clip and Automatic Point Jumps Back Into Barrel.
III.
JENNY BROWNE: "TENSION CREATED IN DOING SOMETHING YOU'RE NOT SUPPOSED TO DO — WHAT MIGHT HAPPEN?"
"When you're uncomfortable, that's where the energy is."
"This is a letter to doing wrong"
FIRST TIME IS DIFFERENT FROM THE 10TH TIME AND DIFFERENT FROM THE 20TH TIME,
WHICH IS DIFFERENT FROM THE 100TH TIME AND THEY are all different you know.
FILL OUT AND MAIL TODAY
Send $1.00 Cash for each 3-Piece Set ordered and we pay postage. If C.O.D., postage is extra.
SEND TO (NAME)
ADDRESS
CITY ZONE STATE
PENMASTER CO., Dept. 29H, 225 N. Michigan, Chicago 1,
Let Us Quote on Quantity Orders for Business Firms
he finds it difficult to fall asleep,

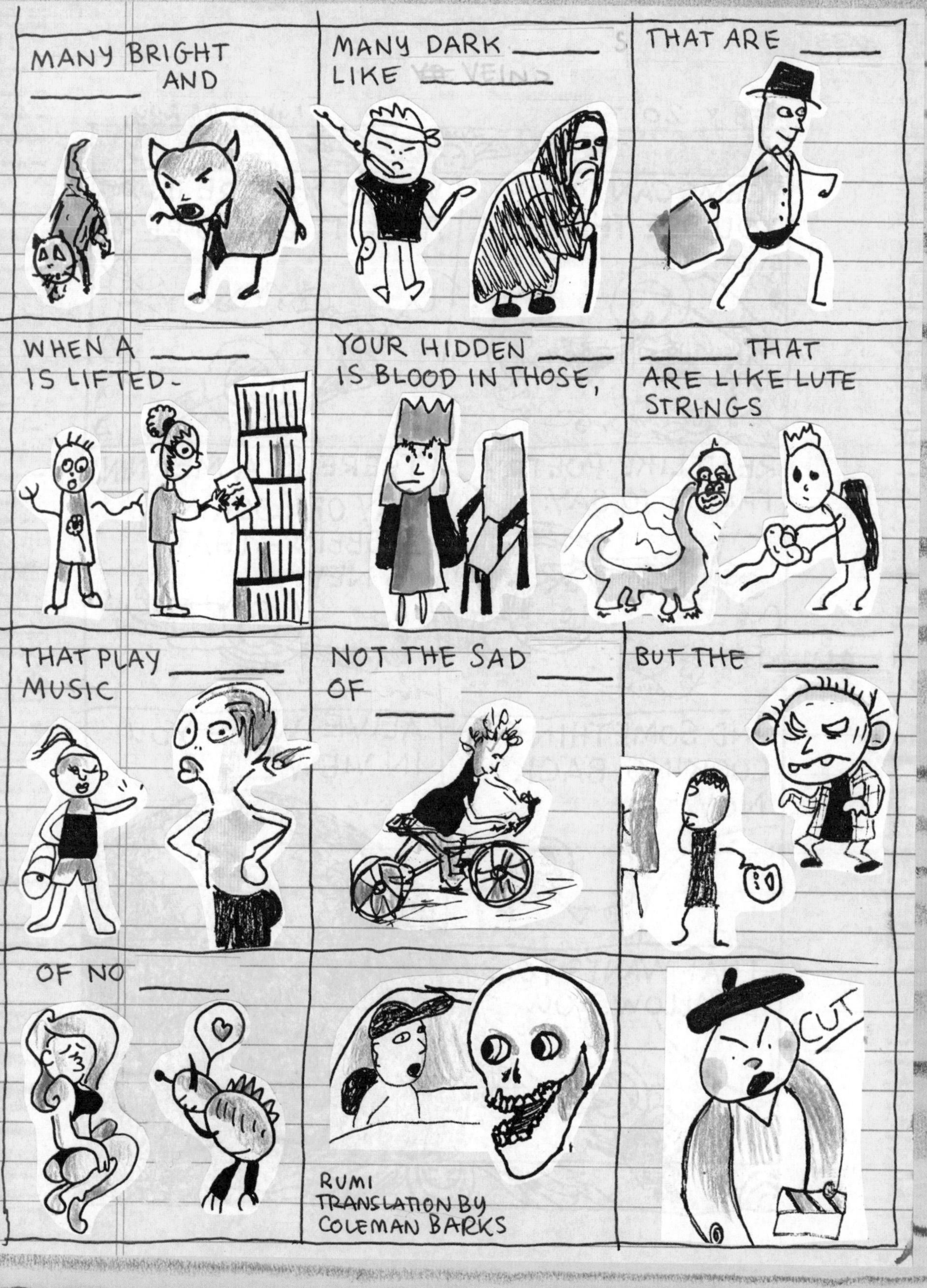
MANY BRIGHT ____ AND
MANY DARK ____ LIKE
THAT ARE ____
WHEN A ____ IS LIFTED.
YOUR HIDDEN ____ IS BLOOD IN THOSE,
____ THAT ARE LIKE LUTE STRINGS
THAT PLAY ____ MUSIC
NOT THE SAD ____ OF ____
BUT THE ____
OF NO ____
RUMI
TRANSLATION BY
COLEMAN BARKS
CUT

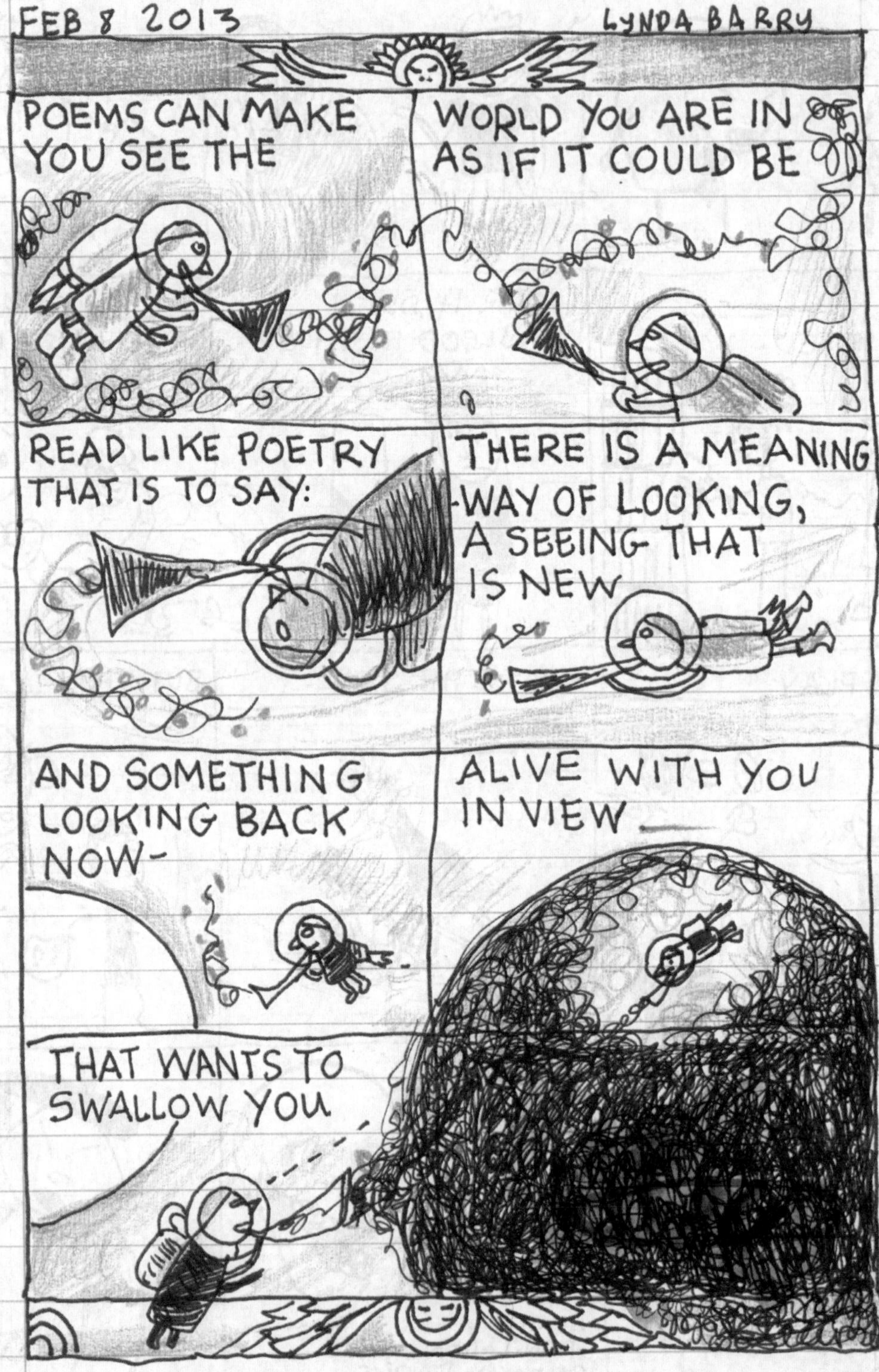
FEB 8 2013
LYNDA BARRY
POEMS CAN MAKE YOU SEE THE
WORLD YOU ARE IN AS IF IT COULD BE
READ LIKE POETRY THAT IS TO SAY:
THERE IS A MEANING -WAY OF LOOKING, A SEEING THAT IS NEW
AND SOMETHING LOOKING BACK NOW-
ALIVE WITH YOU IN VIEW —
THAT WANTS TO SWALLOW YOU

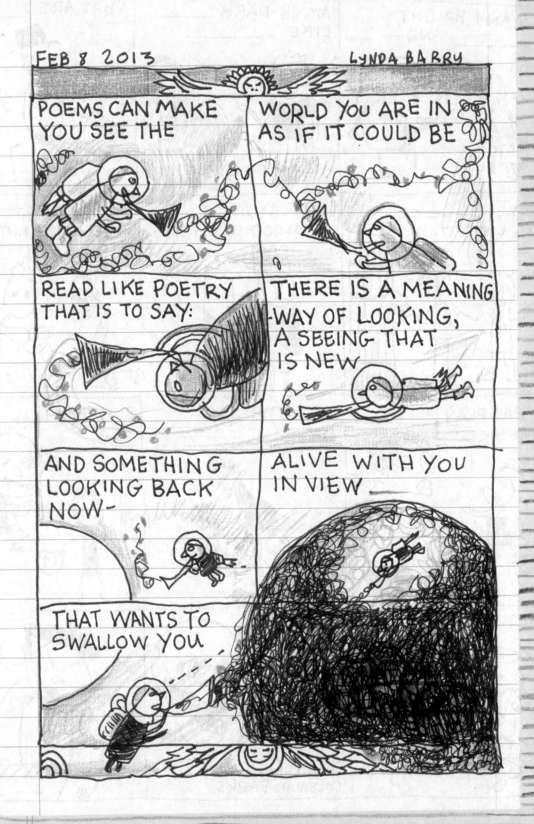

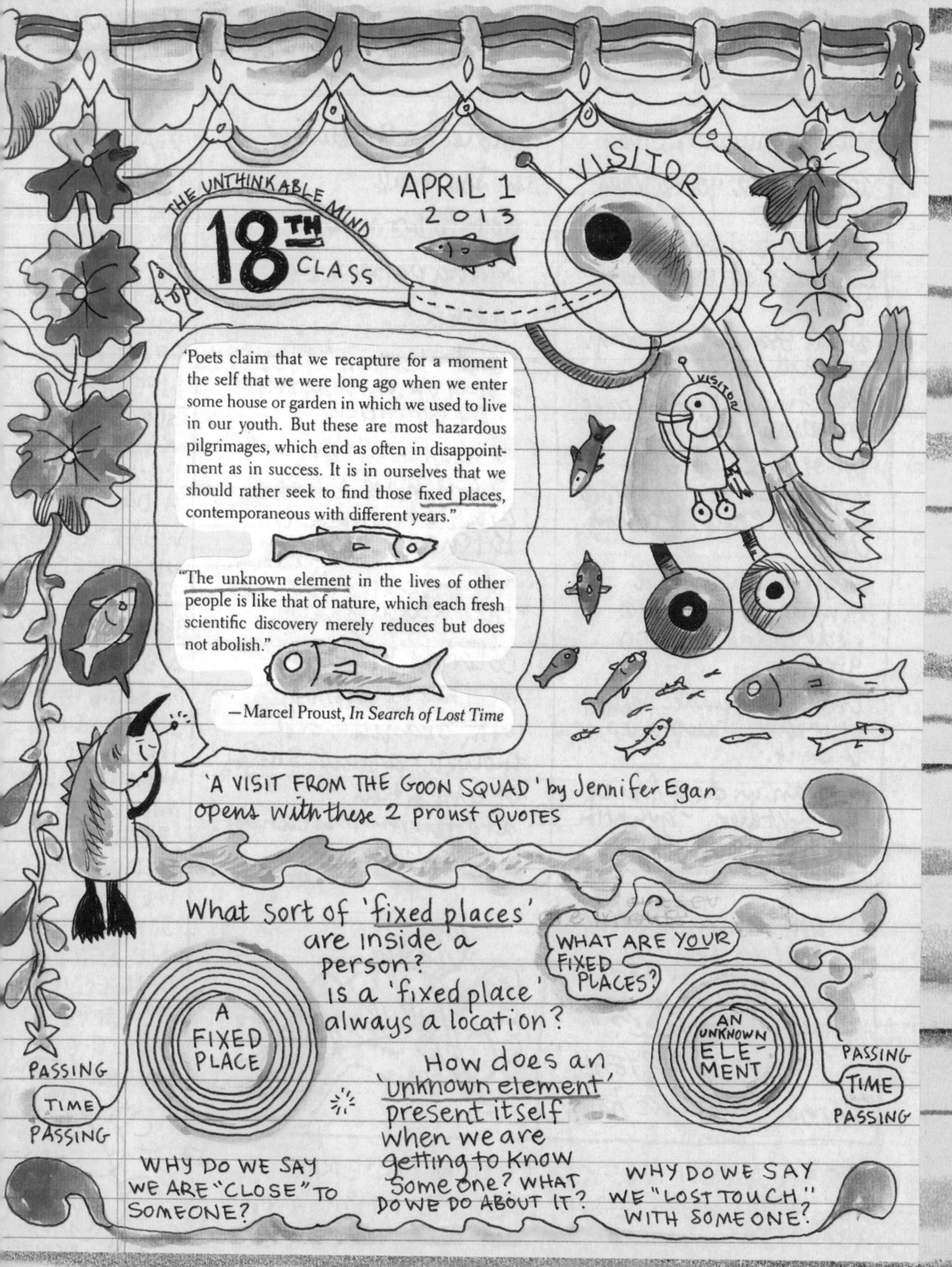

THE UNTHINKABLE MIND
18TH CLASS
APRIL 1 2013
VISITOR
VISITOR
"Poets claim that we recapture for a moment the self that we were long ago when we enter some house or garden in which we used to live in our youth. But these are most hazardous pilgrimages, which end as often in disappointment as in success. It is in ourselves that we should rather seek to find those fixed places, contemporaneous with different years."
"The unknown element in the lives of other people is like that of nature, which each fresh scientific discovery merely reduces but does not abolish."
—Marcel Proust, *In Search of Lost Time*
'A VISIT FROM THE GOON SQUAD' by Jennifer Egan opens with these 2 proust QUOTES
What sort of 'fixed places' are inside a person?
is a 'fixed place' always a location?
WHAT ARE YOUR FIXED PLACES?
A FIXED PLACE
AN UNKNOWN ELEMENT
PASSING TIME PASSING
PASSING TIME PASSING
How does an 'unknown element' present itself when we are getting to know someone? WHAT DO WE DO ABOUT IT?
WHY DO WE SAY WE ARE "CLOSE" TO SOMEONE?
WHY DO WE SAY WE "LOST TOUCH" WITH SOMEONE?

SAW ←——→ DID

SAW	DID
hottmummygurlz.jpeg	· wrote on Birdies card
acorns on 2 young trees in grove.	in Journal.
KK looking down at me from on the grass at SE corner of grove	· Got to work on Sorting papers for TAXES
skull bracelet w/ earrings attached beside bed	· Found 'Luther' after giving up on watching 'the Borgias.'
finding Popkins puzzle on yellow legal par	· drank whiskey w/ K and had a Romp around the grove + Kitchen + Bathroom.
px of grandma and my mother beside carved Indian Chief. Bro sent it.	· ate prociutto for late night snack.
digital image of a mummy fucking a redheaded cartoon girl	· Colored margins of this notebook with crayons and thought about shifts of attention.
cardinal female peeking at window. Jumping up to do it.	· ate too much candy. Loved it.
woman in deep freeze on 'Luther' - guy with his tongue out	
"you remember that girl in shulyn soccer with bad skin so she hung her hair in her face?" "The BUN.GIRL? YEAH. "Peng's kind of like her."	

YOUR DAILY DIARY DOESN'T HAVE TO BE BEAUTIFUL OR LEGIBLE TO OTHERS. IT'S THE PLACE WHERE YOU PRACTICE DIFFERENT SORTS OF WAYS OF REMEMBERING A DAY: WHAT WE DID, WHAT WE SAW, WHAT WE HEARD, AND A DRAWING OF SOMETHING IN OUR DAY. HAVING TO WRITE IT DOWN MAKES US BEGIN TO NOTICE WHEN WE NOTICE SOMETHING. WE REMIND OURSELVES TO 'SAVE' IT FOR THE DIARY

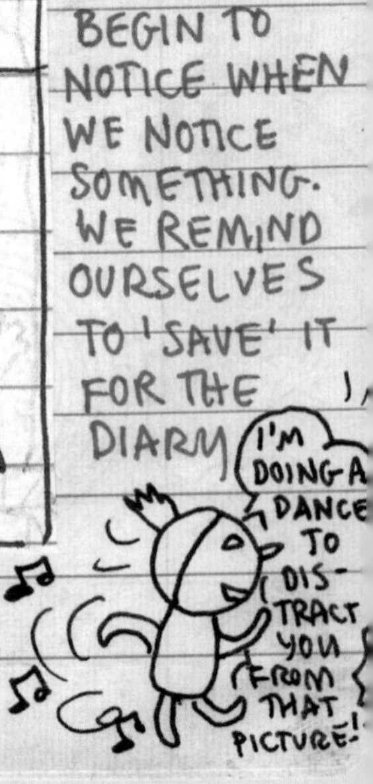

I'M DOING A DANCE TO DISTRACT YOU FROM THAT PICTURE!

AFTER A FEW WEEKS, CERTAIN PATTERNS BEGIN TO EMERGE. WE BEGIN TO KNOW MORE ABOUT THE WATCHING PART OF OURSELVES.

HOMEWORK DUE MON APRIL 8 ²⁰₁₃

VISITOR

☐ USING THE POWERPOINT PRESENTATION STYLE
that Alison Blake *uses in* CHAPTER 12 (pages 234 – 309 OF Egan)
AS A MODEL AND TWO* TO FOUR* sheets of 8.5"X11" paper,
DRAW BY HAND A POWERPOINT STYLE Response Paper
ABOUT KINDS OF CONNECTIONS IN THE BOOK THAT
Struck you as meaningful. YOU CAN follow
persons, places, things — be as EARNEST OR IRONIC
AS YOU WANT *and* use any icons or symbols or
CHART STYLES WITH WORDS CONTROLLED BY THEIR
'SLIDE SPACE' AS *they would be in* POWERPOINT.
use small pieces OF BIG CONNECTIONS *to show*
THE INTER-CONNECTIONS *that* YOU BECAME AWARE OF.
you can use your paper any way you wish —
DIVIDE IT INTO CELLS OR NOT, *but draw it out first*
in NON-PHOTO BLUE PENCIL. THEN INK IT IN WITH
YOUR FLAIR OR UNIBALL PEN.

*no less than 2!
*no more than 4!

☐ CONTINUE DAILY DIARY

DID →
SAW ←
OVERHEARD DIALOG →
← sketch
IN ORIGINAL FORMAT
BUT BE SPECIFIC - Its not just a List to complete

☐ WRITE ⑤ FICTIONAL
STORIES FROM PHOTOS
I GIVE YOU SPEND ABOUT 30 MINUTES FOR ENTIRE EXERCISE FROM START TO FINISH

☐ BEGIN THIS BY SPENDING 5 MINUTES (use a timer) DRAWING THE PICTURE FIRST IN YOUR COMP BOOK, THEN WRITE

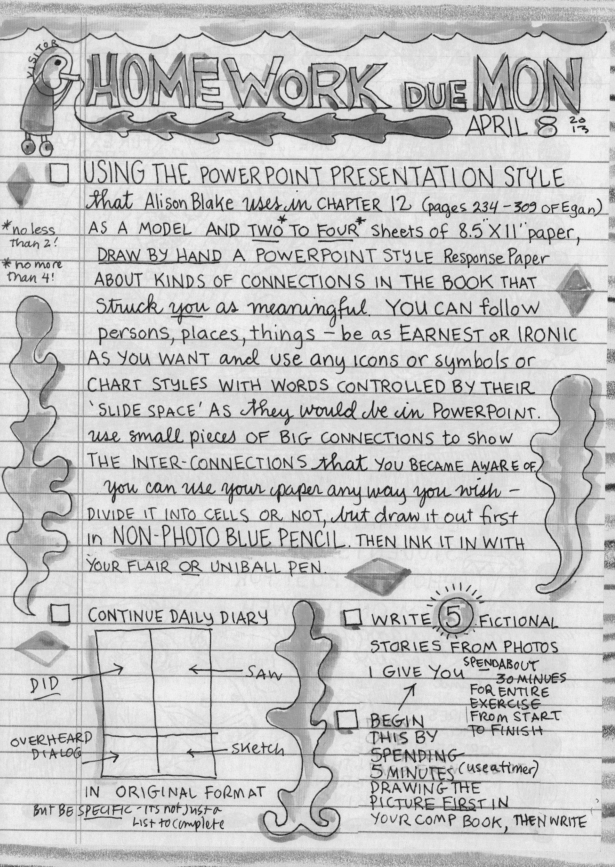

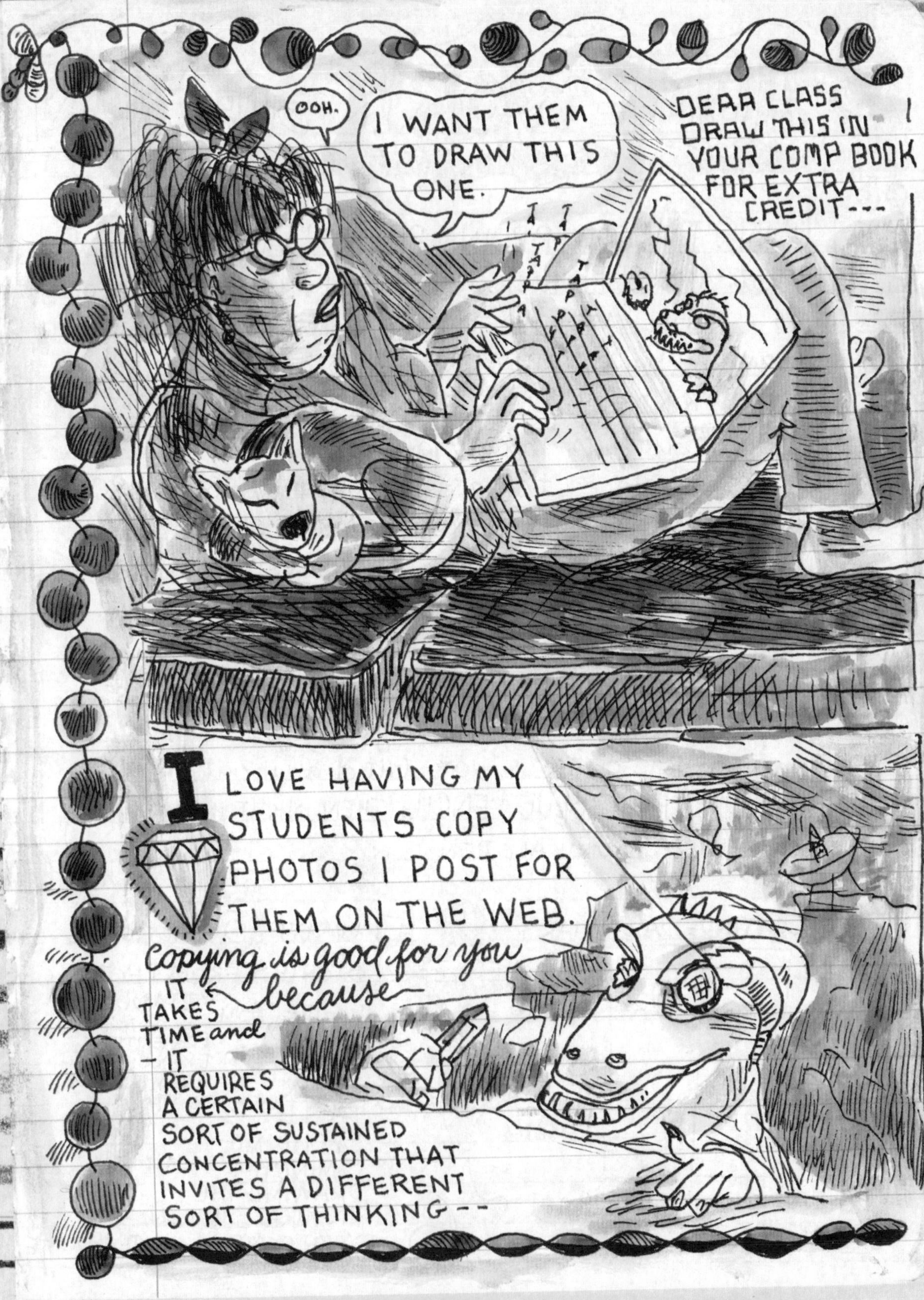
OOH.
I WANT THEM TO DRAW THIS ONE.
DEAR CLASS DRAW THIS IN YOUR COMP BOOK FOR EXTRA CREDIT---
I LOVE HAVING MY STUDENTS COPY PHOTOS I POST FOR THEM ON THE WEB.
Copying is good for you because
IT TAKES TIME and -IT REQUIRES A CERTAIN SORT OF SUSTAINED CONCENTRATION THAT INVITES A DIFFERENT SORT OF THINKING--

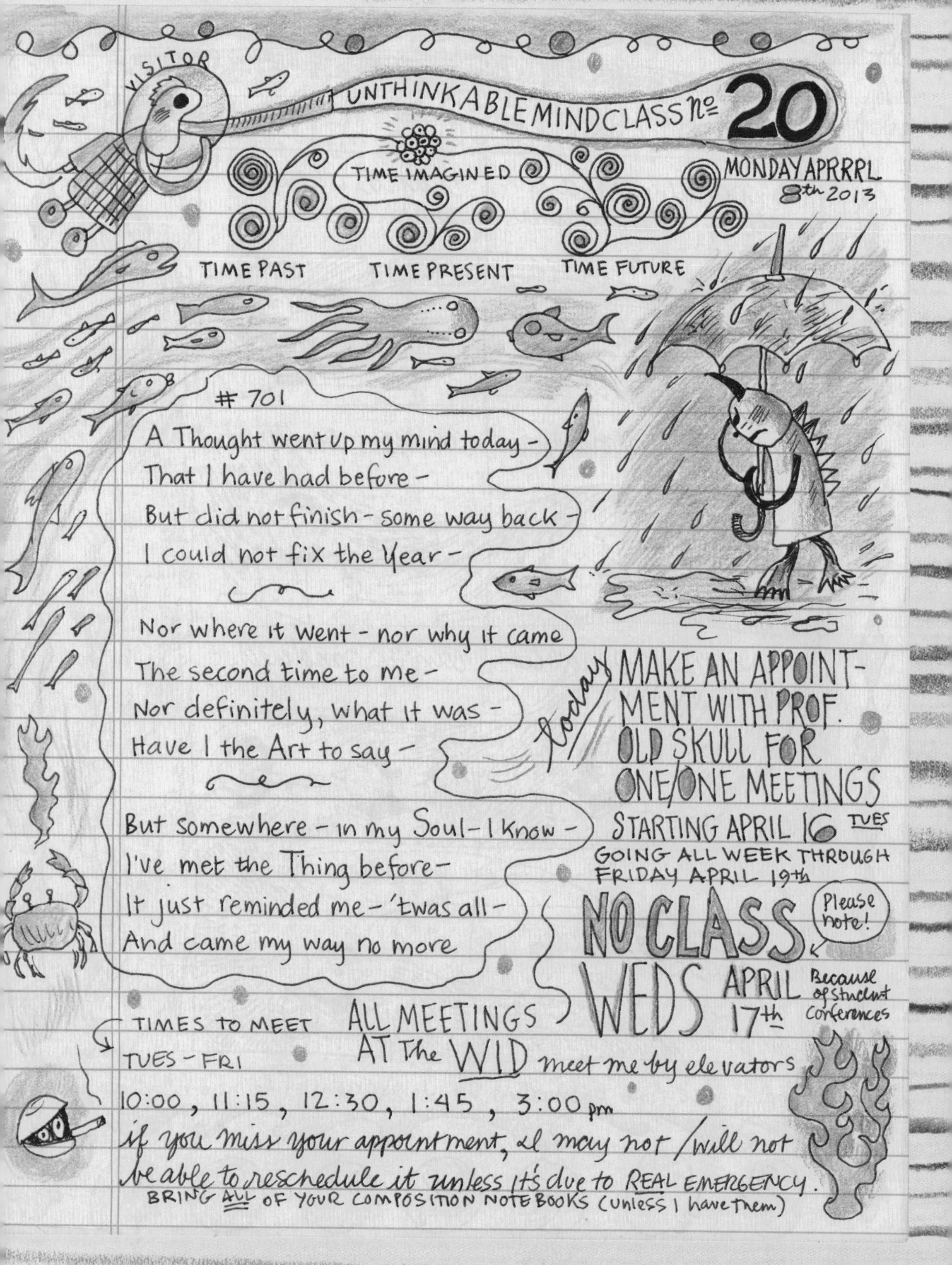
VISITOR
UNTHINKABLE MIND CLASS № 20
MONDAY APRRRL 8th 2013
TIME IMAGINED
TIME PAST
TIME PRESENT
TIME FUTURE
701
A Thought went up my mind today -
That I have had before -
But did not finish - some way back -
I could not fix the Year -
Nor where it went - nor why it came
The second time to me -
Nor definitely, what it was -
Have I the Art to say -
But somewhere - in my Soul - I know -
I've met the Thing before -
It just reminded me - 'twas all -
And came my way no more
today
MAKE AN APPOINTMENT WITH PROF. OLD SKULL FOR ONE/ONE MEETINGS
STARTING APRIL 16 TUES
GOING ALL WEEK THROUGH FRIDAY APRIL 19th
NO CLASS
Please note!
WEDS APRIL 17th
Because of student conferences
TIMES TO MEET
TUES - FRI
ALL MEETINGS AT The WID meet me by elevators
10:00, 11:15, 12:30, 1:45, 3:00 pm
if you miss your appointment, I may not / will not be able to reschedule it unless it's due to REAL EMERGENCY.
BRING ALL OF YOUR COMPOSITION NOTEBOOKS (unless I have them)

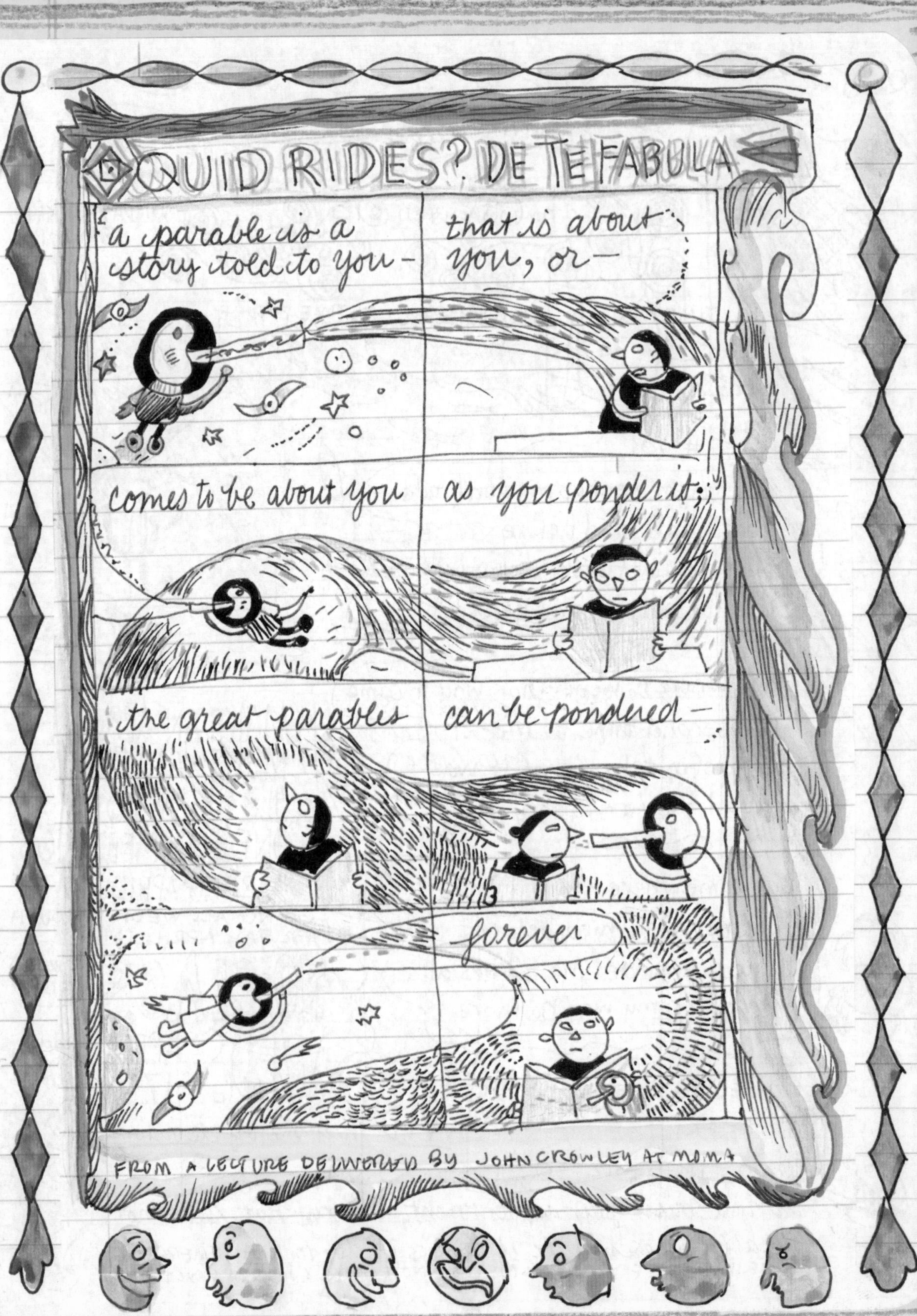
QUID RIDES? DE TE FABULA
a parable is a story told to you -
that is about you, or -
comes to be about you
as you ponder it;
the great parables
can be pondered -
forever
FROM A LECTURE DELIVERED BY JOHN CROWLEY AT MOMA

HOMEWORK

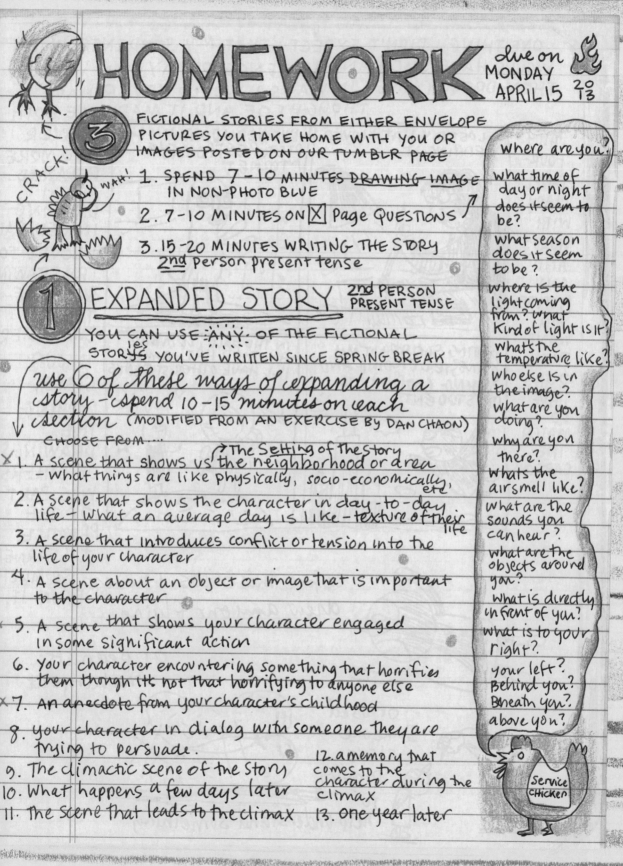

due on **MONDAY APRIL 15** 20 13

CRACK! **WAH!**

3 FICTIONAL STORIES FROM EITHER ENVELOPE PICTURES YOU TAKE HOME WITH YOU OR IMAGES POSTED ON OUR TUMBLR PAGE

1. SPEND 7-10 MINUTES <u>DRAWING IMAGE</u> IN NON-PHOTO BLUE

2. 7-10 MINUTES ON ☒ Page QUESTIONS

3. 15-20 MINUTES WRITING THE STORY <u>2nd</u> Person present tense

1 EXPANDED STORY **2nd PERSON PRESENT TENSE**

YOU CAN USE ·ANY· OF THE FICTIONAL STORYS ies YOU'VE WRITTEN SINCE SPRING BREAK

use 6 of these ways of expanding a story — spend 10-15 minutes on each section (MODIFIED FROM AN EXERCISE BY DAN CHAON)

CHOOSE FROM....

→ The Setting of the Story

X 1. A scene that shows us the neighborhood or area — what things are like physically, socio-economically etc.

2. A scene that shows the character in day-to-day life — what an average day is like — texture of their life

3. A scene that introduces conflict or tension into the life of your character

4. A scene about an object or image that is important to the character

X 5. A scene that shows your character engaged in some significant action

6. Your character encountering something that horrifies them though it's not that horrifying to anyone else

X 7. An anecdote from your character's childhood

8. your character in dialog with someone they are trying to persuade.

9. The climactic scene of the story

10. What happens a few days later

11. the scene that leads to the climax

12. a memory that comes to the character during the climax

13. one year later

---

where are you?

what time of day or night does it seem to be?

what season does it seem to be?

where is the light coming from? what kind of light is it?

what's the temperature like?

who else is in the image?

what are you doing?

why are you there?

whats the air smell like?

what are the sounds you can hear?

what are the objects around you?

what is directly in front of you?

what is to your right?

your left? Behind you? Beneath you? above you?

Service Chicken

187

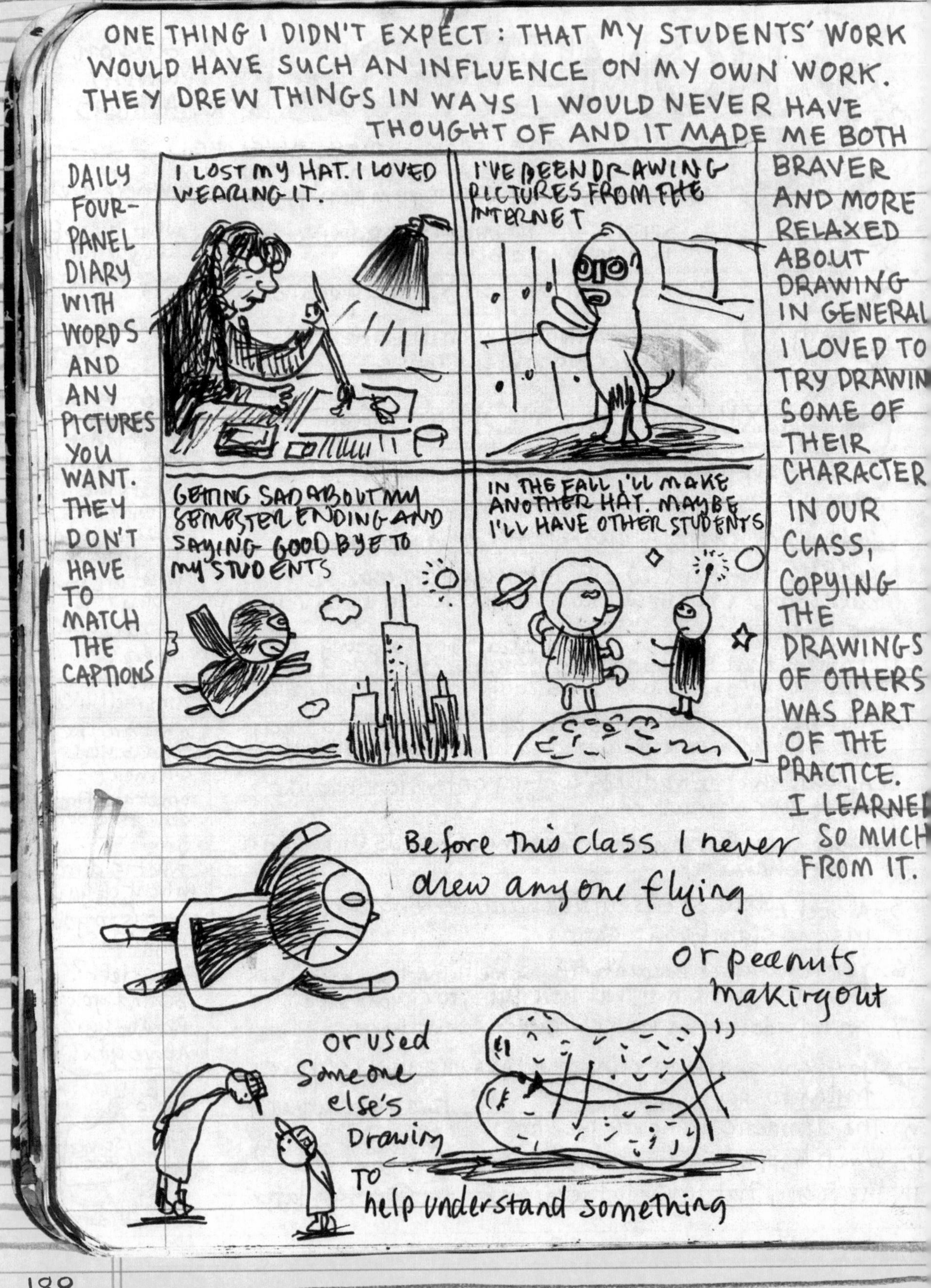
ONE THING I DIDN'T EXPECT: THAT MY STUDENTS' WORK WOULD HAVE SUCH AN INFLUENCE ON MY OWN WORK. THEY DREW THINGS IN WAYS I WOULD NEVER HAVE THOUGHT OF AND IT MADE ME BOTH BRAVER AND MORE RELAXED ABOUT DRAWING IN GENERAL
DAILY FOUR-PANEL DIARY WITH WORDS AND ANY PICTURES YOU WANT. THEY DON'T HAVE TO MATCH THE CAPTIONS
I LOST MY HAT. I LOVED WEARING IT.
I'VE BEEN DRAWING PICTURES FROM THE INTERNET
GETTING SAD ABOUT MY SEMESTER ENDING AND SAYING GOOD BYE TO MY STUDENTS
IN THE FALL I'LL MAKE ANOTHER HAT. MAYBE I'LL HAVE OTHER STUDENTS
I LOVED TO TRY DRAWING SOME OF THEIR CHARACTERS IN OUR CLASS, COPYING THE DRAWINGS OF OTHERS WAS PART OF THE PRACTICE. I LEARNED SO MUCH FROM IT.
Before this class I never drew anyone flying
or peanuts making out
or used someone else's Drawing
TO help understand something

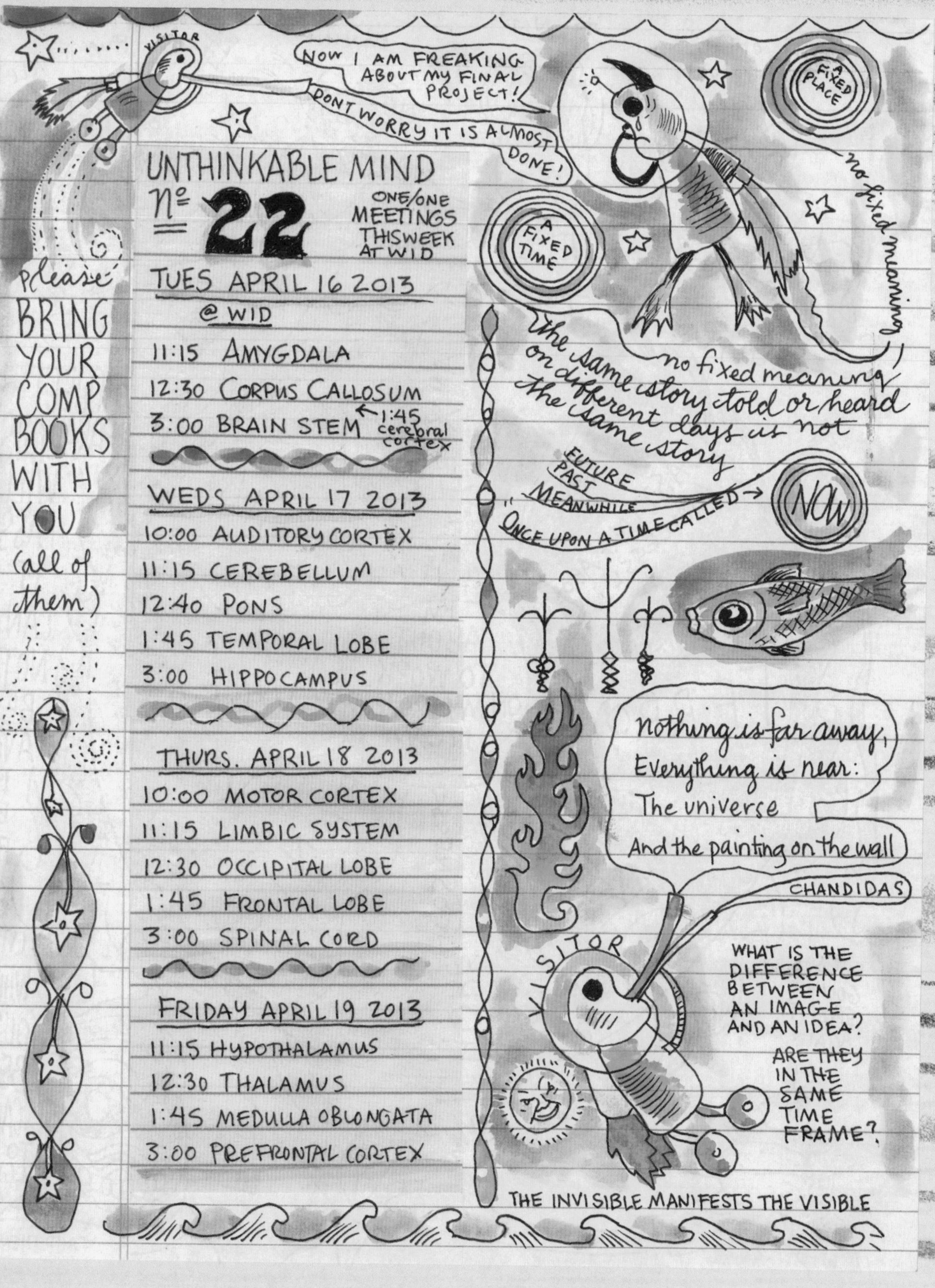
VISITOR
NOW I AM FREAKING ABOUT MY FINAL PROJECT!
DONT WORRY IT IS ALMOST DONE!
A FIXED PLACE
no fixed meaning
A FIXED TIME
UNTHINKABLE MIND
№ 22
ONE/ONE MEETINGS THISWEEK AT WID
TUES APRIL 16 2013
@ WID
11:15 AMYGDALA
12:30 CORPUS CALLOSUM
3:00 BRAIN STEM ← 1:45 cerebral cortex
WEDS APRIL 17 2013
10:00 AUDITORY CORTEX
11:15 CEREBELLUM
12:40 PONS
1:45 TEMPORAL LOBE
3:00 HIPPOCAMPUS
THURS. APRIL 18 2013
10:00 MOTOR CORTEX
11:15 LIMBIC SYSTEM
12:30 OCCIPITAL LOBE
1:45 FRONTAL LOBE
3:00 SPINAL CORD
FRIDAY APRIL 19 2013
11:15 HYPOTHALAMUS
12:30 THALAMUS
1:45 MEDULLA OBLONGATA
3:00 PREFRONTAL CORTEX
please BRING YOUR COMP BOOKS WITH YOU (all of them)
no fixed meaning
the same story told or heard on different days is not the same story
FUTURE
PAST
MEANWHILE
"ONCE UPON A TIME CALLED → NOW
nothing is far away,
Everything is near:
The universe
And the painting on the wall
CHANDIDAS
VISITOR
WHAT IS THE DIFFERENCE BETWEEN AN IMAGE AND AN IDEA?
ARE THEY IN THE SAME TIME FRAME?
THE INVISIBLE MANIFESTS THE VISIBLE

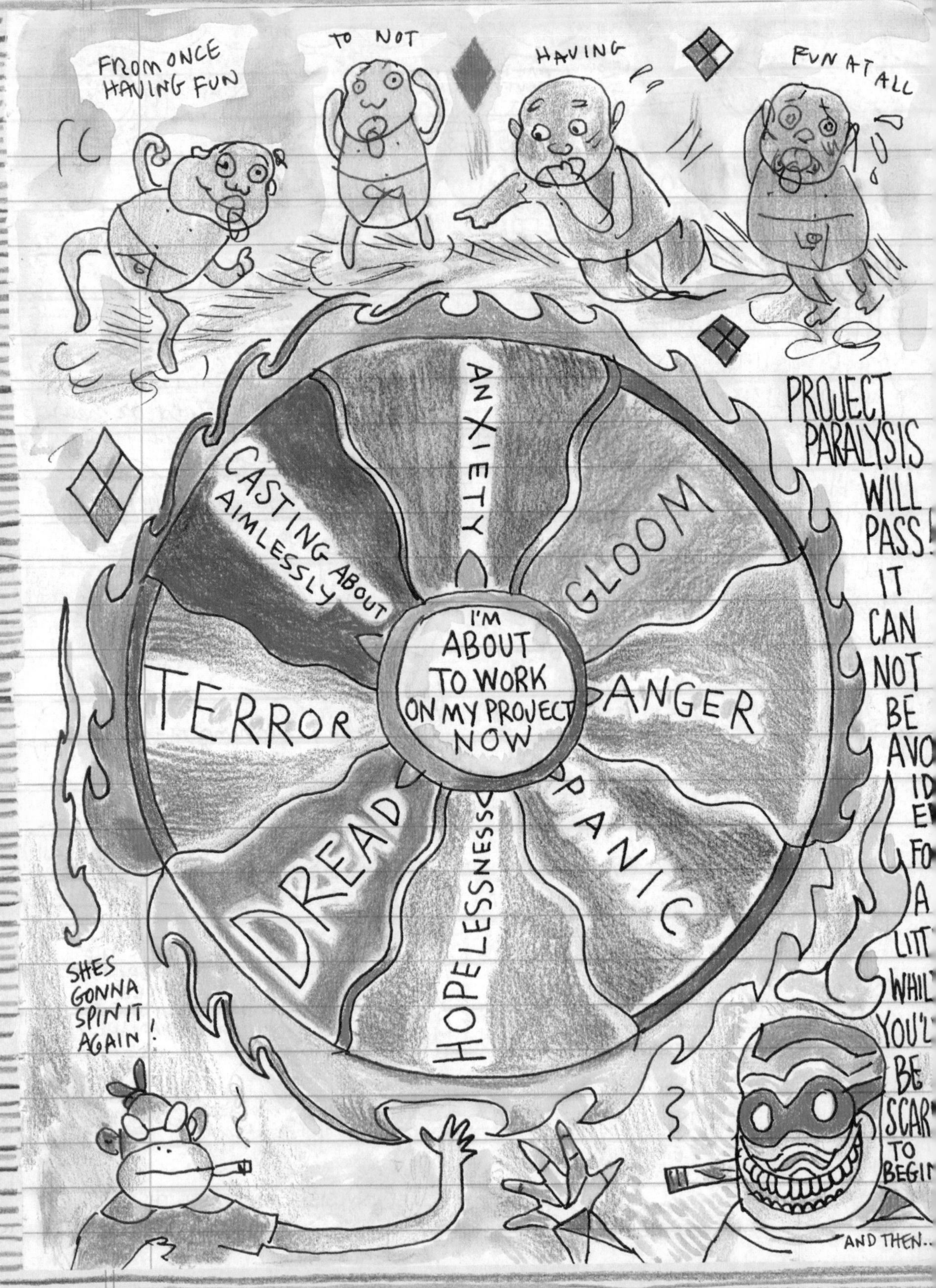
FROM ONCE HAVING FUN
TO NOT
HAVING
FUN AT ALL
CASTING ABOUT AIMLESSLY
ANXIETY
GLOOM
TERROR
I'M ABOUT TO WORK ON MY PROJECT NOW
ANGER
DREAD
HOPELESSNESS
PANIC
PROJECT PARALYSIS WILL PASS! IT CAN NOT BE AVO ID E FO A LIT WHIL YOU'L BE SCAR TO BEGI
SHES GONNA SPIN IT AGAIN!
AND THEN...

HOME WORK

→ NOW IT'S TIME TO BUILD YOUR FINAL PROJECT.
FOR FICTION, AUTOBIOGRAPHY, OR MASH-UP OF BOTH, LOOK
OVER THE PIECES YOU'VE WRITTEN AND SELECT ANY
that seem to qualify thematically OR SUBJECT-WISE,
EVEN ones YOU'RE NOT CRAZY ABOUT RIGHT NOW.

→ AIM FOR 20 PIECES FOR YOUR ROUGH DRAFT.
GIVE EACH ONE A PAGE (OR MORE) IN YOUR PRESENTATION
PORTFOLIO (the one you bought with the plastic sleeves).
THE FIRST PAGE SHOULD BE A TITLE PAGE — You may
not have a title yet, but put a page there anyway.
THE LEFT-HAND SIDE SHOULD be where at

DON'T
FREAK
ON IT!

LET
IT BE
A MESS
AT FIRST!

least ONE VISUAL
element for the story
should go. DON'T WORRY
ABOUT THE LAYOUT YET —

putting your book together this way WILL HELP YOU SEE
WHAT NEEDS TO BE DONE, HOW many visual elements,
How many story elements, HOW many WILD CARD elements
You MAY THROW IN. THIS IS JUST A ROUGH
ROUGH ROUGH DRAFT. Think about the AND
amount of time you usually need to complete KEEP UP
YOUR DAILY DIARY
homework for our class on average and then
DEVOTE THAT AMOUNT OF TIME TO THIS THING
THAT HAS MANIFESTATION ABILITY. YOUR BOOK IS ON ITS WAY!

title

BUT

c. 1861

HAVE THEM MEMORIZE SOME DICKINSON. Important

for Only 25¢

"WHAT EVERY TEACHER IS DOING IS TEACHING SOMEONE HOW TO LOVE SOMETHING"

–JENNY BROWNE
BLOOMINGTON INDIANA
JUNE 9, 2011

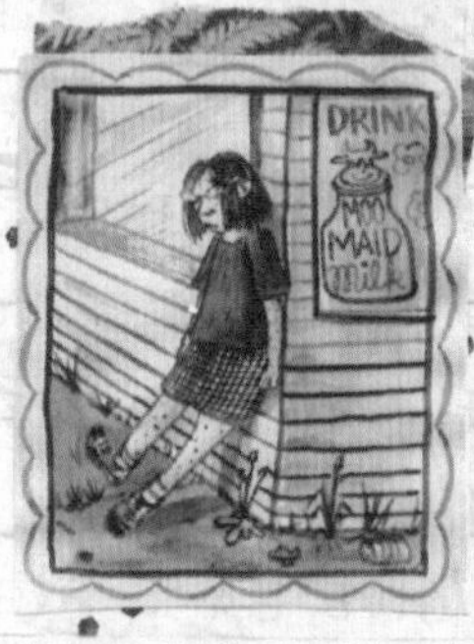

DRINK
MAID

but they are two or three

POETRY IS PART OF IT:
JENNY BROWNE, PANTOUMS

Louisa

269

Bound – a trouble –
And lives can bear it!
Limit – how deep a bleeding go!
So – many – drops – of vital scarlet –
Deal with the soul
As with Algebra!

Tell it the Ages – to a cypher –
And it will ache – contented – on –
Sing – at its pain – as any Workman –
Notching the fall of the Even Sun!

BUILDING A BOOK VS. WRITING A BOOK. GET THEM TO THINK OF IT AS BUILDING

a way to be
d here and I
d the hope of
happy,

SOMETHING – LETTING IT TAKE ACCUMULATED SHAPE OF ACTION – A RECORD OF SINCERE CONTACT WITH THE IMAGEWORLD

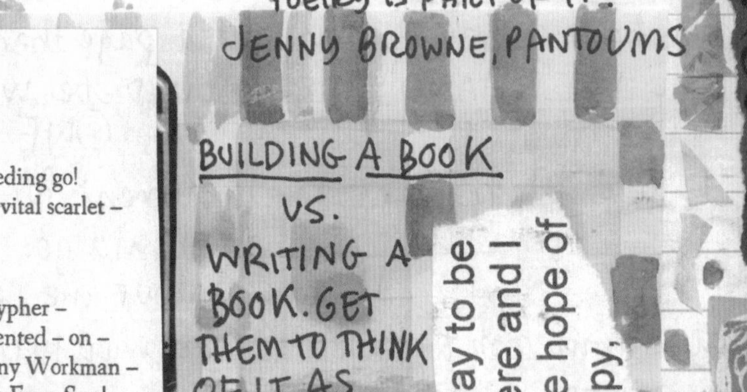

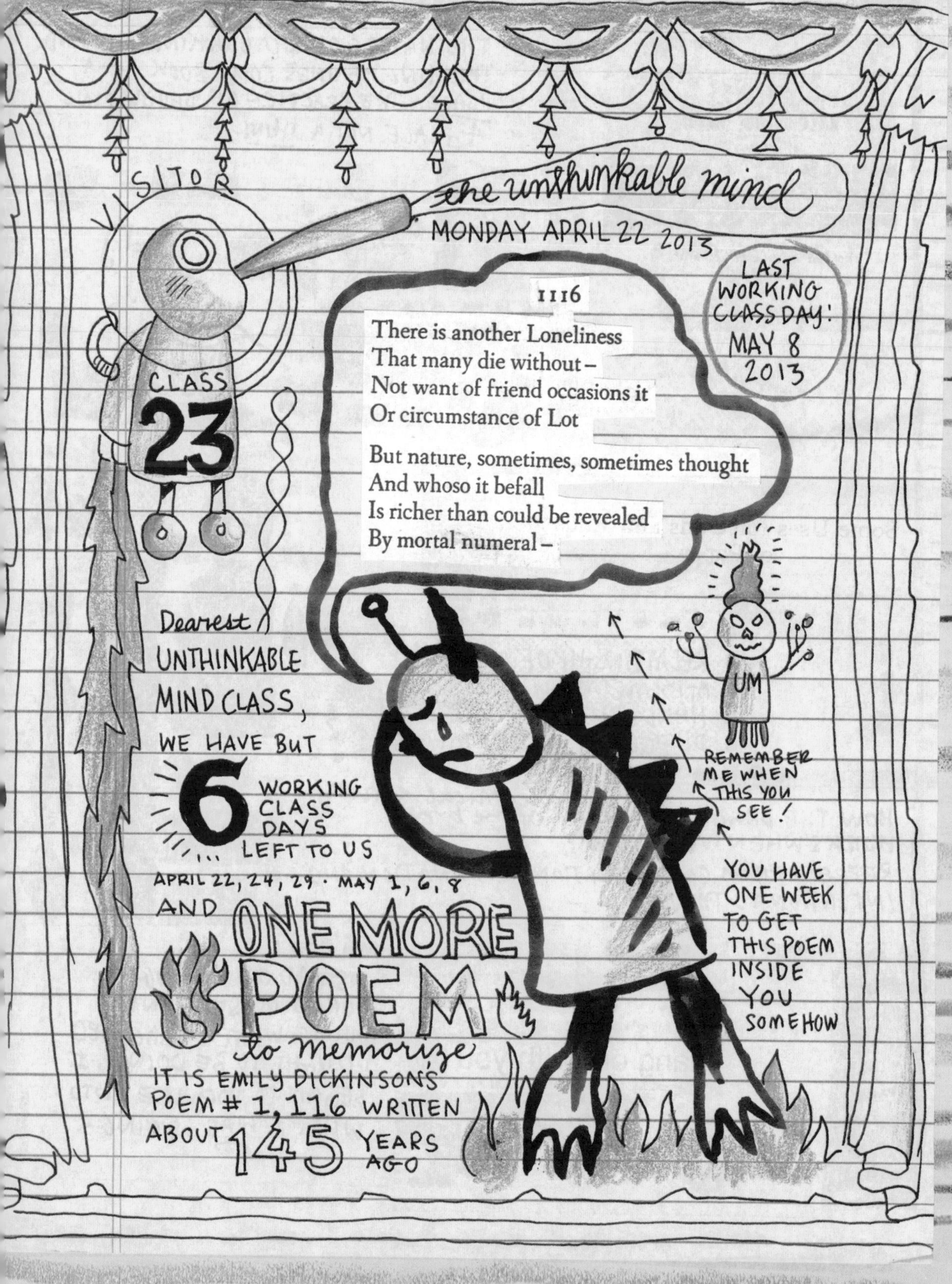

VISITOR
the unthinkable mind
MONDAY APRIL 22 2013
LAST WORKING CLASS DAY: MAY 8 2013
CLASS 23
1116
There is another Loneliness
That many die without –
Not want of friend occasions it
Or circumstance of Lot
But nature, sometimes, sometimes thought
And whoso it befall
Is richer than could be revealed
By mortal numeral –
Dearest UNTHINKABLE MIND CLASS,
WE HAVE BUT 6 WORKING CLASS DAYS LEFT TO US
APRIL 22, 24, 29 · MAY 1, 6, 8
AND ONE MORE POEM to memorize
IT IS EMILY DICKINSON'S POEM # 1,116 WRITTEN ABOUT 145 YEARS AGO
UM
REMEMBER ME WHEN THIS YOU SEE!
YOU HAVE ONE WEEK TO GET THIS POEM INSIDE YOU SOMEHOW

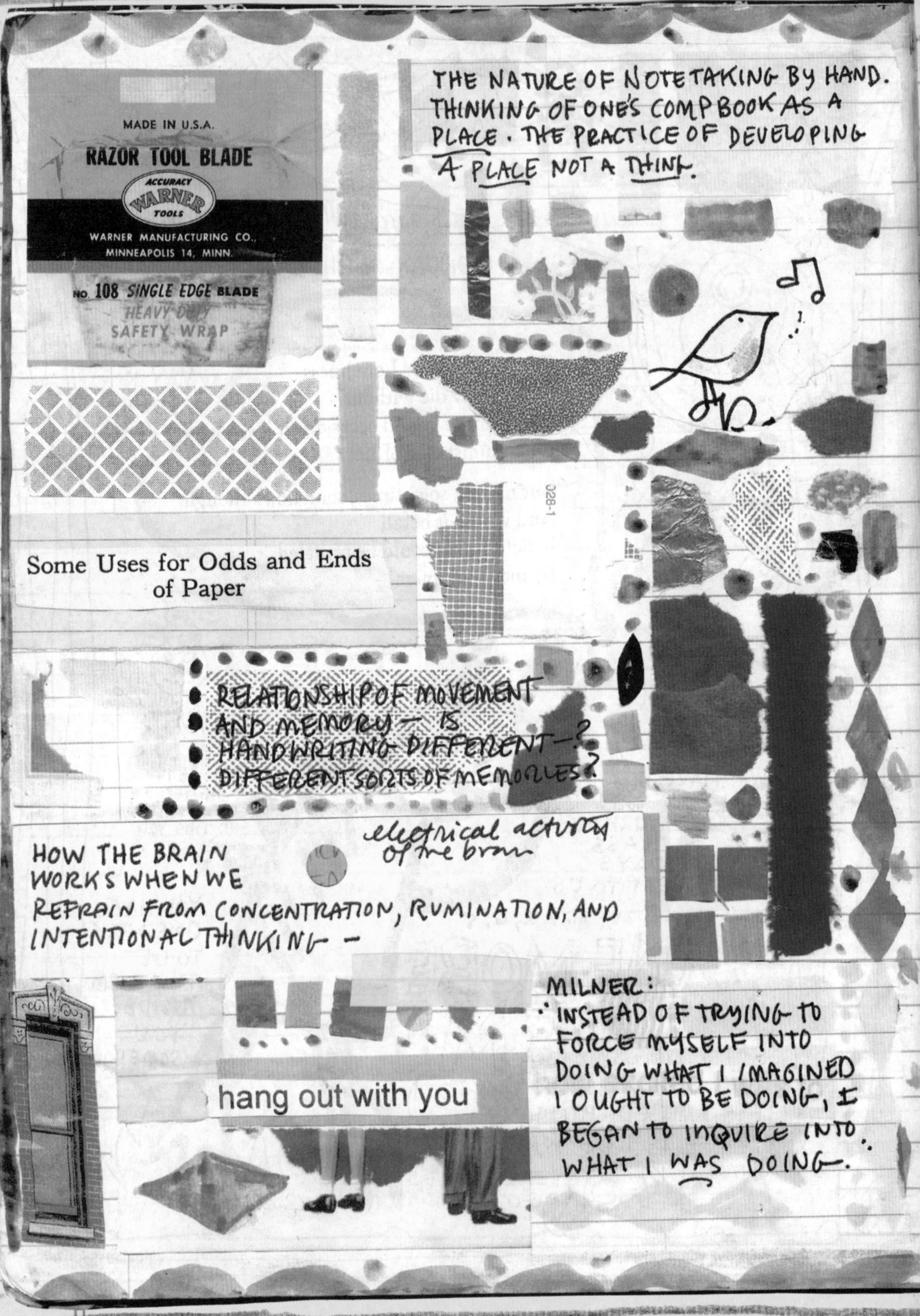
MADE IN U.S.A.
RAZOR TOOL BLADE
ACCURACY
WARNER
TOOLS
WARNER MANUFACTURING CO.,
MINNEAPOLIS 14, MINN.
NO. 108 SINGLE EDGE BLADE
HEAVY DUTY
SAFETY WRAP
THE NATURE OF NOTETAKING BY HAND. THINKING OF ONE'S COMPBOOK AS A PLACE. THE PRACTICE OF DEVELOPING A PLACE NOT A THING.
Some Uses for Odds and Ends of Paper
RELATIONSHIP OF MOVEMENT AND MEMORY — IS HANDWRITING DIFFERENT—? DIFFERENT SORTS OF MEMORIES?
HOW THE BRAIN WORKS WHEN WE REFRAIN FROM CONCENTRATION, RUMINATION, AND INTENTIONAL THINKING —
electrical activity of the brain
hang out with you
MILNER: "INSTEAD OF TRYING TO FORCE MYSELF INTO DOING WHAT I IMAGINED I OUGHT TO BE DOING, I BEGAN TO INQUIRE INTO WHAT I WAS DOING."

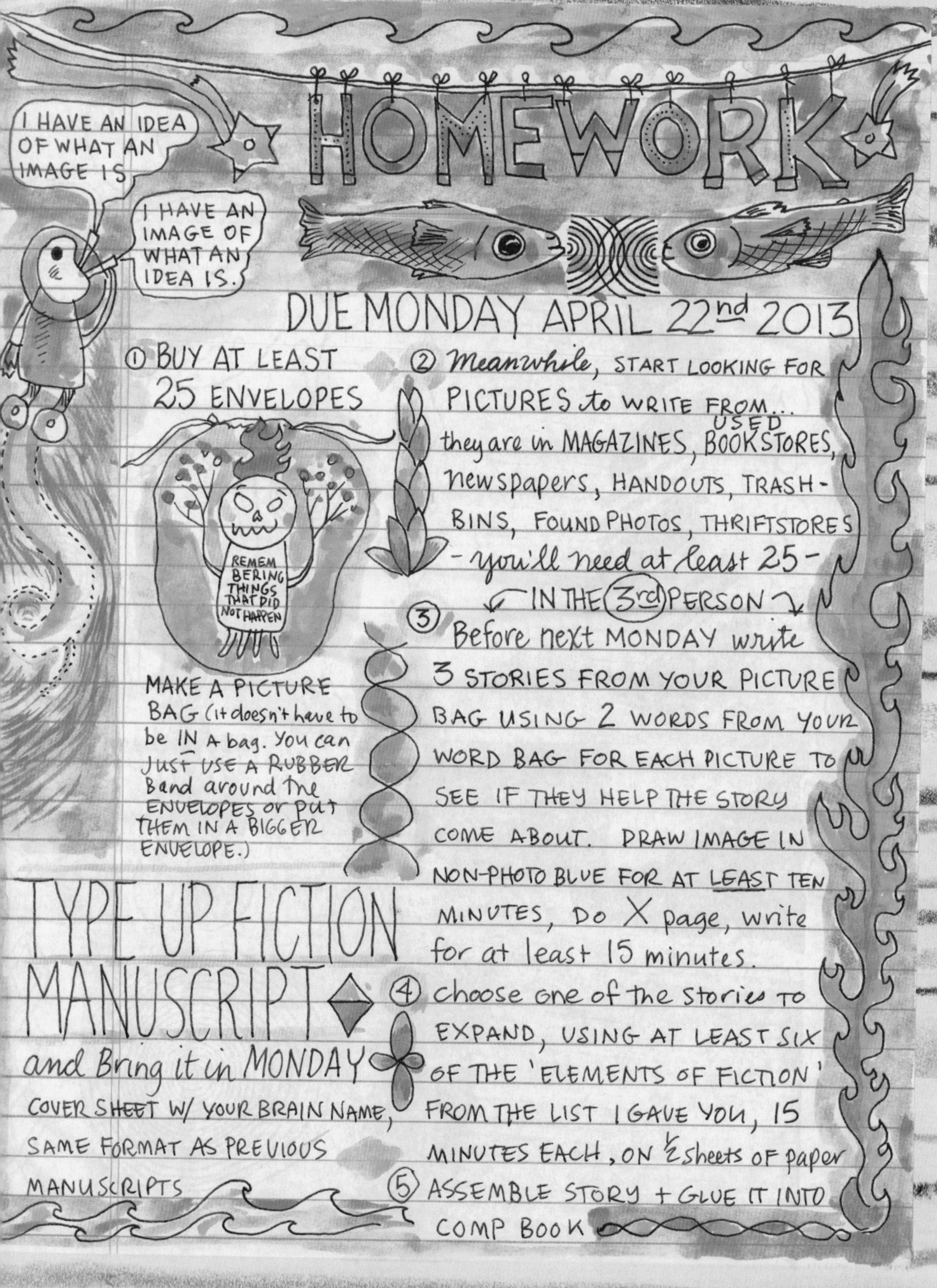
I HAVE AN IDEA OF WHAT AN IMAGE IS
I HAVE AN IMAGE OF WHAT AN IDEA IS.
HOMEWORK
DUE MONDAY APRIL 22nd 2013
① BUY AT LEAST 25 ENVELOPES
REMEMBERING THINGS THAT DID NOT HAPPEN
MAKE A PICTURE BAG (it doesn't have to be IN a bag. You can JUST USE A RUBBER Band around the ENVELOPES or put THEM IN A BIGGER ENVELOPE.)
② Meanwhile, START LOOKING FOR PICTURES to WRITE FROM... they are in MAGAZINES, USED BOOKSTORES, newspapers, HANDOUTS, TRASH-BINS, FOUND PHOTOS, THRIFTSTORES - you'll need at least 25 -
IN THE 3rd PERSON
③ Before next MONDAY write 3 STORIES FROM YOUR PICTURE BAG USING 2 WORDS FROM YOUR WORD BAG FOR EACH PICTURE TO SEE IF THEY HELP THE STORY COME ABOUT. DRAW IMAGE IN NON-PHOTO BLUE FOR AT LEAST TEN MINUTES, DO X page, write for at least 15 minutes.
④ choose one of the stories to EXPAND, USING AT LEAST SIX OF THE 'ELEMENTS OF FICTION' FROM THE LIST I GAVE YOU, 15 MINUTES EACH, ON ½ sheets of paper
⑤ ASSEMBLE STORY + GLUE IT INTO COMP BOOK
TYPE UP FICTION MANUSCRIPT
and Bring it in MONDAY
COVER SHEET W/ YOUR BRAIN NAME, SAME FORMAT AS PREVIOUS MANUSCRIPTS

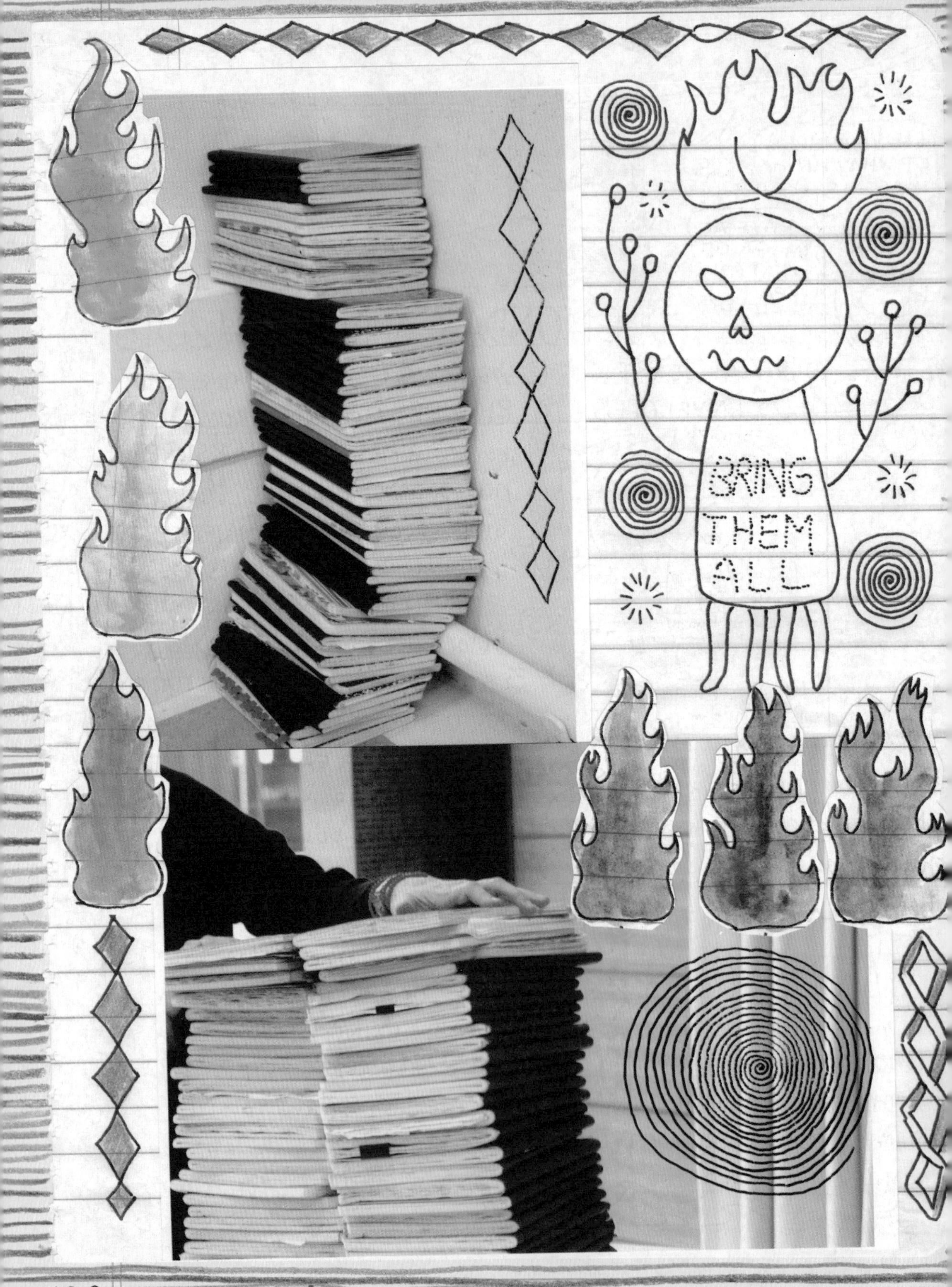
BRING
THEM
ALL

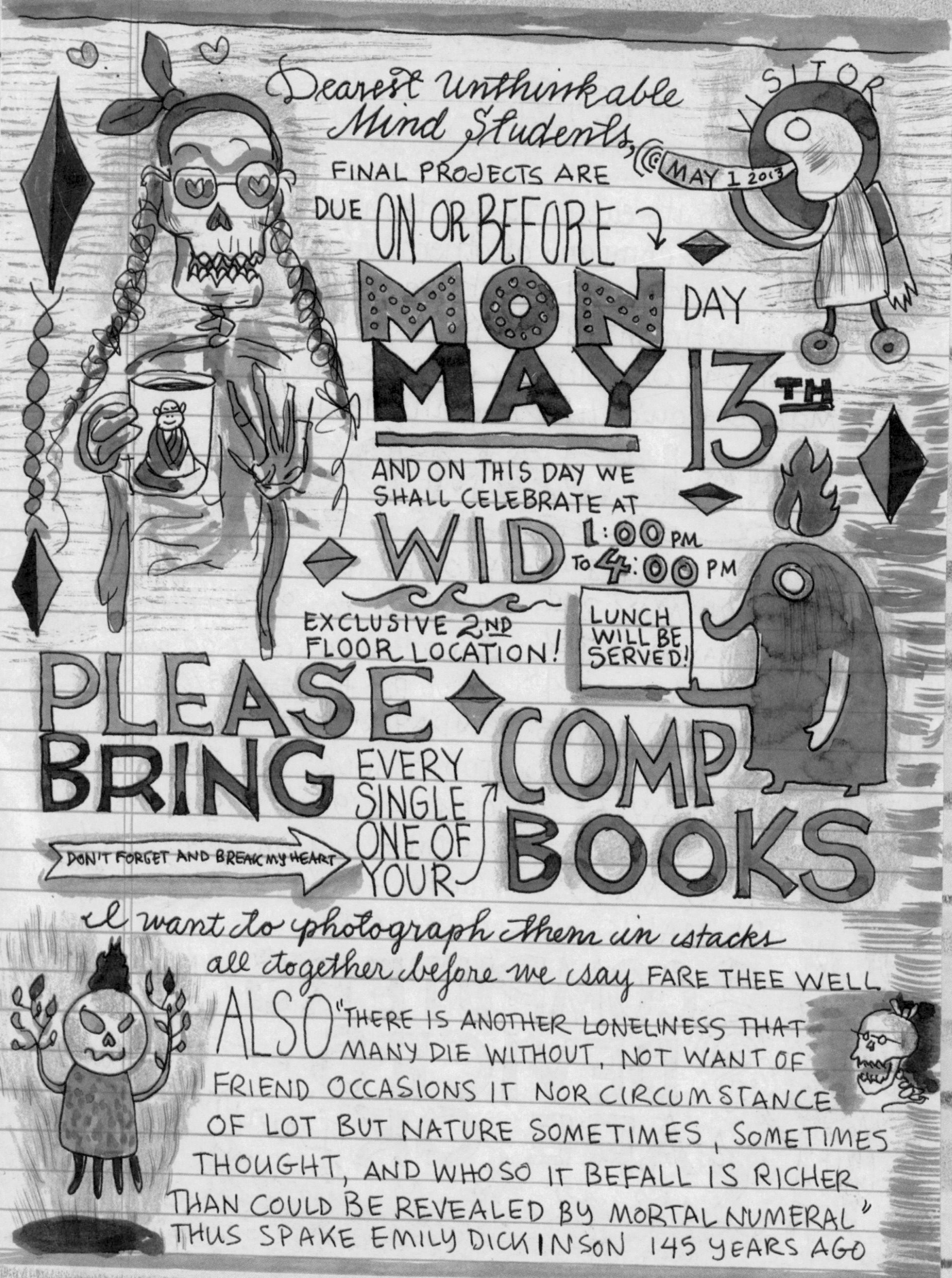
Dearest Unthinkable Mind Students,
MAY 1 2013
FINAL PROJECTS ARE DUE ON OR BEFORE
MON DAY
MAY 13TH
AND ON THIS DAY WE SHALL CELEBRATE AT
WID 1:00 PM TO 4:00 PM
EXCLUSIVE 2ND FLOOR LOCATION!
LUNCH WILL BE SERVED!
PLEASE BRING EVERY SINGLE ONE OF YOUR COMP BOOKS
DON'T FORGET AND BREAK MY HEART
I want to photograph them in stacks all together before we say FARE THEE WELL
ALSO "THERE IS ANOTHER LONELINESS THAT MANY DIE WITHOUT, NOT WANT OF FRIEND OCCASIONS IT NOR CIRCUMSTANCE OF LOT BUT NATURE SOMETIMES, SOMETIMES THOUGHT, AND WHOSO IT BEFALL IS RICHER THAN COULD BE REVEALED BY MORTAL NUMERAL"
THUS SPAKE EMILY DICKINSON 145 YEARS AGO

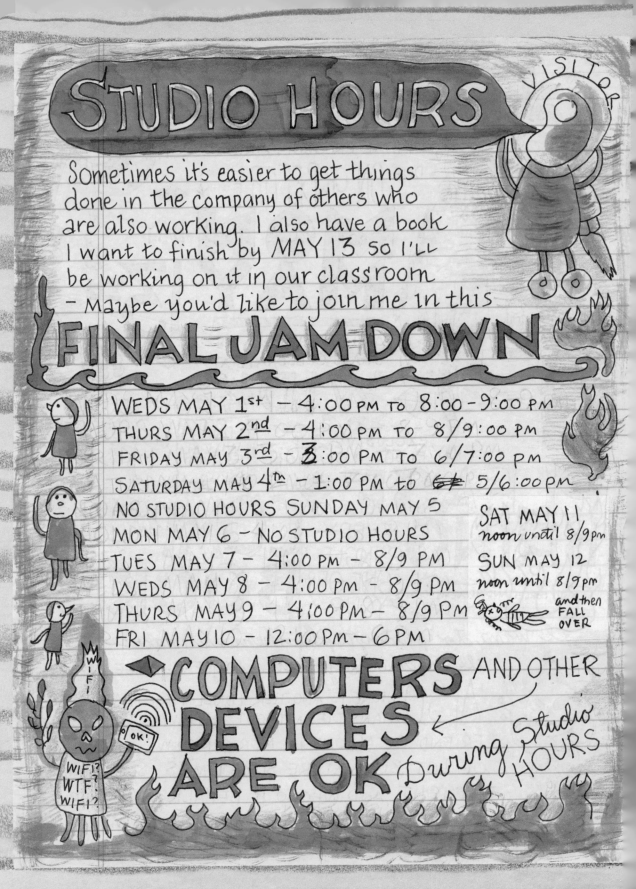

STUDIO HOURS

VISITOR

Sometimes it's easier to get things done in the company of others who are also working. I also have a book I want to finish by MAY 13 so I'll be working on it in our classroom — Maybe you'd like to join me in this

FINAL JAM DOWN

WEDS MAY 1st — 4:00 PM to 8:00-9:00 PM
THURS MAY 2nd — 4:00 PM to 8/9:00 PM
FRIDAY MAY 3rd — 3:00 PM to 6/7:00 PM
SATURDAY MAY 4th — 1:00 PM to ~~6:00~~ 5/6:00 PM
NO STUDIO HOURS SUNDAY MAY 5
MON MAY 6 — NO STUDIO HOURS
TUES MAY 7 — 4:00 PM - 8/9 PM
WEDS MAY 8 — 4:00 PM - 8/9 PM
THURS MAY 9 — 4:00 PM — 8/9 PM
FRI MAY 10 — 12:00 PM — 6 PM

SAT MAY 11
noon until 8/9 pm

SUN MAY 12
noon until 8/9 pm
and then FALL OVER

COMPUTERS AND OTHER DEVICES ← ARE OK During Studio HOURS

WIFI?
WTF?
WIFI?
OK!

umbel...out u...
...aste goes this Winter.
...Love, Orla

SCHOOL IS OUT!

THE UNTHINKABLE MIND · SPRING 2013

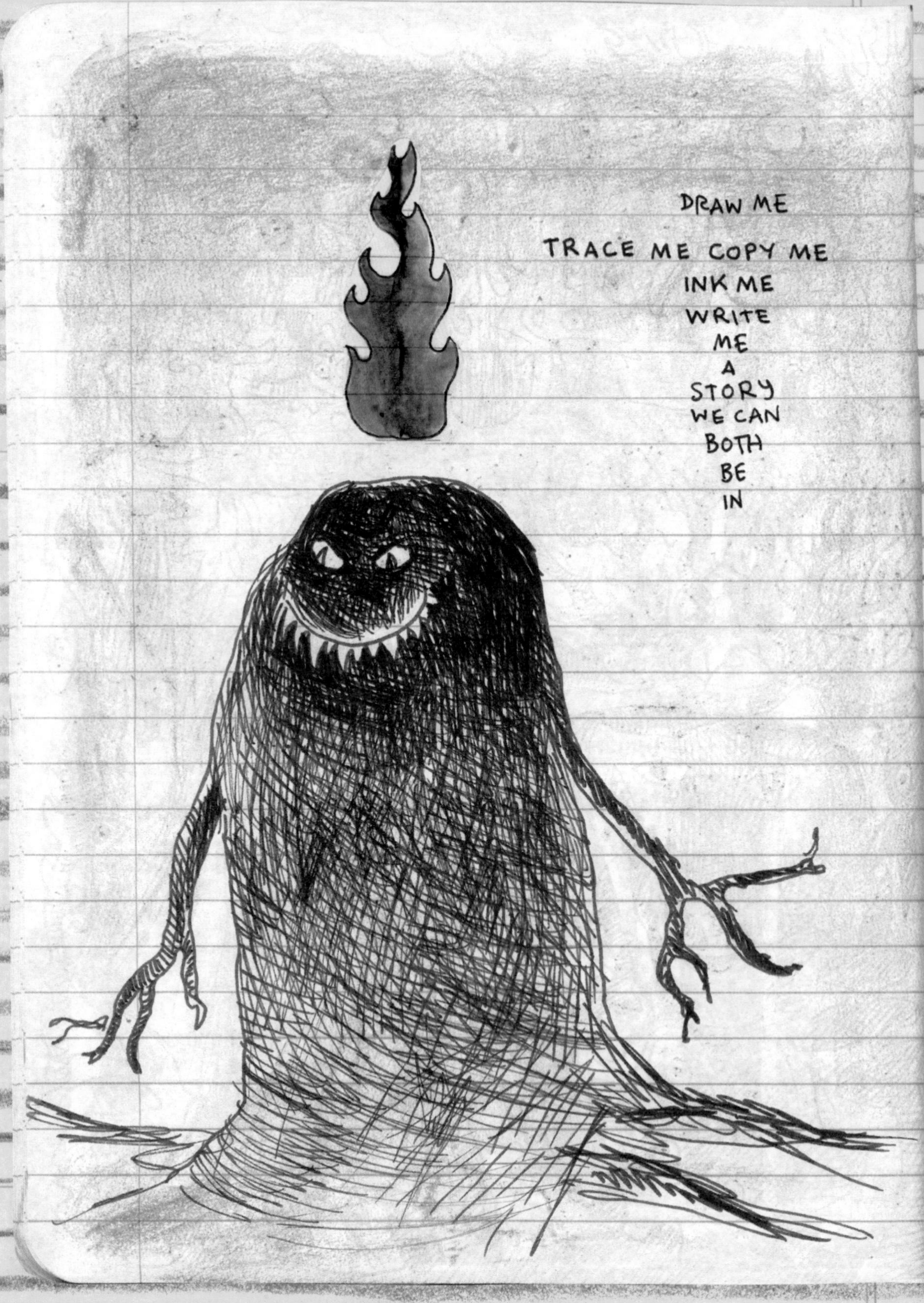
DRAW ME
TRACE ME COPY ME
INK ME
WRITE
ME
A
STORY
WE CAN
BOTH
BE
IN